MANAGING
INNOVATION

The Open Business School

The Open Business School offers a three-tier ladder of opportunity for managers at different stages of their careers: the Professional Certificate in Management; the Professional Diploma in Management; and the MBA. If you would like to receive information on these open learning programmes, please write to the Open Business School, The Open University, Milton Keynes MK7 6AA, England.

This volume is a Course Reader for the Open Business School's MBA course *Creative Management* (B882).

A companion volume, also available from SAGE Publications, is:

Creative Management
edited by Jane Henry

MANAGING INNOVATION

edited by

Jane Henry and David Walker
at the Open Business School

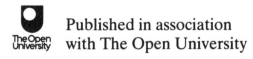 Published in association
with The Open University

 SAGE Publications
London • Newbury Park • New Delhi

First published 1991

 SAGE Publications Ltd
6 Bonhill Street
London EC2A 4PU

SAGE Publications Inc
2455 Teller Road
Newbury Park, California 91320

SAGE Publications India Pvt Ltd
32, M-Block Market
Greater Kailash – I
New Delhi 110 048

British Library Cataloguing in Publication data

Managing innovation.
  I. Henry, Jane   II. Walker, David
  658.4

  ISBN 0–8039–8505–3
  ISBN 0–8039–8506–1 pbk

Library of Congress catalog card number 91–52698

Typeset by Fakenham Photosetting Ltd, Fakenham, Norfolk
Printed in Great Britain by Billing and Sons Ltd, Worcester

Contents

Acknowledgements

This book is the second in two volumes originally prepared as part of the Open University course on Creative Management. The authors would like to thank the following: for their advice and help – John Martin and Robin Roy, both of the Open University, Tudor Rickards of the Manchester Business School; for comments on early proposals – Eion Farmer and David Mayle of the Open University and John Scott from Hamilton University; for hard work and cheerfulness under pressure – Cherry Martin and Judi Moore.

The publishers are grateful to the following for permission to reproduce illustrations: Michael L. Abramson, Chicago for pages 176 and 179; Ampex Corporation, Redwood City, California for page 297; Japan National Tourist Organization for page 319; Mitch Kezar of Kezar Inc., Watertown, Minnesota for page 177; Rover IToC for page 282. If we have inadvertently omitted to mention any other copyright-holders, we shall be glad to include an acknowledgement in any reprint.

We are also grateful to the following for permission to reprint chapters: Basil Blackwell for Chapters 8, 10 and 22; *Business Week* for Chapter 21; Paul Chapman Ltd for Chapter 36; Design Management Institute for Chapter 11; Elsevier Science Publishers B.V. for Chapter 9; Elsevier Science Publishing Co. Inc. for Chapter 13; Gower Publishing Group for Chapter 20; *Harvard Business Review* for Chapters 1, 6 and 25; Rosabeth Moss Kanter for Chapter 5; Alfred A. Knopf Inc. for Chapter 35; McGraw-Hill Inc. for Chapter 32; Macmillan Publishing Company, New York for Chapter 27; Penguin Books USA Inc. for Chapter 23; Pergamon Press for Chapters 26 and 31; *Scientific American* for Chapter 34; *Sloan Management Review* for Chapter 12; The White Rabbit Ltd for Chapters 14–19; John Wiley & Sons Ltd for Chapters 3, 4 and 28.

The authors

Suzanne Berger	Professor of Political Science, MIT, USA
Robert M. Burnside	Center for Creative Leadership, Greensboro, North Carolina, USA
Kim Clark	Professor of Business Administration, Harvard Business School, USA
Colin Clipson	Professor and Director, Architecture, Planning and Research Laboratory, University of Michigan, USA
Robert G. Cooper	Professor of Marketing, Faculty of Business, McMaster University, Ontario, Canada
William Davis	Journalist, formerly Editor of *Punch* and Financial Editor of the *Guardian*, UK
Michael L. Dertouzos	Professor of Electrical Engineering, MIT, USA
Peter F. Drucker	Clark Professor of Social Science, Claremont Graduate School, California; Emeritus Professor of Management, Graduate Business School, New York University, USA
Göran Ekvall	Professor, Swedish Council for Management and Work Life Issues, Stockholm, Sweden
Roger Evans	Director, Creative Learning Consultants, London, UK
Takahiro Fujimoto	Harvard Business School, USA
Jane Henry	Lecturer, Open Business School, Open University, UK
Knut Holt	Professor of Industrial Management, University of Trondheim, Norway
Mariann Jelinek	Professor of Business Administration, College of William and Mary, Ohio, USA
Rosabeth Moss Kanter	Professor of Business Administration, Harvard University, USA
Carol Kennedy	Journalist, USA
John M. Ketteringham	Senior vice-president, Arthur D. Little Inc., Cambridge, Massachusetts, USA
Elko J. Kleinschmidt	Associate Professor of Marketing and International Business, Faculty of Business, McMaster University, Ontario, Canada
Ronnie Lessem	Reader in International Management, City University, Business School, London, UK
Richard K. Lester	Professor of Nuclear Engineering, MIT, USA
Christopher Lorenz	Journalist, Managing Editor, *Financial Times*, UK

Henry Mintzberg   Bronfman Professor of Management, Faculty of
                           Management, McGill University, Montreal,
                           Canada
Russell Mitchell   Journalist, *Business Week*, USA
Akio Morita   CEO, Sony Corporation, Japan
P. Ranganath Nayak   Vice-president, Arthur D. Little Inc.,
                           Cambridge, Massachusetts, USA
R. Charles Parker   Research Fellow, Ashridge Management
                           College, UK
Alan W. Pearson   Director, Research and Development Unit,
                           Manchester Business School, UK
Tom Peters   Founder Tom Peters Group, USA
James Pilditch   Formerly Chairman AID Consultants, UK
Robert B. Reich   School of Government, Harvard University,
                           USA
Peter Reid   Journalist, USA
Robert Rosenfeld   Idea Connection Systems Inc., Rochester, USA
Peter Russell   Consultant, author, broadcaster, UK
Claudia Bird   Professor of Organisation and Management, San
Schoonhoven   Jose State University, USA
Walter K. Schwartz   Innovation Consultant, Vienna, Austria
Jenny C. Servo   Dawnbreaker Inc., Rochester, USA
Gregory P. Shea   Associate Professor, The Wharton School,
                           University of Pennsylvania, USA
Steve Shirley   Director, F I Group, UK
Robert M. Solow   Institute Professor, Department of Economics,
                           MIT, USA
Lester C. Thurow   Professor of Economics and Management, MIT,
                           USA
Pierre Wack   Formerly, Head of Business Environment
                           Division, Royal Dutch Shell UK and Senior
                           Lecturer, Harvard Business School, USA
David Walker   Faculty of Technology, Open University, UK
Frances Westley   Faculty of Management, McGill University,
                           Montreal, Canada

Introduction

David Walker and Jane Henry

Creativity on its own is only a beginning. Human beings are relentlessly creative. Having ideas is relatively easy – having good ideas is slightly more difficult – but the real challenge lies in carrying ideas through into some practical result. The crucial issue then is that creativity must have some tangible outcome – in products, in services, in a new structure or strategy, or more diffusely in a pervasive shift in corporate culture.

Our starting point is that the process from internal thought to external reality seems inhibited and obstructed. These inhibitions rather than a shortage of innovative ideas are the problem taken up in this book.

Let us examine briefly three typical levels of inhibition.

Firstly, at the national level, there seems to be an acute cultural difficulty. The widely accepted view of Britain is that we are good at ideas but bad at carrying them through. We are not so much a nation of shopkeepers as a nation of inventors, who allow others to keep the shop . . . and to profit from our ideas. From a brief comparison of research expenditure and patent activity, it is easy to see that many of our competitors invest more in ideas than we do in the UK.

We belong to a culture which generates many ideas but is hostile to their development. This antipathy manifests itself both economically and managerially in such things as lack of government support, lack of venture capital, lack of supportive organizational structures, lack of incentives, the not-invented-here syndrome and so on. Other countries, such as Japan, Germany, Holland and Scandinavia, have more success, perhaps because their infrastructure is more supportive. Some of our cases are drawn from these countries. By contrast, if you read the study of industrial America in the final part of this book you will find a damning echo of our own national predicament.

Secondly, the innovation process itself is often not very well understood within organizations. Ideas are not generated in any conscious or systematic way. The ideas which are thrown up ad hoc are rarely well managed through the phases of implementation. This has many bad repercussions – for example in the neglect of creative individuals, in the wilful lack of direction and ignorance of the market place and customer wishes, in a narrow obsession with science-based breakthroughs, and an inability to see research design and development as a unified organizational task.

Thirdly, there is some anxiety about the ability of managers to manage the processes of innovation. Here we come close to the heart of this book and its intentions. By 'manage innovation' we mean the ability to trigger, generate, control and steer new ideas through the maze. This is not merely the task of one brilliant manager but a task for teams which include those that generate ideas and those that focus upon constraints, those that innovate and those that adapt: in short, a balanced coalition between original thinkers and those that provide direction and stability. Unhappily there is antagonism between these camps and a widespread lack of respect for creative working. Without trust and mutual support few can operate across the multiple Berlin walls of the professions.

This book provides a contextual framework, knowledge of exemplars, guidance about best practices, and some tools and techniques which may help promote relevant day to day skills. We are not so rash as to offer comprehensive solutions but we present some guidelines which represent the consensus of expert theorists and practitioners.

As you will discover, there are themes which re-occur throughout these readings. They include individual persistence, frameworks for innovation, the place of multidisciplinary teamwork and the need for adaptability in organizations.

Individual leadership and persistence   Ideas may be developed collectively but they begin in a single mind. The individual champion is a vital part of the equation. The driving force behind successful innovation often comes down to a single person who embodies a vision, gives expression to it and in turn inspires others with the same vision. Such a person is the determined product champion and has exceptional qualities of drive, stamina and sheer bloody-mindedness. By traditional criteria this champion may not be a good manager and is likely to be awkward and difficult. Very often these personalities triumph through sheer persistence, and through extraordinary stamina.

Provision of the framework for innovation   Such individuals are rarely locked within the narrow details of the research and development process. They have a large contextual view. They understand the market and the constraints operating upon the organization. They may not even see themselves as very creative, but they have the ability to set up the context within which ideas flow and crackle like electricity. The framework is absolutely crucial in finding a precarious balance between structure and improvisation, between targets and freedom of manoeuvre. The framework provides a sense of orientation but has within it room for others to improvise, to take charge, to take responsibility, to expand to the maximum of their personal energies. In the most innovative companies, this supportive framework takes the form of schemes of intrapreneurship or direct incentives. Individuals can build up teams and gain access to resources for their embryonic ideas. From small, seemingly eccentric, ideas large sectors of the business grow.

Multidisciplinary teamwork   There is an increasing general awareness that more and more complex problems have to be solved by many minds, working co-operatively. This is partly driven by technology wherein no single individual can keep up to date with all relevant developments, and partly driven by new styles of open management. Local knowledge possessed by the most junior members of an organization becomes as valuable as the strategic overviews of management. There is a connected movement away from the hero worship of very visible entrepreneurs to collective creativity and shared responsibilities.

Adaptability and redesigning the organization An additional lesson, emerging from the management of new technologies, makes the strategic tasks of managers even more difficult. The requirement is that the framework must be flexible: it must change according to local pressures. This then leads naturally to the connected notion of an organization periodically redesigning itself, very often and very thoroughly – adapt or die.

The book aims to present an overview of innovative management. It is intended to offer an accessible account of some of the key concepts in the area, with illustrations of applications in practice, along with stories to inspire and a few suggestions for readers to try. The book is unusual in combining reviews of key topics along with case studies illustrating the problems inherent in the management of innovation. It has four parts.

Part One addresses areas in strategic innovation, higher-level management and the organizational environment, including visionary leadership, creative climate and project implementation. Part Two presents mini-case studies which are designed to act as exemplars. They comprise the classic stories of intrapreneurs and innovators, their inventive products and organizations. Part Three offers longer case studies showing how organizations have brought an innovation about, whether in terms of direction finding, product innovation or organizational renewal. These case studies juxtapose a mix of classic accounts (e.g. Shell) and smaller more detailed accounts that may be easier to identify with (e.g. Culpitts). The techniques illustrated range from visioning and scenario planning to idea offices and creative incrementalism. The text discusses pitfalls along the way and offers examples of how creative procedures have been used to develop products and change climate. Part Four approaches the topic from a wider perspective, pointing out the parallels and differences in the process of innovation across different cultures, and presents an overview of principles and strategies that are common in innovative organizations.

We would like to sound some cautionary notes here.

The danger of a book like this, indeed any management textbook, is that it makes everything *sound easy*. John Harvey-Jones calls this the ' "in one mighty bound Jack was free" management book'. In retrospect, from some distance off in the ivory towers of Milton Keynes, after the retrospective rationalizations and the quiet measured analysis, the answers and the recipes for success blandly emerge. Yet this is *not* at all how it feels from within. Any manager with the slightest practical experience knows that answers are far from obvious. When the manager is enmeshed deep in these processes, day to day and minute by minute, the levels of uncertainty are impossibly high, conflict and confrontation are regular events, anxiety generates hysteria, every issue is surrounded by a fuzzy penumbra, every decision is made in a frenzy of haste, and the division between ends and means erodes, the boundary between personal egocentricity and management vision disappears.

So all the good advice we give here can be turned on its head. A vision can be stubborn and misconceived. Personal drive can slip into destructive aggression. Creativity and the seizing upon change can degenerate into anarchy. The organizational framework can become jelly-like and insubstantial. We are familiar with such disasters.

So what does this mean for the creative manager?

It means, first of all, forewarned is forearmed. Principles can turn sour, of course, but this does not totally discredit them. We know there is a certain risk in generalization. Well intentioned advice given here may not apply directly to your immediate circumstances, but given a few modifications and a little time it may be relevant. So be sensitive to shifts in the framework about you and compare your local practices to those exemplified in this book. With patience even the most stubborn organizations will change.

It means, secondly, that *most* acts of creativity are doomed to failure. Ideas themselves are fragile, the processes to which they are subject are uncertain and often hostile, the organizational filters are severely applied, and the world at large might show a quite astonishing indifference to your brilliant brainchild. So for every hundred ideas only one emerges as worth pursuing and maybe only one in a thousand is going to achieve any kind of widespread success. The odds are against you. This is not a matter for pessimism, but something to be faced quite neutrally. It is just the way the world works, and makes it extra important to generate very many good ideas and sharpen up the criteria for assessing them. It also means that, once you are confident in the soundness of an idea, persistence and nerve are needed. The good manager, then, has the ability to sort out the good ideas from the bad ideas, the sense to steer them in the right direction, the stamina to keep going and the resilience to go back and start again.

The extracts in this anthology are chosen to encourage and assist you in those activities, to sharpen up criteria, to give a sense of orientation and context, to demonstrate remarkable cases of brilliance and persistence, and in the end to show that success, against all the odds, is possible.

This book acts as an ideal introduction to the field of managing innovation that will appeal to management students and teachers along with practising managers and trainers with an interest in the field. This volume and its companion, *Creative Management* (J. Henry, 1991, Sage) were both originally prepared for the Open University MBA programme. They are readers for the Open Business School course in Creative Management.

PART ONE

FRAMEWORK – ISSUES IN THE MANAGEMENT OF INNOVATION

Part One of the book deals with creativity and innovation at a general, even theoretical, level. At this level there is a fundamental tension between stability and creativity within organizations. For some this reveals itself as a conflict between the top and the lower tiers of the organization, between strategy making and local autonomy. For some writers, the terms *creative* and *management* themselves are in opposition! As you read, you will have to decide for yourself whether or not there is a deep antipathy within organizations between the forces of stability and the forces of change. Hopefully the book will help you not only to identify the polarities but also to see the means of fruitful reconciliation.

In Section 1 we seek to lay out the main sources and strategies for innovation, and indicate the kind of conflicts that are intrinsic to creative management. Drucker outlines the variety of innovative activity, arguing that 'innovation is work rather than genius' and very much a matter of discipline. Pearson uses the concept of uncertainty to offer a matrix which directs attention to characteristics that might reduce the risks of innovation. Rosenfeld and Servo describe the five-stage office of innovation model used at Kodak and elsewhere.

In Section 2 we cover the personal qualities that are evident in visionary leaders and successful change makers. Westley and Mintzberg draw on the metaphor of the theatre to inform an account of the styles adopted by well known visionary leaders. Moss Kanter describes the personal and interpersonal skills she found in effective change makers. The Reich chapter, by contrast, draws us away from individual heroic figures towards collective creativity.

A further group of extracts in Section 3 considers the role of the organizational setting – the culture, climate and environment which can foster or stifle innovation. Ekvall offers an account of his work on creative climate and its relationship to innovation in organizations. Jelinek and Schoonhoven highlight the difficulties facing managers in the type of strong culture typical of hi-tech companies. Holt features the place of matrix structures and venture teams in organizing innovative projects.

Assuming for the moment we have reached an organizational utopia, and we have a good strategy, driven by a charismatic leader, within a framework that is encouraging, there still remain further thorny problems of implementation. Section 4 addresses some of these developmental problems: Clipson makes the case for the integration of research, design and market information; Clark and Fujimoto paint a picture of the struggle to shorten lead times in the car industry, and Shea gives an account of the role and emerging difficulties of quality circles. Finally, Cooper and Kleinschmidt outline research into factors which lead to success in new product development.

SECTION 1
STRATEGIC INNOVATION

1

The discipline of innovation

Peter F. Drucker

Despite much discussion these days of the 'entrepreneurial personality,' few of the entrepreneurs with whom I have worked during the last 30 years had such personalities. But I have known many people – salespeople, surgeons, journalists, scholars, even musicians – who did have them without being the least bit 'entrepreneurial.' What all the successful entrepreneurs I have met have in common is not a certain kind of personality but a commitment to the systematic practice of innovation.

Innovation is the specific function of entrepreneurship, whether in an existing business, a public service institution, or a new venture started by a lone individual in the family kitchen. It is the means by which the entrepreneur either creates new wealth-producing resources or endows existing resources with enhanced potential for creating wealth.

Today, much confusion exits about the proper definition of entrepreneurship. Some observers use the term to refer to all small businesses; others, to all new businesses. In practice, however, a great many well-established businesses engage in highly successful entrepreneurship. The term, then, refers not to an enterprise's size or age, but to a certain kind of activity. At the heart of that activity is innovation: the effort to create purposeful, focused change in an enterprise's economic or social potential.

Sources of innovation

There are, of course, innovations that spring from a flash of genius. Most innovations, however, especially the successful ones, result from a conscious, purposeful search for innovation opportunities which are found only in a few situations.

Extracted and reprinted by permission from *Harvard Business Review* (May–June), 1985, pp. 67–72. Copyright © 1985 by the President and Fellows of Harvard College; all rights reserved

Four such areas of opportunity exist *within* a company or industry:

- Unexpected occurrences
- Incongruities
- Process needs
- Industry and market changes.

Three additional sources of opportunity exist *outside* a company in its social and intellectual environment:

- Demographic changes
- Changes in perception
- New knowledge.

True, these sources overlap, different as they may be in the nature of their risk, difficulty, and complexity, and the potential for innovation may well lie in more than one area at a time. But among them, they account for the great majority of all innovation opportunities.

Unexpected occurrences

Consider, first, the easiest and simplest source of innovation opportunity: the unexpected. In the early 1930s, IBM developed the first modern accounting machine, which was designed for banks, but banks in 1933 did not buy new equipment. What saved the company – according to a story that Thomas Watson, Sr., the company's founder and long-term CEO, often told – was its exploitation of an unexpected success: the New York Public Library wanted to buy a machine. Unlike the banks, libraries in those early New Deal days had money, and Watson sold more than a hundred of his otherwise unsalable machines to libraries.

Fifteen years later, when everyone believed that computers were designed for advanced scientific work, business unexpectedly showed an interest in a machine that could do payroll. Univac, which had the most advanced machine, spurned business applications. But IBM immediately realized it faced a possible unexpected success, redesigned what was basically Univac's machine for such mundane applications as payroll, and within five years became the leader in the computer industry, a position it has maintained to this day.

The unexpected failure may be an equally important innovation opportunity source. Everyone knows about the Ford Motor Company's Edsel as the biggest new car failure in automotive history. What very few people seem to know, however, is that the Edsel's failure was the foundation for much of the company's later success. Ford planned the Edsel, the most carefully designed car to that point in American automotive history, to give the company a full product line with which to compete with GM. When it bombed, despite all the planning, market research, and design that had gone into it, Ford realized that something was happening in the automobile market that ran counter to the basic assumptions on which GM and everyone else had been designing and marketing cars. No longer did the market segment primarily by income groups; suddenly, the new principle of segmentation was what we now call 'life-styles.' Ford's immediate responses were the Mustang and the Thunderbird – the cars that gave the company a distinct personality and reestablished it as an industry leader.

Unexpected successes and failures are such productive sources of innovation opportunities because most businesses dismiss them, disregard them, and even resent them. The German scientist who around 1906 synthesized novocaine, the first non-addictive narcotic, had intended it to be used in major surgical procedures like amputation. Surgeons, however, preferred total anesthesia for such procedures; they still do. Instead, novocaine found a ready appeal among dentists. Its inventor spent the remaining years of his life traveling from dental school to dental school making speeches that forbade dentists to 'misuse' his noble invention in applications for which he had not intended it.

This is a caricature, to be sure, but it illustrates the attitude managers often take to the unexpected: 'It should not have happened.' Corporate reporting systems further ingrain this reaction, for they draw attention away from unanticipated possibilities. The typical monthly or quarterly report has on its first page a list of problems, that is, the areas where results fall short of expectations. Such information is needed, of course; it helps prevent deterioration of performance.

But it also suppresses the recognition of new opportunities. The first acknowledgement of a possible opportunity usually applies to an area in which a company does better than budgeted. Thus genuinely entrepreneurial businesses have two 'first pages' – a problem page and an opportunity page – and managers spend equal time on both.

Incongruities

Alcon Industries was one of the great success stories of the 1960s because Bill Connor, the company's founder, exploited an incongruity in medical technology. The cataract operation is the world's third or fourth most common surgical procedure. During the last 300 years, doctors systematized it to the point that the only 'old-fashioned' step left was the cutting of a ligament. Eye surgeons had learned to cut the ligament with complete success, but it was so different a procedure from the rest of the operation and so incompatible with it that they often dreaded it. It was incongruous.

Doctors had known for 50 years about an enzyme that could dissolve the ligament without cutting. All Connor did was to add a preservative to this enzyme that gave it a few months' shelf life. Eye surgeons immediately accepted the new compound, and Alcon found itself with a worldwide monopoly. Fifteen years later, Nestlé bought the company for a fancy price.

Such an incongruity within the logic or rhythm of a process is only one possibility out of which innovation opportunities may arise. Another source is incongruity between economic realities. For instance, whenever an industry has a steadily growing market but falling profit margins – as, say, in the steel industries of developed countries between 1950 and 1970 – an incongruity exists. The innovative response: minimills.

An incongruity between expectations and results can also open up possibilities for innovation. For 50 years after the turn of the century, shipbuilders and shipping companies worked hard both to make ships faster and to lower their fuel consumption. Even so, the more successful they were in boosting speed and trimming fuel needs, the worse ocean freighters' economics became. By 1950 or so, the ocean freighter was dying, if not already dead.

All that was wrong, however, was an incongruity between the industry's assumptions and its realities. The real costs did not come from doing work (that is, being at sea) but from not doing work (that is, sitting idle in port). Once managers understood where costs truly lay, the innovations were obvious: the roll-on and roll-off ship and the container ship. These solutions, which involved old technology, simply applied to the ocean freighter what railroads and truckers had been using for 30 years. A shift in viewpoint, not in technology, totally changed the economics of ocean shipping and turned it into one of the major growth industries of the last 20 to 30 years.

Process needs

Anyone who has ever driven in Japan knows that the country has no modern highway system. Its roads still follow the paths laid down for – or by – oxcarts in the tenth century. What makes the system work for automobiles and trucks is an adaptation of the reflector used on American highways since the early 1930s. This reflector shows each car, which other cars are approaching, from any one of a half-dozen directions. This minor invention, which enables traffic to move smoothly and with a minimum of accidents, exploited a process need.

Around 1909, a statistician at the American Telephone & Telegraph Company projected two curves 15 years out: telephone traffic and American population. Viewed together, they showed that by 1920 or so every single female in the United States would have to work as a switchboard operator. The process need was obvious, and within two years, AT&T had developed and installed the automatic switchboard.

What we now call 'media' also had their origin in two process need-based innovations around 1890. One was Mergenthaler's Linotype, which made it possible to produce a newspaper quickly and in large volume; the other was a social innovation, modern advertising, invented by the first true newspaper publishers, Adolph Ochs of the *New York Times*, Joseph Pulitzer of the *New York World*, and William Randolph Hearst. Advertising made it possible for them to distribute news practically free of charge, with the profit coming from marketing.

Industry and market changes

Managers may believe that industry structures are ordained by the Good Lord, but they can – and often do – change overnight. Such change creates tremendous opportunity for innovation.

One of American business's great success stories in recent decades is the brokerage firm of Donaldson, Lufkin & Jenrette, recently acquired by the Equitable Life Assurance Society. DL&J was founded in 1961 by three young men, all graduates of the Harvard Business School, who realized that the structure of the financial industry was changing as institutional investors became dominant. These young men had practically no capital and no connections. Still, within a few years, their firm had become a leader in the move to negotiated commissions and one of Wall Street's stellar performers. It was the first to be incorporated and go public.

In a similar fashion, changes in industry structure have created massive innovation opportunities for American health care providers. During the last 10 or 15 years, independent surgical and psychiatric clinics, emergency centers, and HMOs (health maintenance organizations) have opened throughout the country. Comparable opportunities in telecommunications followed industry upheavals – both in equipment (with the emergence of such companies as ROLM in the manufacturing of private branch exchanges) and in transmission (with the emergence of MCI and Sprint in long-distance service).

When an industry grows quickly – the critical figure seems to be in the neighborhood of a 40% growth rate over ten years or less – its structure changes. Established companies, concentrating on defending what they already have, tend not to counter-attack when a newcomer challenges them. Indeed, when market or industry structures change, traditional industry leaders again and again neglect the fastest growing market segments. New opportunities rarely fit the way the industry has always approached the market, defined it, or organized to serve it. Innovators therefore have a good chance of being left alone for a long time.

Demographic changes

Of the outside sources of innovation opportunity, demographics are the most reliable. Demographic events have known lead times; for instance, every person who will be in the American labor force by the year 2000 has already been born. Yet, because policymakers often neglect demographics, those who watch them and exploit them can reap great rewards.

The Japanese are ahead in robotics because they paid attention to demographics. Everyone in the developed countries around 1970 or so knew that there was both a baby bust and an education explosion going on; half or more of the young people were now staying in school beyond high school. Consequently, the number of people available for traditional blue-collar work in manufacturing was bound to decrease and become inadequate by 1990. Everyone knew this, but only the Japanese acted on it and they now have a ten-year lead in robotics.

Much the same is true of Club Méditerranée's success in the travel and resort business. By 1970, thoughtful observers could have seen the emergence of large numbers of affluent and educated young adults in Europe and the United States. Not comfortable with the kind of vacations their working-class parents had enjoyed – the summer weeks at Brighton or Atlantic City – these young people were ideal customers for a new and exotic version of the 'hangout' of their teen years.

Managers have known for a long time that demographics matter, but they have always believed that population statistics change slowly. In this century, however, they don't. Indeed, the innovation opportunities that changes in the numbers of people and their age distribution, education, occupations, and geographic location make possible are among the most rewarding and least risky of entrepreneurial pursuits.

Changes in perception

'The glass is half-full' and 'the glass is half-empty' are descriptions of the same phenomenon but have vastly different meanings. Changing a manager's perception of a glass from half-full to half-empty opens up big innovation opportunities.

All factual evidence indicates, for instance, that in the last 20 years, Americans' health has improved at unprecedented speed – whether measured by mortality rates for the newborn, survival rates for the very old, the incidence of cancers (other than lung cancer), cancer cure rates, or other factors. Even so, collective hypochondria grips the nation. Never before has there been so much concern with health or so much fear about health. Suddenly everything seems to cause cancer or degenerative heart disease or premature loss of memory. The glass is clearly half-empty.

Rather than rejoicing in great improvements in health, Americans seem to be emphasizing how far away they still are from immortality. This view of things has created many opportunities for innovations: markets for new health care magazines, for all kinds of health foods, and for exercise classes and jogging equipment. The fastest growing new US business in 1983 was a company that makes indoor exercise equipment.

A change in perception does not alter facts. It changes their meaning, though – and very quickly. It took less than two years for the computer to change from being perceived as a threat and as something only big businesses would use to something one buys for doing income tax. Economics do not necessarily dictate such a change; in fact, they may be irrelevant. What determines whether people see a glass as half-full or half-empty is mood rather than fact, and change in mood often defies quantification. But it is not exotic or intangible. It is concrete. It can be defined. It can be tested. And it can be exploited for innovation opportunity.

New knowledge

Among history-making innovations, those based on new knowledge – whether scientific, technical, or social – rank high. They are the superstars of entrepreneurship; they get the publicity and the money. They are what people usually mean when they talk of innovation, though not all innovations based on knowledge are important. Some are trivial.

Knowledge-based innovations differ from all others in the time they take, in their casualty rates, and in their predictability, as well as in the challenges they pose to entrepreneurs. Like most superstars, they can be temperamental, capricious, and hard to direct. They have, for instance, the longest lead time of all innovations. There is a protracted span between the emergence of new knowledge and its distillation into usable technology. Then, there is another long period before this new technology appears in the market-place in products, processes, or services. Overall, the lead time involved is something like 50 years, a figure that has not shortened appreciably throughout history.

To become effective, innovation of this sort usually demands not one kind of knowledge but many. Consider one of the most potent knowledge-based innovations: modern banking. The theory of the entrepreneurial bank – that is, of the purposeful use of capital to generate economic development – was formulated by the Comte de Saint-Simon during the era of Napoleon. Despite Saint-Simon's extraordinary prominence, it was not until 30 years after his death in 1826 that two of his disciples, the brothers Jacob and Isaac Pereire, established the first entrepreneurial bank, the Crédit Mobilier, and ushered in what we now call 'finance capitalism.'

The Pereires, however, did not know modern commercial banking, which developed at about the same time across the channel in England. The Crédit Mobilier failed ignominiously. Ten years later, two young men – one an American, J.P. Morgan, and one a German, Georg Siemens – put together the French theory of entrepreneurial banking and the English theory of commercial banking to create the first successful modern banks, J.P. Morgan & Company in New York and the Deutsche Bank in Berlin. Another ten years later, a young Japanese, Shibusawa Eiichi, adapted Siemens' concept to his country and thereby laid the foundation of Japan's modern economy. This is how knowledge-based innovation always works.

The computer, to cite another example, required no fewer than six separate strands of knowledge: binary arithmetic; Charles Babbage's conception of a calculating machine in the first half of the nineteenth century; the punch card, invented by Herman Hollerith for the US census of 1890; the audion tube, an electronic switch invented in 1906; symbolic logic, which was created between 1910 and 1913 by Bertrand Russell and Alfred

North Whitehead; and the concepts of programming and feedback that came out of abortive attempts during World War I to develop effective anti-aircraft guns. Although all the necessary knowledge was available by 1918, the first operational computer did not appear until 1946.

Long lead times and the need for convergence among different kinds of knowledge explain the peculiar rhythm of knowledge-based innovation, its attractions, and its dangers. During a long gestation period, there is a lot of talk and little action. Then, when all the elements suddenly converge, there is tremendous excitement and activity and an enormous amount of speculation. Between 1880 and 1890, for example, almost 1,000 electrical apparatus companies were founded in developed countries. Then, as always, there was a crash and a shakeout. By 1914, only 25 of these companies were still alive. In the early 1920s, 300 to 500 automobile companies existed in the United States; by 1960, only 4 remained.

It may be difficult, but knowledge-based innovation can be managed. Success requires careful analysis of the various kinds of knowledge needed to make an innovation possible. Both J.P. Morgan and Georg Siemens did this when they established their banking ventures. The Wright bothers did this when they developed the first operational airplane.

Careful analysis of the needs and, above all, the capabilities of the intended user is also essential. It may seem paradoxical, but knowledge-based innovation is more market dependent than any other kind of innovation.

De Havilland, a British company, designed and built the first passenger jet airplane, but it did not analyze what the market needed and therefore did not identify two key factors. One was configuration – that is, the right size with the right payload from the routes on which a jet would give an airline the greatest advantage. The other was equally mundane: how the airlines could finance the purchase of such an expensive plane. Because De Havilland failed to do an adequate user analysis, two American companies, Boeing and Douglas, took over the commercial jet aircraft industry.

Principles of innovation

Purposeful, systematic innovation begins with the analysis of the sources of new opportunities. Depending on the context, sources will have different importance at different times. Demographics, for instance, may be of little concern to innovators in fundamental industrial processes like steel making, although Mergenthaler's Linotype machine became successful primarily because there were not enough skilled typesetters available to satisfy a mass market. By the same token, new knowledge may be of little relevance to someone innovating a social instrument to satisfy a need that changing demographics or tax laws have created. But – whatever the situation – innovators must analyze all opportunity sources.

Because innovation is both conceptual and perceptual, would-be innovators must also go out and look, ask, and listen. Successful innovators use both the right and left sides of their brains. They look at figures. They look at people. They work out analytically what the innovation has to be to satisfy an opportunity. Then they go out and look at potential users to study their expectations, their values, and their needs.

To be effective, an innovation has to be simple and it has to be focused. It should do only one thing; otherwise it confuses people. Indeed, the greatest praise an innovation can receive is for people to say: 'This is obvious! Why didn't I think of it? It's so simple!' Even the innovation that creates new users and new markets should be directed toward a specific, clear, and carefully designed application.

Effective innovations start small. They are not grandiose. They try to do one specific thing. It may be to enable a moving vehicle to draw electric power while it runs along rails, the innovation that made possible the electric streetcar. Or it may be the elementary idea of putting the same number of matches into a matchbox (it used to be 50). This simple notion made possible the automatic filling of matchboxes and gave the Swedes a world monopoly on matches for half a century. By contrast, grandiose ideas of things that will 'revolutionize an industry' are unlikely to work.

In fact, no one can foretell whether a given innovation will end up a big business or a modest achievement. But even if the results are modest, the successful innovation aims from the beginning to become the standard setter, to determine the direction of a new technology or a new industry, to create the business that is – and remains – ahead of the pack. If an innovation does not aim at leadership from the beginning, it is unlikely to be innovative enough.

Above all, innovation is work rather than genius. It requires knowledge. It often requires ingenuity. And it requires focus. There are clearly people who are more talented as innovators than others but their talents lie in well-defined areas. Indeed, innovators rarely work in more than one area. For all his systematic innovative accomplishments, Edison worked only in the electrical field. An innovator in financial areas, Citibank for example, is not likely to embark on innovations in health care.

In innovation as in any other endeavor, there is talent, there is ingenuity, and there is knowledge. But when all is said and done, what innovation requires is hard, focused, purposeful work. If diligence, persistence, and commitment are lacking, talent, ingenuity, and knowledge are of no avail.

There is, of course, far more to entrepreneurship than systematic innovation: distinct entrepreneurial strategies, for example, and the principles of entrepreneurial management, which are needed equally in the established enterprise, the public service organization, and the new venture. But the very foundation of entrepreneurship – as a practice and as a discipline – is the practice of systematic innovation.

2

Managing innovation: an uncertainty reduction process

Alan W. Pearson

Innovation means change. Such changes can be incremental or radical, evolutionary or revolutionary, enabling or disruptive. They can have different effects upon producers and users.

Case studies show the variety of forms innovation takes.

- In the public mind the era of antibiotic discoveries began in 1928 with Alexander Fleming's famous contaminated petri dish. An air-borne mould fell into the culture of a bacterial pathogen, and where the mould grew the pathogen died. What Fleming saw at St Mary's Hospital, London, was an example of microbial antagonism, a phenomenon familiar to all bacteriologists at the time. Louis Pasteur had observed it in 1877, but even he was not the first to do so. In Fleming's time, most bacteriologists would simply have thrown the spoiled culture away, but he looked for the cause. (Conover, 1984)

- The polyethylene terephthalate (PET) plastic bottle was developed at Du Pont by Wyeth. He thought that if you could orient molecules in yarn or film – just as Wallace Carothers did when he invented nylon in the same company in the 1930s – why couldn't you apply the same technique to plastic bottles to make them stronger? Unfortunately the results of some very crude cold-blown bottle tests were disastrous. Trying to convince people the project was worth pursuing was not easy, and over a long period personal time had to be carved out to work on the project from time allocated to a variety of other activities ranging from textile fibres to films and even to electronics. (Wyeth, 1988)

- Chester Carlson came from a poor background and after graduating from Cal-Tech in physics in the 1930s found himself unemployed. He subsequently went to law school and became a patent attorney, where he noticed how difficult and expensive it was to make copies of documents. He then spent many years at night in the New York public library searching for an alternative method, and eventually discovered one in reading about the well-known principle of the photoconductor – a substance that will hold a charge of electricity in the dark, but not in the light. Working on his idea in his kitchen for about five or six years he got his first crude image in 1938. From 1938 to 1944 he talked to many companies, including Kodak and IBM, to no avail. In the mid 1940s Battelle took an interest in developing the process further, and at a later date it was exploited through the

Haloid Corporation after a research person had read about the technology in a journal. (Lamb, 1987)

- Sony Corporation's Tape Recorder Division tried to redesign a small portable tape recorder so that it gave stereophonic sound. But they failed to reduce the size sufficiently and ended up with a prototype that couldn't record anything – so the engineers used it to play their favourite music cassettes while they worked. Mr Ibuka, a honorary chairman, popped into the room, saw this and remembered a project on developing lightweight portable headphones going on elsewhere in the building. The rest is history – the Walkman. (Nayak and Ketteringham, 1986)

- When a sufficiently large electric field is applied to certain fluids, they undergo marked changes in their rheological properties. They can in a matter of milliseconds make a transition from the liquid state to a 'weak solid' state with solid-like properties. Although the mechanism responsible for this phenomenon is still far from understood, the implications for hydraulic systems and common mechanical devices are significant. Not only do ER (electro-rheological) fluids reduce the need for complicated interfaces, but they offer the advantages of rapid responses, significant reduction in space and weight requirements, simpler devices and improved reliability. They could bring about fundamental changes in many everyday devices; for example braking systems, robotics, valves, clutches, shock absorbers, activators and vibration dampers are all applications currently being studied and developed. (Brooks, 1989)

- In the late 1940s Howard Head, an aerospace designer, metals expert and ski enthusiast, began to design, build and test metal skis. Despite disparaging comments from professionals he persuaded to test them, and three years of broken and twisted skis, he persisted, being described as 'possessed by his idea' and 'a fanatic'. He ran out of money and had to sell off 40% of his company, and only after six to seven years and scores of design failures did he finally begin to make some money from his enterprise. Hundreds of others had tried to design metal skis but had failed. Head's skis worked so well they were called 'cheaters'. They sold for $100 in a market used to paying only $25 and helped to create the ski boom of the 1950s. (Quinn, 1979)

- Post-it notepads were made possible by Spencer Silver's research which produced an unexpected outcome – a less aggressive adhesive. Unfortunately the worst thing about this unsticky adhesive was that, for five years, it had no perceptible application. It was a solution looking for a problem. The search was for a better glue, not a worse one. Company support slipped away and the adhesives programme died a natural death. But not for Silver. Persistence and the 15% personal interest time he could call upon kept him going until he found a potential end use and a person willing to put time and effort into developing the idea into a truly innovative and useful product. (Nayak and Ketteringham, 1986)

- Centralized, computer-based management information systems have done much to help people to manage resources. But some applications require data tracking in environments ill-suited for on-line solutions. In these cases it is more desirable to have the person or item carry the required information. This has now become feasible through the use of portable data carrier (PDC) products – or 'smart cards' as they are commonly referred to. (Brownstein and Rosen, 1989)

● The punch card lock system for hotels was developed using brainstorming involving representatives of guests, lobby staff, security people, maintenance crew, local and corporate management. (Holt, 1988)

These nine examples drawn from a vast literature illustrate many of the key issues of innovation: the importance of observant people, the value of experience, the linking of different technologies to turn failure into success, the need for perseverance, the contribution of group problem solving techniques, the potential for opening up a wide range of opportunities and for changing, even destroying, existing organizational and market structures. More detailed analysis of these and other cases provides confirmation of the findings of more systematic research into the factors which influence the success or failure of innovations: for example, the importance of communication, the role of product champions, the matching of technological and market opportunities, and the value of understanding user needs (Rothwell, 1977).

These examples show that technological innovation is a messy process which is not easily managed. This will not surprise many people. In the words of one researcher, 'technology tends to advance in a bubbling, intuitive, tumultuous process – more akin to a fermentation vat than a product line. Individual discoveries tend to be highly individualistic and serendipitous, advances chaotic and interactive, and specific outcomes unpredictable and chancy until the very last moment' (Quinn, 1986).

Drucker (1985), in writing about innovation, poses the question, 'How can managers expect to plan for – or count upon – a process that is itself so dependent on creativity, inspiration, and old-fashioned luck?' and then goes on to answer it by saying 'There are, of course, innovations that spring from a flash of genius. Most innovations, however, especially the successful ones, result from a conscious purposeful search for innovation opportunities which are found only in a few situations.' He goes on to cite examples of such situations including incongruities, process needs, industry and market changes, demographic changes and new knowledge. There is obviously much truth in this analysis, although it must be pointed out that even the most obvious process need may be very difficult to achieve. For example, a reduction in the cost of grinding and polishing plate glass was made possible by the float process, but it took a long time and a great deal of money to make it work. Maidique (1980) states that 'month after month, Alastair Pilkington faced the firm's directors with a new request for $280,000 of operating funds and with promises of progress on the project. For a company with net profits of about $400,000 per month, this was a major risk.'

The views of different researchers in the field of innovation are not necessarily incompatible, that is, planning and serendipity can both be important and be intertwined. But a question to be answered and the one addressed in this chapter is – can we map the innovation process in such a way as to provide a better understanding about how it might be more effectively managed?

Uncertainty and the innovation process

The examples cited in the previous section serve to illustrate the complexity of innovative activity. That is why we have had so many research studies in this area, and why we have such a wide variety of interesting cases of both successful and less successful projects which are extremely valuable starting points for analysis. Drawing on this database and combining it with current research into the planning of innovative activities in R & D departments has yielded a framework which provides useful insights into the innovation process.

The impetus for the development of this framework was the realization that a common point in discussions with managers of innovative activities was the issue of uncertainty. And this uncertainty could be usefully divided into two independently identifiable dimensions which can be described as:

- uncertainty about *ends* or focus, i.e. what the output from the activity is aimed at or is likely to result in, and
- uncertainty about *means* or approaches, i.e. how such an endpoint is likely to be arrived at.

In retrospect, information about both of these dimensions can be obtained from the case studies, in prospect it has to be inferred by those most closely connected with the work. It is on their best judgement that decisions are made, resources allocated and, as more information becomes available, changes put forward to take into account the new knowledge. Such changes may include decisions to accelerate, decelerate, or even stop expenditure on the project. The nature of the uncertainty present and the way it changes over time therefore becomes the focus of the framework shown in Figure 1.

Considering each of the quadrants in turn and relating them to various types of work, we arrive at the following conclusions. Activities in Quadrant 1 are those in which the form of output is not clear and the means by which the work will be carried out cannot be precisely specified. It would be surprising to find a great deal of this type of activity in any organization, although it would be sad to see none. This work might best be termed *exploratory*, possibly to be left in the hands of the most competent and confident scientists and technologists. Feedback on performance is likely to be slow and not very visible to the outside world, and intrinsic as distinct from extrinsic motivation would be a key factor. Alternatively, some of this type of work could well be done on the side, that is, alongside work of a more directed nature where rewards are more easily identifiable. It might well fit into the category often referred to as 'bootlegging'.

Quadrant 2 contains those activities where goals and outputs are more

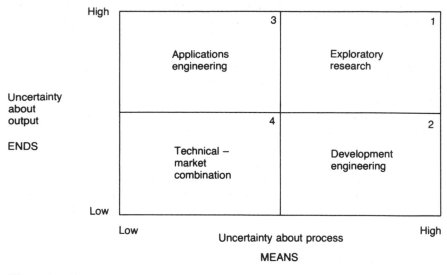

Figure 1   *The uncertainty map*

clearly defined but the means to achieve them are not. It can be argued that many projects fall into this category, perhaps usefully called *development engineering*. The Pilkington float process, metal skis, xerography, are success stories, but only after a long time period, much effort and many technical difficulties. It is almost certain that the presence of a product champion can be an advantage in such circumstances. However, it is also an area where great failures can occur, despite or perhaps because of the presence of such people. Factors influencing success include the likelihood of alternative technologies being chosen. Lengthy timescales often mean a changing external environment into which the innovation has to be introduced, and impact upon the benefits.

Activities in Quadrant 3 are those in which the technology is relatively well-known and the major issue is how it might best be used. *Applications engineering* is a title which is descriptive. There are many examples which fit well into this area, including fluidized bed engineering, freeze drying, laser technology and smart cards. For example, in the case of the latter it has been stated that

> with the variety of potential applications, as well as the assortment of PDC (portable data carriers – a phrase used to describe 'smart cards') it is not surprising that identifying effective applications and integrating systems has become especially important. At Battelle we have had the opportunity to examine and apply PDC technology in a wide variety of application areas. Through this experience, we have found that a systematic approach to applications engineering is needed to identify whether a PDC concept is appropriate to solve a specific problem, and, if so, what set of data carriers and other system elements is best suited for the application. (Brownstein and Rosen, 1989)

The issues raised in this area therefore focus on identifying appropriate customers and working closely with them (Von Hippel, 1986). Not over-stretching by trying to cover too wide a range of applications simultaneously is also important. Prioritization is a keyword.

Quadrant 4 covers the type of innovative activities where the goals and outputs can be fairly well specified and the means to achieve them are relatively clear. The problems here often arise in the area of speed – how quickly can the *technical–market combination* be put together. Competition is potentially high – if it's easy why can't everybody do it? Appropriability and complementary assets may be necessary ingredients of success (Teece, 1987). The Sony Walkman would fit into this quadrant. In such cases the competition can usually respond by introducing similar products or services if they so wish, and where they do, the price is forced down and technical improvements are rapidly introduced to maintain leadership.

Theory, practice and residual risks

The uncertainty map is a concept developed from working on-line with managers as well as from retrospective case analysis. Its characteristics have been briefly described. Its real value lies in its ability to help identify important characteristics which if taken into account will reduce the risks of innovation. Ideas can, and do, occur in a variety of ways, and the process of translating them into successful innovations can be understood better through the uncertainty map. For example, ideas arising from work in Quadrant 1 may well not be easily recognizable as potentially useful by those concerned with the practical aspects of managing organizations. Communication links between the 'explorers' and the 'implementers' need to be strong, although they are just as likely to be based on informal as distinct from formal communications patterns and networks. Ideas that arise in Quadrant 4 may be very exciting to the person concerned, but be seen as trivial by those who have to implement them, with the result that the innovation process is less effective than it might be. Motivation in this area can be a big issue.

Creativity and innovation in Quadrant 3 is more about where 'known' technologies, recent breakthroughs, etc. might be most usefully exploited, and about how to recognize which markets to enter first and what strategies to use to ensure the most effective implementation. The risks are frequently related to spreading resources too thinly across too many market opportunities. Karl Kroyer pointed out that one of the greatest obstacles to success in innovation is the availability of choice, and the consequent tendency toward indecision. After you have decided which product to pursue, you must be absolutely single-minded in your dedication to the profitable introduction of this one product, and this one only. Quadrant 2 is an area in which innovative projects frequently end up, and it is risky. If the potential rewards are high it is worth pursuing, but knowing when to stop is not easy, and formalized methods of planning are not always easy to apply.

A number of different management issues are therefore raised by the uncertainty map. For example, it suggests that Quadrant 1 might best be left to the 'scientists', with 'cultivate' instead of 'manage' being the modus operandi (Breton and Gold, 1987). People who spend much of their time in this type of activity will probably have already built up a reputation in the area.

Broadcasting objectives and market data among technical people, rather than channelling specific kinds of information to individuals, and being non-directive in work assignments might be an appropriate management strategy here. However, it must be remembered that

> where a research problem has not been tightly structured, the solutions – even if found – are not always obvious. An essential skill of the technical manager is his ability to recognize technically or commercially significant results. The history of invention is replete with instances, like Carothers' discovery of nylon, where a flash of insight to the possibilities of totally unanticipated results led to great discoveries that would otherwise have been missed. (Ansoff and Stewart, 1967)

Work in this area might usefully go on as part of a larger, more focused programme. Such activity might be seen as part of the '15% free time' which most R & D directors say their staff have to work on their personal interests. Bednorg makes this point when discussing the work on superconductivity for which he was jointly awarded the Nobel Prize with Alex Mueller (Rae and Forgan, 1989). In answer to the question 'How about the attitude of your employers over the years? Were they always prepared to support a long-term speculative research project?' – he stated 'Apart from superconductivity I had a main project on insulating oxides where I felt I had solid ground under my feet, at least under one foot. Alex and I were convinced that even if we would not discover new superconductivity materials, our work on the metal oxides would yield very interesting results.' Unfortunately many researchers report that they don't seem to be able to find time for such 'extra' activities because of overload from other more pressing work.

Quadrant 2 is certainly the area where the risks are high. Development shoot-outs as suggested by one researcher may be a way of widening the solution arena (Quinn, 1986), but if the uncertainties are too high even this approach may be of little value. Knowing when to get out is not easy, particularly when the external environment is changing and/or the competition is proving to be more successful. But getting out too quickly is also a danger. Product champions are almost essential and the role of Alastair Pilkington in the float process is often cited in this respect. A similar story applies in the case of Tagamet, the ulcer drug developed by James Black – another Nobel Prize winner – for Smith Kline and French. The promises Black made to management about the likely technical success by specific time periods were continually broken and again only the support of a product champion kept the work from being stopped (Nayak and Ketter-ingham, 1986).

In such cases, personality and the possibility of very high rewards to the organization at the end of the day are likely to be the major influences. Unfortunately, when individuals such as product champions get it wrong the almost inevitable consequence is bankruptcy, or at least much reduced profitability, with other possibly longer-term consequences. Sometimes partial fulfilment of goals in a shorter timescale is a more sensible path to pursue – changing directions may be useful, changing the management and the organizational structure may be necessary. Milestone planning and monitoring can indicate the need for such rethinking; it cannot, however, answer all the questions.

If urgency is not a major issue 'bootlegging' may play a big part in the process. From Wyeth's description this seems to have been the approach followed in the PET case. There can be a vital need for the encouragement of this type of activity, but it may be that a more conscious and directed effort by Dupont would have led to an earlier breakthrough and increased profitability from the work.

It could be argued that 'skunk works' might be useful in Quadrant 2, but a special interest session of the Industrial Research Institute 1986 Fall Meeting concluded that such an approach is less likely to succeed when, for example, the project requires too advanced a technology and/or the tran-sition to manufacturing is complex and requires very large scale-up. From an examination of some of the success, it seems that the chances are better when well-known technology is involved. This suggests this might be a more suitable approach for use in Quadrant 3 type activities.

There has been much discussion of the need to increase the speed at which new products are brought to the marketplace and a 'rugby team' in contrast to a 'relay' approach to project management has been suggested as a way of making faster progress (Takeuchi and Nonaka, 1986). This would seem to be most applicable to Quadrant 4 types of innovations, and may well be counterproductive in the other areas.

People, projects and future research

In describing the framework, we have not focused on the types of individ-uals who might be most productive and, probably at the same time, most comfortable in each quadrant, although there has been much speculation about this in our discussions with managers and researchers. Would we, for example, expect adaptors to feel better when working on projects in the Q4 area, and innovators in the Q1 area (Kirton, 1976)? How would the Myers-Briggs types map onto this framework?

Gordon (1966) discussed the characteristics of individuals needed under different combinations of predictability and urgency, the former referring to the extent to which the administrators of a project feel that the steps necessary to achieve their research objectives are predeterminable, and the latter to the need of the organization for rapid research results. Although no empirical data were offered to support the hypothesis, he suggested that for low urgency areas the toleration of tangents would be high, whereas the reverse would be true of high urgency. It was suggested that tolerance for ambiguity would be most needed by individuals faced with low predictability work and that the ability to cope with pressure would be most critical when the urgency was high. None of these hypotheses would seem to contradict what has been said about the management styles and organizational forms identified as likely to be appropriate in each quadrant of the uncertainty map. This therefore appears to be a very fruitful area for research, with obvious implications for individuals and for the organization.

Concluding remarks

Nayak and Ketteringham (1986) stated that 'as a manager, as an organisation, you can get a breakthrough whether you deserve it or not', and that 'new, extraordinary ideas can emerge from any environment'. If this is accepted, the obvious caveats about the need for having a balanced portfolio and for not having too many eggs in one basket, etc. seem too obvious to require any amplification. In this chapter it has been argued that the uncertainty map can be of great help in managing such a portfolio. It focuses attention on the nature of the uncertainty and raises issues of ideas, people, organizational structure and strategy.

Examples from retrospective case studies suggest that the uncertainty map relates to and in fact provides an integrative framework for much of the innovation research to date. It can provide information regarding the possible need to change management style, to accelerate, decelerate or even terminate the activity earlier and hence save scarce resources which can be used to good effect elsewhere. It can therefore be a valuable aid to the better understanding and management of what is inevitably a very complex process.

Its application in practice shows that it focuses attention on critical issues and highlights areas for management intervention, or not, as the case may be. It raises important questions about issues such as clarity of objectives, coordination and commitment, roles in teams, the value of planning techniques and of milestone monitoring. These are key areas for attention which are highlighted in the project management literature. If attention is paid to these, then some of the uncertainty which is inevitably present in innovative activities will be more effectively managed.

References

Ansoff, I.H. and Stewart, J.M. (1967) 'Strategies for a technology-based business', *Harvard Business Review*, November–December, pp. 71–83.

Breton, E.J. and Gold, R.J. (1987) 'Cultivating invention', *Research Technology Management*, September–October, pp. 9–12.

Brooks, D. (1989) 'Fluids get tough', *Physics World*, 2 August, pp. 35–8.

Brownstein, B.J. and Rosen, R.D. (1989) 'Smart cards: tools for research management', *International Journal of Technology Management*, vol. 4, no. 3, pp. 361–6.

Conover, L.H. (1984) 'Discovering tetracycline', *Research Technology Management*, September–October, pp. 17–22.

Drucker, P. (1985) 'The discipline of innovation', *Harvard Business Review*, May–June, pp. 67–72; also Chapter 1, this volume.

Gordon, G. (1966) 'Preconceptions and reconceptions in the administration of science', in M.C. Yovits et al. (eds) *Research Program Effectiveness: proceedings of the conference sponsored by the Office of Naval Research, Washington DC, 1965*, Gordon & Breach, New York and London.

von Hippel, E. (1986) 'Lead users: a source of novel product concepts', *Management Science*, vol. 32, no. 7, July.

Holt, K. (1988) 'The role of the user in product innovation', *Technovation*, 7, pp. 249–58.

Kirton, M.J. (1976) 'Adaptors and innovations: a description and measure', *Journal of Applied Psychology*, 61, pp. 622–9.

Lamb, R.B. (1987) *Running American Business*, Basic Books, pp. 137, 138 and 144.

Maidique, M.A. (1980) 'Entrepreneurs, champions, and technological innovation', *Sloan Management Review*, Winter, pp. 59–76.

Nayak, P.R. and Ketteringham, J.M. (1986) *Breakthroughs*, Rawson & Associates, pp. 130–50.

Quinn, J.B. (1979) 'Technological innovation, entrepreneurship and strategy', *Sloan Management Review*, vol. 20, no. 3, Spring.

Quinn, J.B. (1986) 'Innovation and corporate strategy: managed chaos', in Mel Horwitch (ed.) *Technology in the Modern Corporation: a strategic perspective*, Pergamon, p. 128.

Rae, A. and Forgan, T. (1989) 'The art of the possible', *Physics World*, October, pp. 25–8.

Rothwell, R. (1977) 'The characteristics of successful innovators and technically progressive firms (with some comments on innovation research)', *R&D Management*, vol. 7, no. 3, pp. 191–206.

Takeuchi, H. and Nonaka, I. (1986) 'The new product development game', *Harvard Business Review*, January–February, pp. 137–46.

Teece, D.J. (1987) 'Profiting from technological innovation implications for integration, collaboration, licensing and public policy', in D.J. Teece (ed.) *The Competitive Challenge: strategies for industrial innovation and research*, Ballinger.

Wyeth, N.C. (1988) 'Inventing the PET bottle', *Research Technology Management*, vol. 31, no. 4, July–August, pp. 53–5.

3

Facilitating innovation in large organizations

Robert Rosenfeld and Jenny C. Servo

Carl greeted us with a soft-spoken voice. His stature was slight. As he spoke his eyes danced. It was clear that we were about to interview a corporate treasure.

We entered his office in the Research Labs. What a sight! Yellow Post-it notes, glowing with the thoughts of the day, stuck to the shelves of his voluminous bookcase.

'What are all the Post-its, Carl?' we asked.

'There are no provisions for new ideas, so I keep them posted in my office until I need them,' he said.

Within large organizations innovation faces special problems. As size increases, there is a tendency towards greater depersonalization coupled with a decrease in lateral and vertical communication. Many employees feel like faceless numbers – their position in the structure clearly identified by job descriptions and departmental assignments. In an attempt to protect the growing organizational assets, procedures are put in place. Over time, the organization becomes more rigid and the culture more uniform. Such organizations recognize that within the dynamic world in which we all exist, innovation is essential. Yct, large organizations face a dilemma. They must allow for change while still maintaining a high degree of organizational integrity. It practice, this is extremely difficult to do (Adams, 1976; Andrews, 1975; Shephard, 1967; Van Gundy, 1985).

The intent of this chapter is to present a model referred to as the 'Office of Innovation', which has been implemented within more than ten Fortune 200 corporations. It is an employee involvement program which draws upon the human resources of the organization. From a financial perspective this model offers a high return on investment; from an administrative perspective it allows one to pace the rate of change; from a humanistic perspective it allows the 'mavericks' a way to contribute more fully to the organization. To understand the model and its adaptation to different environments, attention will initially be given to definitions, roles, and communication gaps.

Differences between creativity and innovation

Many people believe 'creativity' and 'innovation' are synonymous, but they are different. Creativity refers to the generation of novel ideas – innovation to making money with them. Creativity is the starting point for any innovation: in many cases, a solitary process, conjuring up the image of an eccentric scientist buried under mounds of papers, or of an artist surrounded by half-finished canvases and multicolored palettes. Innovation is the hard work that follows idea conceptions and usually involves the labor of many people with varied, yet complementary, skills. The challenge is to transform creative ideas into tangible products or processes that will improve customer services, cut costs and/or generate new earnings for an organization (Levitt, 1963; Rosenfeld and Servo, 1984).

Simply put,

Innovation = Conception + Invention + Exploitation.

In this context, the word 'conception' refers to an idea that is novel with respect to some frame of reference (individual, departmental, organizational, or all accumulated knowledge); the word 'invention' applies to any novel idea that is transformed into reality; and the word 'exploitation' refers to getting the most out of an invention. Therefore, 'exploitation' normally implies wide acceptance and/or profitability resulting from the invention. 'Conception, invention, and exploitation' are all necessary ingredients for innovation. The challenge facing large organizations of all types is to reduce the time among these three stages. This can be accomplished by wisely releasing the creative potential of individual employees and empowering them to contribute to the goals of the corporation.

Harnessing an idea and transforming its potential into reality requires turning around the thinking of many people holding claim to resources needed to fuel an idea's growth (financing, information, human resources). Innovation almost always involves a prolonged battle amongst numerous people and requires tremendous stamina and confidence on the part of a champion (Schon, 1963; Servo, 1988).

Innovation players

Most large organizations contain individuals who informally promote innovation through their roles as 'ideators', 'inventors', 'technology gatekeepers', 'champions', 'sponsors', and 'entrepreneurs (or intrapreneurs)'. With the exception of inventors and entrepreneurs, these players are frequently not distinguishable to themselves or others. Individuals do not tend to think of themselves as champions, technology gatekeepers, or sponsors. Human Resource departments are also unaccustomed to classifying employees according to these informal roles that are so vital to innovation. Instead, they tend to focus on formal job descriptions, as these are key to performance appraisals. The recognition of these players within an organization is an important first step in facilitating innovation.

An 'ideator' is a prolific idea generator who, by definition, does not like to 'reduce ideas to practice' (i.e. make a prototype), but would rather restrict the ideas to the realm of mental gymnastics. Ideation appears to almost be a form of play. As soon as the ideator's feet hit the floor in the morning, he or she starts to generate countless possibilities. The motivation for the ideator is quite varied: playfulness, fear of failure, and stress reduction are but a few. In many situations, this process is difficult for the ideator to control – ideas just flow.

'Inventors' like to reduce ideas to practice; in fact, they savor it. For them, the challenge is in solving the problem – in putting the solution into a tangible form. More likely than not, their inventions are not initially in a marketable form. There is a *New Yorker* cartoon which depicts various inventions for 'keeping warm': prominent among these are a waterbottle tie and a catnip comforter covered, of course, with cats – practical solutions in the inventor's mind, but would require a master salesman!

Organizations often forget that for an inventor, the joy comes in savoring the solution. With R & D environments, a project may frequently be stopped or transferred to another department before the inventor has had the opportunity to reap the joy that comes from full explorations of their work. 'It's like a Christmas present,' one inventor said. 'If it's for you, you would want to open it yourself. You wouldn't just hand it over to someone else to open. You'd like to delight in its unveiling. Once you've had an opportunity to enjoy it, to see it, you wouldn't mind letting others share it.'

Another important role that is frequently overlooked is that of 'technology gatekeeper'. Often they are viewed by their organizations as technology experts and are used by the organization and individuals for 'reality checks'. For technology gatekeepers, the motivation is to keep on the 'cutting edge'.

A 'champion' has status or clout and advocates on behalf of others. Champions, in fact, help legitimize the idea originator, serving as a bridge, or a translator between the sometimes unconventional idea originator (ideator or inventor) and the more traditional organization.

A 'sponsor' usually has higher status within an organization and a proven track record. By definition, the sponsor also has resources (money, people, equipment) and applies them towards the development of an idea. His or her motivation is usually for strategic gain of their organization, the corporation, or the individual. By connecting with other players in the innovation process, this role ultimately brings great benefit to the corporation in increased earnings and development of personnel.

Finally there is 'the entrepreneur', the individual, calculated risk-taker whose primary drive is to start and develop a new organization, new product, or new process that will profit and thrive.

All of these players are essential for innovation. Yet in American culture, we tend to make folk heroes only of the inventors and entrepreneurs.

Perhaps the champions, technology gatekeepers, and sponsors suffer from a lack of press – little glamour or apparent risk attached to their roles. Their roles, however, are essential. Imagine, if you will, a beaver standing at the base of Hoover Dam, saying 'Well, it was my idea'. You can see the absurdity of 'single-handed acceptance' of the responsibility for making anything a commercial success.

Innovations as a relay race

This cast of players exists without designation in every large organization embedded within a formal structure characterized by bureaucracy, strategic focus, budgetary constraints, and limited time. Innovation players, in their effort to get their idea through the corporate labyrinth, play what can best be likened to a relay race. However, unlike the relay races to which we are accustomed, a player in this team will not, at the outset, know the names of the other players, nor their location within the organization (Rosenfeld, 1984).

The idea itself is analogous to the baton. Each member of the relay race needs to entice others to be on the team. Frequently this is accomplished by changing the baton's form as it is in motion. At times, the relay race may have the appearance of a rugby game, as players move downfield together at the same time, each playing their specific role. However, the goal line may be unclear and the rules of the game are constantly being revised.

The innovation process is complex. If one does not appreciate the complexity of the process , both the ideas and the players will falter. Common places for an idea to be dropped within complex organizations are with (1) the idea originator, (2) middle management, and (3) across organizational boundaries.

Communication gaps

A communication gap occurs at each juncture where an idea may be dropped. The *first communication gap* lies within the idea originator. He or she may fail to take the idea to another for fear of ridicule. This is not without cause. We tend to 'turn each other off' very readily with a casual phrase or sneer. An idea or an invention, however, is like someone's child. The use of a 'killer phrase' such as 'Well, if that's such a great idea, why hasn't someone else done it?' is like telling a parent that their child has no talent.

Fear of the idea's theft, lack of time, or lack of incentives may also be deterrents to the idea originator. We inadvertently tend to reinforce individuals for keeping their ideas to themselves. Often, the risk of sharing is far greater than keeping an idea to oneself. When stepping forth with an idea, an individual may open himself up to personal rejection. 'I don't care how good the idea is, I don't like you and won't give it the time of day.' Such statements are not explicitly stated to the idea originator, but frequently surface behind closed doors.

If an employee overcomes this first hurdle and exercises one of the various informal roles in innovation through the traditional corporate structure, his or her efforts may be poorly received. If an idea originator takes the idea to management prematurely, he or she may get little action. Many managers are chronically overextended and may view a new idea as an annoyance, or at best, a distraction that interferes with assigned objectives.

Additionally, if the idea is extremely complex or tangential to a manager's assigned work, he may simply not know what to do with it. Many organizations fail to disclose the corporate mission, strategy, and business objectives to their employees, fearing that knowledge of this would provide the competition with an advantage. A consequence of this approach is that many managers within one division will not know what is important to another division, as well as the overall corporation. It is, therefore, unreasonable to expect that first-line or even middle management would necessarily have the perspective or information needed to deal effectively with all ideas that are brought to their attention (*second communication gap*).

In actuality, the expertise needed to evaluate complex ideas is housed within different sectors of large, highly bureaucratic, and mature organizations: in research and development, marketing, manufacturing, administration, finance, etc. However, the physical separation, differences in jargon, and differences in mode of operation present yet a *third communication gap*.

Crossing organizational barriers is very difficult. The 'not invented here (NIH)' phenomenon is quite prevalent in many organizations. Many times an idea will be rejected simply because it has come from outside the department. It is viewed as a 'foreign body' invading the department, rather than something which could be of potential value.

Idea connections

There are numerous opportunities for an idea to be dropped and few occasions for it to be carried through. Many formal and informal approaches have been instituted to prevent ideas from faltering. Heroic efforts have been made by inventors to push their ideas through bureaucratic mazes. Individuals such as Charles Kettering, former Director of R & D for General Motors, have taken it upon themselves to 'buck the system' by developing their own style for dealing with the organizational barriers to innovation. They have bootlegged time (i.e. used discretionary time on the job), found contact people in various sectors of the company, and in general done outlandish things in order to get a hearing for their idea.

However, not every idea originator has the know-how, the drive, and the aggressiveness to do so. Many employees and organizations could benefit from a structure that acts as a conduit to help ideas flow more readily through an organization.

The Office of Innovation

Various structures have been initiated to help facilitate innovation including the 'Office of Innovation' model developed at the Eastman Kodak Company during the late 1970s. This type of model has been implemented by many other large organizations including American Greeting Cards, Amoco Chemical Company, Atomic Energy of Canada, Bell Canada, Electronic Surveillance Command of the United States Air Force, Northwestern Bell, and Union Carbide. This system provides a mechanism for drawing together a cast of informal innovation players around ideas which are often not part of one's assigned work (Rosenfeld and Servo, 1988).

The 'Office of Innovation' is the name of a process that is used to evaluate complex ideas. In other organizations this model may be referred to as 'The New Ideas Process', 'Aviary', 'Discovery', 'The Innovation Network' and the like. The 'Office of Innovation' (OI) transcends the interests of individual departments, thereby allowing for cross-fertilization of ideas among divisions. It operates as a conduit for ideas to flow freely throughout an organization. This model coexists with other idea systems within the organization that are designed to handle different types of ideas and/or clientele (i.e. suggestion systems and quality circles).

An OI can be a highly decentralized network of individual offices located in various client areas (marketing, sales, manufacturing, R & D). The more decentralized the network, the greater the success. It is in essence a 'point of sale' operation located in various client areas. The office is a physical location that is readily discernible to employees and is staffed by facilitators, referred to as innovation facilitators, connectors, idea facilitators, etc. The idea flow rate is directly proportional to the number of 'Office' sites – the more sites, the greater the idea flow. These staff members have the designated responsibility to seek out and attract individuals who informally play various roles within the innovation process. In this model, people who bring their ideas to the OI (ideators and inventors) are referred to as idea originators; technology gatekeepers serve as consultants; and champions and sponsors are designated in the traditional way.

It takes considerable time and ingenuity to find out who these informal players are, but once discerned, the model performs very well and can be relied upon to enrich, screen, and find sponsorship within the organization, for a good number of complex ideas. For example, after several years of operation within the Eastman Kodak Company, the estimated value of ideas harvested in one year alone was approximately $300 million (over the lifetime of the idea) while the cost of connecting the ideas through an OI network containing 19 offices was only 0.3% of the potential revenue (Rosenfeld and Servo, 1988).

Very few ideas that are taken to an OI will be adopted (e.g. four out of 100 at Eastman Kodak Company, 1979–88). Yet after 10 years in operation at the Eastman Kodak Company, satisfaction with the process remains high for idea originators, with over 90% of those responding to surveys indicating that they would continue to use OI. This high rate of satisfaction is attributed to the philosophy which guides each OI (see Table 1).

Table 1   *The philosophy of the Office of Innovation*

1	Ideas are fragile (so are people).
2	Ideas are organic and need to be nurtured (so do people).
3	All ideas have value and should be given a hearing.
4	The originator of an idea needs assistance in idea enhancement and in promoting the idea internally.
5	The originator is the initial advocate of an idea and should be actively involved in its development.
6	Only ideas which have been enhanced and demonstrate potential value will be brought to management.
7	Both marketing and technical issues need to be addressed in the development of an idea.
8	Differences among people constitute a strength, not a weakness. Individuals can benefit from the opportunity to interact with other professionals from different perspectives.
9	A mediator is often necessary to facilitate the communication of people from different cultures and who may possess clashing personalities.
10	The most effective way to proceed is not necessarily the most efficient.

This philosophy serves as the foundation for the model's success. Each facilitator implements the process with regard to his or her cultural area, in a way consistent with the philosophy. The process used (see Figure 1) provides a systematic approach for idea development, autonomy to an idea originator, and weaves in other players at appropriate times. There are five stages to the process:

1   Idea generation
2   Initial screening
3   Group review
4   Seeking sponsorship
5   Sponsorship.

The process begins with a meeting between the idea originator and a facilitator. The facilitator functions as an advocate of the originator, their guide through the corporate labyrinth, and as their bridge to management. During idea generation, the idea is enriched. The process includes asking the originator to describe the idea, obtaining the reasons for his or her belief of its potential value to the company, and discussing the degree to which technical and marketing concerns have been addressed. If the idea originator wishes to proceed, he or she is then asked to prepare a brief, one or two page description, sometimes referred to as an idea memorandum

STAGES

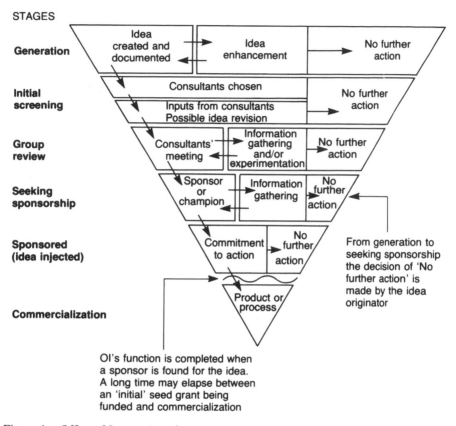

Figure 1 *Office of Innovation idea connection process*

(IM). Generally, the idea's progress through the process is dependent not only on the quality of the idea and its enhancement, but also upon the amount of drive the originator exerts. If the originator is unable to put in the time and effort required, the OI can only be of limited help (Rosenfeld and Servo, 1985).

If the originator chooses to proceed, he or she enters the next phase, referred to as initial screening. Here the facilitator and originator jointly select a group of experts within the organization to review the idea. Many of these are *technology gatekeepers*, and are referred to as consultants. The consultant's involvement is voluntary. Between five and 15 consultants chosen from a large pool of employees are typically called upon to review any given idea memorandum. This pool of employees is not a fixed stable of designated experts.

The consultants are sent a copy of the idea memorandum along with a brief questionnaire requesting their comments in many areas including: novelty, market needs, and technological feasibility; additions that they would make to improve it; and whether or not they wish to be involved in any further review and/or elaboration of this idea. At the originator's request this stage can proceed as a blind-review, with the originator's name withheld.

The reviews are collected and another meeting scheduled between the facilitator and the idea originator. The goal of this meeting is to review the information provided by the reviewers and to decide jointly how to proceed. The facilitator's role is always similar – responding to the originator's ideas, asking probing questions in a subtle but directive manner, and requiring the individual to make decisions. The decision as to whether or not to proceed is always made by the originator, thus allowing for his or her growth.

If the decision is made to go ahead, the originator enters the group review stage. This is an individual meeting or series of face-to-face meetings with consultants. The purpose of these meetings is to gather more information and hopefully some assistance and/or resources. If the group review process goes well, the next step may include some experimentation, market research, or prototype development. These tasks may be conducted by the originator or one or more of the consultants who may have expressed a willingness to help. Any time invested by the originator or consultants is on a voluntary or bootleg basis.

As more and more information is gathered and the idea is further enhanced, its value to the organization becomes more apparent. It soon becomes necessary to shift to the fourth stage of the process, referred to as seeking sponsorship. Here, the major objective is to find at least a champion, and hopefully an internal sponsor for the idea. The idea has now reached dimensions where it requires some assistance by individuals with stature and/or money to legitimize its growth. The bootleg efforts have reached their limits. More often than not champions and sponsors have a management position within the formal structure. Thus, this stage marks the beginning of the transition from the informal to formal channels of the organization.

As an idea moves through this process, its progress can be charted. An individual facilitator's performance can be viewed by looking at the percentage of ideas that move successfully from one stage to the next (see Figure 2). Based on Kodak's experience, one should expect that 40% to 60% of ideas should be lost during the first two stages, with the idea originators having screened themselves out of the process as a consequence of the feedback they received through the review process. The last stage shown in Figure 2 is the 'champion' stage, referring to an idea's advocacy by individuals other than the idea originator. Eighteen percent of the ideas reached this stage. 'Seed' sponsored (a subset of the champion stage) designates that funding has been provided by a department as a clear budgeted line-item. Nine percent of the ideas reached this stage. At this point it is up to the host organization to nurture further development of the idea. The Office of Innovation's role is completed.

Another benefit of such a system is that it enables one to learn about the human resources of the organization in a different way:

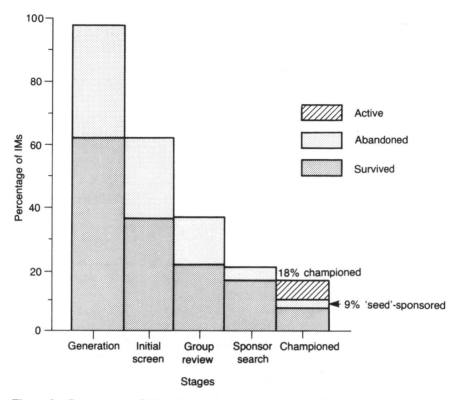

Figure 2   *Progression of IMs (idea memoranda) by stage (1985–86) in the Eastman Kodak Company*

'Until recently,' Carl said, 'there were no provisions for new ideas, so I kept them in my files until a need arose. If someone needed something, then I would contribute solutions from my file; but unless there was a need, it was a waste of time to try and peddle them.

Then the emphasis came on innovation. I was really surprised to see that the Innovation System worked. They disseminated my ideas, found interested people, and sponsors for a number of them.'

This idea originator was modest. His ideas were not only prolific, but extremely valuable to the company. Within the space of just three years, he submitted approximately 15 proposals, more than half of which found champions or sponsors, with projected value in the millions of dollars.

Using an Idea-O-Graph, the contributions of individuals can be charted (see Figure 3). The Idea-O-Graph is a plot of different levels of corporate commitment to an idea over a period of time. The level of commitment increases monetary outlay as the corporation commits to higher levels of an idea's growth. The slope of the line indicates how efficiently an organization implements an idea's growth from origination through commercialization. The slope will vary according to the type of idea being implemented. For example, a sales idea will be easier to implement and show a

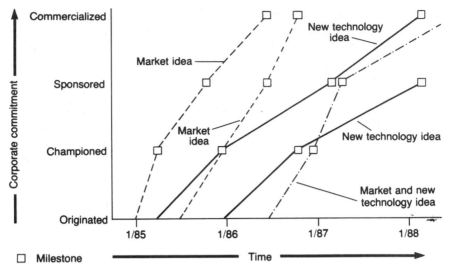

Figure 3   *Idea-O-Graph*

steeper slope (e.g. takes less time from origination to commercialization) than one requiring a new technology involving research and development. By comparing similar projects and their slopes along the graph, one learns how long it takes the organization to transform an idea into a business reality. This graphic representation of idea growth provides information that will assist in the optimization of the stages of the innovation process. This can be extremely valuable knowledge for an organization, making them aware of special skills and how ideas evolve in their company.

Office of Innovation facilitators can act as a guide for those involved with innovation. They make the organizational labyrinth less treacherous, make it easier to find the other team members, help groom the baton before passing it along, assist management by providing them with mature ideas for review and generally increase the odds of getting a hearing for ideas within the organization.

Summary

The mood in American industry today is highly analytical. There is the tendency to look for quick formulas, for ways to maximize efficiency, and as mentioned at the outset, to view employees in a depersonalized way. Often employees are moved around an organization with the same consideration that one would have for a table or chair. In this climate, it is likely that people may look at the Office of Innovation model through analytical eyes.

However, what makes the innovation process work is a truly personalized interaction between facilitators and the cast of innovation players. Not everyone can play the role of a facilitator, who, like 'the invisible man', helps to make things happen. This personalized process aims at releasing human potential in a way that will benefit the corporation.

In this regard, we can take a lesson from Japanese corporations. It appears that due to the history and cultural values of Japan, it is easier for the Japanese to suppress their 'egos', focusing instead on the greater good. Transforming an idea into reality therefore becomes less of a problem as individuals are less likely to pose barriers. But they will, instead, 'fall in line' to move an innovation ahead. The difficulty for Japanese corporations is the front end of the innovation process. Their devotion to the group makes it less likely that they will think in creative ways that are tangential to, or radically different from, those of the group.

The problems facing American industry are the opposite and are likewise steeped in our culture. Americans have many creative ideas and find it easier to think tangentially. We have a cultural attachment to images of the 'rugged individualist' and the 'sharp shooters of the old west'. Therefore, we find it difficult to 'line up' behind a common cause. The result is that in large American industry, 'egos' and 'politics' frequently get in the way and often are the rate-limiting steps to innovation and growth of new business opportunities.

One of the positive manifestations of the American 'free-spirit' is entrepreneurial behavior. The Japanese demonstrate unified action. The task, therefore, is to merge the Eastern and Western processes into a new paradigm that will unleash the creative potential and 'free-up' innovative activities while focusing on unified goals of the organization.

References

Adams, J.S. (1976). Structure and dynamics of behavior in organization boundary roles. In M.D. Dunnette (Ed.), *Handbook of Industrial and Organization Psychology*. Chicago: Rand McNally.

Andrews, F.M. (1975). Social and psychological factors which influence the creative process. In I.A. Taylor and J.W. Getzels (Eds), *Perspectives in Creativity*. Chicago: Aldine.

Levitt, T. (1963). Creativity is not enough. *Harvard Business Review*, May, 72–83.

Rosenfeld, R. (1984). Innovation through investment in people: The consideration of creative styles. *Creativity Week VII: 1984 Proceedings*. Center for Creative Leadership.

Rosenfeld, R. and Servo, J. (1984) Making ideas connect. *The Futurist*. August, 21–26.

Rosenfeld, R. and Servo, J. (1985) The first step to implementing new and better ideas. *Intrapreneurial Excellence*, November, 4, 6–7.

Rosenfeld, R. and Servo, J. (1988). Innovation through investment in people. Unpublished manuscript.

Schon, A. (1963). Champions for radical new inventions. *Harvard Business Review*, March–April, 84.

Servo, J. (1988). Creativity by itself reaps no profits. *Rochester Business Journal*, No. 21–27, 7.

Shephard, H.A. (1967). Innovation-resisting and innovation-producing organizations. *Journal of Business*, 48, 91–102.

Van Gundy, M. (1985). Organizational creativity and innovation: a review and needed future research. In S.G. Isaksen (Ed.), *Frontiers of Creativity Research: Beyond the Basics*. Buffalo: Bearly Limited.

SECTION 2

PERSONAL QUALITIES

4

Visionary leadership and strategic management

Frances Westley and Henry Mintzberg

A strange process seems to occur as concepts such as culture and charisma move from practice to research. Loosely used in practice, these concepts, as they enter academia, become subjected to a concerted effort to force them to lie down and behave, to render them properly scientific. In the process they seem to lose their emotional resonance, no longer expressing the reality that practitioners originally tried to capture.

Leadership is another such concept. Somewhere along the line, as Pondy has argued, 'we lost sight of the "deep structure", or meaning of leadership' (1978: 90). In attempting to deal with the observable and measurable aspects of leadership behaviour, and perhaps to simplify for normative purposes, leadership research has focused on a narrow set of styles – democratic, autocratic, and *laissez-faire*, for example. We agree with Pondy that instead 'we should be trying to document the variety of styles available' (1978: 90).

Strategy may also be such a concept. Much effort has been dedicated in strategic management to narrowing it, to pinning it down (as in the attention to 'generic' strategies), likewise to narrowing the process by which it forms (in the attention to 'planning'). Again, in attempting to dissect a living phenomenon, the skeleton may be revealed while the specimen dies.

More recently, the concepts of strategy and leadership have been combined into that of strategic vision. In academia (Bennis, 1982; Mendell and Gerjuoy, 1984) as well as practice (*Business Week*, 1984; Kiechel, 1986). This has been hailed as a key to managing increasingly complex organizations. Consultants have responded with workshops (e.g. Levinson and Rosenthal, 1984) that promise to train managers to be visionary leaders. In general, however, efforts to turn the creation of strategic vision into a

Extracted from *Strategic Management Journal*, 10 (1989), pp. 17–32, © 1989 by John Wiley & Sons Ltd. Reproduced by permission of John Wiley & Sons Ltd manageable process, one that can be researched, taught, and adopted by managers, risk robbing it of its vitality.

Of special concern should be the tendency to subsume strategic vision under leadership in general, in other words to perceive it as just another category of leadership style (e.g. 'transformative'; Tichy and Devanna, 1986). Most writings seem to agree that leadership vision, or 'visioning', as the process has sometimes been called, can be broken down into three distinct stages: (1) the envisioning of 'an image of a desired future organizational state' (Bass, 1987: 51) which (2) when effectively articulated and communicated to followers (Bennis and Nanus, 1985; Tichy and Devanna, 1986; Gluck, 1984) serves (3) to empower those followers so that they can enact the vision (Sashkin, 1987; Srivastva, 1983; Conger and Kanungo, 1987; Robbins and Duncan, 1987). Such a view posits enormous control in the hands of the individual leader (Bennis and Nanus, 1985; Meindl, Ehrlich and Dukerich, 1985; Gupta, 1984).

If the field of strategic management is to render the concept of strategic vision suitable for its own purposes it must deal with it in a unique way. That is what we set out to do in this paper, proceeding from three assumptions that differ from those of the traditional leadership literature. First, we assume that visionary leadership is a dynamic, interactive phenomenon, as opposed to a unidirectional process. Second, we assume that the study of strategic vision must take into consideration strategic content as well as the strategic contexts of product, market, issue, process, and organization. Third, we assume that visionary style can take on a variety of different forms.

In this chapter we shall deal with each of these assumptions in turn. We build our description on a survey of biographical and autobiographical publications of a number of well-known leaders generally thought to be visionary, including Lee Iacocca of Chrysler, Jan Carlzon of SAS, Edwin Land of Polaroid, René Lévesque of the Parti Quebécois, and Steven Jobs, formerly of Apple Computer.

Visionary leadership as drama

As noted, visionary leadership is increasingly being defined as a process with specific steps, by and large as follows:

vision (idea) → communication (word) → empowerment (action)

The process, in its emphasis on active leadership and unidirectional flow, may be likened to a hypodermic needle, with the active ingredient (vision) loaded into a syringe (words) which is injected into the patient (subordinate) to effect change. Stripped to its essence, this model takes on a mechanical quality which surely robs the process of much of its evocative appeal.

An alternative image of visionary leadership might be that of a drama.

Here action and communication occur simultaneously. Idea and emotion, actor and audience, are momentarily united in a rich encounter which occurs on many symbolic levels. Peter Brook (1968), the legendary director of the Royal Shakespeare Company, has suggested that the magic of the theatre lies in that moment when fiction and life somehow blend together. It may be brief, but it is the goal of playwright, director, actor and audience, the result of 'rehearsal', the 'performance' itself, and the 'attendance' of the audience. Brook, however, finds these words too static, and prefers the French equivalents 'repetition', 'representation' and 'assistance' (p. 154), all of which, coincidentally, have special meanings in English. We wish to suggest that these words may equally be substituted to describe strategic vision, suggesting a dynamic model as follows, each stage of which we then discuss in turn.

repetition   ⟷   representation   ⟷   assistance
   (idea)   (vision)   (emotion and action)

Repetition

Repetition, according to Brook, beautifully captures the endless practice in which every artist must engage. He notes that Lawrence Olivier would repeat his lines again and again until he had so trained his tongue muscles to say them that he could perform effortlessly (p. 154). Repetition is likewise the musician practising her scales until she can be consistent every time, so that while she performs she can think about the music itself rather than the individual notes.

For the strategic visionary, repetition has a similar role – to develop an intimacy with the subject at hand, to deal with strategy as 'craft', as one of us has noted elsewhere:

> Craft evokes the notions of traditional skill, dedication, perfection through the mastery of detail. It is not so much thinking and reason that spring to mind as involvement, a sense of intimacy and harmony with the materials at hand, developed through long experience and commitment. (Mintzberg, 1987a: 66)

Like the craftsman, the strategic visionary would appear to develop strategic perception as much through practice and gut-level feel for the business, product, market and technology as through conscious cognition. Lee Iacocca 'grew up' in the auto industry. When he left Ford he went to Chrysler because cars were 'in his blood' (Iacocca, 1984: 141). Jan Carlzon hailed as a visionary for his turnaround at SAS airlines, has spent his entire career (beginning in 1968) in the travel business, since 1978 in the airline industry.

Consider how Edwin Land describes his invention of the Polaroid camera:

> One day when we were vacationing in Santa Fe in 1943 my daughter, Jennifer, who was then 3, asked me why she could not see the picture I had just taken of

her. As I walked around that charming town, I undertook the task of solving the puzzle she had set for me. Within the hour the camera, the film and the physical chemistry became so clear that with a great sense of excitement I hurried to the place where a friend was staying to describe to him in detail a dry camera which would give a picture immediately after exposure. In my mind it was so real that I spent several hours on this description. (Land, 1972a: 84)

Reading this description, it is easy to focus on the element of inspiration, of an idea seemingly springing fully blown, from nowhere. What might be forgotten is that Land had spent years in the laboratory perfecting the polarization process, schooling his scientific and inventive abilities, practising and repeating, learning his craft. His inspiration fell on fertile ground, prepared by endless repetition. As Land himself said:

It was as if all that we had done . . . had been a school and a preparation both for that first day in which I suddenly knew how to make one-step dry photographic process and for the following three years in which we made the very vivid dream into a solid reality. (Wensbergh, 1987: 85)

In a sense the strategic visionary practises for the moment of vision, much as the actor practises for the moment of performance. But for strategy to become vision, craft is not enough. Repetition can become deadly, rigidifying innovation into imitation. Strategic visionaries are leaders who use their familiarity with the issues as a springboard to innovation, who are able to add value by building new perceptions on old practices.

Representation

For the actor, the performance itself is what must transform repetition into success. Brook chooses the word 'representation' to describe this transformation. To represent means to take the past and make it live again, giving it immediacy, vitality. In a sense, representation redeems repetition, turning it from craft into art.

But what corresponds to the work of art for the strategic visionary? It is, of course, the vision itself. But not the vision as a private mental image. Rather, it is the vision articulated, the vision *represented* and communicated, in words and in actions. Just as a leader cannot exist without followers, so too strategic vision cannot exist without being so recognized by followers.

For this reason we equate visionary leadership not just with an idea *per se*, but with the communicated idea. Here we are concerned with the profoundly symbolic nature of visionary leadership. What distinguishes visionary leadership is that through words and actions, the leader gets the followers to 'see' his or her vision – to see a new way to think and act – and so to join their leader in realizing it. *How* the vision is communicated thus becomes as important as *what* is communicated. Edwin Land understood this as well. He argued that inventions have two parts: the product itself, which must be 'startling, unexpected and come to a world which is *not* prepared', and the 'gestalt' in which the product is embedded:

> The second great invention for supporting the first invention is finding how to relate the invention itself to the public. It is the public's role to resist. All of us have a miscellany of ideas, most of which are not consequential. It is the duty of the inventor to build a new gestalt for the old one in the framework of society. And when he does his invention calmly and equitably becomes part of everyday life and no one can understand why it wasn't always there. But until the inventor has done both things [product and gestalt] nothing has any meaning. (Land, 1975: 50)

And how is such a gestalt created? Here again, the metaphor of drama is useful. When the actor represents the play, he or she draws upon a variety of verbal and non-verbal resources. The voice, the face, the gesture, the language itself, the timing, the costume, the lighting, the staging, all combine in an intricate weave to arouse and inspire the audience to create a living gestalt. There is much to suggest that the visionary leader shares many of the actor's skills in representing his or her strategic vision.

For example, one is hard-pressed to find an example of a visionary leader who was not also adept at using language. Language has the ability to stimulate and motivate, not only through appeals to logic but also through appeals to emotion (Burke, 1950; Pfeffer, 1981; Edelman, 1964). Rhetoricians since Aristotle have carefully observed the potential of linguistic devices such as alliteration, irony, imagery and metaphor, among other things, to provoke identification and emotional commitment among listeners. The speeches of famous visionary leaders such as Winston Churchill and Martin Luther King offer good examples of the skilful use of such rhetorical devices, which allow their listeners to 'see' the visions as if they were real. Analysis of Lee Iacocca's leadership in the Chrysler turnaround suggests that much of the power of his strategic initiatives resided in his use of metaphors to unite stakeholders behind him (Westley and Mintzberg, 1988). Likewise, Edwin Land inspired his employees not only with his inventions, but also with the evocative imagery with which he surrounded them. In a short statement on photography (Land, 1972a), Land suggested that it was a way of retaining the shifting, fleeting world of childhood and thus giving the child 'a new kind of security'. Sharing photographs was to him an act of intimacy; to show someone a photograph you took was to give them a 'deeper insight into you as well as what you discerned'. Land presented his new camera as follows:

> It will help [the photographer] to focus some aspect of his life and in the process enrich his life at that moment. This happens as you focus through the view finder. It's not merely the camera you are focusing: you are focusing yourself. That's an integration of your personality, right that second. Then when you touch the button, what's inside you comes out. It's the most basic form of creativity. Part of you is now permanent. (Land, 1972a: 84)

In a similar fashion, Steven Jobs described the Macintosh as an 'insanely great' product, which will 'make a difference'. He described his co-workers as 'the people who would have been poets in the sixties and they're looking at computers as their medium of expression rather than language' (Jobs, 1984: 18). On the Apple Computer Company itself, Jobs said: 'There's something going on here . . . something that is changing the world and this is the epicenter' (Jobs, 1984: 18). As Steve Wozniak, the co-founder with Jobs of the Apple Computer Company, tersely noted: 'he can always couch things in the right words' (Patterson, 1985).

In addition to language, the visionary leader can use a range of drama-turgical devices capable of stimulating and arousing responses. Non-verbal elements such as gesture (Hall, 1959), glance (Goffman, 1959), timing (Wrapp, 1967), movement and props are also able to evoke similar re-sponses. For example, Steve Jobs organized the Apple office as a circle of work areas around a central foyer. There stood a grand piano and a BMW. 'I believe people get ideas from seeing great products,' Jobs claimed (Wise, 1984: 146).

In sum, the media of communication for the visionary are many and varied. By wedding perception with symbols the visionary leader creates a vision, and the vision, by evoking an emotional response, forms a bridge between leader and follower as well as between idea and action.

Assistance

Brook argues that for repetition to turn into representation requires more than practice, more than craft, more than the power of word and gesture. An audience is needed. But not a passive audience. It must be active, hence the importance of 'assistance'.

Brook tells of an ingenious experiment to show what audience assistance entails (1968: 27–9). During a lecture to a lay group he asked a volunteer to come to the front and do a reading. The audience, predicting that the volunteer would make a fool of himself, began to titter. But Brook had given the volunteer a passage from Peter Weiss' play on Auschwitz, which recounted with great clarity a description of the dead. The volunteer was too 'appalled' by what he was reading to pay much attention to the titters, and something of his attitude was communicated to the audience. It became quieter. As the volunteer was moved by what he was reading, he delivered the text with exactly the right pacing and intonations, and the audience responded with 'shocked, attentive silence' (p. 28).

Next Brook asked for a second volunteer. This time the text was a speech from Henry V listing the names of English and French dead at the battle of Agincourt. Recognizing Shakespeare, the volunteer launched into a typically amateur rendition: false voice, stilted phrasing, etc. The audience grew restless and inattentive. At the finish Brook asked the audience why the list of the dead at Agincourt did not evoke the same response as the description of the dead at Auschwitz. A lively discussion ensued. Brook then asked the same volunteer to read again, but to stop after each name. During the short silence the audience was to try to put together the images of Auschwitz and Agincourt. The reader began. Brook recounts:

> As he spoke the first name, the half silence became a dense one. Its tension caught the reader, there was an emotion in it, shared between him and them and it turned all his attention away from himself on to the subject matter he was speaking. Now the audience's concentration began to guide him: his inflections were simple, his rhythms true: this in turn increased the audience's interest and so the two-way current began to flow. (1968: 29)

Like a performance, a strategy is made into vision by a two-way current. It cannot happen alone, it needs assistance. Elsewhere we have argued that part of what made René Lévesque and Lee Iacocca effective as leaders was the temporal significance of their vision: they appealed powerfully to the specific needs of specific stakeholders at a specific time. Indeed, there are important instances when the 'followers' stimulate the leader, as opposed to the other way around. In most cases, however, it would appear that leader and follower participate together in creating the vision. The specific content – the original idea or perception – may come from the leader (though it need not, as in the case of Lévesque), but the form which it takes, the special excitement which marks it, is co-created. As Brook put it: 'there is only a practical difference between actor and audience, not a fundamental one' (1968: 150). Recall Land's description of hurrying to tell his friend of his vision of the camera. Why was he not content to keep the idea to himself? For the same reason an actor is not content to perform before the mirror. Vision comes alive only when it is shared.

This is captured dramatically in this century's most infamous example of visionary leadership. Shortly before Adolf Hitler came to power, Albert Speer attended one of his lectures. Arriving sceptical, Speer left a convert.

> I was carried away on the wave of enthusiasm which, one could almost feel this physically, bore the speaker along from sentence to sentence. It swept away any skepticisms, any reservations ... Hitler no longer seemed to be speaking to convince; rather, *he seemed to feel that he was expressing what the audience, by now transformed into a single mass, expected of him*. It was as if it were the most natural thing in the world ... (Speer, 1970: 18; italics added)

Thus the visionary leader not only empowers his audience; it also empowers him. On leaving Apple, Steve Jobs was described as 'its heart and soul' (Patterson, 1985) and Lévesque was seen as speaking for the little people of Quebec, the average French Canadians whom he loved.

One final word about our analogy. The early Greek and Roman rhetoricians were particularly sensitive to the need for integrity among those who used the power of word and gesture (Burke, 1950). In this sense visionary leadership is distinct from theatre. The actor can play a different person each month and still be considered a good actor. Ironically, the visionary leader who, through similar inconsistency, is labelled a good actor, risks losing credibility. Even before Steven Jobs left Apple, accusations that he was facile, inconsistent, and lacked integrity surfaced. 'He should be running Walt Disney. That way every day when he has some new idea, he can contribute to something different,' one Apple manager complained (Cocks, 1983: 26). In contrast, Edwin Land's belief that other people in the organization should have the same rich, varied job as himself, the fact that he used similar symbols to describe his products, his organization, and his own life (as we shall describe in greater detail below) enabled stakeholders to trust him. They knew that the same power he used to move them moved him. It is this integrity – this sense of being truly genuine – which proves crucial to visionary leadership, and makes it impossible to translate into a general formula.

In summary, the use of the metaphor of drama has allowed us to construct an alternative model of visionary leadership, one of dynamic interaction rather than unidirectional flow, a process of craft and repetition rather than simple cognition, brought to bear in the communication of affect as well as effect. Vision as leadership is a drama which takes place in time. As in theatre, a leader can have a 'bad house' – a passive, unresponsive organization. Only at the right time with the right leader and the right audience can strategy become vision and leadership become visionary.

Varieties of visionary leadership

All that we have described so far we believe to be common to visionary leadership in general. But in other regards contexts vary, issues vary, leaders vary. If vision is a drama, then script, direction, actors, staging, and audience may all vary; many combinations can produce vivid, exciting representation.

What drives the strategic visionary? What is the nature of his or her particular attributes, his or her particular ideas?

Firstly, just as recent theories of the mind suggest there is not one but multiple kinds of intelligence (Gardner, 1983), so too the notion of vision seems to involve a variety of mental capacities, what can be called *visionary style*. In particular, vision has been equated with a capacity for 'imagination', 'inspiration', 'insight', 'foresight' and 'sagacity' (*Oxford English Dictionary*). An analysis of some of the visionary leaders we have encountered in our research suggests that individual leaders exhibit characteristic styles in which certain of these capacities are salient, while the others, though present, remain secondary.

Secondly, visionary style is expressed through *strategic process*. We identify two elements of this – its mental origin and its evolution. *Mental origin* refers to that combination of mental and social dynamics, particular to the individual, that gives rise to the vision in the first place. For example, vision may arise primarily through introspection or interaction, or through the combination of the two. *Evolution* refers to the deliberateness and pace of development of the vision. Some visions develop more deliberately, through controlled conscious thought. Others emerge through a less conscious learning process. Also, some appear suddenly (like a visitation), others build up gradually, piece by piece over time in an incremental process. We might also note the aspect of intensity, which refers to the degree to which the vision possesses the visionary and those surrounding him/her, and durability, which refers to the persistance of the vision, ranging even beyond the career of the visionary as it infuses the behaviour of an organization for generations.

Thirdly is the *strategic content* of the vision. Vision may focus on products, services, markets, or organizations, or even ideals. This is its strategic component, the central image which drives the vision. We refer to this as the *core* of the vision. In addition to this, every vision is surrounded by a kind of halo designed to gain its acceptance. It is this component, comprising its symbolic aspects of rhetorical and metaphorical devices, which we refer to as its circumference. Often, however, unless the vision focuses on a very tangible product (such as Land's camera), the line between core and circumference is blurred. We should also note that the value added by the visionary may lie in the circumference alone, the core alone, or in the core and circumference in a gestalt combination. That is, leaders can sometimes charge rather ordinary products or markets, etc. with strategic vision, or create novel products or markets. The most exciting cases, however, inevitably involve novelty of both, integrated together.

Fourthly, and last, there are variations in *external context* that influence the visionary process. The nature of the organization itself can vary, in ownership, in structure, in size, in developmental stage, etc., for example, being public or private, developing entrepreneurial or mature turnaround. So too can the industry and the broader environment, from traditional mass production to contemporary high technology, etc.

In a previous paper (Westley and Mintzberg, 1988), we probed into the relevance especially of the contextual and stylistic factors through a comparison of the visionary leadership of Lee Iacocca and René Lévesque. Here we draw on that material and also extend the analysis to some of the other factors in considering these two visionary leaders alongside three others – Edwin Land, Steve Jobs and Jan Carlzon. Four of the people we shall discuss, Land, Jobs, Iacocca and Carlzon, are business leaders widely recognized and admired for their visionary abilities. The fifth, René Lévesque, likewise recognized for his visionary leadership, was the premier of Quebec between 1976 and 1985 who brought that province to the brink of separation from the rest of Canada. As shown in Table 1, we consider these men to have exhibited five distinct styles of visionary leadership. [A detailed examination follows in the original paper.]

Conclusions

We have suggested that visionary leadership can vary importantly from leader to leader. The style of the leader may vary, as may the content of

Table 1 *Varieties of leadership style*

Characteristic style	Salient capacities	Content	Process	Organization content	Product/market context	Target group
Creator (Edwin Land)	Inspiration, imagination, foresight	Product focus	Sudden, holistic; introspective, deliberate	Start-up, entrepreneurial	Invention and innovation, tangible products, niche markets	Independent consumer, scientific community
Proselytizer (Steven Jobs)	Foresight, imagination	Market focus	Emergent, shifting focus, interactive, holistic	Start-up, entrepreneurial	Tangible product, adaptation, mass market	Collective market, competitor infrastructure
Idealist (René Lévesque)	Imagination, sagacity	Ideals focus	Deliberate, deductive, introspective, incremental	Turnaround, public bureaucracy	Political concepts, zero-sum market	General population, 50% market share
Bricoleur (Lee Iacocca)	Sagacity, foresight, insight	Product/organization focus	Emergent, inductive, interactive, incremental	Revitalization, turnaround, private and public bureaucracy	Product development; segmented, oligopolistic markets	Government (in Chrysler), union, customers
Diviner (Jan Carlzon)	Insight, sagacity, inspiration	Service focus	Incremental, sudden crystallization, interactive	Revitalization, bureaucracy	Service development and innovation, mass oligopolistic market	Employees

the leader's vision and the context in which it takes root. The core of the vision may focus on product or service, market, process, organization or ideals; its circumference involves the rhetoric and metaphor of persuasion. The envisioning process may be ignited by introspection or interpersonal interaction. It may be experienced by the leader as deliberate or emergent, and as a sudden visitation or a series of incremental revelations. It may vary in intensity and in duration. The possibilities are enormous; other leaders may reveal other categories. Our intention has not been to present any firm typology so much as to indicate the possibilities for variations in visionary style, and to map out some important dimensions of visionary leadership.

This *strategic vision* is part style, part process, part content, and part context, while *visionary leadership* involves psychological gifts, sociological dynamics and the luck of timing. True strategic visionaries are both born and made, but they are not self-made. They are the product of the historical moment.

Our research suggests that, despite their great skills, it is a mistake to treat leaders such as those discussed here as possessing superhuman qualities. They are the product of their times, of their followers, of their opportunities. As times and contexts change the visionaries of yesterday fade into obscurity or, worse, become the villains of today. Iacocca is currently in danger of losing his status as a visionary leader, Carlzon has likewise run into difficulties. Polaroid and Land eventually parted company, as did Apple and Jobs, and Lévesque lost his election and quit his party in frustration. It did not seem to be the man or his capacities that changed in these cases, so much as the needs and expectations of his followers, organizations, and markets.

We should emphasize that visionary leadership is not always synonymous with good leadership. All of our leaders had reputations for being difficult to work with in some ways. Land 'wore out and exhausted his employees' (Wensbergh, 1987: 128). Some claimed that Jobs could be tyrannical and destructive (Butcher 1988: 117–126). Leaders in many contexts can be effective without being visionary, and their organizations may be happier places.

A dramaturgical model of vision raises a number of intriguing questions for further research. What is the exact nature of the symbols and processes visionary leaders employ in their 'representations'? What kind of interactions characterize the 'assistance' that the visionary receives from his or her organization? What kind of psychological, social, or technical 'repetition' forms the different visionary styles?

Careful analysis of speeches, reports, autobiographies, and interviews using techniques of textual analysis (Kets de Vries and Miller, 1987) should reveal similarities and differences in 'representation' technique across styles. Further collection of biographical information with a larger sample of visionary leaders should be oriented toward uncovering patterns of similarities and differences in the process of repetition or rehearsal. Assistance must likely be uncovered through direct observation, or through accounts of people who worked with the visionary. We might expect to find regularities in the roles team members play in relation to the visionary, but this has yet to be established.

Overall, the study of visionary leadership and strategic vision offers the opportunity for a rewarding and revitalizing interchange between the fields of leadership studies and strategic management. Concepts of strategy introduce consideration of market forces, environmental pressures, and organizational imperatives which form the backdrop for visionary initiatives. Against these features it is to their credit that even the gifted individuals we discussed were able to have such an impact on their organizations and on history. Consideration of that impact – more attention to issues of insight and inspiration, communication and commitment – can help to humanize considerations of strategic management while restoring to leadership study itself some of the flavour that Selznick (1957) sought (largely in vain) to instil 30 years ago.

In the closing lines of his book, Brook makes an observation about the relationship between life and the theatre:

> In everyday life, 'if' is a fiction, in the theatre 'if' is an experiment.
> In everyday life, 'if' is an evasion, in the theatre 'if' is the truth.
> When we are persuaded to believe in this truth, then the theatre and life are one.
> This is a high aim. It sounds like hard work.
> To play needs much more. But when we experience the work as play, then it is not work any more.
> A play is play. (p. 157)

If we substitute 'organization' for 'life' and 'vision' for 'theatre', we may begin to understand why strategic vision is stimulating so much interest. The visionary leader is a transformer, cutting through complex problems that leave other strategists stranded. Visionary leadership encourages innovation – fiction becomes experiment. Visionary leadership inspires the impossible – fiction becomes truth. In the book *The Soul of a New Machine*, Tracy Kidder quotes a secretary who worked for the Eagle Team under the visionary Tom West. Asked why she didn't leave when so overworked and underappreciated, she replied: 'I can't leave ... I just have to see how it turns out. I just have to see what Tom's going to do next' (1981: 58). Visionary leadership creates drama; it turns work into play.

Bibliography

Bass, Bernard M. (1987) 'Charismatic and inspirational leadership: what's the difference?' *Proceedings of Symposium on Charismatic Leadership in Management*, McGill University, Montreal.

Bello, Francis (1959) 'The magic that made Polaroid', *Fortune*, April, pp. 124–164.

Bennis, Warren (1982) 'Leadership transforms vision into action', *Industry Week*, 31 May, pp. 54–56.

Bennis, Warren and Burt Nanus (1985) *Leaders: The Strategies for Taking Charge*, Harper and Row, New York.

Braybrooke, David and Charles E. Lindblom (1963) *A Strategy of Decision*, Free Press, New York.

Brook, Peter (1968) *The Empty Space*, Penguin, Books, Markham, Ontario.

Burke, K. (1950) *A Rhetoric of Motives*, Prentice-Hall, Englewood Cliffs, NJ.

Business Week (1984) 'A new breed of strategic planner', 17 September, pp. 62–68.

Butcher, Lee (1988) *Accidental Millionaire*, Paragon House Publications, New York.

Carlzon, J. (1987) *Moments of Truth*, Ballinger, Cambridge, MA.

Cocks, J. (1983) 'The updated book of Jobs', *Time*, 3 January, pp. 25–27.

Conger, Jay A. and Rabindra N. Kanungo (1987) 'Towards a behavioral theory of charismatic leadership in organizational settings', *Academy of Management Review*, 12(4), pp. 637–647.

Edelman, M. (1964) *The Symbolic Uses of Politics*, University of Illinois Press, Urbana, IL.

Forbes (1981) Vol. 127, 12 April, p. 32.

Fraser, Graham (1984) *René Lévesque and the Parti Quebecois in Power*, Macmillan of Canada, Toronto.

Gardner, H. (1983) *Frames of Mind*, Basic Books, New York.

Gluck, Frederick W. (1984) 'Vision and leadership', *Interfaces*, 14(1), pp. 10–18.

Goffman, Erving (1959) *The Presentation of Self in Everyday Life*, Doubleday, New York.

Gupta, Anil, K. (1984) 'Contingency linkages between strategy and general manager characteristics: a conceptual examination', *Academy of Management Review*, 9, pp. 399–412.

Hall, E. (1959) *The Silent Language*, Doubleday, New York.

Hofer, Charles W. 'Turnaround strategies', in Glueck, W.F. (ed.), *Business Policy and Strategic Management*, McGraw-Hill, New York, pp. 271–278.

Iacocca, Lee with William Novak (1984) *Iacocca: An Autobiography*, Bantam Books, New York.

Jobs, Steven (1984) 'What I did for love', *Advertising Age*, 3 September, p. 18.

Kets de Vries, M. and D. Miller (1987) 'Interpreting organizational texts', *Journal of Management Studies*, 24(3), May, pp. 233–247.

Kidder, T. (1981) *The Soul of a New Machine*, Aron Books, New York.

Kiechel, W. (1986) 'Visionary leadership and beyond', *Fortune*, 21 July, pp. 127–128.

Land, E. (1972a) 'The most basic form of creativity', *Time*, 26 June, p. 84.

Land, E. (1972b) 'If you are able to state a problem, it can be solved', *Life Magazine*, 27 October, p. 48.

Land, E. (1975) 'People should want more from life . . .', *Forbes*, 1 June, pp. 48–50.

Lévesque, René (1986) *Memoirs* translated by Philip Stratford, McClelland and Stewart, Toronto.

Levinson, H. and S. Rosenthal (1984) *CEO: Corporate Leadership in Action*, Basic Books, New York.

Lévi-Strauss, Claude (1955) 'The structural study of myth', *Journal of American Folklore*, 68, pp. 428–444.

Lieberson, S. and J. F. O'Connor (1982) 'Leadership and organizational performance: a study of large corporations', *American Sociological Review*, 37, pp. 117–130.

Marbach, W. (1984) 'Reviewing the Mac', *Newsweek*, 30 January, p. 56.

Meindl, James R., Sanford B. Ehrlich and Janet M. Dukerich (1985) 'The romance of leadership', *Administrative Science Quarterly*, 30, pp. 78–102.

Mendell, Jay S. and Herbert G. Gerjuoy (1984) 'Anticipatory management or visionary leadership: a debate', *Managerial Planning*, 33, pp. 28–31, 63.

Mintzberg, Henry and James A. Waters (1982) 'Tracking strategy in an entrepreneurial firm', *Academy of Management Journal*, 25, pp. 465–499.

Mintzberg, Henry and James A. Waters (1985) 'Of strategies, deliberate and emergent', *Strategic Management Journal*, 6, pp. 257–272.

Mintzberg, Henry (1987a) 'Crafting strategy', *Harvard Business Review*, July–August, pp. 66–75.

Mintzberg, Henry (1987b) 'Five P's for strategy', *California Management Review*, 30, Fall, pp. 11–24.

O'Reilly, B. (1988) 'Steve Jobs tries to do it again', *Fortune*, 23 May, pp. 83–88.

Patterson, William P. (1985) 'Jobs starts over – this time as a multi millionaire', *Industry Week*, 30 September, pp. 93–98.

Pfeffer, Jeffery (1981) 'Management as symbolic action: the creation and maintenance of organizational paradoxes', in Straw, B.M. (ed.), *Research in Organizational Behavior*, Vol. 3, JAI Press, Greenwich, CT, pp. 1–52.

Pondy, Louis R. (1978) 'Leadership is a language game', in McCall, M. J. and M. W. Lombardo (eds), *Leadership: Where Else Can We Go?*, Duke University Press, Durham, NC, pp. 87–99.

Quinn, James Brian (1980) *Strategies for Change: Logical Incrementalism*, Richard D. Irwin, Homewood, IL.

Robbins, S. R. and Robert B. Duncan (1987) 'The formulation and implementation of strategic vision: a tool for change'. Paper presented to the seventh Strategic Management Society Conference, Boston, MA, 14–17 October.

Rogers, M. (1984) 'It's the Apple of his eye', *Newsweek*, 30 January, pp. 54–56.

Sashkin, Marshall (1987) 'A theory of organizational leadership: vision, culture and charisma', *Proceedings of Symposium on Charismatic Leadership in Management*, McGill University, Montreal.

Selznick, Philip (1957) *Leadership in Administration: A Sociological Interpretation*, Harper and Row, New York.

Speer, A. (1970) *Inside the Third Reich*, Macmillan, New York.

Srivastva, Suresh and Associates (1983) *The Executive Mind*, Jossey-Bass, San Francisco, CA.

Tichy, N. and D. Ulrich (1984) 'Revitalizing organizations: the leadership role', in Kimberly, J. R. and R. E. Quinn (eds), *Managing Organizational Transitions*, Richard D. Irwin, Homewood, IL.

Tichy, Noel M. and Mary Anne Devanna (1986) *The Transformational Leader*, John Wiley and Sons, New York.

Time (1961) 'Edwin-Herbert Land', 17 March, p. 88.

Uttal, Bro (1985a) 'Behind the fall', *Fortune*, 5 August, pp. 20–24.

Uttal, Bro (1985b) 'The adventures of Steve Jobs (cont'd)', *Fortune*, 14 October, pp. 119–124.

Weber, M. (1978) *Economy and Society*, University of California Press, Berkeley, CA.

Wensbergh, Peter C. (1987) *Land's Polaroid*, Houghton Mifflin, Boston, MA.

Westley, F, and H. Mintzberg (1988) 'Profiles of strategic leadership: Lévesque and Iacocca', in Conger, J. and R. Kanungo (eds), *Charismatic Leadership: The Elusive Factor in Organizational Effectiveness*, Jossey-Bass, San Francisco, CA.

Wise, D. (1984) 'Apple's new crusade', *Business Week*, 26 November, pp. 146–156.

Wrapp, H. Edward (1967) 'Good managers don't make policy decisions', *Harvard Business Review*, 45, May–June, pp. 91–99.

5

Change-master skills: what it takes to be creative

Rosabeth Moss Kanter

Corporate entrepreneurs are people who envision something new and make it work. They don't start businesses; they improve them. Being a corporate entrepreneur, what I call a 'change master,' is much more challenging and fun than being a nonentrepreneur. It requires more of a person, but it gives back more self-satisfaction.

Change masters journey through three stages. First they formulate and sell a vision. Next they find the power to advance their idea. Finally they must maintain the momentum. I discovered the skills of change masters by researching hundreds of managers across more than a half-dozen industries. I put change-master skills in two categories: first, the personal or individual skills and second, the interpersonal ones, how the person manages others.

Kaleidoscope thinking

The first essential skill is a style of thinking, or a way of approaching the world, that I have come to call 'kaleidoscope thinking.' The metaphor of a kaleidoscope is a good way of capturing exactly what innovators, or leaders of change, do. A kaleidoscope is a device for seeing patterns. It takes a set of fragments and it forms them into a pattern. But when the kaleidoscope is twisted, shaken, or approached from a new angle, the exact same fragments form an entirely different pattern. Kaleidoscope thinking, then, involves taking an existing array of data, phenomena, or assumptions and being able to twist them, shake them, look at them upside down or from another angle or from a new direction – thus permitting an entirely new pattern and consequent set of actions to take place.

Change masters, or the makers of change, are not necessarily more creative than other people, but they are more willing to move beyond received wisdom to approach problems from new angles. This is a classic finding in the history of any kind of innovation – that it takes challenges to

From Chapter 11 in R. Kuhn (ed.), *Handbook for Creative and Innovative Managers* (New York: McGraw-Hill, 1988). Copyright © 1985 Rosabeth Moss Kanter beliefs to achieve a breakthrough. A large proportion of important innovations are brought about by people who step outside of conventional categories or traditional assumptions. They are often *not* the experts or the specialists. Rather they are 'boundary crossers' or 'generalists' who move across fields or among sectors who bypass what everybody else is looking at to find possibilities for change.

Kaleidoscope thinking begins with experience not associated with one's own field or department. Moving outside for broadened perspectives was the common foundation of every innovation I studied. A woman change master at a computer company began an important project this way. She got her assignment, and the first thing she did was leave her area and roam around the rest of the organization, talking it over with nearly everyone she could find, regardless of field, looking for new directions, new perspectives, new ways to approach it – so what she could bring back would be new and creative. She did not start with what she already knew. She started with what other people could bring her; she crossed boundaries to do that.

This is how many important changes have been seeded. For example, frozen vegetables were invented by Clarence Birdseye, owner of a produce business at the turn of the century. The conventional wisdom of his time, like that of our time, held that the best way to run a business (or a department) was to 'mind the store' – managing one's field and only one's field, watching it like a microscope image, getting better and better at knowing and doing just one thing. But Birdseye was an adventurer, and so, like many change masters, he wandered away from his store and his scope; he passed beyond his territory, quite literally, and went on expeditions. On one of his adventure trips, fur-trapping in Labrador, he discovered that fish caught in ice could be eaten much later with no ill effects. He brought that idea back and transformed his business from a local produce store to the beginnings of national distribution.

Organizations that seek innovation ought to learn from this kind of experience: allow people to move outside of the orthodoxy of an area, to mix and match, to shake up assumptions. One chief executive believed that such thinking was so important to his organization's success in a high-tech field that he staged a highly imaginative top management meeting. He took his top fifty officers to a resort to hold their annual financial planning meeting. Though it started out just like their usual meetings, he wanted this year to be different. He was concerned that they were getting stuck in a rut and that he was not getting much creative thinking, though his company needed innovation for survival. He made the point symbolically. Halfway through his talk, the meeting was suddenly interrupted by a cadre of men dressed as prison guards; these rather realistic toughs burst into the room, grabbed everybody there, and took them out to a set of waiting helicopters, which flew the bewildered executives off to a second meeting site. 'Now we'll begin again,' said the CEO, 'and we will bury all the thinking we were doing in the last meeting and approach everything from a new angle. I want new thinking out of you.' He continued to punctuate the meeting with sets of surprises, like a parade of elephants on the beach. First there was a small elephant and it had the natural financial goal painted on its side, then along came a bigger elephant with a bigger number, and then a huge elephant with a huge number, and he said, 'Go for it! Stretch your thinking!' The symbolism of the whole meeting was to stretch, move outside, challenge assumptions, twist that kaleidoscope.

Communicating visions

The second conclusion I drew about change masters' individual skills was their ability to articulate and communicate *visions*. New and creative ideas and better ways to do things come not from *systems* but from *people*. People leading other people in untried directions are the true shapers of change. So behind every change, every innovation, every development project, there must be somebody with a vision who has been able to communicate and sell that vision to somebody else (even when the change begins with an assignment, not a self-directed initiative).

Though innovation is a very positive term, it is important to remember that any *particular* innovation is only positive in retrospect, *after* it has worked. Before that, because change by definition is something no one has seen yet (despite models that may exist elsewhere), it has to be taken at least partially on faith. For example, why a continuing education program now? Why use funds to develop a new product when there are so many already on the market? Why take the risk of decentralizing the accounting office? In short, unless there is somebody behind the idea willing to take the risk of speaking up for it, the idea will evaporate and disappear. One reason there is so little change in most traditional burcaucratic organizations, I argue, is that they have conditioned out of people the willingness to stand up for a new idea. Instead, people learn to back off at the first sign that somebody might disapprove.

This second change-master skill can be called 'leadership.' Martin Luther King's famous speech in the March on Washington personified this as 'I have a dream.' He didn't say, 'I have a few ideas; there seem to be some problems out there. Maybe if we set up a few *committees*, something will happen.' But when I see managers present their ideas in just this sort of well-if-you-don't-like-it-that's-all-right way, I can understand why so many are so ineffective in getting new things done. Each innovation, shift, or novel project – even the noncontroversial and apparently desirable ones – requires somebody getting behind it and pushing, especially when things get difficult, as they always do when change is involved. This kind of leadership involves communication plus conviction, both energized by commitment.

Persistence

Leaders of innovation persist in an idea; they keep at it. When I examined the differences between success and failure in change projects or development efforts, I found that one major difference was simply *time* – staying with it long enough to make it work.

To some extent, *everything* looks like a failure in the middle. There is a point or points in the history of every new product, every original effort, every fresh idea when discouragements mount, and the temptation to stop is great. But pulling out at that moment automatically yields failure. There is nothing to show just yet. The inevitable problems, roadblocks, and low spots when enthusiasm wanes are the critical hurdles in achieving a healthy return on the investment of time and resources. Without persistence, important changes never happen.

In large organizations, the number of roadblocks and low points can seem infinite, particularly when something new is being tried. There are not only all the technical details of how the new program is going to work, but there are also all the political difficulties of handling the critics. Naysayers are more likely to surface in the middle than at the beginning because now the project is more of a threat, more a challenge to their own perceived status. There is little incentive for critics to tie up political capital by confronting the project until it looks like it actually may happen. This is a reality of organizational life.

At one major consumer products company, this phenomenon was demonstrated all too well. Today, the company has a highly successful new product on every supermarket's shelves. But when this project was in the development stage, it was known as 'Project Lazarus' because it 'rose from the dead' so many times. Four times people at higher levels tried to kill it off, and four times the people working on it came back and fought for it, argued for it, provided justification and evidence for why it should continue: 'Just give us a little more time; we know we can make it work.'

Every organization has examples like this one. If the team had stopped, the effort would have been a total loss – confirming, in a circular way, the critics. But arguing for the additional time and money and confronting the critics transformed a potential failure into a ringing success.

Coalition building

In addition to the personal skills of change masters, interpersonal and organizational skills are also required. The first of these is coalition building. At the point at which there is a creative idea, with someone with vision behind it willing to persist, it still has to be sold to other people in the organization in order to get implemented.

Though the literature on organizational politics has emphasized one-on-

one relationship building, my research moves the emphasis to the coalition. What makes people effective in organizations is the ability to create a whole set of backers and supporters, specifically for projects of innovative activities, that helps lend the power necessary to vitalize those activities. In this sense entrepreneurs inside a corporation are just like entrepreneurs outside: They have to find bankers, people who will provide the funds; they have to find information sources; and they have to find legitimacy and support, people who will champion the project to other powerholders.

Multiple, rather than single, sponsors and backers make the difference. An attractive young woman who now holds one of the top six positions in an American corporation began as assistant to the chairman and was subjected to many innuendoes about their relationship. But she proved to be a highly effective change master in her organization, responsible for many successful new projects, because she is a superb coalition builder, drawing hardly at all on her relationship with the CEO. She brings others into projects; she works with peers and people below to make them feel included. She creates multiple relationships and teams around her by giving people 'stakes' in each project, solidified by promised personal benefit. Because of her coalition-building skills, she led successful change projects that in turn brought her recognition and early promotions.

Coalitions are especially important when change is needed because innovation – new projects or developments – generally involve going outside of current sources of organizational power. My research found that managers who wanted to innovate, or try something new, almost invariably needed more resources, information, and support than they had. They often needed money above and beyond their budget (though sometimes not much) – because usually their budget was for the routine things they were doing, and if they wanted to do something novel, they had to find extra funds. They also needed higher levels of support because innovations sometimes interfere with ongoing things in an organization. Change is often resisted because it can be a nuisance and an interference; it requires other people to stop what they are doing or redirect their thinking. And new efforts also tend to require special information, more data, new sources of knowledge. Thus, the change masters I studied *had* to build a coalition in order to find the backers or 'power sources' to provide information, support, and resources for their projects.

Coalition building not only attracts needed power to a project, it also tends to help guarantee success. Once others are brought in and contribute their money or support to a project, they also have a stake in making it work. Their reputations (and egos) are now on the line. As a result, the innovator is not out there all by herself, trying to convince a reluctant organization to do something. There are now other people to serve as cheerleaders.

This process of coalition building is so well-known that some companies have invented their own language around it. They call the whole process one of getting 'buy-in' or generating wider 'ownership' of a project from key supporters. First is a low-key step of gathering intelligence and plant-ing seeds – just finding out where people stand and leaving behind a germ of the idea to let it blossom. Then the serious business of coalition building begins in the process they call 'tincupping.' The manager, symbolically, takes his or her 'tin cup' in hand and walks around the organization 'beg-ging' for involvement, seeing who has a little bit to chip in, who has a few spare budget dollars to invest, who has a staff member to lend, who will be on the advisory committee, or who has key data. In the process of tin-cupping, two vital organizational functions take place that guard against failures. First is the 'horse trading' required. For everything that is dropped into the tin cup, people have to feel that they get something back. Thus, one person's project has to be translated into something of wider benefit around the organization – which helps ensure success because it has sup-port. And, second, in the course of tin-cupping, an innovator also gets a 'sanity check' – feedback from 'older and wiser heads' helping reshape the idea to make it more workable. (The only failures at innovation that I saw in high-tech firms occurred when the manager thought he or she already had so much power that coalition building was unnecessary.)

Coalition building, therefore, provides not just personal or political advantage; it is also an important process for making sure that the ideas that do get developed have merit and broad support. It is a form of peer control, a way of screening out bad or nonimplementable proposals. For this reason, top management at one computer company is more likely to provide large allocations for ideas that come with a coalition already formed around them.

Working through teams

Once a group of supporters has been generated, it is time to get down to the actual project work. Now the next interpersonal–organizational skill comes into play: the ability to build a working team to carry out the idea.

Very few ideas and very few projects of any significance are imple-mented by one person alone: Other people's effort makes it happen – whether they are assistants, subordinates, a staff, a special project team, or a task force of peers assembled just for this effort. But regardless of who the people are, it is critical that they feel like a *team* in order to make any new idea work. My research documents the importance of participative management when change is involved even if it is not necessary for manag-ing the routine. Full involvement turns out to be critical when the issue is change.

For a routine operation in which everybody knows what they are doing high involvement and high intensity are less critical. But change requires above-and-beyond effort on the part of everybody involved. It requires their creativity and their commitment. Without such general cooperation, those trying to make something significant happen in an organization run forever uphill. Help is hard to find. Peers find other priorities; reports are late. When dependent on other people to get the job done, one must engage them. Everybody in an organization has at least one form of power – the 'pocket veto.' Even without directly challenging an idea, all one has to do is sit on it for a while, put it in his or her pocket, not respond, find other projects more important – and the change effort will be stalled. Loss of momentum occurs when other people are not motivated to do their part.

The development of a new computer at Data General illustrates the process of team building. Tom West, the middle manger behind this development team, worked extraordinarily hard to create a self-conscious sense of *team* – team play, ownership, and identification. He led young engineers who were just out of school to perform engineering 'miracles' – record-time achievements that no one predicted. Their intense sense of ownership came from a team identity, symbolized by names (the 'microkids' and the 'Hardy boys'). The team genuinely had a mission. They also had fun together. They were given full responsibilty and were always informed. They had room to make mistakes. West, the manager, supported by two assistants, did not impose his ideas on the team. Indeed, when he had solutions to problems, he sometimes went to the lab late at night and left his ideas on slips of paper for people to find in the morning – without knowing how they got there. Thus, he created an atmosphere in which people felt autonomous and in control and consequently became incredibly dedicated and committed to the project.

Sharing the credit

Finally, bringing innovation full circle, people who lead changes share credit and recognition – making everyone a 'hero.' Instead of simply taking individual credit, change masters make sure that everyone who works on their effort gets rewarded. This behavior brings back benefit to the change master. I saw this dramatically illustrated in an insurance company. A manager had led a series of employee involvement projects that improved productivity in his region and boosted the firm's overall profits. At bonus time, his superiors were going to reward him with a fat check. He asked if he could also have bonus money for the people below who had also contributed to his efforts. Management, unfortunately, turned him down. So he took several thousand dollars from his own pocket, collected contributions from peers, and made up his own bonus pool for everyone down to the clerks who had contributed. That made people feel that their least effort was rewarded and they looked forward to participating in the next organizational improvement. Change became an opportunity rather than a threat.

For many people, projects of change and innovation become the most significant things they have ever done in their work lives. I have interviewed people who had spent 30 years in a big bureaucracy who said that the 6-month development task force was the only thing they were excited by and the only thing they would be remembered for – change was their mark on the organization.

Change, the development of something new, unleashes people's creative energy. It is exhilarating, stimulating personnel in a way that routine work cannot do. Giving people the opportunity for innovation and recognizing them for it fulfills both organizational and individual needs.

6

Entrepreneurship reconsidered: the team as hero

Robert B. Reich

'Wake up there, youngster,' said a rough voice.
Ragged Dick opened his eyes slowly and stared stupidly in the face of the speaker, but did not offer to get up.
'Wake up, you young vagabond!' said the man a little impatiently; 'I suppose you'd lay there all day, if I hadn't called you.'

So begins the story of *Ragged Dick, or Street Life in New York*, Horatio Alger's first book – the first of 135 tales written in the late 1800s that together sold close to 20 million copies. Like all the books that followed, *Ragged Dick* told the story of a young man who, by pluck and luck, rises from his lowly station to earn a respectable job and the promise of a better life.

Nearly a century later, another bestselling American business story offered a different concept of heroism and a different description of the route to success. This story begins:

All the way to the horizon in the last light, the sea was just degrees of gray, rolling and frothy on the surface. From the cockpit of a small white sloop – she was 35 feet long – the waves looked like hills coming up from behind, and most of the crew preferred not to glance at them ... Running under shortened sails in front of the northeaster, the boat rocked one way, gave a thump, and then it rolled the other. The pots and pans in the galley clanged. A six-pack of beer, which someone had forgotten to stow away, slid back and forth across the cabin floor, over and over again. Sometime late that night, one of the crew raised a voice against the wind and asked, 'What are we trying to prove?'

The book is Tracy Kidder's *The Soul of a New Machine*, a 1981 tale of how a team – a crew – of hardworking inventors built a computer by pooling their efforts. The opening scene is a metaphor for the team's treacherous journey.

Separated by 100 years, totally different in their explanations of what propels the American economy, these two stories symbolize the choice that Americans will face in the 1990s; each celebrates a fundamentally different version of American entrepreneurship. Which version we choose to embrace will help determine how quickly and how well the United States adapts to the challenge of global competition.

Horatio Alger's notion of success is the traditional one: the familiar tale of triumphant individuals, of enterprising heroes who win riches and rewards through a combination of Dale Carnegie-esque self-improvement, Norman Vincent Peale-esque faith, Sylvester Stallone-esque assertiveness, and plain, old-fashioned good luck. Tracy Kidder's story, by contrast, teaches that economic success comes through the talent, energy, and commitment of a team – through *collective* entrepreneurship.

Stories like these do more than merely entertain or divert us. Like ancient myths that captured and contained an essential truth, they shape how we see and understand our lives, how we make sense of our experience. Stories can mobilize us to action and affect our behavior – more powerfully than simple and straightforward information ever can.

To the extent that we continue to celebrate the traditional myth of the entrepreneurial hero, we will slow the progress of change and adaptation that is essential to our economic success. If we are to compete effectively in today's world, we must begin to celebrate collective entrepreneurship, endeavors in which the whole of the effort is greater than the sum of individual contributions. We need to honor our teams more, our aggressive leaders and maverick geniuses less.

Heroes and drones

The older and still dominant American myth involves two kinds of actors: entrepreneurial heroes and industrial drones – the inspired and the perspired.

In this myth, entrepreneurial heroes personify freedom and creativity. They come up with the Big Ideas and build the organizations – the Big Machines – that turn them into reality. They take the initiative, come up with technological and organizational innovations, devise new solutions to old problems. They are the men and women who start vibrant new companies, turn around failing companies, and shake up staid ones. To all endeavors they apply daring and imagination.

The myth of the entrepreneurial hero is as old as America and has served us well in a number of ways. We like to see ourselves as born mavericks and fixers. Our entrepreneurial drive has long been our distinguishing trait. Generations of inventors and investors have kept us on the technological frontier. In a world of naysayers and traditionalists, the American character has always stood out – cheerfully optimistic, willing to run risks, ready to try anything. During World War II, it was the rough-and-ready American GI who could fix the stalled jeep in Normandy while the French regiment only looked on.

Horatio Alger captured this spirit in hundreds of stories. With titles like *Bound to Rise*, *Luck and Pluck*, and *Sink or Swim*, they inspired millions of readers with a gloriously simple message: in America you can go from rags to riches. The plots were essentially the same; like any successful entrepreneur, Alger knew when he was onto a good thing. A fatherless, penniless boy – possessed of great determination, faith, and courage – seeks his fortune. All manner of villain tries to tempt him, divert him, or separate him from his small savings. But in the end, our hero prevails – not just through pluck; luck plays a part too – and by the end of the story he is launched on his way to fame and fortune.

At the turn of the century, Americans saw fiction and reality sometimes converging. Edward Harriman began as a $5-a-week office boy and came to head a mighty railroad empire. John D. Rockefeller rose from a clerk in a commission merchant's house to become one of the world's richest men. Andrew Carnegie started as a $1.20-a-week bobbin boy in a Pittsburgh cotton mill and became the nation's foremost steel magnate. In the early 1900s, when boys were still reading the Alger tales, Henry Ford made his fortune mass-producing the Model T, and in the process became both a national folk hero and a potential presidential candidate.

Alger's stories gave the country a noble ideal – a society in which imagination and effort summoned their just reward. The key virtue was self-reliance; the admirable man was the self-made man; the goal was to be your own boss. Andrew Carnegie articulated the prevailing view:

'Is any would-be businessman . . . content in forecasting his future, to figure himself as labouring all his life for a fixed salary? Not one, I am sure. In this you have the dividing line between business and non-business; the one is master and depends on profits, the other is servant and depends on salary.'[1]

The entrepreneurial hero still captures the American imagination. Inspired by the words of his immigrant father, who told him, 'You could be anything you want to be, if you wanted it bad enough and were willing to work for it,' Lee Iacocca worked his way up to the presidency of Ford Motor Company, from which he was abruptly fired by Henry Ford II, only to go on to rescue Chrysler from bankruptcy, thumb his nose at Ford in a best-selling autobiography, renovate the Statue of Liberty, and gain mention as a possible presidential candidate.[2] Could Horatio Alger's heroes have done any better?

Peter Ueberroth, son of a traveling aluminium salesman, worked his way through college, single-handedly built a $300 million business, went on to organize the 1984 Olympics, became *Time* magazine's Man of the Year and the commissioner of baseball. Steven Jobs built his own computer company from scratch and became a multimillionaire before his thirtieth birthday. Stories of entrepreneurial heroism, come from across the economy and across the country: professors who create whole new industries and become instant millionaires when their inventions go from the laboratory to the marketplace; youthful engineers who quit their jobs, strike out on their own, and strike it rich.

In the American economic mythology, these heroes occupy center stage:

'Fighters, fanatics, men with a lust for contest, a gleam of creation, and a drive to justify their break from the mother company.'[3] Prosperity for all depends on the entrepreneurial vision of a few rugged individuals.

If the entrepreneurial heroes hold center stage in this drama, the rest of the vast work force plays a supporting role – supporting and unheralded. Average workers in this myth are drones – cogs in the Big Machines, so many interchangeable parts, unable to perform without direction from above. They are put to work for their hands, not for their minds or imaginations. Their jobs typically appear by the dozens in the help-wanted sections of daily newspapers. Their routines are unvaried. They have little opportunity to use judgment or creativity. To the entrepreneurial hero belongs all the inspiration; the drones are governed by the rules and valued for their reliability and pliability.

These average workers are no villains – but they are certainly no heroes. Uninteresting and uninterested, goes the myth, they lack creative spark and entrepreneurial vision. These are, for example, the nameless and faceless workers who lined up for work in response to Henry Ford's visionary offer of a $5-per-day paycheck. At best, they put in a decent effort in executing the entrepreneurial hero's grand design. At worst, they demand more wages and benefits for less work, do the minimum expected of them, or function as bland bureaucrats mired in standard operating procedures.

The entrepreneurial hero and the worker drone together personify the mythic version of how the American economic system works. The system needs both types. But rewards and treatment for the two are as different as the roles themselves: the entrepreneurs should be rewarded with fame and fortune; drones should be disciplined through clear rules and punishments. Considering the overwhelming importance attached to the entrepreneur in this paradigm, the difference seems appropriate. For, as George Gilder has written, 'All of us are dependent for our livelihood and progress not on a vast and predictable machine, but on the creativity and courage of the particular men who accept the risks which generate our riches.'[4]

Why Horatio Alger can't help us anymore

There is just one fatal problem with this dominant myth: it is obsolete. The economy that it describes no longer exists. By clinging to the myth, we subscribe to an outmoded view of how to win economic success – a view that, on a number of counts, endangers our economic future:

- In today's global economy, the Big Ideas pioneered by American entrepreneurs travel quickly to foreign lands. In the hands of global competitors, these ideas can undergo continuous adaptation and improvement and reemerge as new Big Ideas or as a series of incrementally improved small ideas.
- The machines that American entrepreneurs have always set up so efficiently to execute their Big Ideas are equally footloose. Process

technology moves around the globe to find the cheapest labor and the friendliest markets. As ideas migrate overseas, the economic and technological resources needed to implement the ideas migrate too.

- Workers in other parts of the world are apt to be cheaper or more productive – or both – than workers in the United States. Around the globe, millions of potential workers are ready to underbid American labor.
- Some competitor nations – Japan, in particular – have created relationships among engineers, managers, production workers, and marketing and sales people that do away with the old distinction between entrepreneurs and drones. The dynamic result is yet another basis for challenging American assumptions about what leads to competitive success.

Because of these global changes, the United States is now susceptible to competitive challenge on two grounds. First, by borrowing the Big Ideas and process technology that come from the United States and providing the hardworking, low-paid workers, developing nations can achieve competitive advantage. Second, by embracing collective entrepreneurship, the Japanese especially have found a different way to achieve competitive advantage while maintaining high real wages.

Americans continue to lead the world in breakthroughs and cutting-edge scientific discoveries. But the Big Ideas that start in this country now quickly travel abroad, where they not only get produced at high speed, at low cost, and with great efficiency, but also undergo continuous development and improvement. And all too often, American companies get bogged down somewhere between invention and production.

Several product histories make the point. Americans invented the solid-state transistor in 1947. Then in 1953, Western Electric licensed the technology to Sony for $25,000 – and the rest is history. A few years later, RCA licensed several Japanese companies to make color televisions – and that was the beginning of the end of color television production in the United States. Routine assembly of color televisions eventually shifted to Taiwan and Mexico. At the same time, Sony and other Japanese companies pushed the technology in new directions, continuously refining it into a stream of consumer products.

In 1968, Unimation licensed Kawasaki Heavy Industries to make industrial robots. The Japanese took the initial technology and kept moving it forward. The pattern has been the same for one Big Idea after another. Americans came up with the Big Ideas for videocassette recorders, basic oxygen furnaces, and continuous casters for making steel, microwave ovens, automobile stamping machines, computerized machine tools, integrated circuits. But these Big Ideas – and many, many others – quickly found their way into production in foreign countries: routine, standardized production in developing nations or continuous refinement and complex applications in Japan. Either way, the United States has lost ground.

Older industrial economies, like our own, have two options: they can try to match the low wages and discipline under which workers elsewhere in the world are willing to labor, or they can compete on the basis of how quickly and how well they transform ideas into incrementally better products. The second option is, in fact, the only one that offers the possibility of high real incomes in America. But here's the catch: a handful of lone entrepreneurs producing a few industry-making Big Ideas can't execute this second option. Innovation must become both continuous and collective. And that requires embracing a new ideal: collective entrepreneurship.

The new economic paradigm

If America is to win in the new global competition, we need to begin telling one another a new story in which companies compete by drawing on the talent and creativity of all their employees, not just a few maverick inventors and dynamic CEOs. Competitive advantage today comes from continuous, incremental innovation and refinement of a variety of ideas that spread throughout the organization. The entrepreneurial organization is both experience-based and decentralized, so that every advance builds on every previous advance, and everyone in the company has the opportunity and capacity to participate.

While this story represents a departure from tradition, it already exists, in fact, to a greater or lesser extent in every well-run American and Japanese corporation. The difference is that we don't recognize and celebrate this story – and the Japanese do.

Consider just a few of the evolutionary paths that collective entrepreneurship can take: vacuum-tube radios become transistorized radios, then stereo pocket radios audible through earphones, then compact discs and compact disc players, and then optical-disc computer memories. Color televisions evolve into digital televisions capable of showing several pictures simultaneously; videocassette recorders into camcorders. A single strand of technological evolution connects electronic sewing machines, electronic typewriters, and flexible electronic workstations. Basic steels give way to high-strength and corrosion-resistant steels, then to new materials composed of steel mixed with silicon and custom-made polymers. Basic chemicals evolve into high-performance ceramics, to single-crystal silicon and high-grade crystal glass. Copper wire gives way to copper cables, then to fiber-optic cables.

These patterns reveal no clear life cycles with beginnings, middles, and ends. Unlike Big Ideas that beget standardized commodities, these products undergo a continuous process of incremental change and adaptation. Workers at all levels add value not solely or even mostly by tending machines and carrying out routines, but by continuously discovering opportunities for improvement in product and process.

In this context, it makes no sense to speak of an 'industry' like steel or

"We've decided to tell individuals we treat them
like institutions, and tell institutions we treat them like
individuals."

automobiles or televisions or even banking. There are no clear borders around any of these clusters of goods or services. When products and processes are so protean, companies grow or decline not with the market for some specific good, but with the creative and adaptive capacity of their workers.

Workers in such organizations constantly reinvent the company; one idea leads to another. Producing the latest generation of automobiles involves making electronic circuits that govern fuel consumption and monitor engine performance; developments in these devices lead to improved sensing equipment and software for monitoring heartbeats and moisture in the air. Producing cars also involves making flexible robots for assembling parts and linking them by computer; steady improvements in these technologies, in turn, lead to expert production systems that can be applied anywhere. What is considered the 'automobile industry' thus becomes a wide variety of technologies evolving toward all sorts of applications that flow from the same strand of technological development toward different markets.

In this paradigm, entrepreneurship isn't the sole province of the company's founder or its top managers. Rather, it is a capability and attitude that is diffused throughout the company. Experimentation and development go on all the time as the company searches for new ways to capture and build on the knowledge already accumulated by its workers.

Distinctions between innovation and production, between top managers and production workers blur. Because production is a continuous process of reinvention, entrepreneurial efforts are focused on many thousands of small ideas rather than on just a few big ones. And because valuable information and expertise are dispersed throughout the organization, top management does not solve problems; it creates an environment in which people can identify and solve problems themselves.

Most of the training for working in this fashion takes place on the job. Formal education may prepare people to absorb and integrate experience, but it does not supply the experience. No one can anticipate the precise skills that workers will need to succeed on the job when information processing, knowhow, and creativity are the value added. Any job that could be fully prepared for in advance is, by definition, a job that could be exported to a low-wage country or programed into robots and computers; a routine job is a job destined to disappear.

In collective entrepreneurship, individual skills are integrated into a group; this collective capacity to innovate becomes something greater than the sum of its parts. Over time, as group members work through various problems and approaches, they learn about each others' abilities. They learn how they can help one another perform better, what each can contribute to a particular project, how they can best take advantage of one another's experience. Each participant is constantly on the lookout for small adjustments that will speed and smooth the evolution of the whole. The net result of many such small-scale adaptations, effected throughout the organization, is to propel the enterprise forward.

Collective entrepreneurship thus entails close working relationships among people at all stages of the process. If customers' needs are to be recognized and met, designers and engineers must be familiar with sales and marketing. Salespeople must also have a complete understanding of the enterprise's capacity to design and deliver specialized products. The company's ability to adapt to new opportunities and capitalize on them depends on its capacity to share information and involve everyone in the organization in a systemwide search for ways to improve, adjust, adapt, and upgrade.

Collective entrepreneurship also entails a different organizational structure. Under the old paradigm, companies are organized into a series of hierarchical tiers so that supervisors at each level can make sure that subordinates act according to plan. It is a structure designed to control. But enterprises designed for continuous innovation and incremental improvement use a structure designed to spur innovation at all levels. Gaining insight into improvement of products and processes is more important than rigidly following rules. Coordination and communication replace command and control. Consequently, there are few middle-level managers and only modest differences in the status and income of senior managers and junior employees.

Simple accounting systems are no longer adequate or appropriate for monitoring and evaluating job performance: tasks are intertwined and interdependent, and the quality of work is often more important than the quantity of work. In a system where each worker depends on many others – and where the success of the company depends on all – the only appropriate measurement of accomplishment is a collective one. At the same time, the reward system reflects this new approach: profit sharing, gain sharing, and performance bonuses all demonstrate that the success of the company comes from the broadest contribution of all the company's employees, not just those at the top.

Finally, under collective entrepreneurship, workers do not fear technology and automation as a threat to their jobs. When workers add value through judgment and knowledge, computers become tools that expand their discretion. Computer-generated information can give workers rich feedback about their own efforts, how they affect others in the production process, and how the entire process can be improved. One of the key lessons to come out of the General Motors–Toyota joint venture in California is that the Japanese automaker does not rely on automation and technology to replace workers in the plant. In fact, human workers still occupy the most critical jobs – those where judgment and evaluation are essential. Instead, Toyota uses technology to allow workers to focus on those important tasks where choices have to be made. Under this approach, technology gives workers the chance to use their imagination and their insight on behalf of the company.

The team as hero

In 1986, one of America's largest and oldest enterprises announced that it was changing the way it assigned its personnel: the US Army discarded a system that assigned soldiers to their units individually in favor of a system that keeps teams of soldiers together for their entire tours of duty. An Army spokesperson explained, 'We discovered that individuals perform better when they are part of a stable group. They are more reliable. They also take responsibility for the success of the overall operation.'

In one of its recent advertisements, BellSouth captures the new story. 'BellSouth is not a bunch of individuals out for themselves,' the ad proclaimed. 'We're a team.'

Collective entrepreneurship is already here. It shows up in the way our best run companies now organize their work, regard their workers, design their enterprises. Yet the old myth of the entrepreneurial hero remains powerful. Many Americans would prefer to think that Lee Iacocca single-handedly saved Chrysler from bankruptcy than to accept the real story: a large team of people with diverse backgrounds and interests joined together to rescue the ailing company.

Bookstores bulge with new volumes paying homage to American CEOs. It is a familiar story; it is an engaging story. And no doubt, when seen through the eyes of the CEO, it accurately portrays how that individual experienced the company's success. But what gets left out time after time are the experiences of the rest of the team – the men and women at every level of the company whose contributions to the company created the success that the CEO so eagerly claims. Where are the books that celebrate their stories?

You can also find inspirational management texts designed to tell top executives how to be kinder to employees, treat them with respect, listen to them, and make them feel appreciated. By reading these books, executives can learn how to search for excellence, create excellence, achieve excellence, or become impassioned about excellence – preferably within one minute. Managers are supposed to walk around, touch employees, get directly involved, effervesce with praise and encouragement, stage celebrations, and indulge in hoopla.

Some of this is sound; some of it is hogwash. But most of it, even the best, is superficial. Lacking any real context, unattached to any larger understanding of why relationships between managers and workers matter, the prescriptions often remain shallow and are treated as such. The effervescent executive is likely to be gone in a few years, many of the employees will be gone, and the owners may be different as well. Too often the company is assumed to be a collection of assets, available to the highest bidder. When times require it, employees will be sacked. Everybody responds accordingly. Underneath the veneer of participatory management, it is business as usual – and business as usual represents a threat to America's long-term capacity to compete.

If the United States is to compete effectively in the world in a way designed to enhance the real incomes of Americans, we must bring collective entrepreneurship to the forefront of the economy. That will require us to change our attitudes, to downplay the myth of the entrepreneurial hero, and to celebrate our creative teams.

First, we will need to look for and promote new kinds of stories. In modern-day America, stories of collective entrepreneurship typically appear in the sports pages of the daily newspaper; time after time, in accounts of winning efforts we learn that the team with the best blend of talent won – the team that emphasized teamwork – not the team with the best individual athlete. The cultural challenge is to move these stories from the sports page to the business page. We need to shift the limelight from maverick founders and shake-'em-up CEOs to groups of engineers, production workers, and marketers who successfully innovate new products and services. We need to look for opportunities to tell stories about American business from the perspective of all the workers who make up the team, rather than solely from the perspective of top managers. The stories are there – we need only change our focus, alter our frame of reference, in order to find them.

Second, we will need to understand that the most powerful stories get told, not in books and newspapers, but in the everyday world of work. Whether managers know it or not, every decision they make suggests a story to the rest of the enterprise. Decisions to award generous executive bonuses or to provide plush executive dining rooms and executive parking places tell the old story of entrepreneurial heroism. A decision to lay off 10% of the work force tells the old story of the drone worker. Several years ago, when General Motors reached agreement on a contract with the United Auto Workers that called for a new relationship based on cooperation and shared sacrifice, and then, on the same day, announced a new formula for generous executive bonuses, long-time union members simply nodded to themselves. The actions told the whole story. It is not enough to acknowledge the importance of collective entrepreneurship; clear and consistent signals must reinforce the new story.

Collective entrepreneurship represents the path toward an economic future that is promising for both managers and workers. For managers, this path means continually retraining employees for more complex tasks; automating in ways that cut routine tasks and enhance worker flexibility and creativity; diffusing responsibility for innovation; taking seriously labor's concern for job security; and giving workers a stake in improved productivity through profit-linked bonuses and stock plans.

For workers, this path means accepting flexible job classifications and work rules; agreeing to wage rates linked to profits and productivity improvements; and generally taking greater responsibility for the soundness and efficiency of the enterprise. This path also involves a closer and more permanent relationship with other parties that have a stake in the company's performance – suppliers, dealers, creditors, even the towns and cities in which the company resides.

Under collective entrepreneurship, all those associated with the company become partners in its future. The distinction between entrepreneurs and drones breaks down. Each member of the enterprise participates in its evolution. All have a commitment to the company's continued success. It is the one approach that can maintain and improve America's competitive performance – and America's standard of living – over the long haul.

Notes

1   Andrew Carnegie, *The Business of Empire* (New York: Doubleday, Page, 1902), p. 192.
2   See Lee Iacocca and William Novak, *Iacocca: An Autobiography* (New York: Bantam Books, 1984).
3   George Gilder, *The Spirit of Enterprise* (New York: Simon and Schuster, 1984), p. 213.
4   Ibid., p. 147.

SECTION 3
ORGANIZATIONAL ENVIRONMENT

7

The organizational culture of idea-management: a creative climate for the management of ideas

Göran Ekvall

The appearance of the concept and phenomenon of idea-management or idea-handling is due to several forces of change in industrial developed societies. One is the accelerating rate of development in technological fields, which enforces almost continuous changes in products and pro-cesses. Another is fast, world-wide commerce, giving the individual com-pany a more flexible and uncertain market to compete in. A third force is the frequent fluctuation in the life-styles and preferences of customers due to international media, communications and travel, secularization, affluent conditions and so on. A fourth is new values, ambitions and attitudes at work, which result in demands from employees to participate in problem-solving and decision-making. Companies need the ideas and the support of all their employees in the implementation of the new. Idea-management then becomes a necessary activity.

The concept of idea-management is about finding and taking care of ideas for change in the organization's operations, concerning both products and processes. It is a much broader concept than R & D management, as ideas are sought from all quarters. Idea-management has two sides. One concerns general features of the organization which stimulate or hamper innovation, the other includes special formal systems and procedures for idea-finding and use.

I have, for the last ten years, been carrying out a research programme about organizational conditions for creativity and innovation, covering both soft aspects like values, climate and leadership styles as well as harder qualities of the organization like structure, strategies and special systems for innovation. Studies have been done in small and large industrial organizations, banks, airlines, newspaper offices, broadcasting corporations, universities and hospitals.

Among the general features of organizations my research group has especially focused on, one of the more subjective, softer aspects is the emotional climate. Among formal structures and procedures for idea-handling, we have studied suggestion systems extensively, but also touched on several others, such as innovation offices, internal development funds, idea-hunts, idea-promotors, and training programmes in entrepreneurship.

Climate has to do with behaviour, attitudes and feelings which are fairly easily observed. Culture, on the other hand, refers to more deep-rooted assumptions, beliefs and values which are often on a preconscious level, things that are taken for granted. If we include climate in the culture concept, we can look upon climate as a manifestation, on a more superficial level, of the deeper, basic cultural element.

I regard organizational climate as an intervening variable which affects the results of the operations of the organization. The climate has this moderating power because it influences organizational processes such as communications, problem-solving, decision-making and the psychological processes of learning and motivation. The organization has resources of different kinds – people, money, machines, etc. – which are used in its processes and operations. These operations bring out effects of many kinds and on different levels of abstraction: high-quality or low-quality products or services; radically new products or only small improvements in the old ones; high or low job satisfaction among employees; commercial profit or loss. Climate has an important influence on these outcomes. But the effects in turn influence both resources and climate. The causal picture (seen in Figure 1) becomes complicated.

We measured creative/innovative climate through a questionnaire, consisting of 50 items forming 10 different scales with 5 items in each. The organizational climate score is an aggregated score based on the scores of the members of the organization. This instrument was thoroughly constructed and standardized by a series of factor analyses.

To give you some insight into the kind of research we have been doing in order to grasp the concept of innovative climate, I will present two sets of data.

Table 1 shows the mean scores for the climate dimensions from 27 different organizations. 'Organization' here stands for a separate small company or a self-governed part of a large company. All employees or a representative sample answered the questionnaire. The figures in the table are thus mean scores of the means for the organizations in the three groups. Very rigorous criteria were applied when putting organizations in the 'innovation' and 'stagnated' groups. The criterion of innovation is based on product innovations. (The classification was of course made independently of the climate scores, by a researcher from a business school who had developed a method to rate the innovativeness of a company's strategies and products.) The reliability of the climate scales permits a mean

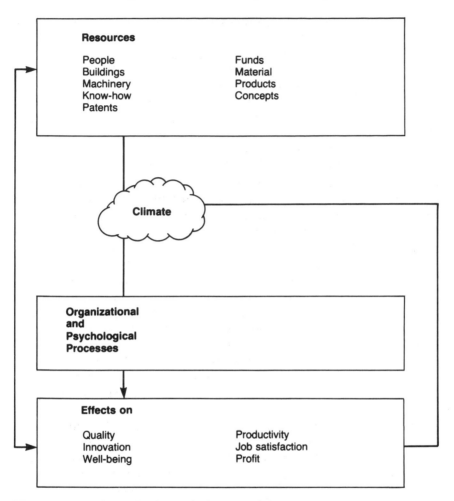

Figure 1   *The relationship between climate and the organization*

Table 1   *Mean climate scores for 27 Swedish organizations*

| Climate dimension | Organizations | | |
	Innovative N = 8	Stagnated N = 4	Average N = 15
Challenge	2.35	1.64	1.90
Freedom	2.17	1.52	1.74
Idea-support	2.09	1.31	1.64
Trust	1.82	1.37	1.60
Dynamism	2.31	1.30	1.55
Playfulness	2.16	1.29	1.69
Debates	1.54	0.92	1.28
Conflicts	0.71	0.85	0.88
Risktaking	2.34	0.95	1.12

score difference between any two organizations of 0.25 to be considered significant (provided that the means are based on a substantial sample of individuals).

The tendency in the table is evident. The innovative group has the highest mean scores of all three groups on all dimensions, with the exception of 'conflicts', and the stagnated group has the lowest mean scores, also except for 'conflicts'. But the opposite difference on the 'conflicts' scale is not strong. The 'conflict' climate aspect is a tricky one in relation to creativity and innovation. Personal, emotional conflicts can be seen as blocking creativity whereas ideas-controversies ('debates') are stimulating, but in some highly creative organizations both types of tension are markedly present. Those organizations, however, seem to be creative in spite of the personal tensions, not because of them.

Research results of this kind indicate that climates are different in innovative and stagnated organizations.

Table 2 *Mean climate scores for the extremes of a US industrial company*

Climate dimension	Innovative dept.	Stagnated dept.
Challenge	2.32	2.25
Freedom	1.92	0.95
Idea-support	1.85	1.00
Trust	1.62	1.25
Dynamism	1.97	1.50
Playfulness	1.62	1.35
Debates	1.52	1.10
Conflicts	1.10	1.40
Risktaking	1.27	0.40
Idea-time	1.50	1.00

In Table 2 the results from a study in an American industrial company are presented. A translation of the Swedish version of the creative climate questionnaire was applied in eight independent product departments belonging to the same division. The top management of the division rated one of the departments as creative and innovative and one as very problematic from that aspect. In the table only the results from these two 'extreme groups' are included. The scores are the means of the group members' scores. The results are very much the same as in the Swedish material, with the exception of 'challenge', where no difference was observed. Compared to all the other seven departments the 'stagnated' had the lowest score on all dimensions except 'challenge' (where it was in the middle) and 'conflicts' (where it had the highest score). The 'innovative' department, however, did not show the most supportive climate of all departments.

On the relation between organizational climate and formal systems for idea-handling (such as suggestion schemes), our results are clear-cut and the conclusions straightforward:

- No idea-handling system can work successfully without a supportive climate in terms of the dimensions I have referred to.
- An idea-handling system can make a good climate even better.
- An idea-handling system which is set up in an organization where the climate is bad tends to make that climate still worse. The system becomes another area of conflict and distrust.

When it comes to the more basic aspects of organizational culture – the beliefs and values concerning leadership and organization – that lay behind the concrete organizational phenomena, a model relating culture to idea-management has evolved in our research efforts.

The three broad value orientations affecting leadership and organization that have appeared in western societies during this century form different patterns which distinguish organizations from each other. These patterns imply very differing conditions for idea-management. Let me label the orientations 'structure', 'people' and 'change'.

'Structure-orientation' was the first on the historical scene of industrial society. It is articulated in Taylor's 'scientific-management' concept, in Weber's bureaucratic principles and in Fayol's classical management teachings. It is also seen in leadership-style concepts such as 'initiating-structure' (the Ohio leadership studies), and 'production-centeredness' (the Michigan school). In Burns' and Stalker's famous book *The Management of Innovation* (1961), structure-oriented organizations are described by the metaphor 'mechanistic'.

'People-orientation' is based on human relations and has had many variants. McGregor's theory Y is perhaps the strongest. 'Participation' is another but it also has other sources. The leadership style described as 'consideration' (Ohio group) or 'employee-centered' (Michigan) belongs here. Nowadays the concept of 'human resources' seems to be the most vivid representative of this orientation.

'Change-orientation' is the youngest and it is gaining ground. It is prevalent in the 'organismic' organizations described by Burns and Stalker. Leadership terms such as 'entrepreneurial' and 'transformational' leaders mirror this orientation. The modern distinction between leader and manager, between the person who creates meanings and goals for others and the one who administrates information and decisions, is clearly a result of this value-orientation being strong.

In the Swedish industrial culture where I do the main part of my research, four types of profiles on these three orientations are discernible. They are presented in Table 3.

Table 3 *Profiles of value orientations*

| Value orientation | Culture patterns | | | |
	A	B	C	D
Structure	++	++	0	0
People	0	+	0	++
Change	0	0	++	+

Type A is a *bureaucratic* culture with an *authoritarian* face. In such an organization in Swedish society it is not possible to run an idea-handling system successfully. The employees keep their ideas to themselves. If they hand in an idea, by mail or in the suggestion box, they do so anonymously and the idea is a joke or an impertinence.

Type B is a *bureaucracy* with a *human* face, a well-ordered culture where people's needs, feelings and relationships are considered, mostly in a formal, administrative way. Our research shows that in such a culture an idea-handling system can work. Many of the large Swedish industrial companies are of this type. Several of them have effective systems of idea-handling. But because of the weak change-orientation in these cultures, the idea-handling remains at a relatively low level of creativity. Improvements and refinements of processes and products turn up but no radically new concepts.

The type C pattern constitutes the classic *entrepreneurial* culture headed by a pushing, idea-rich and dominating person. This situation often characterizes the early phases of an organization's history. In a culture of this kind there is no need for a special procedure to handle ideas. Everything that occurs in the organization is in one way or another idea-handling. The pace of ideation is for the most part so great that a more formal procedure of idea-handling would be obstructive and pointless.

Type D may best be described as a culture of relations and *co-operation*, where opportunities exist for creative thinking. Innovation is seen as vital for the survival of the organization. Expansion through innovation is the main strategy. Renewal is sought in team-work and networks. It is assumed, in this type of organization, that creativity and innovation result when different people and their differing thoughts and experiences meet. Patterns of this kind have been called 'greenhouse cultures'. As long as the organization is small, there is no need for a formal idea-handling procedure. But as it grows and the number of people and ideas becomes large, even in an idea-stimulating culture and climate such as this one, a more formal procedure seems required to take care of the creative potential of the employees. In a type-D culture we have no doubt the best conditions for a successful idea-handling system, one that brings forth both improvements and new concepts.

Idea-management thus has very different prospects according to the cultural pattern of the organization. In some organizations it is futile to try to implement an idea-handling procedure of any kind, because it will be rejected like an unfit transplanted organ, the immune defence being the prevalent values, norms, attitudes and analogous actions. In other organizations formal procedures of idea-handling are possible but not necessary. When the organization is small, the people-orientation strong and the change-orientation marked, then a climate exists which allows all members of the organization to speak and have their ideas considered as a matter of course.

But when organizations grow to a level where it is impossible for all the members to know each other, where the division of work between individuals and groups becomes more strict, where communications are restricted by physical and administrative distances and boundaries – in such a situation the need for an idea-handling system arises even in an organization where the cultural and climate conditions support creativity and innovation.

This is a paradox, that formal procedures are needed to take care of employees' ideas in organizations with creativity-stimulating values and climates. Bureaucracy and formalism are enemies of creativity and innovation, but nevertheless we do need formal procedures and routines to be able to utilize the creative potential existing in the organization. It seems that formalism must be resisted by its own means.

The paradox can be explained in two ways. One explanation is that human beings as well as organizations function far from perfectly. Even in organizations that work well, correctives are needed for inappropriate actions. Formal procedures of idea-handling are, in this perspective, correctives of inadequate behaviour such as idea-suppression, force of habit, status-quo thinking, self-righteousness and territory protection. The formal procedure is seen as a substitute for a more spontaneous flow and nurture of ideas.

Another explanation is that organizations are systems that are structured and composed of separate sub-systems, which are of vital importance for the survival of the total system, the organization. Idea-handling is such a structured sub-system, and it is becoming more and more important.

Reference

Burns, T. and Stalker, G. *The Management of Innovation* (London: Tavistock, 1961).

8

Strong culture and its consequences

Mariann Jelinek and Claudia Bird Schoonhoven

Local knowledge in high-technology firms

Decades ago, it was recognized that managers don't 'do.' Instead, they
depend on others to do, while they see to resources, mind details of co-
ordination, keep track of morale and so on. Similarly, it appears that
managers for the most part do not make strategic decisions. Instead, their
contribution has more to do with co-ordination, management of collaboration and complexity, ensuring widespread input and engagement, and,
finally, validating or ratifying the commitment of the firm to a course of
action. In short, high-technology managers recognize quite explicitly that
they depend upon their people and their people's 'local knowledge' – their
detailed expertise in and familiarity with technology, markets, production
realities, and all the myriad details of how to understand what is happening, and how to actually implement any plan (Baba, 1988; Geertz, 1983).

Local knowledge, a concept drawn from anthropology, is special knowledge that is context-specific. It exists in discrete pockets, is shared among
the 'locals' there, and may or may not be noticed, appreciated or acknowledged by those outside the locale. While local knowledge is not a special
characteristic of strong cultures, it is an inevitable consequence of differences in expertise, experience, and attention. What is characteristic of
strong cultures, and in particular the strong cultures of our sample companies, is that management is deeply respectful of employees' special knowledge. Together with informality, this recognition permeates these firms;
they draw upon local knowledge, seek it out, cherish it, and consciously
accept their dependence on it as part and parcel of the open, participative
culture they strive to maintain.

'Local knowledge' is special knowledge tied intimately to the locale in
which it occurs. These firms make particular use of technical knowledge
about equipment, procedures, designs, or production processes; and
marketplace knowledge – detailed familiarity with a customer's problem or
proposed use for a product. This knowledge evolves in only one way: by
close contact with the technology (technical local knowledge) or with the

Extracted from Chapter 11 in M. Jelinek and C.B. Schoonhoven, *The Innovation Marathon*
(Oxford: Basil Blackwell, 1990)

customer (local market knowledge). These firms' use of local knowledge is visible in their universal policy of ensuring close contact between engineers and customers, and between designers and manufacturing engineers.

The close contact is explicitly fostered, in order that detailed familiarity can result, and thus be available for problem-solving when needed. The close links between open communication in general in these firms, and access to local knowledge which will be held by lower-level individuals, should be clear. Local knowledge in other industries certainly exists, but it is often ignored. Here, local knowledge is anticipated and counted upon: it is an important contribution from 'front line' personnel, those in direct contact with technology or with customers. Perhaps more importantly, because local knowledge is taken seriously and included in decision making, it is ratified and legitimated in our sample firms.

Other forms of local knowledge are also important. One of these is appreciation of a business unit's limitations, knowing what it can or cannot expect to undertake successfully. This knowledge can direct decisions to attempt or to abandon a particular opportunity. Another form of local knowledge is recognition of how developments or discoveries elsewhere apply to the local situation. Because innovation is so often thought of in purely product feature terms, these connections are especially important: they are the almost invisible understanding of the immediate situation that can spell ultimate success or failure in the marketplace . . .

Developing local knowledge

Developing this local knowledge is an important facet of managing corporate culture. It forms part of the process of socializing juniors into the firm and its culture; one aspect of such socialization, which transforms the juniors from outsiders to insiders, is the acquisition of appropriate perspectives on local knowledge. Local knowledge matters in these firms, it supports innovation, and thus it is to be fostered. By ensuring the transmission of local versions of organizational 'common sense' (that 'you've got to include the minions,' as one wag had it) these firms help to push the essential decision criteria and the wherewithal for decision making well down into the organization.

What is important here is not so much the content of what seniors convey as the process of doing so. Juniors come to recognize that the local, situation-specific knowledge they are expected to acquire is important, that it will be called upon, and that it is their responsibility to develop and communicate it, to be sure it gets into the decision process. Dan Dooley described the process at National Semiconductor, where new engineers are 'raised by hand' to develop market sense and strategy sense for how National does business:

Generally what we do for the engineers that come in [is], we put them up with a senior guy, to go on the system, and bring them up that way . . . Tutoring them, if you will.

Dan Dooley, National Semiconductor

Local knowledge is a key concept here, along with the idea of the strong culture as a pervasive, permeable essence that links people, both within and outside formal systems. Formal systems and checkpoints guide and drive strategy and operations, but only through substantial informal inter-action among employees. What knowledge is needed cannot be specified in advance; people must develop it for themselves, must assess it, and must communicate it. In essence, formal systems and procedures *depend on* local knowledge. Thus much time, attention, and effort are devoted to encouraging local knowledge.

Managers in the companies we studied recognize that they depend on the inputs of those who know. Managers cannot tell these people what, specifically, to find out. Thus it is not at all surprising to find managers acknowledging the importance of local knowledge. In stark contrast to much early thinking that assigned the formal systems to management and informal systems to employees, often in adversarial roles (e.g. Dalton, 1950; Gouldner, 1954; Homans, 1950; Roethlisberger and Dickson, 1939; Roy, 1952, 1954; Selznick, 1943), here we see formal systems working closely with informal systems, relying on local knowledge. Indeed, these firms cannot operate without it, because knowledge is developing too fast – by the time it's written down and formalized, it's obsolete. So they capture 'enough' in the documentation, and rely on local knowledge for the rest. Equally, the firms cannot ensure that decisions will be made according to what they see as appropriate criteria unless those criteria are built into the decision process. This means, of course, that the criteria must be widely disseminated and widely accepted.

Shared criteria also constitute a double-edged sword: once those criteria are widely shared, people are able to recognize the importance of their local knowledge. Recognizing it, they will feel entitled to consideration in strategic decisions. If people are to accept responsibility for outcomes, they will insist upon being substantively included in the decision process. They will have, and will articulate, their opinions and insights. Only by broadly and substantively including people can innovation be fostered (Carlzon, 1987; Kanter, 1983).

Our research shows that local knowledge can be encouraged: people can be sensitized to the need for it via congruent formal and informal means. And strong cultural norms of open participation, shared communication, and emphasis on task-relevant knowledge as the basis for credibility and authority provide a vehicle for bringing the local knowledge into decision making. In other words, local knowledge can contribute essential strength to decisions, but it requires a different management style, and a surrender of older ideas about hierarchy and status if it is to function properly. Intense personal involvement is another outcome of depending on local knowledge; and that also carries costs, as we have shown.

Dependency costs for managers

Two important sources of stress for managers in our sample companies are
technological change and dependency on subordinates. It isn't always easy
for North American managers to live with constant change, and with the
dependency on those whom they supervise that that change implies. At
one company, a technical manager described 'the Screaming Room.' This
person's manager, who had profit and loss responsibility for a large division
within the company, was warmly and favorably described as 'non-political':

> [That] means he's very honest. It means he can see. He doesn't do things for
> stupid personal reasons. He can see good and bad. He tends to be very
> pragmatic.
>
> Anonymous high-technology manager

Yet nevertheless, this well–regarded manager occasionally succumbs to
the pressure, and subordinates bear the brunt:

> Suddenly the human part of him is falling apart. He's bitching at me all of the
> time, he's complaining, and he's apt to be yelling at me, too. I'm not a yeller,
> but the only way I can handle him if he gets like that is, I yell back. We had a
> room built for him, which we call 'the Screaming Room.' I said '[Name], if
> you've got to scream, would you run for the room, so we don't disrupt the whole
> area?' When he would start this [yelling], productivity would drop to zero, and I
> don't like the effect on the people.

In such a case, subordinates must manage the boss's reaction to pressure,
and this manager did:

> Finally, it got to the point where he was driving me nuts, because I couldn't even
> find out the reason he was screaming so. He would give a reason, but that wasn't
> the real reason. At first, I was missing it, but then I finally realized: 'Oh, yeah.
> He's really uncomfortable [technologically] with the program.' So I said, 'I think
> we need some tutorials. We're going to spend four hours a week, and I'm going
> to sit down ... and give you educational lectures.' This guy, [whom] I had
> worked with for seven years, is really very bright. He's a really good man, who is
> suffering from 'technology shock,' and reacting by some heavy psychological
> things. I do a big education job for management [when it's needed].

'Training up' is notoriously difficult, and 'training' *per se* is not an explicit part of this anonymous manager's job. Nevertheless, it was independently undertaken, in a very matter-of-fact way, to assist a respected
superior in coping. Such efforts are, of course, eminently consistent with
local knowledge in the open communication culture we have been describing, in terms of shared expertise and taking personal responsibility, and
also in terms of managerial dependency. They are also quite atypical of
large-company manager–subordinate relations in traditional firms.

Managers and executives faced with their own likely technical obsol-
escence are in some senses confronted with their own professional mortality. Understandably, this is a difficult recognition to make, and not all

acknowledge it, or accept it gracefully. We might expect such a recognition to be especially difficult in strong cultures, where investment of self in the work of the firm is most profound. The cost to a superior involves the humbling experience of admitting limits, further undercutting the status differentials captured in organizational hierarchy and calling them further into question. The cost to subordinates, beyond the frustrations of trying to communicate past erroneous assumptions and obsolete knowledge, may include contending with training. All is not roses in high-technology firms; people work hard at working well with one another.

Time to manage culture costs

The effort to deliberately manage culture is necessarily expensive of managerial time. To begin with, it is an attempt to influence a great deal that is beyond management's direct sphere of influence. As one anthropologist suggested:

> To an anthropologist, the conscious creation of a culture by management is amusing, because all human groups have culture by nature, and these systems of values and beliefs are shaped by experience, tradition, class position, and political circumstances – all powerful forces that are extremely refractory to directed change, particularly by occasional committee. (Reynolds, 1986)

In our sample firms, the 'occasional committee' Reynolds mentions was not even considered as the mode of culture management. Instead, the effort to build and manage culture was a serious, constant, iterative, 'hands on' activity. It entailed enormous amounts of time spent in communicating to people, sharing ideas and views, articulating goals, encouraging, and hearing out. Of course, organizational culture will emerge even without management attention, regardless of management's wishes. Its values and norms, in that instance, may be very different from those management would have chosen. Seeking to influence corporate culture, management in our sample companies must invest substantial amounts of time, energy, attention, and conscious effort. 'Endless meetings' and 'endless explanations' are symptoms of this cost category.

Even so, culture will not be wholly within management's control. External culture (ethnic culture, the national culture within which the firm operates, and the like) also play a generally underappreciated role (Hofstede, 1984). Although we will not spend time on it, 'external culture' enters our sample firm in the form of enormous variety – personnel on a production line speaking ten or more languages other than English, for instance. This reality creates very different culture problems for North American managers in, say, California, than for Japanese managers in Tokyo facing an essentially homogeneous workforce. These complexities are only one item of culture's cost for managers in our sample companies.

The management of innovation efforts, particularly in terminating activities that do not make business sense, can be delicate as well as time-consuming – the more so since administrative fiat is not an acceptable solution. An account from Motorola highlights the difficulty, and the consummate care of the managers for their innovative contributor:

It turns out that we went far enough with [an experimental project] to determine that, unfortunately, it was going to be too expensive and could not be made large enough to approach the market as a whole. What we did at that point, was to get together a task force of people to examine the idea and where it was going: the people doing the work and the people who were likely to understand the most likely market – put them together in one room to reason their way through to the fact that we really ought to drop the project. It turns out the inventor by then had come to the conclusion that 'I really ought to go off and look at something else now.' It was sort of a group kind of thing, but there wasn't somebody telling him, 'You can't do that.' It was an attempt to lead him to the realization that this was something that wouldn't work . . .

You don't want to turn him off, because his next winner might be a real winner . . . It turned out that he was the one who made the presentation and suggested we get out of it.

Bill Howard, Motorola

Meetings, and time for them, are a serious management expense in strong culture organizations. Because so much communication is deliberately informal, it is not recorded on paper. Thus it involves massive amounts of reporting, in person or on paper, to keep everyone up to date:

Fifty to eighty percent of my time goes to meetings, either with one of my engineers or in development meetings, or in planning functions, or – we have a series of meetings set up with this group since they provide a service to us – and oh, I don't know – ten to twenty percent of my time [is spent] on the phone . . . and the rest of my time, either in filling out forms that I have to fill out or thinking, sometimes. That's a rough estimate.

Kim Kokkonen, Intel

Constant meetings and interface requirements exacerbate time pressure, widely recognized as exasperating. Multiple meetings, among parties with differing agendas and often conflicting needs, are also a source of stress and 'interaction fatigue,' as well as time-expensive.

As to formal written reports, in our sample firms we also saw efforts to reduce the number of them, and to facilitate their production – for instance, by substituting computer programs for manual information collection and transmittal. Nevertheless, despite such efforts, the management effort required to co-ordinate, collaborate and integrate innovation activities is great:

There are a number of mechanisms in place that are good by themselves, but when I add it together, it's a very large time segment that we are always fighting. That's something that we've argued about a lot. I personally don't feel that all the indicators [reports and briefings, based on data collected and analyzed] we do are essential. However, there is a strong proponent for each indicator in upper-level management.

Kim Kokkonen, Intel

Shared information is the foundation of participation in decisions, yet as the number of people to be co-ordinated rises, the number of potential communication links, be they by computer, telephone, paper or in person rises dramatically. Ultimately, the cost is overload and the response of people to overload is stress, prioritizing, queuing of information (or problems), and, ultimately, degraded performance.

Some portion of these costs must be due to the particular sort of culture – surprisingly uniform, across these very different companies – that our sample firms sought to induce: a high participative one. Nevertheless, the old aphorism applies here, 'TANSTAAFL' – There Ain't No Such Thing As A Free Lunch. Especially in trying to foster a culture of open communication and widely shared ideas, managers and others must spend enormous time communicating and sharing ideas. *Too much* time is spent on committees, teams, and meetings, according to some.

Les Vadasz (Senior Vice-President, Planning at Intel) remarked that pruning committees and interfaces was somewhat difficult. His comment is worthy of attention, especially in the context of such high change organizations as those we studied. Even there, even with all the change, people find it difficult to cut back on activities in which they have invested themselves over time.

Committees and complex, multiple reporting relationships, which are necessary, can get out of hand. This danger, and the maintenance task of overseeing organizational arrangements and seeing to them, are very real costs of a strong culture. Time and attention must be expended in managing these relationships. Yet it can seem burdensome, or even dysfunctional. According to Vadasz – and, we might add, many other managers we talked to in our sample firms – cutting back to avoid 'meeting overload' and an over-elaborate structure of relationships is a never-ending task:

> We try to do that. We're more conscious of these things than we used to be, before. But in fact, we had one senior individual in the company who was spending most of his time trying to clean up some organizational messes. That doesn't make sense. But, you know, when you explain these concepts to the people who are part of that committee, or they are the chairman of that committee – it's very easy to say, 'Yeah, that other committee is really bad. It's not me. It's them.'

Les Vadasz, Intel

The phenomenon of meeting overload highlights another managerial cost to the sort of culture we have been describing. The committees and working groups are certainly participative, and are intended to be arenas for wide input from a variety of sources. However, they cannot be allowed to operate as completely autonomous or ad hoc bodies. Their functioning must be managed, and this takes management time. As Vadasz noted, 'somebody has to do the supervising.'

In essence, managerial time – supervisory effort – is being put in as the transaction cost to ensure effective committee efforts. The dual tasks of supervising committee operation and pruning committees and other such relationships back when they are no longer necessary are real management costs in strong culture firms. The alternative, allowing individuals or individual committees to operate without supervision, would also incur costs. The firms we studied have universally decided that ad hoc, undirected teams are simply too expensive in terms of creative effort and participative input. Therefore they elect to manage these activities.

What we see here are costs brought into management's account: an internal structuring cost, via committees; an on-going maintenance cost, for repeated pruning; and an internalized transaction cost, via management time. These costs, formerly borne by the individual employees if the necessary co-ordination was to take place, now accrue to their managers. This makes sense if and only if these committees and interfaces produce more innovation and more efficient innovation than the alternatives. Of course, committees can fail. The participants can fail to express their views, the experts' expertise can be withheld, people can fail to attend, fail to contribute, or fail to follow through. All these contributions and more, in addition to the required time, must be forthcoming if the committees and interfaces are in fact to produce the close coupling and co-ordinated collaboration these firms need.

Values, norms, and expectations – the very stuff of culture – must provide a context within which open communication, personal responsibility for outcomes, and shared focus on problem-solving can occur. Local knowledge can be brought to bear, but only if its possessors share with management a common vision that values contribution of one's special understanding, particularly when that understanding is different from that of others. Scattered experts will contribute to complex team interfaces, but only if frequent pruning ensures that their scarce time isn't wasted on needless meetings. In short, management of values, and management consistent with values, is a constant, and difficult, task.

The management of corporate culture is expensive of time to *do* it – the endless meetings that people participate in. It is also expensive of *management time* – the careful fostering of innovation's context, of the value of listening, and the patient explanation of goals and norms and targets, and the willing 'open association' policy, even at very senior levels. Managing culture comes full circle: the need to instill values is driven by the need for those values to be available to guide people's activities.

Conclusion

The tour of cultures contained in this chapter has highlighted the costs of strong culture and methods for its management. Strong culture's benefits do not come unalloyed, nor without cost. Our discussion has centered upon individual costs – particularly personal and interpersonal costs – and managerial costs, as well as organizational cost.

References

Baba, M.L. (1988) 'The local knowledge content of technology based firms', Presentation at the University of Colorado conference on Managing High Technology Firms.

Carlzon, J. (1987) *Moments of truth*, Cambridge MA: Ballinger.

Dalton, M. (1950) 'Conflicts between staff and line managerial officers', *American Sociological Review*, 15 June, pp. 342–51.

Geertz, C. (1983) *Local knowledge*, New York: Basic Books.

Gouldner, A.W. (1954) *Patterns of industrial bureaucracy*, New York: The Free Press.

Hofstede, G. (1984) *Culture's consequences*, Cross cultural research and methodology series, 5, Beverly Hills CA: Sage.

Homans, G.C. (1950) *The Human Group*, New York: Harcourt, Brace and World.

Kanter, R. Moss (1983) *The change masters: innovation for productivity in the American corporation*, New York: Simon and Schuster.

Reynolds, P.C. (1986) 'Corporate culture on the rocks', *Across the Board* 23:10 October, pp. 51–6.

Roethlisberger, F.J. and Dickson, W.J. (1939) *Management and the worker*, Cambridge MA: Harvard University Press.

Roy, D. (1952) 'Quota restriction and goldbricking in a machine shop', *American Journal of Sociology*, 57:5 March, pp. 430–7.

Roy, D. (1954) 'Efficiency and the fix: informal intergroup relations in a piecework machine shop', *American Journal of Sociology*, 60:3, pp. 255–66.

Selznick, P. (1943) 'An approach to a theory of bureaucracy', *American Sociological Review*, 8, pp. 47–57.

9

What is the best way of organizing projects?

Knut Holt

Innovation projects are of an interdisciplinary nature and require co-operation between people with various talents. They can be performed within the permanent organization, but often it is practical to use temporary, problem-oriented project groups. Several departments and levels may be represented in the groups which come together and accomplish more or less well defined objectives and then disperse. There are numerous definitions of the term 'project', but it appears to be impossible to find a good one. I will not attempt to compete with the many existing ones, but use an indirect definition by listing the most important characteristics of innovative projects:

- a specific objective: this is related to the needs of those involved.
- resource constraint: the project must be completed with the manpower, equipment, and financial resources allocated to it.
- time constraint: the project must be completed within a certain time limit.
- interdisciplinary approach: people with various skills participate.
- control: a special approach is required for monitoring the project.
- organization: responsibility for the project must be clearly defined and a special arrangement made for co-ordination purposes.

The items listed appear to cover most projects. However, there are exceptions.

> At Philips, a world-wide international corporation with 400,000 employees, most innovation projects are undertaken within 14 product divisions. However, when the firm wants to move into a new area, a special project organization may be created for this purpose. An example is the development of new energy systems for the heating of homes. A project organization was created, consisting of six full-time employees, two with marketing backgrounds, the others with technical and administrative backgrounds. The group reports directly to the 'Board of Management', the highest administrative level of the company. The

Extracted from Chapter 4 in Knut Holt, *Innovation: A Challenge to the Engineer* (Oxford: Elsevier, 1987) group meets about every second month with representatives from the board and discusses results and further plans. The approach is flexible, and there are no limitations with regard to time.

The scope of a project varies considerably. Many projects start when an idea or a proposal is accepted for realization. There are also cases where a project includes the whole process, from idea conception to practical application. In other cases, separate project organizations are used for idea generation and idea realization. Many projects start with a small group and are gradually expanded as they move ahead. Due to the great variety of approaches for organizing innovative projects, it is difficult to classify them. Here, we will distinguish between the basic structure, the matrix organization, the independent project organization, and the venture team.

The basic structure

Here, the project is planned and implemented within the permanent structure. It moves from department to department in a pre-arranged sequence like the baton in a relay race. The solution requires an elaborate planning and control procedure. It is used for improvements and new applications of existing products, and for new products with a low degree of novelty. The project must have attributes which allow sequential processing.

With the involvement of several departments, the responsibilities must be clearly defined. One alternative is total responsibility; one department is then responsible for the whole project. This will facilitate overall co-ordination and monitoring, which is important when unexpected events occur. On the other hand, it may be difficult to implement and it may also create human problems.

Another alternative is divided responsibility; it then rests with the functional departments involved and changes from department to department as the project moves ahead.

> An example of divided responsibility is found at Danfoss. Projects are authorized by divisional product committees. The authorization is based on a detailed product specification, a market evaluation, a time schedule, a project budget, and in some cases, a solution concept. The project starts in the R & D department where one engineer is made responsible for it. This includes both the work in the department and contact with marketing, quality control and production engineering. When the first pilot run is completed and approved, responsibility for the project is transferred to the manufacturing department.

Some firms divide the responsibility between two or more departments.

> An example is Volvo Penta, a large producer of diesel engines for marine purposes. Each functional manager appoints a representative who is responsible for the project within his department. The technical director feels there is a need for a special unit for total co-ordination and monitoring. However, the departments involved are heavily loaded, and none of them want to contribute a key person for this purpose. There is also a general feeling that a co-ordination unit

will result in more pressure and control on functional departments. Some argue that such a solution will require more personnel and thus be more expensive. Others claim that projects will be handled better and result in a net saving. The solution is strongly opposed by the R & D staff, who usually make the largest contribution to the project in terms of effort. Their view is that the co-ordinator will not necessarily come from the R & D department, which will reduce its influence. They, therefore, prefer to retain the present approach.

The sequential processing requires special measures in order to integrate the activities involved. Often there is strong pressure on the departments to give top priority to short-term problems, such as minor product changes, in order to satisfy needs of special users, and assistance to manufacturing and marketing in connection with trouble shooting. Such situations allow little opportunity for innovative behaviour and may cause a great strain on the staff; good planning and skilful leadership are required if innovative projects are not going to suffer too much. The time-pressure may cause serious problems, particularly in small departments where a few engineers have to handle all problems related to product technology.

One example is Unitor. This firm makes equipment for electrical welding that is sold all over the world. Here, engineers complain that the work situation is dominated by assignments in connection with modifications to product design in order to meet national requirements of the various countries. Long-term work of an innovative nature is given low priority and has to be done between short-term assignments.

When using the basic structure for processing of innovative projects, the challenge is to find a proper balance between short-term projects, which require a considerable amount of order and discipline, and innovative projects, which require more freedom and flexibility.

The matrix organization

Here, one person is appointed as manager and given full responsibility for achieving the objectives of the project. This will involve performance, cost, and time. Depending on the situation, he may report to the chief executive, to a functional manager, or to a steering committee. For important projects, one may also use an advisory board representing those who will be most influenced by the project.

The project manager makes agreements with the heads of functional departments which provide the necessary resources in terms of manpower and equipment. The staff is assigned to the project on a full-time or part-time basis.

Characteristic of the matrix organization is dual relationship as indicated in Figure 1. The symbols indicate that project P1 has one part-time member from marketing, two full-time and one part-time member from R & D, two part-time members from manufacturing, and one part-time member from finance. The figure also shows that three projects, P1, P2,

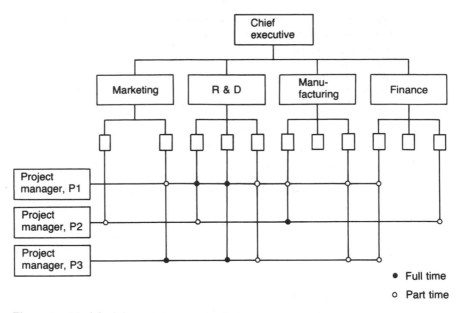

Figure 1   *Model of the matrix organization*

and P3, are processed simultaneously, each cutting across the authority lines of the functional departments.

The matrix approach is best suited for complex projects which require the simultaneous efforts of experts from several disciplines. Typical applications are found in companies with several medium-sized projects, i.e. ranging from one half to five man-years.

One example is the Aanonsen company. The R & D department has three engineers who spend most of their time improving existing products. When the chief executive wants to take up a new product, he selects one of them as 'project engineer'. This engineer then reports directly to him and is responsible for the formulation of project specifications, finding the technical solution concept, developing the product technology, testing and modification of the prototype, making manufacturing drawings, determination of manufacturing processes and operations, determination of time-standards for manufacturing and assembly operations, estimating product costs, and supervision of pilot runs. Most often the project engineer does not have enough know-how for all these tasks. He then gets support through informal contacts with employees in the R & D department, in the industrial engineering department, and in the production control department. No formal procedure is used for monitoring the project, but the chief executive follows it with interest and talks informally with the project engineer from time to time.

The matrix approach can be used in connection with large projects. The project manager then has a special staff to assist him. He may also have a contact man in each functional department responsible for co-ordination and monitoring of the work within the department.

An example of such an organization is General Electronics that produces military products such as radar, underwater defence, and missile systems. The business development department is responsible for assessment of long-term user needs, long-term planning, and co-operation with research, which attempts to solve technological problems associated with future requirements. Marketing is responsible for customer relations, sales, and contract administration. The development department is broken down into product-oriented sectors which, in turn, are divided into discipline-oriented units. When a contract for a weapon system is received, a project manager is appointed. He is responsible for planning and control of the project, and for ensuring that cost estimates and project schedules are realistic, that time and money are properly budgeted between functional departments, and that the staff is doing a good job. In order to perform his duties, he has a project staff. In all but the largest projects, the functions are performed by having most of the staff members located in their functional departments reporting to their functional managers. However, normally one contact man from each of the units is transferred to the staff of the project manager and is responsible to him for the work that is done in his unit.

The application of the matrix model for projects with a high degree of novelty, creates a difficult planning situation. Such projects require a creative environment and flexible plans with ample room for unforeseen delays. On the other hand, co-ordination of those involved, and completion of the project within the established time and budget limits, require an elaborate procedure for planning and control.

An important task of the project manager is to break down the project into independent activities, to specify what shall be done and when the work must be finished, and to make agreements with functional managers about their contributions. He must also come to an agreement with the customer with regard to performance characteristics, key schedule dates, costs, and funding. Furthermore, he must keep them informed about progress of the project – what they will get, when they will get it, and what it will cost.

The managers in the functional departments are responsible for determining how to make their contributions considering other tasks which they have to perform. This creates complicated relationships between project managers and functional managers. According to Kampfrath (1970), one can distinguish between three different situations:

– functional orientation: the project manager orders a certain result from the functional departments. Each functional manager acts as a subcontractor responsible for delivery of the result on time, at the right cost, and with the right quality. The functional staffs perform the work under supervision of their own managers.
– intermediate orientation: the project manager supervises the functional staff. He determines the type of activities required and their timing. The functional managers are responsible for choosing the right staff, for instructing them and for the result with regard to quality, quantity and cost.

− project orientation: the project manager is furnished with staff and
   equipment from the functional departments. He is responsible not only
   for the results, but also for giving orders and for the amount, quality
   and cost of the contributions. The functional managers are responsible
   for the material resources and the suitability of the staff in terms of
   motivation, know-how, capacity, etc. This is a difficult situation for
   those involved and should be thoroughly explained.

Due to the complicated relationships, the matrix organization has potential conflicts built in; it almost appears to be designed for social problems.
If you get the job of project manager, you must recognize that you have
one of the most complex and demanding tasks you can get. You must be
able to develop good, informal contact with functional managers. They are
not your subordinates. Often they are at the same or higher levels. The
matter is further complicated if you have to compete with other project
managers for the same resources.

Another problem comes from the fact that many staff members spend
only part of their time on a project. They have to cope with one or more
project managers, and to take orders from their own department head.
Another difficulty is that new forms of co-operation must be established
between individuals who have little knowledge about each other, who are
placed temporarily under new managers, and who often feel closely
attached to their functional departments. Many staff members, particularly
those who are working full-time on long projects, feel insecure over what is
going to happen when the project is finished.

The project manager may have problems in motivating people to work
for him. If he does not have authority to give the staff financial rewards or
the possibility of developing themselves, they may go to their functional
managers in order to satisfy their economic and professional ambitions.

The independent project organization

This is a self-contained group consisting of full-time members with skills in
marketing, R & D, manufacturing, finance, etc. The project manager has
full responsibility for the project and is given necessary resources for
planning and implementation. He usually reports to the head of the company or to a steering committee composed of high-level executives. In
order to justify a separate organization, the project must be of such a
magnitude that it is possible to employ experts from the required disciplines, on a full-time basis. As a supplement, one may use external consultants and part-time experts from the basic organization.

When a new solution, or a new product is wanted, one may use an
independent project organization. When the project is completed, the
group members are transferred back to the basic structure, or they are
given operating responsibility for the new product in a new unit.

An example of an independent project organization is found at Philips. The group, which works with development of new energy systems, can use outside consultants and experts from the company when this is practical. The whole approach is flexible and has a great strength in the direct link to the highest administrative body. If the project is successful, it will be transferred to one of the existing product divisions, or a new product division will be organized for further exploitation.

In order to get a well integrated group, the members should be located together. However, thereby they lose contact with the professional environment in the basic organization. In order to counter this, specific measures should be undertaken on long-lasting projects to update the professional competence of those involved.

The independent project organization appears to be the best approach from a social point of view. However, there are also problems related to this model. At the start of a project there is often a pressure on functional managers to provide qualified people for the project. This may cause disturbances in the basic organization. The staff members that are transferred may have a frustrating period before they become acquainted and learn to work together on the project. At the end of a long project there may be a difficult situation if functional managers in the meantime have staffed their departments with new members.

The venture team

This is a variation of the independent project organization that is used in order to promote entrepreneurial behaviour. It is often called 'intrapreneurship'. Copulsky and McNulty (1974) state, 'A new wind is blowing, and it is a strong one. Corporate life is changing as companies realize that they need more than young managers who demand high starting salaries, work a standard day, keep in line, and concern themselves about security. Business has come to recognize the need to foster entrepreneurship; failure to do so may result in a kind of in-house recession.'

According to Hanan (1969), a venture team is characterized by being relatively small, by being composed of members from various functional areas working full-time on the project, by being willing to take risks, by having a broad objective that is not well defined at the start, by having sufficient resources, by being segregated from the permanent organization, and by having great freedom with a minimum of corporate rules and regulations. The venture group not only generates new ideas, but is also responsible for development and exploitation of them.

An example of a venture team is found in connection with the development of robots at Cincinnati Milacron. A team of six engineers were hired and given great freedom in assessing user needs, and generating, developing and exploiting the ideas. During the exploitation stage, the group hired its own salesman and operated as a small independent business unit.

Concept	one should have an idea for a workable product
Technology	one should have the means and skills to produce and sell the product
Resources	one should have sufficient financial support and enough time
Management	one should have a person who is able and willing to take a career risk by being identified with the venture
Market	one should make a market test after the prototype has been developed in order to study the need beyond that implied in the original concept
Organization	one should clarify long-term objectives, degree of freedom of the venture, and how closely it will be connected with the original sponsor

Figure 2   *Requirements of a successful venture (Mueller, 1973)*

If a venture team is to succeed, the requirements shown in Figure 2 should be fulfilled. And above all, top management must really want and stimulate people to be innovative. In actual practice, one or more of the items are often missing and this may explain the high failure rate of new ventures. The idea behind the venture team is to create a climate for innovation by simulating the qualities of the small entrepreneurial firm.

It is difficult to define the venture concept. Although it is widely used, there are no generally accepted definitions. However, it appears that most ventures are characterized by investments in a project where the uncertainty is so great that it is not possible to evaluate it by means of ordinary criteria for analysis of projects.

References

Copulsky, W. and McNulty, H.W. (1974) *Entrepreneurship and the Corporation*, New York: AMACOM.

Hanan, M. (1969) Corporate growth through venture management, *Harvard Business Review*, January–February, pp. 43–61.

Kampfrath, A. (1970) Organizing for Innovation, Paper presented at the 10th European Federation of Productivity Services Conference, The Hague, 10 June.

Mueller, R.K. (1973) Venture vogue: boneyard or bonanza?, *Management Review*, pp. 56–8.

SECTION 4

IMPLEMENTATION

10

Innovation by design

Colin Clipson

Throughout the 1970s the big three automobile companies in Detroit and their counterparts in the United Kingdom foundered in the face of competition from Japan, Germany and Scandinavia. Poorly organized to meet rapidly changing markets, energy crises and customer performance shifts, they lost sight of their customers, and lost a grip on emerging technologies necessary to competitiveness. Products of poor quality, poor performance and short life cycle had little chance against high quality, dependable Japanese and European products.

It is taking a long time to redesign the business processes of these industries. In some sectors of manufacturing there has been almost a reluctance to change. Poorly trained managers who found themselves faced with new, rapidly changing technologies developed technophobia out of fear of things they did not understand.

New and improved products are essential to the well-being of any business. Unless a firm can upgrade its products and services to remain ahead of the competition, the margin of profitability will be significantly reduced with attendant loss of market share.

However, historical reviews of business failure rates show that the incidence of new product failure is very high and costly. In a classic study of product development, Booz-Allen and Hamilton reported that only two out of ten new products were a commercial success and that seven out of eight hours of technical effort failed to result in commercial success (Jain 1984). As Bacon and Butler (1981) point out, the seriousness of this problem is not generally recognized; most firms are poorly equipped to deal with the technical change and continue to operate with organizations that themselves are poorly designed. Why have these conditions become more critical in recent years?

From Chapter 33 in M. Oakley (ed.), *Design Management* (Oxford: Basil Blackwell, 1990), pp. 313–21

Technological change

If we look at the development of computers over the past 30 years we see accelerated change of a phenomenal nature. From its first operation in the 1920s, the computer only reached commercial feasibility and success in 1964. Similarly, the transistor took decades to become incorporated into commercial products such as hearing aids, navigational instruments and computers. The silicon microchip and integrated circuit followed similar if shorter processes from invention to commercial realization. In the last two decades, rates of change have become much shorter with more rapid translation of technical advances into commercialized products. Since 1953 the United States has been subjected to rapidly reduced lead time on computer innovation, from several years' lead time in the 1950s and 1960s to zero and lag time in the 1980s.

The implications of this accelerated diffusion of technology and rapid translation into innovative products are that companies have very little time to rest on the strength of any one currently successful product. The cost of developing new innovative products is extremely high; companies must be able to defray the high front-end cost associated with translating inventions into commercially successful products by marketing them as widely as possible around the world.

Economies of scale in product development may be achieved by companies who manage to work together, or find some cooperative ways to share the costs of developing new products. Even when adding new products to the product line, a company can avoid going through product development by joining with other firms, acquiring other firms or getting products from them (Terpstra 1984).

'The bottom line is that companies that choose to develop domestic markets may find themselves totally blocked out by competitors that are well entrenched and ready to launch offensives on others' home markets' (Ohmae 1985). Significant differences can be detected in the technological edge of the high technology industries over the medium technology industries:

High technologies Electronics, computers, communication equipment, fine chemicals, pharmaceuticals, office equipment.
Medium technologies Steel, light electrical industry, automobiles, petroleum refining, textiles, non-ferrous metals, paper and paper products, fabricated metal products, ceramics, earth and stone.

In a comparison of Organization for Economic Cooperation and Development (OECD) nations, the high technology group had 1.49 times the sales growth, 2.8 times the productivity growth and 2.75 times the profit growth of the medium technology industries. It is becoming very difficult to make a profit in old line industries (Figure 1). For example, VCR products are growing at three times the rate of other audiovisual products (Ohmae 1985).

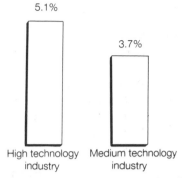

Figure 1 *Technological change: net profit/sales ratio for the world's leading companies, weighted average 1980 and 1981 (Japanese Ministry of International Trade and Industry, 1982)*

Redesigning organizations

Given the problems implied by technological change and the blurring of the traditional divisions between various sections of the manufacturing and marketing systems, corporations themselves have to be redesigned in order to withstand the rigours of change and adaptation to new market conditions. Some general conditions of sound organization design are as follows (Clipson 1985):

1 The chief executive officer and corporate management understand the critical link between design engineering and manufacturing engineering in their business and believe that effective design for quality is an essential part of the corporate business strategy.
2 The corporation understands that design is not merely styling and market hype.
3 The corporation values long-term profits and does not heavily rely on discounted cash flow analysis. Investment in research is a key business strategy.
4 Organizations are managed by people who know the business and know how the various aspects of the business are related and how they operate. This implies an orientation obtained through practical experience in an industry rather than reliance on the belief that a good manager can manage anything.
5 Organizations that have horizontal and adaptive structures are able to meet the changes in market need more readily than those with cumbersome hierarchical structures, and create multifunctional development groups to plan new product developments.
6 Organizations that stay close to their customers' needs have a competitive edge.

The road to profitable innovation is littered with well-intentioned wreckage. Bacon and Butler (1981) summarize a few of the short cuts and legends to be avoided:

- *The better mousetrap*   All you have to do is build a better version of brand X and the world will beat a path to your door.
- *Another Xerox*   All you have to do is find another superproduct with a powerful technology to exploit.
- *The gift of genius*   Find a brilliant inventor to set loose in the laboratory and your problems are solved; the new products will start to roll off the line immediately.

More and more companies are taking R & D abroad but many still prefer to centralize this critical activity at home. The numerous advantages of centralization include realization of economies of scale, easier communication, better protection of knowledge, more leverage with domestic government, and ease of coordination between R & D, marketing and production. On the other hand, undertaking R & D abroad is encouraged in response to subsidiary pressure and foreign government incentives. It serves in the adaptation of home products abroad, makes use of local talent and is considered an effective public relations tool. Carrying out R & D abroad also broadens the base for seeking new product ideas, is cost saving, and is closer to markets. Finally, it could be carried out as a continuation of the R & D activities of a firm acquired abroad. In general, it is expected that the future will see more companies enlarging their R & D activity abroad, using the sharing or transferring of technology as an effective way to enter these markets (Jain 1984).

In well-designed organizations, the ability to change and remain dynamic is a key ingredient of continued competitiveness. Design implies change and improvement, solving technical problems and meeting new needs. Translating inventions into marketable products and services requires a delicate balance between uniformity and diversity; innovation flourishes in this milieu and needs the pressure of both. *Uniformity* implies standardization and common procedures; the pressure for uniformity includes the economies of standardization, the need for interchangeability in product systems, the need for control of processes, the need for a standard quality product, specialization of markets and the need for common management controls. On the other hand, there will be pressures for *diversity* in a dynamic environment. This is expressed in a number of ways such as regional and marketing diversifications, the attraction and risk of moving into new and untested product markets, broadening and changing technological resources and, more radically, changing the fundamental directions and goals of the organization.

The twin pressures of diversity and uniformity are tangible phenomena in the design process. The relationship between innovation and design at a company such as Hewlett-Packard is not a simple linear action, but a holistic process of interrelated actions – technical, social, economic, strategic and aesthetic – all subject to these twin pressures. Innovation is acknowledged to contribute to economic growth, social benefit and survival in the competitive world, yet many organizations are not innovative and mimic the innovators to stay in the race. Consumer product manufacturers such as Philips have remained successful in their international markets by redesigning both their approach to product development and their product manufacture. According to Robert Blaich, Director of Design, design for manufacture and assembly is at the centre of Philips's compacted development time.

Most organizations have difficulty in being innovative and designing well. There is evidence to suggest that many corporations do not have an organizational structure and process that allow the lateral integration of marketing, research, design engineering, financing and manufacturing for the successful conclusion of their business enterprises; in these organizations, ideas get thrown over the wall rather than worked on collaboratively. Many corporations have top heavy, vertical organization structures and new ideas just take too long to move through the business process. Such organizations can be said to be poorly designed. If a product or service is to be successful in the marketplace, then the organization itself must be designed to meet its conditions. The interrelationship of organizational attributes is the key to any successful business/design activity. Neither invention nor innovation and translation by design can take place in an inflexible or chaotic environment; nor can they take place if flexible design procedures for capitalizing on new market conditions are lacking.

One of the most critical problems for organizations in designing well and competitively is their response or lack of response to change and, more specifically, to rates of change in markets' technical and economic conditions.

> It must be remembered that there is nothing more difficult to plan, more uncertain of success, or more dangerous to manage than the creation of a new order of things. For the initiator has the enmity of all who would profit by the preservation of the old institutions, and merely lukewarm defenders of all who would gain by new ones. (Machiavelli 1948)

New product strategies

Basically, new product development takes place in two ways. In the first a company or industry discerns the need for a new product or product range, develops markets and sells to the widest possible market. To do this, it has to not only come up with single products but be able to place them in product systems and even combine them in innovative ways. Using existing unconnected product breakthroughs, Sony took a small tape player, married it to lightweight headphones and made the Walkman an entirely new product that, after a slight hesitation, became a world beater. The company originated and broke through with a new idea, using high quality elements from its flexible audio product system.

In the second the end user develops an idea for a new product that is beyond the present vision of the industry and brings it to the attention of a manufacturer or industry. Many medium to high tech industries have 'users as innovators'. For example, at IBM in the Installed User Programs (IUP) Department, 30 per cent of IBM leased software for large and medium computers is developed by users. In other cases, such as medical electronics, commercial applications very often lag behind the clinical front line until user specialists take a hand.

More and more companies are taking account of these two approaches to commercial innovation. Companies like 3M, Honda, United Technologies and Apple are providing the means by which new ideas can be recognized and commercialized whether they are insider or outsider generated.

Successful companies use integrated design management as a means of ensuring that all products, communications and services of the organization are serving the overall business. Organizations that are successful in integrated designing are often started and run by outstanding individuals who know the business, like Morita, Hewlett and Packard. They are people dedicated to seeing that corporate goals and cultures do not deviate from the chosen path. Accelerated rates of change demand improved organization and procedures to increase the ability to adapt to new conditions and to conserve money by well-designed, economical manufacturing; keeping this in focus often requires a single vision.

Three business strategies have to interface with designing:

1 Develop market/user understanding thoroughly before design development.
2 Focus on commercially viable translation of ideas, i.e. innovation for successful commercial products.
3 Design a well-integrated organization to support product development in the milieu of ever changing conditions, with product systems or cascading development from one product to the next.

> Invention is the first stage in the process of technological innovation. A tidy distinction between invention and innovation does not exist, even though there is a qualitative difference in the activities. They are frequently inextricably linked ... Invention is best treated as the subset of patentable technical innovations. Inventions typically involve minor improvements in technology. Three general theories of invention exist: one attributes invention to the individual genius; another considers it to be an inevitable historical process, proceeding under stress of necessity, where need dictates and technology complies; and the third and most realistic approach sees invention arising from a cumulative synthesis of what has preceded. (Parker 1974)

According to this view, the occurrence of invention is not certain; an act of insight is required. It is likely to occur to an individual directly concerned with the problem. This individual, however, is not suddenly struck by a brilliant idea. When and if the act of insight takes place, it is conditioned by the specific problems encountered, and occurs through a synthesis of previous knowledge. By this synthesis and the act of insight, the inventor may overcome a discontinuity. This theory conforms with the concept of technology building on technology, where progress is not a random process but a synthesis of what has gone before. It is true, however, that necessity hustles invention forward and that great inventors do exist, but these are not typical occurrences. Theories of invention must describe the usual. Economic factors are predominant in the motivation to invent. The primacy of economic forces, however, does not imply how research should be organized. Keeping the sources of invention as wide and diffuse as possible is considered to be the best approach.

Innovation may occur after a considerable time interval from invention. Successful innovation can greatly improve the economic performance of companies, enhancing growth and profit rates. The term 'innovation' covers all the activities of bringing a new product or process to the market. It tends to be a time-consuming transformation process which is both management and resource intensive, and is more expensive than invention. Development risks are divided into technical and market risks. The amount of technical risk involved depends upon the size and complexity of the desired advance. The market risk is, to a much larger extent, beyond the control of the company, being dependent on the achievement of an adequate market. When selecting projects, the criteria applied by management indicate a fear of the high risk of the market. Research allocations are typically modest and payback periods required tend to be short.

R & D is expensive but is a necessary cost. Commitment to research differs among industries, depending upon technological push and customer pull. The relationship between a company's size and its technological capabilities is unclear. Large companies do not appear to be unchallenged. In terms of relative expenditure, very big companies may carry out proportionately less research than smaller ones. In terms of major inventions, lone inventors and small companies may have a comparative advantage, while the large company's forte may lie in development and follow-up improvements. The same ambiguity seems to exist regarding the influence of specific market structures. The most crucial factor in the organization of R & D probably relates to the number of independent centres of initiative. By having numerous potentially creative units, an enterprise may greatly improve its chances (Parker 1974).

Conclusion

An 'invention is the solution to a problem, often a technical one, whereas innovation is the commercially successful use of the solution'; so say Bacon and Butler (1981). From the start, new product development activity must focus on innovation and continuous product improvement. By examining all aspects of innovation prior to major expenditures on development – such as market need, technical, production and marketing requirements, and a basis for protecting the product from competition – the product solution can be found. Designing in its various forms (product, graphic, packaging, advertising, etc.) is the key to translating the invention into a commercially viable innovation (Figure 2). Effective designing is the *only* activity that can make this tangible.

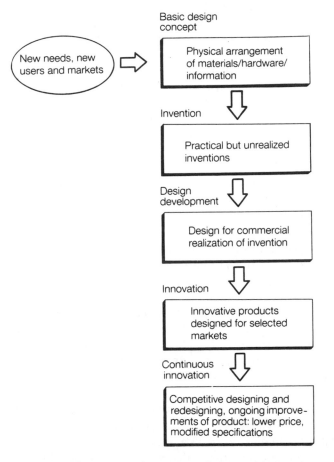

Figure 2   *The process of invention, design and innovation*

References and further reading

Bacon, F. and Butler, T. (1981) *Planned Innovation*. Ann Arbor: University of Michigan.
Clipson, C. (1985) *Business/Design Issues*. Ann Arbor: University of Michigan and the National Endowment for the Arts, The Competitive Edge Project.
Clipson, C. (1987) *Design for World Markets*. Ann Arbor: University of Michigan.
Jain, S.C. (1984) *International Marketing Management*. Boston: Kent.
Japanese Ministry of International Trade and Industry (1982) *Economic Analysis of World Enterprise: International Comparison*. Tokyo.

Machiavelli, N. (1948) *The Prince*. Chicago: Great Books Foundation.
Ohmae, K. (1985) *Triad Power: the Coming Shape of Global Competition*. New York: Free Press.
Parker, J.E.S. (1974) *Economics of Innovation*. London: Longman.
Terpstra, V. (1984) The role of economies of scale in international marketing. In Hampton, G.M. and van Gent, A.P. (eds): *Marketing Aspects of International Business*. Boston: Kluwer-Nijhoff.

11

Reducing the time to market: the case of the world auto industry

Kim Clark and Takahiro Fujimoto

Recently, reduction of the time to market has attracted significant attention as market needs become increasingly unpredictable and unstable, as technology is diversified and changes rapidly, and as competition intensifies.[1] The international automobile industry is a typical case where shortening the product development lead time is recognized as a valuable competitive weapon.[2] In particular, this strategy offers three major advantages:

- it contributes to better market forecasting at the concept stage of development;
- it compresses the model renewal interval, which increases the opportunities to modify designs and make better use of new technologies; and
- it enables firms to introduce products more quickly in response to competition.

But while there is agreement on the benefits of this approach, there is not much information on implementing such a policy. Indeed, many executives harbor misconceptions, believing it is merely a matter of adding extra engineering and design personnel or introducing the latest computer-aided design (CAD) technology. Nor will managers succeed by putting greater emphasis on planning or simply overlapping various stages in the development process. Reductions in time to market are the result of more subtle initiatives. Two are particularly critical: effective communication between upstream and downstream members of the design team and better working relationships with die manufacturers and suppliers.

Several authors have addressed these issues using case studies or practical experience, but few have probed them quantitatively. That is the contribution of this analysis. Begun in 1984, the scope of the study is international, using data collected from three car-producing corporations in the United States, nine in Western Europe and eight in Japan. Comparisons were compiled on 29 projects, all of which are either new models or major

From *Design Management Journal*, 1(1), 1989, pp. 49–57

model changes. The variables examined include product development performance (lead time, engineering hours, design quality, etc.), project characteristics (product complexity, supplier involvement, parts commonality, etc.), development processes and organizational systems. And although this research is industry-specific, the hope is that it offers insights and design lessons applicable in many areas.

Background: the Japanese advantage in lead time

As in any investigation of this nature, the first step is to gather the facts. These emerge most clearly by dividing the development process into six stages (concept generation, product planning, advanced engineering, product engineering, process engineering, and pilot run) and comparing the Japanese (12 cars), US (6 cars) and European (11 cars) project schedules. In some sense the results (see Figure 1) are as expected, but the statistics still seem startling:

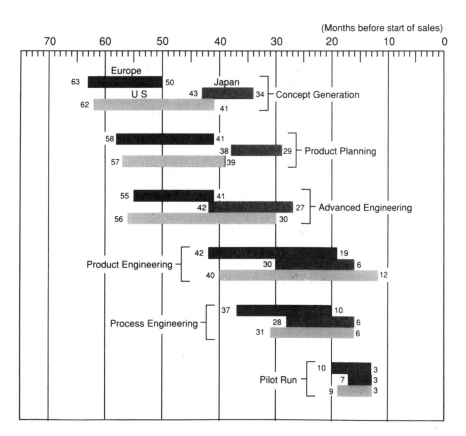

Figure 1 *Development lead time: Europe, Japan and the United States*

- First, in Japan, the average overall project lead time, or time between concept generation and market introduction, is about 3.5 years. In the US and Europe, it is about 5 years.
- Second, subdividing overall lead time into planning lead time (from concept generation to product planning) and engineering lead time (from product engineering to market introduction), the Japanese average is again dramatically shorter: 14 months versus 22–23 months for planning; and 30 months versus 40–42 months for engineering.[3]

The next question is to ask if the gaps are primarily due to differences in project characteristics. The Japanese examples, for instance, include micro-mini cars, while there are no such models in the US and European samples. In another contrast, the average complexity of the products (as measured by price) is low in Japan. A third variation is the degree of supplier participation in engineering, which is highest in Japan and lowest in the US. Yet one more distinction is the conclusion that the Japanese use more unique parts – elements designed specifically for a particular model. Technically it is possible to adjust for these discrepancies by applying regression coefficients to the data, but even after this is done, major Japanese lead-time advantages – of 13 to 14 months – remain.[4]

In explaining this situation, it might be possible to point to sources inherent to Japan – its culture, mentality, religion, or geography. Such approaches are intellectually valuable but of limited applicability. To identify more universal models, the focus of this effort is on general competitive patterns, processes that can be duplicated in other countries. Specifically, the Japanese market has been quite volatile, with many competitors, slow growth, direct product rivalry, unstable consumer needs, rapid changes in technology, and short product renewal cycles.[5] Over time, Japanese companies have adapted to this environment by designing a highly integrated organizational framework. This is the advantage that merits thorough consideration, a topic that, in this article, is analyzed from the perspective of engineering problem solving, manufacturing capability, and the capability of suppliers.[6]

Stage overlapping and communication patterns

Development lead time is directly affected by the nature of engineering problem solving. In theory, assuming that a project consists of a number of stages, lead time can be shortened in two ways: (1) overlapping upstream and downstream engineering activities on the critical path; and/or (2) shortening each step on the critical path. The benefit of the first method is that it cuts total lead time while leaving each individual stage length unchanged. As such, overlapping seems to be particularly effective at the engineering stages where companies want to avoid the technical problems associated with sharp reductions in individual stage length.

Based on this knowledge and looking at charts that plot the timing of stages, it is no surprise that the average Japanese project seems to exercise a higher degree of overlap between product engineering and process engineering than is true in the US and Europe. This is confirmed by calculating an 'overlap ratio' for each project as the sum of product engineering, process engineering and pilot run stage length divided by engineering lead time. As expected, the average ratio in the Japanese projects (1.63) was higher than that of their US (1.53) and European (1.37) counterparts.[7]

However, simply overlapping the engineering stages is not a complete answer. This has to be achieved without adversely affecting design quality, a task that can prove quite challenging. Overlapping upstream and downstream cycles means that the downstream has to start solving problems before the problems (inputs) themselves are completely defined. And, without appropriate information processing between the two stages, this technique tends to cause excessive engineering changes which prolong, rather than shorten, development and lead to deterioration of product quality due to poor coordination.

A series of in-depth interviews with project engineers concerning a critical upstream–downstream relationship – product engineering (upstream) and die development (downstream) – revealed to some degree how automobile manufacturers address the communications issue. There were several interesting Japanese/US comparisons:[8]

- Although the length of each activity varied, both the Japanese and US projects had a significant overlap between product and process engineering.
- It was not the overlap timing in general, but the timing of resource commitment that distinguished Japanese from US projects. For example, the Japanese process engineers start detailed die design on or before the completion of the first-generation prototypes, and start cutting dies before the second-generation prototypes are complete. By contrast, in a typical US company, both designing and cutting happen only after the second-generation prototypes are complete. This means that the Japanese die engineers face a higher risk of engineering changes than their US colleagues.
- In spite of this risk, the Japanese experience lower costs for engineering changes. As an indicator of downstream problems, the ratio of engineering change cost to total die development cost was 5 to 20% in Japan, versus 30 to 50% in the US.[9] In Japan, there are three formal engineering releases from body to die engineering; in the US, there are only two such releases. Also, other data suggest that the informal exchange of preliminary information between the product and process engineers is more frequent in Japan than the US.

With respect to organizational design, the implications of these facts are quite instructive. The Japanese manage overlapping differently. They frequently exchange preliminary information across stages, which apparently enables them to shorten lead time without much confusion downstream and without incurring costs commonly associated with an early commitment to die engineering. In the US on the other hand, firms have not been able to realize the potential advantage of overlapping. Overall engineering lead time is longer and there is a higher degree of downstream confusion. The missing component seems to be effective communication, which must be combined with overlapping if this last strategy is to pay off.

As an organizational model, this finding can be summarized in these terms: the efficient linking of the stages in product development depends both on timing and how information is transferred. Obviously, there are many variations in this relationship but the most straightforward – and one that continues to be used in technically complex projects such as those undertaken by NASA – can be described as the 'Phased Approach.' In this situation, the downstream stage starts only after completion of the upstream stage, with no timing overlap between the two. Usually a complete set of information about the final result of the upstream cycle is transmitted to the downstream in one shot. There is no uncertainty about the upstream output, and although lead time is extended, there is an appropriate match between the timing of stages and the sharing of information.

A second type is called the 'Overlapping Approach,' where portions of the up- and downstream stages occur simultaneously. This can shorten the lead time, but to be effective it must be accompanied by the correct information processing pattern. As an illustration, the combination of the Overlapping Approach with the batch information processing only at the end of the upstream stage is a mismatch. What happens here is that the downstream has to start its resource commitment without any clues regarding upstream output. And when that information is finally released, it often includes surprises that cause confusion that, in turn, extends the length of the downstream stage to the point where it offsets the advantages of overlapping. Unfortunately, this relationship was too common in the US die development cases.

There is, however, an alternative in the Overlapping Approach category. It might be referred to as 'intensive information processing,' where data on upstream events are continually released downstream, and vice versa (see Figure 2). In this piece-by-piece transmission, the downstream stage uses preliminary information to forecast the final outcome of upstream activities. The result is that overlapping contributes to lead-time efficiency with the minimum of confusion. This technique is typical of the Japanese projects.

The difficulty is that many US corporations neglect to complement an overlapping strategy with the required intensive information processing. They make a few modest changes in their product development systems, but ignore the larger problem of redesigning their organizations to foster other necessary attitudes and skills. To make the most of overlapping, then, the following metamorphoses are essential:

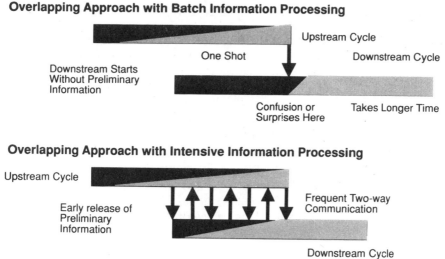

Figure 2   *Overlapping approach with and without intensive information processing*

- As cross-functional information flows become frequent and fragmented, integration mechanisms (project teams, task forces, liaisons, product managers, etc.) have to be built into the structure.
- Attitudes on information handling and responsibility have to change. Upstream engineers must be willing to release preliminary information even though it is subject to change. They must avoid a 'perfectionist' mentality. Downstream people must be willing to take risks based on their best possible estimate of the future. They must avoid a 'wait and see' mentality. Together, the two players in the development process must have a sense of mutual responsibility for projects.
- Skills and capabilities for information processing need to be enhanced. The downstream group has to forecast more reliably the final form of upstream output. Alternatively, the upstream team has to articulate better the consequences of its decisions. It must also reduce changes due to carelessness and miscommunication. Individuals downstream, on the other hand, have to acquire the flexibility to cope with unexpected change, being able to reach quick – but accurate – diagnoses and remedies.
- Finally, certain manufacturing capabilities are crucial for effective overlapping. In the case of the automobile industry, for instance, sophisticated expertise in die manufacturing is necessary to judge the trade-offs between the risk of changes and the benefits of early die making. Another requirement to respond to unanticipated change is a short production cycle. Indeed, manufacturing capability seems to have such a major impact on product development that it is worth examining in greater detail.

The power of manufacturing capability

The conventional academic literature tends to emphasize the dichotomy between production management and R & D management. The argument usually goes that because the nature of effective production (e.g. stable, rigid, discipline-oriented) and the nature of effective R & D (e.g. fluid, organic, creativity-oriented) are so diametrically opposed, the two functions have to be managed by entirely different principles. A corollary of this hypothesis is that there are no direct relationships between an organization's capability in manufacturing and its capability in R & D.

In the automobile industry, the reality is just the opposite – companies that are good at manufacturing are also good at development. This is true for two reasons. First, the effective management of development – and perhaps basic research as well – has many of the same goals as manufacturing: faster throughput time, reduction of inventory, better upstream–downstream communication, continuous improvement, subtle balances between discipline and creativity, quick problem solving, etc. Second, the product development process contains critical activities which are essentially manufacturing, including prototype fabrication, tools/equipment fabrication, and implementing the pilot run.

The result of this link is that the most efficient producers tend to have the shortest development lead time.[10] This is especially evident in prototype fabrication and die development.[11] In Japan, for example, the average time between the earliest parts drawing release to completion of the prototype vehicle was 6 months versus 12 in the US and 11 months in Europe. Interestingly after the last drawing release, the time to prototype completion is not so different – three months in Japan, three in the US and five in Europe – implying that the scheduling of drawing releases and/or control of prototype parts suppliers are the main sources of inefficiencies.

With respect to die development (and these comparisons are based on studies of a die set for the most complicated body panel), the time between the release of the first rough part drawings to completion of tryouts was 14 months in Japan versus 25 and 28 months in the US and Europe, respectively (see Figure 3). Since most of the gap occurs between the final parts drawing release and delivery of the dies, differences can be attributed to the die manufacturing process. In working with US manufacturers, die shops are confronted with many engineering changes and historically have had an adversarial relationship with auto companies. The result is that shops use a work-in-process inventory to buffer themselves against problems and uncertainties, a situation where each station has a long queue of semifinished elements. This necessarily causes delay. In Japan, on the other hand, die shops are better at dealing with engineering changes and have a generally cooperative relationship with car manufacturers. The shops operate more like just-in-time factories with a streamlined work flow that drastically reduces manufacturing time and expense.

In the automobile industry, then, current methods contradict traditional

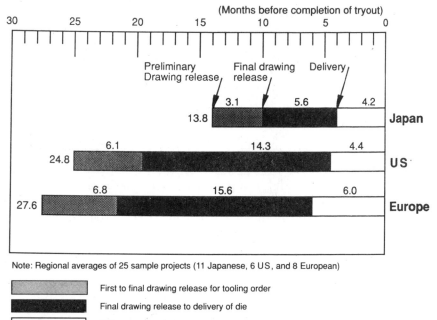

Note: Regional averages of 25 sample projects (11 Japanese, 6 US, and 8 European)

[shaded box] First to final drawing release for tooling order

[solid box] Final drawing release to delivery of die

[empty box] Delivery to completion of tryout

The numbers do not add up exactly because some respondents reported total die lead time only

Figure 3   *Lead time for a set of dies for a major body panel*

wisdom. The development process is, indeed, affected by manufacturing capability. In particular, lead time can be shortened through the optimum design of drawing release, purchasing strategies and fabrication procedures in the shop.

Planning lead time

Beyond overlapping and manufacturing, planning is a third area where lead time can be reduced.[12] Without any loss in quality, the average Japanese project takes about 14 months to complete these stages (concept study and product planning) while the same activities take 24 months in the US and 22 months in Europe. Interestingly, the Western producers may be caught in a kind of vicious cycle. The longer planning time means there is a greater chance the environment will change, which subsequently forces companies to revise the plan. Not unexpectedly, this causes confusion and delays. In addition, as the total lead time increases, model change cycles also get longer. This, in turn, requires more significant technical and conceptual changes, which take more planning time in order to build consensus. The only way out may simply be to mandate a shorter planning period, an alternative the Japanese have demonstrated does not have to come at the expense of quality.

Another potential planning advantage is the engineering capability of parts suppliers.[13] Thanks to the greater design sophistication of this group in Japan, car manufacturers there can subcontract out many parts engineering jobs and thereby simplify inter-parts coordination during the planning stage. This not only helps reduce lead time but also tends to minimize reliance on carried-over parts, whose excessive use can have adverse effects on quality.

Myths

In any balanced analysis, it is as valuable to comment on strategies that do not work as those that do. One such point relates to the classical hypothesis, widely accepted by project engineers, that adding people to a stage shortens the length of that stage. This argument assumes an inverse relationship between engineering hours and lead time. In this study, however, the data indicate just the opposite. That is, the Japanese projects consume fewer engineering hours (1.2 million) than the non-Japanese projects (3.5 to 3.6 million).[14] This was the case even after adjusting for differences in project content. The probable explanation is that lead time drives engineering hours, rather than vice versa. Although counter-intuitive, by taking action to minimize lead time, executives may actually create circumstances that simultaneously reduce the number of changes and improve engineering productivity.[15]

The extensive implementation of computer-aided design (CAD) and computer-aided manufacturing (CAM) is another explanation given for shorter development time in Japan. And certainly, interviews suggest that efficiency motivates Japanese firms to adopt CAD-CAM systems. One producer even estimated that lead time was cut by six months through the introduction of 250 CAD-CAM terminals. The problem is that US and European corporations also exploit the technology. Thus, while this is an important tool in speeding up product design, it does not explain the Japanese advantage.

Conclusions

In summary, careful statistical and comparative research indicates that the main source of the shorter lead time in Japanese projects is an organizational design that emphasizes stage overlapping, intensive communication, manufacturing capability, and supplier engineering. In enumerating these specific areas, however, there is a caveat. Executives must know that no one focus is sufficient. Nor is it enough to pursue these capabilities independently. Successful product development emerges from an overall pattern, a coherent system that integrates attitudes, skills and capabilities within a larger design management strategy.

Notes

1 See, for example, Imai *et al.* (1985), Takeuchi and Nonaka (1986), Uttal (1988), Peters (1988) and Stalk (1988) for the issues of managing the time to market.
2 For recent analysis of international competition in the auto industry, see Abernathy *et al.* (1983), Altshuler *et al.* (1984), Graves (1987), Sheriff (1989), and Krafcik (1988).
3 Japanese averages are different from the non-Japanese averages at 5% level of significance in all of the above categories. The differences between US averages and European averages are not significantly different.
4 For further technical details of the adjustment, see Clark *et al.* (1987), Clark and Fujimoto (1989a), and Fujimoto (1989).
5 For further details of the relations between competitive patterns and lead-time performance, see Clark and Fujimoto (1989b).
6 More detailed studies on the sources and consequences of shorter development lead time include Clark and Fujimoto (1987), Clark *et al.* (1987), Clark (1988), Clark and Fujimoto (1989a, 1989b), and Fujimoto (1989).
7 Note that this ratio is only a rough indicator of overlapping since the ratio does not reflect overlapping of more detailed engineering activities.
8 The European cases showed some variety, but they were rather similar to the US ones.
9 Note that the number of engineering changes itself is not as important as the consequences of the changes. Although some American managers apparently believe that the Japanese reduce the number of engineering changes to a near-zero level at an early point of engineering (e.g. after final engineering release), our study revealed that the Japanese also made many engineering changes even after final release. Thus, the number of engineering changes in the Japanese case was far from negligible, although it may have been significantly smaller than typical US cases.
10 According to the authors' study of fourteen producers, Spearman rank-order correlation between speed of development (inverse of lead time) and manufacturing productivity was 0.56 when one-tail critical value at 5% level was $+/-0.46$. See Fujimoto and Sheriff (1989).
11 For statistical analysis for this, see Clark and Fujimoto (1989a), in which regression analysis showed significant impacts of both prototype lead time and die development lead time on engineering lead time.
12 For further conceptual and empirical works, see Clark and Fujimoto (1989a).
13 For further details, see Clark and Fujimoto (1989a).
14 After adjustment for project content similar to the case of lead time, the Japanese advantages came down to about a 2 to 1 margin, but significant differences still remained. For further technical details, see Clark *et al.* (1987), Clark and Fujimoto (1989b), and Fujimoto (1989).
15 For details of the statistical analysis of lead time–productivity relations, see Clark *et al.* (1987) and Fujimoto (1989).

References

Abernathy, William; Clark, Kim; and Kantrow, Alan (1983). *Industrial Renaissance.* New York: Basic Books.
Altshuler, Alan; Anderson, Martin; Jones, Daniel; Roos, Daniel; and Womack, James (1984) *The Future of the Automobile.* Cambridge: The MIT Press.
Clark, Kim (1988) 'Project Scope and Project Performance: The Effect of Parts Strategy and Supplier Involvement on Product Development.' Harvard Business School Working Paper #88–069. Also in *Management Science*, forthcoming.
Clark, Kim; Chew, Bruce; and Fujimoto, Takahiro (1987) 'Product Development in the

World Auto Industry: Strategy, Organization and Performance.' *Brookings Papers on Economic Activity*: 729–771.

Clark, Kim, and Fujimoto, Takahiro (1987) 'Overlapping Problem Solving in Product Development.' Harvard Business School Working Paper #87–048. Also in Ferdows (ed.). *Managing International Manufacturing.* Amsterdam, North Holland (1989): 127–152.

Clark, Kim, and Fujimoto, Takahiro (1989a) 'Lead Time in Automobile Product Development: Explaining the Japanese Advantage.' *Journal of Technology and Engineering Management*, Vol. 1, No. 1 (forthcoming).

Clark, Kim, and Fujimoto, Takahiro (1989b) 'Product Development and Competitiveness.' Paper for the International Seminar on Science, Technology and Economic Growth by OECD, Paris, June 1989.

Fujimoto, Takahiro (1989) 'Organizations for Effective Product Development – The Case of the Global Automobile Industry.' Unpublished DBA dissertation, Harvard Business School.

Fujimoto, Takahiro, and Sheriff, Antony (1989) 'Consistent Patterns in Automotive Product Strategy, Product Development, and Manufacturing Performance – Road Map for the 1990s.' A paper for International Policy Forum, International Motor Vehicle Program, MIT, May.

Graves, Andrew (1987) 'Comparative Trends in Automotive Research and Development.' A paper for International Policy Forum, International Motor Vehicle Program, MIT, May.

Imai, Ken-ichi; Nonaka, Ikujiro; and Takeuchi, Hirotaka (1985) 'Managing the New Product Development,' in Clark and Hayes (eds), *The Uneasy Alliance*. Cambridge: HBS Press.

Krafcik, John (1988) 'Triumph of the Lean Production System.' *Sloan Management Review*, Fall.

Peters, Thomas (1988) *Thriving on Chaos*. New York: Alfred A. Knopf.

Sheriff, Antony (1989) 'Product Development in the Automobile Industry: Corporate Strategies and Product Performance.' Unpublished MSM dissertation, Sloan School of Management.

Stalk, George, Jr (1988) 'Time – The Next Source of Competitive Advantage.' *Harvard Business Review*, July–August.

Takeuchi, Hirotaka, and Nonaka, Ikujiro. (1986) 'The New New Product Development Game.' *Harvard Business Review*, January–February.

Uttal, Bro (1988) 'Speeding New Ideas to Market.' *Fortune*, 2 March.

12

Quality circles: the danger of bottled change

Gregory P. Shea

The record to date

Interestingly, Japanese managers tend not to quantify the costs and benefits of quality control circles. Rather, they utilize anecdotal data and intuition, an approach that makes sense given their use of quality control circles.[1] Cole states that the Japanese 'were concerned with getting things done, getting on with their initiatives, experimenting with a wide range of techniques, and writing fairly sketchy reports to spread lessons'.[2] The Japanese began quality control circles as part of a program of decentralization, hence that was their overall concern.[3] Furthermore, the technical nature of quality control circles and their heavy use of statistical analysis meant that quantifiable problems (e.g. defect rates) either were being solved or were not being solved (e.g. defect rates decreased or did not decrease). 'Hard progress' in improving quality was easy enough to check if anyone wanted to do so, but the objective of improving quality, like the objective of decentralization, was what mattered, not the specific cost/benefit of one or more circles. The Japanese therefore have both a more purely technical, even mechanistic view of the purposes and nature of quality circles than do Americans and a less formal approach to their evaluation. The technical nature of the work and the clarity of the reasons why Japanese organizations have quality control circles serve to free Japanese managers from the necessity of precise cost/benefit measures of their circles.[4]

Americans, on the other hand, tend to view quality circles as a stand-alone program which has to pay for itself. Cole (1982) reviews evidence that American managers often do not require detailed cost/benefit analysis when innovating, especially when innovating as part of a fad. He goes on to suggest that the attitude that quality circles have to justify themselves surfaces because of the threat to American management (namely participatory organizations) implicit in quality circles. Regardless of the appropriateness of this view, if American managers see quality circles as a program to solve specific, quantifiable problems, then numbers matter, and if American managers see quality circles as part of an effort to alter fundamentally an organization's work, then duration matters. And so we come to two criteria: (1) Is it cost effective? and (2) Does it last?

The first criterion is self-explanatory while the second merits further comment. A productivity program either yields savings or does not. However, full-fledged formal organizational change efforts often require at least three to five years to become established (a reality painfully apparent, for instance, in the quality of work life literature). Programs that expire in less time are less likely to have met their objectives and to have achieved enduring organizational change.

Applying these criteria returns us to the problem of confusion among American managers about quality circles. If, as has been argued, such confusion exists, then it would produce failures within organizations (e.g. the mixed-message scenario for failure sketched above). After all, the likelihood of success depends in large part on knowledge of what success looks like and what is required from all actors to achieve it. Furthermore, how can anyone measure something without knowing what it is? Mixed messages within an organization and markedly different uses of quality circles in different organizations should yield a track record of the following sort:

1 Few hard data about the cost effectiveness of quality circles
2 Mixed indications that they are cost effective
3 A sizable percentage of quality circle programs that fail to last as long as three years.

Cost effectiveness

Limited data exist concerning the performance of quality circles.[5] Yager places the standard break-even point for American quality circles at three to five months after startup and a profit-to-cost return ratio of six to ten to one after a year of operation, while Simmons and Mares report claims of ratios from two to eight to one in years one and two of circle operation.[6] Mohrman and Novelli report a slight positive change in productivity in their case study as well as difficulty in determining the role of quality circles in the change. Platten presents findings from a survey of ninety-two quality circle members and eighty-three nonmembers in a manufacturing plant and his findings indicate that quality circles are an effective way of increasing the productivity and quality of work in remedial departments,[7] while Ferris and Wagner cite evidence indicating that even at Lockheed, the beachhead for quality circles in America, '... quality circles have languished since their initial promoters left the firm to consult elsewhere.'[8] Wood, Hull, and Azumi offer these sobering comments:

1 Many success stories come from people who stand to benefit from news of the success (e.g. managers or consultants).
2 Two surveys of quality circle programs (total combined sample of seventy firms) each found that approximately 70 percent of the sample reported saving-to-cost ratio of less than one.
3 A change in management and capital investment (apart from quality circle recommendations) may have far more to do with reported successes than quality circles programs.
4 Anyone familiar with the Hawthorne effect (or the legacy of 'productivity consultants') knows that paying more attention to people in and of itself can produce temporary improvements in productivity and morale.[9]

Overall, Wood, Hull, and Azumi describe 'The current state of information regarding the effectiveness of QCs ... as a long list of claimed benefits, supported by anecdotal data and isolated cases which do not adequately establish the validity or generality of the benefits claimed.'[10] Ferris and Wagner go even further: 'Unfortunately, most of the literature appraising the effectiveness of American QCs has consisted of anecdotal case data presentations; little rigorous research exists. This lack of scholarship is especially alarming in light of recently reported failures of American QCs.'[11] In other words, the available data is as hypothesized above: findings few in number and limited in quality.[12]

Duration of quality circles

Available data concerning the duration of quality circles is even scantier, a result of limited research, the recency of the explosion in the number of quality circles, and a probable reluctance to advertise failures. Wolff reports that within one year two of the three sites that he studied had started and ended formal quality circles.[13] Mohrman and Novelli report that two of the four quality circles they studied disbanded within about one year of forming.[14] And Lawler has stated that in his extensive research he found that quality circles rarely lasted more than nine months and has written that '... it is likely that few [quality circle] programs will be institutionalized and sustained over a long time period.'[15] Causes of the demise of quality circles include:[16]

1 Running out of problems to solve
2 Lack of support and/or disaffection (supervisory, managerial, and occasionally union)
3 Lack of change (connection to day-to-day operating style of workgroup and company) and/or failure to implement quality circle recommendations
4 Development of a 'what's in it for me?' attitude by circle members (often precipitated by the failure of management to share gains precipitated by circle recommendations with circle members).

Summary

An explanation for the record of quality circles in the US is the apparent general state of understanding (or misunderstanding) regarding the purpose, not the *technology*, of quality circles. Little hard data exists and what does tells, at best, a mixed tale: great and no financial success and little success in institutionalizing quality circles. A serious question exists as to whether quality circles generally survive long enough to affect organizational culture substantially.

Learning from the past

The above indicates the need to clarify the purpose of quality circles and to recommend how best to use them. Below is an attempt to do so.

Quality circles can serve various purposes and serve them well, provided they are used in consonance with *a* selected purpose. Managers can choose to employ quality circles to solve problems and/or to change work relations. Furthermore, managers can use quality circles with a short-term or a long-term perspective. The purpose dictates how a manager should approach a quality circles program and, more important, how he or she should present the program to others, especially would-be participants. A typology appears in Figure 1 and, while the categories are not discrete or absolute, it limits the confusion (and the danger) surrounding quality circles.

Lessons learned: the short term

Problem solving/short term. The purpose here is participation of affected, involved, or knowledgeable parties in selecting and solving specific problems related to improving quality. Such problems might be high reject rates, rising warranty work, introduction of a new technology, consolidation/expansion of work areas, or merging of work units. These problems are not new; traditionally they are handled by managers, often working in *ad hoc* groups. Quality circles provide a way of involving, in a specifically structured and trained way, anyone affected or informed about a problem in the handling of that part of the problem that concerns his or her work. A quality circles program can provide both the opportunity to contribute as well as the skills and structure necessary for more people to work more effectively in groups. Managers and nonmanagers alike may learn considerable amounts about the problem (and its solution) while also learning about how to function better in groups.

Quality circles under such circumstances can mobilize parts of an organization to solve a quality problem. All involved should expect quality circles to be discontinued once the problem has been addressed. This self-contained, self-limited use of quality circles may have special appeal for American managers because it does not present the specter of large-scale

Improved problem solving	Short term	Long term
Purpose	Mobilization of specific parts of the organization to solve specific problems.	Continued improvement in organizational problem-solving ability.
Benefits	Problem solution; camaraderie; skill development; mobilization experience.	Problem solutions; dissemination of problem-solving skills and practice throughout the organization; experience in collaborative problem solving.
Risks	Broader expectations/sense of manipulation; crisis management; burnout.	Misunderstanding (especially by top management) of nature of participative decision-making and change process; corresponding impact of large-scale failure.
'To do's'	Clarity of purpose; empower circle members; preemptive orientation.	Informed commitment by top management; inclusion of all organizational members.
Improved work relations		
Purpose	Short-term improvement in general work relations.	Overall change in working relations throughout the organization.
Benefits	Short-term improvement in problem solution; skill development.	More thoroughly based, hence more secure, SOP (including problem solving).
Risks	Strong sense of manipulation; alienation; erosion of trust; anger.	Failure by management to appreciate enormity of cultural change; general negative impact on work relations.
'To-do's'	Do not. Do not use quality circles for this end.	Education (including experiential) of top management and the rest of the organization; special importance of active, ongoing top management involvement in the process.

Figure 1   *A typology of purposes for using quality circle programs*

change in organizational culture and operating style. Organizational benefits could include solving a problem, improving communication, creating a
sense of teamwork, disseminating skills about group problem solving, and
developing the ability to construct a quality circles program quickly.

The risks associated with this use of quality circles are:

1   Great expectations about the organization 'going participative.'
2   A sense of manipulation, particularly by workers. 'We get to partici-
    pate only when management wants and only on those problems they
    can't handle. We do their job and they get the profit.'
3   Failure to own the problem. Mobilization requires a shared sense of
    immediacy which in turn requires that each group member understand

the consequences of a problem for him or her *and* believe that he or she
can contribute to a solution
4 Mobilization and burnout. Crisis management develops and people
burn or opt out
5 A call throughout the organization to participate more in more
decisions.

Minimizing these risks entails:

1 Clearly and repeatedly stating the purpose of the quality circles program, namely, 'to solve quality problem X'
2 Clear, explicit identification of consequences of the problem needing
solving and of the opportunities that circle members have to counter
those consequences
3 Provision of necessary skills and resources
4 Anticipatory or proactive use of quality circles, i.e. using them to avoid
and not to meet crises.

Improving work relations/short term. The purpose here is the short-term
improvement of general work relations (not just problem-solving ability)
by providing training in cooperative problem solving and the regular occasion to practice cooperation on actual workplace problems. Many quality
circle programs may end up looking as if this were their purpose (namely,
they do not last long and do not pay for themselves); however, this
approach is fraught with dangers, including:

– a strong sense of manipulation
– alienation of lower and middle management ('So top management
thinks *we*'re the problem?!')
– a corresponding erosion of trust and decreased likelihood of worker
involvement in future improvement efforts.

The best way to avoid these dangers is *not* to employ quality circles for
these ends. Short-term improvements in working relations are frustrating
enough when unplanned. Add to that a sense that management actively
manipulates people by pursuing *short*-term improvements and the frustration can easily become directed anger.

Lessons learned: the long term

Organizational change and quality circles. One choice facing anyone out
to change organizational culture, to manage the norms of an organization,
is whether to start at the top and work down or to start at the bottom and
work up. The issue is how serious top management is about change and
when it wishes to confront changing its own behavior (as distinct from
concentrating on changing other people's behavior). Quality circles can
generate organizational dynamics common to a bottom-up change strategy
whether such dynamics are planned or not.

Managers who begin quality circles are, unquestionably, starting problem-solving groups. They are also choosing to create the potential for:

- A vehicle for employee involvement in traditionally managerial activities
- An occasion for employees to become more involved in and more committed to their work
- An opportunity for employees to learn more about their work and the work of the organization as a whole
- The chance for employees to learn more about what it takes to make the organization function
- A statement about a belief in the capacity of employees to contribute to organizational success in nontraditional ways
- The possibility that employees will come to know more of what management knows, both information-wise and skill-wise, and that management as an activity will be demystified
- Grounds for hopes about a more participative and open organization.

Why these creations? Because people want more say over their jobs and their working conditions: once people start having a say they want more. The truism holds – on the shop or office floors of America and in the shipyards of Gdansk. Consequently, quality circles are not experienced by their members as simply problem-solving groups. They are, undeniably, problem-solving groups, but humans form them and invest them with meaning – their meaning. Quality circle members therefore set about their work with items on their agenda other than solving quality problems. Participants can experience quality circles as a bottom-up change effort, or, more accurately, as a springboard for such an effort, regardless of the intention of upper management. Whereas the preceding section on short-term lessons dealt with managing quality circles in order to limit that experience, this section concerns managing in order to maximize it.[17]

Problem solving/long term. The interest here is the continued long-term improvement in the ability of the organization to identify and resolve performance-related problems. Quality circles constitute a way to realize this goal by starting at the bottom of the organization. The orientation critical to this use of quality circles is: that these are tools to realizing an objective; that the objective is a process; that the process must envelop the organization; and that the process will occur/endure only with the conscious and continued involvement (as distinct from mere advocacy) of key organizational actors.

Quality circles can thereby serve these ends:

1 Dissemination of training and experience in cooperative problem solving
2 Visible support for the notion of collaborative problem solving

3 Expansion of the appreciation by organizational members of the effort
   involved in participative decision making
4 A springboard to expanded participation and a testing ground for large-
   scale participation.

Recommendations consonant with these ends are as follows:

1 Management commitment to a long-term change in how the organization solves problems before asking others to do so. Personally trying
   out quality circles or other group problem-solving technologies first for
   an extended period (like three to six months) would greatly help management make an informed, responsible choice, as well as convince
   organization members of management's commitment.
2 Inclusion of all organizational members in the program, i.e. managerial
   and non-managerial quality circles.
3 Recognition that long-term change involves pressures for expansion
   and for elimination of the efforts.
4 Education about the process of change and explicit attention to expanding the nature and scope of change.

Improving work relations/long term.   The focus in this case is on a broader
range of processes than mere problem solving. The objective includes an
overall pattern of relationships, encompassing, but not limited to, collaborative problem solving. How people communicate, handle conflict, and
manage authority are as important as problem solving. The main argument
in favor of this orientation is that without a general change in the organization, enduring change in group problem solving will not occur, and,
therefore, overall organizational effectiveness will not improve.

Points made about long-term improvement in problem solving apply
here too, only more so. To say that the objective is full-scale, encompassing cultural change, is to invite an explosion of expectations, hopes, and
fears. Doing so raises the ante for everyone and demands even more
expertise and involvement from key actors in key choices, expectation
management, education, and the process of change.

Conclusion

Confusion has surrounded quality circles from the time that Americans
'discovered' them in Japan. Westerners were confused about their purpose
in Japan and then about their purpose in America. That confusion has
manifested itself in the alteration of the quality circle technology (including
considerably more emphasis on human relations skills), in the presentation
(selling) of quality circles to American organizations as a multipurpose
technology (often bordering on being a panacea), and in the data available
(the amount and nature of it as well as the tale it tells).

Quality circles are a technology, a tool – one replete with potential. The technology is not the challenge: its use *is*, and that is what managers must clarify before they implement or evaluate quality circles. Managers must decide what they are trying to accomplish. Failure to do so sets up the program (and those associated with it) to fail and invites a string of casualties. Indeed, developing clarity about behavioral objectives, communicating such goals, and acting consistently with them could be the biggest, most difficult, and most noteworthy aspect of any quality circles program. It might also prove to be the most beneficial.

Figure 1 presents a typology that can help organize thinking about quality circles (and other kinds of technologies designed to change behavior in organizations). The discussion summarized in Figure 1 suggests these rules of thumb for managers considering the installation of quality circles:

1 *Decide why you want quality circles.* The reasons have everything to do with the success or failure of the program, in everyone's eyes, managers and employees.

2 *Try it yourself first.* This rule has special saliency the more the purpose of quality circles is organizational change, but the point remains that being a participant will help you manage the program by helping you know what you are managing.

3 *Manage expectations, your own included.* Keep yourself and others informed about what is happening and why. Expectations, including your own, are like anything else that matters in organizations – they need managing.

4 *Make the quality circle option a universal one.* This will help to limit resistance based on feelings of being excluded and facilitate the dissemination of quality circles if it is desired.

5 *Mark the program boundaries clearly and walk the line yourself.* Just because you and others were clear once upon a time about what quality circles were and why they were installed does not mean that you or they still are. Check.

Notes

1 R.E. Cole (1982) 'Diffusion of Participatory Work Structures in Japan, Sweden, and the United States' in P.S. Goodman and Associates (eds), *Change in Organizations* (San Francisco: Jossey-Bass).

2 Ibid.

3 R.E. Cole (1979) *Work, Mobility and Participation* (Berkeley: University of California Press) provides evidence supporting the success of decentralization: estimates of inspector/worker ratios at GM manufacturing and assembly plants (1:10 and 1:17) and Toyota (1:25 and 1:30).

4 Cole (1982) argues convincingly for the point of view presented here. Nissan, however, does have suggestion quotas for its circles (Public Television Networks (1984) 'We Are Driven,' *Frontline*) and G. Munchus III (1983) 'Employer–Employee based Quality Circles in Japan: Human Resource Policy Implications for American Firms,' *Academy of Management Review*, 8:255–61 reports the existence of mandatory suggestion rates at

Toyota. Suggestion quotas or rates indicate that Japanese management does have short-term measures of quality control circle performance although not traditional cost/benefit.

5 P. Gibson (1982) 'Quality Circles: An Approach to Productivity Improvement,' *Work in American Institute Studies in Productivity* (New York: Pergamon); S. Mohrman and L. Novelli, Jr (1982) 'Beyond Testimonials: Learning from a Quality Circles Program,' USC Graduate School of Business Administration, Center for Effective Organizations, G82–10 (29), revised; R. Wood, F. Hull, and K. Azumi (1983) 'Evaluating Quality Circles: The American Applications,' *California Management Review*, Fall, pp. 37–53.

6 E. Yager (1979) 'Examining the Quality Control Circle,' *Personnel Journal*, October, pp. 683–684 and E. Yager (1980) 'Quality Circle: A Tool for the '80s,' *Training and Development Journal*, August, pp. 60–62; J. Simmons and W. Mares (1985) *Working Together: Employee Participation in Action* (New York: New York University Press). As for the cost of installation, the first circle runs from $8,000 to $15,000, given the use of an outside consultant (Yager, 1980). Subsequent circles cost less to install, given the development of internal training capacity, and start-up of the first circle may cost less if the organization has the capacity to train in-house.

7 P. Platten (1983) 'The Investigation of Organizational Commitment as a Source of Motivation in Quality Control Circles,' unpublished PhD dissertation (New York University).

8 G.R. Ferris and J.A. Wagner III (1985) 'Quality Circles in the United States: A Conceptual Reevaluation,' *Journal of Applied Behavioral Science* 21: 155–167.

9 Wood, Hull and Azumi (1983).

10 Ibid.

11 Ferris and Wagner (1985).

12 Gibson (1982) and P. Thompson (1982) *Quality Circles: How to Make Them Work in America* (New York: AMACON) suggest concrete measures of the impact of quality circles on individuals and organizations.

13 P. Wolff II (1984) 'Quality Circles at King James County,' paper presented at the 44th Annual Meeting of the Academy of Management.

14 Mohrman and Novelli (1982).

15 E. Lawler and S. Mohrman (1984) 'Quality Circles: A Self-Destruct Approach?' USC Graduate School of Business Administration, Center for effective organizations, G84–1(49); E. Lawler (1984), question-and-answer period following: 'A Report on Research Concerning the Problems and Failures of Some Employer–Employee Work Innovations,' presentation at the Second National Labor–Management Conference, Washington DC, June.

16 K. Bradley and S. Hill (1983) 'After Japan: The Quality Circle Transplant and Productive Efficiency,' *British Journal of Industrial Relations*, November, pp. 291–311; E. Lawler and S. Mohrman (1985) 'Quality Circles After the Fad,' *Harvard Business Review*, January–February, pp. 65–71; Simmons and Mares (1985); Thompson (1982); Wolff (1984); Wood, Hull, and Azumi (1983).

17 A reader interested in more detailed discussion of how to link quality circles to larger change efforts should consult Lawler and Mohrman (1984, 1985) or E. Trist and C. Dwyer (1982) 'The Limits of Laissez-faire as Sociotechnical Change Strategy' in R. Zaeger and M. Rosow, editors, *Innovative Organizations: Productivity Programs in Action* (New York: Pergamon).

13

New products: what separates winners from losers?

Robert G. Cooper and Elko J. Kleinschmidt

Critical management questions

What makes a new product a success? And what separates new product winners from losers? The answers to these questions are critical to effective new product management. An understanding of new product success factors is important for two reasons: it provides guidelines to the screening of new product projects; and it leads to insights into the way the new product project should be managed.

We set out to resolve the success-vs.-failure issue by studying 203 new products – both winners and losers – that were launched into the market place. A thorough review of past studies and literature resulted in a conceptual model of new product success and failure – a model that links project outcomes to a number of key project descriptors. Ten hypotheses were derived from the model. These hypotheses were then tested using the 203 actual case histories. The results are provocative; besides lending support to the conceptual model, the results also have important managerial implications in terms of screening criteria and new product management approaches.

Previous research

New products are vital to the growth and prosperity of most manufacturing firms. Booz-Allen and Hamilton estimate a doubling of new product introductions in the 1981–1986 period, and that by the end of 1986, new products introduced during these five years will have accounted for 40% of corporate sales [4]. New products are also high-risk endeavors, approximately 46% of the resources devoted to product development and commercialization go to unsuccessful projects [4], and 35% of products launched fail commercially [14,17].

Adapted and reprinted by permission of the publisher from *Journal of Production Innovation Management*, 4 (1987), pp. 169–84. Copyright 1987 by Elsevier Science Publishing Co., Inc.

Early research in the field of product innovation sought to identify those characteristics that were common to new product successes. An extensive descriptive study of 567 successful innovations by Myers and Marquis showed that most successes were market-derived (market pull) ventures and that only 21% were technology push. [26] A descriptive process model, consisting of five major steps and eight activities, portrayed the process typically followed in these innovations.

The ingredients of success in Globe's study of ten radical innovations were dominated by internal and technical factors [18]. Success factors included: a recognition of a technical opportunity; market need recognition; proficient R & D management; well-executed venture decisions; ample development resources; and a technical entrepreneur. An investigation of six successful innovations at GE Labs by Roberts and Burke showed a close link to market needs as the key to success [30]. Market needs were typically recognized, and R & D was targeted at satisfying these needs; when a technical breakthrough did not have a specific market need, the product was adapted to suit an identified need.

A study of highly successful Canadian case histories revealed that the new product process was a goal directed, stepwise process, involving a series of information acquisition activities and evaluation points [12,13]. Extensive market inputs, including, for example, marketing research, were common to the successes, especially near the beginning of the project, and played a key role in shaping the success of the products. In a similar vein, Townsend's study of one radical innovation and subsequent incremental innovations showed that success hinged on close collaboration between user and innovator; a well-defined market need; a technical champion; strong internal communication; and highly developed screening and testing procedures [37].

Another research direction has been the investigation of new product failures. The premise underlying such exploratory research is that a retrospective analysis of past failures would identify pitfalls and problems in product innovation, that management can then take steps to overcome or avert in the future.

Three *Conference Board* studies over a 16-year period all identified marketing variables as the major weaknesses in firms' new product failures [19,20,27]. Inadequate market analysis, product defects, the lack of an effective marketing effort, high costs, bad timing, and competitive strength were uncovered as major failure reasons. Recommendations from these studies called for more and better marketing research and marketing efforts, careful product positioning, better concept testing and test marketing, and improved project evaluation, notably early screening. Another large sample study (114 failure cases) identified particularly weak activities in the new product process, notably market research and market studies; test marketing; and financial evaluation [10,11]. Many of these failures could be described as a 'better mousetrap no one wanted,' a product conceived and developed in the absence of market information and with no clearly identified market need [6]. A second popular failure type was the 'me too product meeting a competitive brick wall,' a product similar to competitors' products but offering no advantages to the user.

Success vs. failures

The problem with both research directions above is that they only looked at one type of product – either commercial successes or commercial failures – but not both types in the same study. In short, there was no control group or group for comparison. In order to uncover success factors, one must identify characteristics which discriminate between commercial successes and failures, hence the need for both types of projects in the analysis.

The first study to undertake such a comparison was Project SAPPHO, which employed a pairwise comparison methodology [33]. Forty-three pairs of projects – success versus failure – were studied, and 41 variables were found to be statistically significant in their relationship to project outcomes. The most important discriminators were:

1   Understanding of users' needs;
2   Attention to marketing and publicity;
3   Efficiency of development;
4   Effective use of outside technology and external scientific communication; and
5   Seniority and authority of responsible managers.

A similar study was undertaken in Hungary and revealed a parallel set of success factors, notably market need satisfaction; effective communication; efficient development; a market orientation; and the role of key individuals [33,34]. Kulvik's success/failure study in Finland yielded similar results to the above, but identified additional facilitators, including a good 'company/product fit,' the utilization of technical 'know-how' of the company, and familiarity with both the product's markets and technologies [22]. Another study on European and Japanese successes vs. failures identified marketing proficiency, product advantage, early market need recognition, a high degree of customer contact, and top management initiation as the keys to success [38].

Fifty-four significant facilitators for success were identified in Rubenstein's study of US new products [35]. High on the list were the existence of a product champion, marketing factors such as need recognition, superior data collection and analysis, planned approaches to venture management, and strong internal communications.

Project NewProd was an exploratory study into success vs. failure, which sought to identify those characteristics that separated 102 new product successes from 93 failures in 102 firms [9,11,12]. The use of factor analysis and multiple regression analysis revealed a set of success factors, the most important being:

1   Having a unique, superior product in the eyes of the customer, one with a real differential advantage in the market;
2   Having strong market knowledge and market inputs, and undertaking the market research and marketing tasks well; and
3   Having technological and production synergy and proficiency.

The most recent success/failure study was undertaken by Maidique and Zirger, the Stanford Innovation Project [25]. The researchers used a variety of methodologies, including unstructured interviews, a structured survey, and an analysis of paired case histories. The authors conclude that success is likely to be greater under the following circumstances:

1   The developing organization, through in-depth understanding of the marketplace and customers, introduces a product with a high performance-to-cost ratio.
2   The company is proficient in marketing, and commits a significant amount of resources to selling and promoting the product.
3   The product yields a high contribution margin to the firm.
4   The R & D process is well planned and executed.
5   The create, make, and market functions are well interfaced and coordinated.
6   The product is introduced into the market early.
7   The markets and technologies of the new product benefit from the strengths of the firm.
8   There is a high level of management support for the project from the development stage through to launch.

A conceptual model

The results of these empirical investigations have helped to identify the possible factors that underlie new product success. Many of the results of these studies were consistent, in spite of obvious methodology, sample type, and location differences. One result of these studies is the development of conceptual models of new product outcomes. For example, both NewProd and the Stanford Innovation Project propose tentative conceptual models. The research to date, however, has been largely exploratory: to identify variables and propose explanatory models rather than to test models and hypotheses.

The current research takes the next step and involves model and hypotheses testing. The model, shown conceptually in Figure 1, is based on previously proposed models and previous research results, as well as on other literature that proposes what factors should be key to success. The

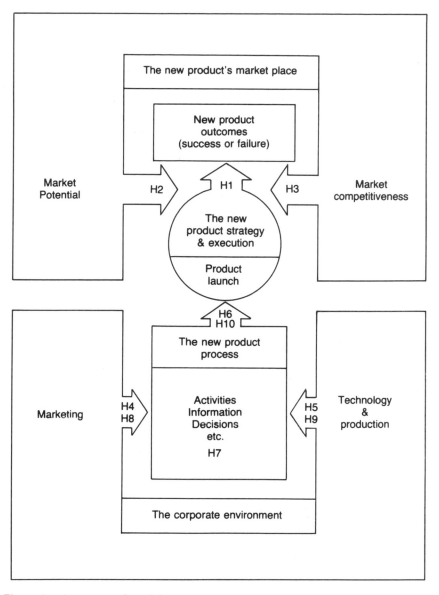

Figure 1 *A conceptual model of new product outcomes*

model postulates that new product outcomes (success or failure) are determined from the interaction of the market environment and the new product strategy and execution. The new product strategy and execution includes both the product itself (e.g. product design, product advantages) as well as the launch. The new product strategy and execution is the result of the new product process, a series of activities that move the product from idea to launch. Finally, this process takes place within a corporate environment consisting of resources, experience, and skills in marketing, production, and technology.

A set of ten hypotheses was next derived from the conceptual model, from previous research findings on new product outcomes, and from other research and writings on business or product success. Each hypothesis and its rationale are presented below, while Figure 1 shows how each hypothesis links constructs in the conceptual model. (Not all the possible hypotheses that might have been derived from the model are tested in the current research; further, the hypotheses are presented in the positive, rather than null form, for style reasons, although it is the null hypothesis that is being tested here.) Later in the article, the tests of these hypotheses are presented, where 'product success' is measured in a variety of ways.

Hypotheses

H1: New product success is positively related to product advantage

Rationale: The product itself – its design, features, attributes, and advantages – is the leading edge of the new product strategy, as shown in Figure 1. It is the new product strategy interacting with the market environment that yields product outcomes. In previous research, product advantage has been uncovered as a success factor. Maidique and Zirger concluded that products that are better matched to users' needs and that feature a higher benefit-to-cost ratio are more likely to be a success [25]. NewProd identified product superiority and product economic advantage to the user as success factors [9–11]. The PIMS studies (Profit Impact of Market Strategy) revealed that product quality was a major determinant of profitability in the case of on-going products [5,36]. Further, studies into new product failures have revealed that product deficiencies and lack of product advantage are major failure causes [10,19]. Finally, conceptual articles cite product advantage as important to success: for example, Kotler argues that product design is a strategic tool [21]. Bennett and Cooper propose their 'product value' concept [3]; and Corey cites product advantage as an important evaluation criterion in analyzing the chances for success for a new product [15].

H2: New product success is positively related to market potential for the new product

Rationale: Market attractiveness and market potential are obvious descriptors of the market environment, which is postulated to interact with product strategy to yield product outcomes (Figure 1). Moreover, previous research has identified market size, growth rate, and market need level as factors in success [9–11]. Additionally, Maidique and Zirger [24] found environmental factors, including market characteristics, to be a consideration in new product success (cited by managers 14% of the time in the unstructured interview phase of the Stanford study). Market attractiveness is also an important dimension in various strategy models used to allocate resources to new and existing businesses and products [1,23]. Finally, market characteristics were found to be useful screening criteria for project selection [14].

H3: New product success is negatively related to the level of competitiveness in the new product's market

Rationale: Market competitiveness as a negative success factor is a logical corollary to H2, and represents the negative facet of the market environment in Figure 1. Maidique and Zirger identified the competitive situation as one factor in project outcomes, but it was not nearly so frequently or strongly cited in the unstructured interview phase as other factors [25]. Similarly, NewProd identified the competitive situation as a negative, albeit minor, factor in project outcomes [9–11]. Nonetheless, business strategy literature, particularly recent writings, emphasizes the competitive situation and competitive analysis as key to strategy [1,29]. The strength of arguments in the conceptual literature, together with the fact that market competitiveness was uncovered in previous exploratory work, led to its inclusion as a hypothesis in the current research.

H4: New product success is positively related to marketing synergy or fit – the ability of the project to build from the firm's existing marketing resources

H5: New product success is positively related to technological synergy or fit – the ability of the project to build from the firm's existing development and production resources

Rationale: Synergy is the common thread that binds the new business to the old, according to Ansoff [2]. Peters and Waterman, in *In Search of Excellence*, make a strong case for 'sticking to the knitting,' that is, building on existing strengths, skills, and experience rather than seeking new opportunities far from one's experience and resource base [28]. Both marketing and technological synergy were found to be important success determinants in the Stanford Project, in NewProd, and in Kulvik's study [9–11,22,25]. Synergy also plays a role in many strategy selection models: for example, the 'business position' dimension in Abell and Hammond's portfolio model, which is similar to many such portfolio models, closely parallels the notion of business fit or synergy [1].

H6: New product success is positively related to project definition or 'protocol' – how well defined the project strategy is prior to product development

H7: New product success is positively related to the proficiency of the 'up-front' or predevelopment activities of the new product process

Rationale: The predevelopment activities of the new product process – those activities that precede the product development phase – are increasingly seen as key to success. Booz-Allen and Hamilton note that successful US firms spend more on these 'up-front' activities, and that the Japanese spend still more [4]. In previous research, effective project evaluation, market studies, and marketing research, and a well-defined market need early in the process were identified as success factors [9–11,19,24,25,31–33,38]. The empirical evidence and conceptual arguments led to the inclusion of this hypothesis in the study.

Closely related to these 'up-front' activities is predevelopment strategy definition. Crawford makes a strong case for all-party predevelopment agreement on the product strategy: target market definition, product benefits to be delivered, etc. [16]. He calls this strategy agreement or step the 'protocol.' The logic and strength of Crawford's proposition led to the inclusion of protocol and its impact on success as a hypothesis in the current research.

H8: New product success is positively related to the proficiency of the market-related activities of the new product process

H9: New product success is positively related to the proficiency of the technological (development and production) activities of the new product process

Rationale: How well the activities of the new product process are undertaken has been found to be related to project outcomes in previous research. For example, a strong market orientation, marketing proficiency, undertaking market research, and effective advertising, promotion, and launch have all been found to be correlates of success [9–11,19,24,25,31–35]. Similarly, the technological activities – the management of the R & D phase and efficient product development – have been found to be linked to outcomes [25,32–34].

H10: New product success is positively related to the degree of top management support for the project

Rationale: The SAPPHO studies were among the first to identify the important role of top management support in product success [31–34]. The European/Japanese new product study undertaken by Utterback et al. revealed top management initiation to be a positive success factor [38]. Further, the Stanford Innovation Project showed that success likelihood was higher when there was a high level of top management support for the product from the development stage through to launch [25]. Based on these empirical studies, top management support as a success factor was included as a hypothesis in the current study.

[The research methods are fully explained in the original paper. Here we look at their results.]

Key success factors

Of the ten hypothesized success factors, nine were found to be significantly related to new product success, three of these in a very strong way. Moreover, all of the significant relationships were in the hypothesized direction of effect. The strongest success factors, measured in terms of numbers of correlations and strength of correlation, were:

1   *Product advantage*. The product offered unique features for the customer; was higher quality; reduced customers' costs; was innovative; was superior to competing products in the eyes of the customer; and solved a problem faced by the customer. (H1)
2   *Proficiency of predevelopment activities*. Undertaking proficiently a set of 'up-front' activities, namely initial screening; preliminary market assessment; preliminary technical assessment; detailed market study or marketing research; and business/financial analysis. (H7)
3   *Protocol*. There was a clear definition, prior to the product development stage, of the target market; customers' needs, wants, and preferences; the product concept; and product specifications and requirements. (H6)

There were five other, relatively strong, success factors. These second level factors included:

- Proficiency of technological activities (H9)
- Proficiency of market-related activities (H8)
- Technological synergy (H5)
- Market potential (H2)
- Marketing synergy (H4).

There was one relatively weakly related success factor, namely Top Management Support. It would appear that failure projects had almost as much top management commitment and involvement as did the successes.

Finally, one hypothesis – market competitiveness – was not supported at all by the research findings. The failure of this one hypothesis comes as no great surprise: even during the hypothesis development phase, the role of market competitiveness was in question. The hypothesis was included largely because of arguments in speculative writings, not on the basis of past research results.

The fact that nine of the ten hypotheses were supported lends partial support to the conceptual model from which they were derived (Figure 1). While tests of these ten hypotheses do not represent a complete test of the model, it is important to note that none of the results were in conflict with the model. The conceptual model of Figure 1 appears to be a reasonable representation or model of new product outcomes, and certainly merits further testing.

What the results mean to managers

Besides yielding a test of ten hypotheses and lending support to a conceptual model, the research results have managerial implications:

Product superiority is the number one factor in success.   This finding has implications for both new product screening decisions and for the management of the new product process. There were six items that comprised product superiority:

- Unique benefits for the customer
- Product quality
- Reduced customers' costs
- Product innovativeness
- Product superiority in the eyes of the customer and
- Solution to a customer's problem.

This list provides a useful checklist of questions in assessing the odds of success of a proposed new product project. In short, these items logically should be top priority questions in a project screening model or checklist.

The second implication focuses on how the process is managed. The development of a product with real advantages becomes the number one objective in the new product process. Simply being equal to competition, or having a good 'product–market fit' is not enough: rather, one must seek a product advantage: the goal must be superiority. If the proposed product is weak on all or most of the above six items, then every effort must be made to build in product superiority as the final product takes shape. Some of these efforts might include, for example, extensive market research to understand customers' needs, wants, and preferences, and to gain an insight into what constitutes 'a better product in the eyes of the customer': creativity techniques and creative problem solving methods to arrive at novel technical solutions: and extensive field trials and tests with customers to ensure that the final product design scores high on customer acceptance and preference.

Project definition and the 'up-front' activities are vital to success.   These two hypotheses – protocol and the proficiency of predevelopment activities – are closely related. The most critical steps in the new product process are those that occur before the product development gets underway. These include: initial screening, preliminary technical and market assessments, marketing research, and business/financial analysis. One implication is that management must recognize the importance of these up-front steps, and be prepared to devote the necessary resources – people, time, and money – to see that they are carried out well. The research evidence suggests otherwise: that these steps are currently weakly handled. Further, the Booz-Allen and Hamilton study notes that the Japanese devote considerably more resources to these 'homework' stages than does the typical US firm [4].

A second implication is that these five key predevelopment activities should be built into the new product process as a matter of routine rather than by exception. The recommendation is that firms adopt a game plan or process model that incorporates these five up-front activities as an integral and vital part of the process.

The role of protocol – gaining agreement on target market and product strategy prior to charging ahead with product development – supports Crawford's plea for such a step in the new product process [16]. The recommendation is that managers build into their new product process a protocol step or check point. This step should occur just prior to product development, and hence logically after the completion of the five up-front steps cited above. Here, there must be agreement on:

- The target market: exactly who the product will be aimed at.
- The customers' needs, wants, and preferences: the customers' 'wish list.'
- The product concept: what benefits the product will deliver, and how it will be positioned in the market.
- The product's attributes, features, specifications, and requirements.

If the five up-front activities are carried out well, then defining a protocol should be relatively straightforward.

Synergy – both marketing and technological – is a key factor in success. The proponents of synergy as an ingredient in success appear to be correct, according to the results of this research. While synergy was not the most important success determinant, it was nonetheless a significant factor. Marketing synergy means having a good 'project–company' fit in terms of a variety of marketing resources and skills, varying from the sales force through to the service department. Technological synergy included project-company fit in terms of R & D, engineering, and production resources and skills. These two factors, and the list of items that comprise each, become important checklist questions in the screening of new product ventures.

Controllable variables, rather than situational or environment variables, are the dominant factors in success.   The ten hypothesized success factors can be approximately categorized into two groups:

Controllable factors: those factors over which the project manager and team have control and can affect in the short term. Such factors include:

- Proficiency of predevelopment activities
- Proficiency of market-related activities
- Proficiency of technological activities
- Product advantage
- Protocol.

Situational/environmental factors: those factors that are more or less fixed, and describe the setting for the project. They include:

- Market potential.
- Market competitiveness.
- Market synergy.
- Technological synergy.

One factor, top management involvement, fits into both categories – partly controllable, partly noncontrollable by the project leader and team.

A review of the two lists – controllable vs. situational/environmental variables – reveals that the strongest success factors are in the controllable category. Indeed, the top three success factors – product advantage, proficiency of predevelopment activities, and protocol – are all factors within the control of the project manager and team. This finding has important implications. First, it means that the way the new product process is managed and executed – the activities that people undertake and how well they do them from idea to launch – largely decide project outcomes. This points to the need for a carefully conceived plan of action or blueprint of activities to ensure that key steps are carried out, and that sufficient resources are made available. Second, the environmental/situational variables, such as market potential, market competitiveness, marketing synergy, and technological synergy remain valid screening criteria for project selection. They are not the most important correlates of success, however.

Conclusion

New product development remains one of the riskiest yet most important management challenges. A better understanding of what makes a new product a success – what separates winners from losers – is essential to improved project selection and management. This research, by testing certain success factor hypotheses, has identified and confirmed the importance of a number of success determinants. The research has also lent support to a model of new product outcomes, and yielded results that have action implications to managers.

References

1 Abell, D.F. and Hammond, J.S. *Strategic Market Planning*. Englewood Cliffs. NJ: Prentice-Hall, 1979.
2 Ansoff, I.H. *Corporate Strategy*. New York: McGraw-Hill, 1965. p. 103.
3 Bennett, R.C. and Cooper, R.G. The product life cycle trap. *Business Horizons*, 27:7–16 (September–October 1984).
4 Booz-Allen & Hamilton. *New Product Management for the 1980's*. New York: Booz-Allen & Hamilton. Inc., 1982.
5 Buzzell, R.D., Gale, B.T., and Sultan, R.G.M. Market share – a key to profitability. *Harvard Business Review* (1975).
6 Calantone, R. and Cooper, R.G. New product scenarios: prospects for success. *Journal of Marketing* 45:48–60 (Spring 1981).
7 Cooper, R.G. The performance impact of product innovation strategies. *European Journal of Marketing* 18:3–54 (1984).
8 Cooper, R.G. An empirically derived new product project selection model. *IEEE Transactions on Engineering Management* EM-28:54–61 (August 1981).
9 Cooper, R.G. Project NewProd: factors in new product success. *European Journal of Marketing* 14:277–292 (1980).
10 Cooper, R.G. The dimensions of industrial new product success and failure. *Journal of Marketing* 43:93–103 (Summer 1979).
11 Cooper, R.G. Identifying industrial new product success: project NewProd. *Industrial Marketing Management* 8 (May 1979).
12 Cooper, R.G. Introducing successful new products. *MCB Monographs, European Journal of Marketing* 10 (1976).
13 Cooper, R.G. *Winning the New Product Game*. Montreal: McGill University, 1976.
14 Cooper, R.G. and de Brentani, U. Criteria for screening new industrial products. *Industrial Marketing Management* 13:149–156 (1984).
15 Corey, E.R. *Industrial Marketing*. Third Ed., Englewood Cliffs. NJ: Prentice-Hall, 1983. pp. 201–233 (see Hartford case: see also teaching notes to the case in question).
16 Crawford, C.M. Protocol: new tool for product innovation. *Journal of Product Innovation Management* 2:85–91 (1984).
17 Crawford, C.M. New product failure rates – facts and fallacies. *Research Management* 9–13 (September 1979).
18 Globe, S., Levy, G.W., and Schwartz, C.M. Key factors and events in the innovation process. *Research Management* 16:8–15 (July 1973).
19 Hopkins, D.S. and Bailey, E.L. New product pressures. *The Conference Board Record* 8:16–24 (June 1971).
20 Hopkins, D.S. *New Product Winners and Losers*. Conference Board Report No. 773, 1980.
21 Kotler, P. and Rath, G.A. Design: a powerful but neglected strategic tool. *The Journal of Business Strategy* 5:16–21 (Fall 1984).
22 Kulvik, H. *Factors Underlying the Success or Failure of New Products*. Helsinki: University of Technology. Report No. 29. Finland, 1977.
23 Luck, D.J. and Ferrell, O.C. *Marketing Strategy and Plans*. Second Ed. Englewood Cliffs. NJ: Prentice-Hall, 1985. pp. 78–83.

24 Maidique, M.A. and Zirger, B.J. The new product learning cycle. Research Report Series. Innovation & Entrepreneurship Institute. School of Business Administration. University of Miami. Coral Gables, FL. February 1985. pp. 85–101.

25 Maidique, M.A. and Zirger, B.J. A study of success and failure in product innovation: the case of the U.S. electronics industry. *IEEE Transactions in Engineering Management* EM-31:192–203 (November 1983).

26 Myers, S. and Marquis, D.G. Successful industrial innovations. *National Science Foundations* NSF 69–17 (1969).

27 National Industrial Conference Board. Why new products fail. *The Conference Board Record*. New York: NICB, 1964.

28 Peters, T.J. and Waterman, R.H. Jr. *In Search of Excellence*. New York: Harper & Row, 1982.

29 Porter, M.E. *Competitive Advantage: Creating and Sustaining Superior Performance*. New York: Free Press, 1985.

30 Roberts, R.W. and Burke, J.E. Six new products – what made them successful. *Research Management* 16:21–24 (May 1974).

31 Rothwell, R. Innovation in textile machinery: some significant factors in success and failure. *SPRU Occasional Paper Series*. No. 2. Brighton, Sussex, United Kingdom (June 1976).

32 Rothwell, R. The 'Hungarian Sappho': some comments and comparison. *Research Policy* 3:30–38 (1976).

33 Rothwell, R. Factors for success in industrial innovations, from *Project SAPPHO – A Comparative Study of Success and Failure in Industrial Innovation*. Brighton, Sussex: SPRU, 1972.

34 Rothwell, R., Freeman, C., Horsley, A., Jervis, V.T.P., Robertson, A. B., and Townsend, J. SAPPHO updated – Project Sappho Phase II. *Research Policy* 3:258–291 (1974).

35 Rubenstein, A.H., Chakrabarti, A.K., O'Keefe, R.D., Sounder, W.E., and Young, H.C. Factors influencing success at the project level. *Research Management* 16:15–20 (May 1976).

36 Schoeffler, S., Buzzell, R.D., and Heany, O.F. Impact of strategic planning on profit performance. *Harvard Business Review* 137–145 (March–April 1974).

37 Townsend, J.F. Innovation in coal machinery: 'The Anderton Shearer Loader' – the role of the NCB and the supply industry in its development. *SPRU Occasional Paper Series*, No. 3, Brighton, Sussex, United Kingdom. December 1976.

38 Utterback, J.M., Allen, T.J., Holloman, J.H., and Sirbu, M.H. The process of innovation in five industries in Europe and Japan. *IEEE Transactions in Engineering Management* 3–9 (February 1976).

PART TWO
SHORT EXEMPLARS

Whereas the opening extracts set up the overall framework, we now move on to consider some examples of practice. Each extract is quite short. Collectively, you might like to consider them a series of snapshots of creativity in action. We start with a raft of well known names – Honda, Jobs, Land, Pilkington, Sinclair and Roddick. The emphasis moves from people in Section 5 to processes and products in Section 6, although in most examples, as in life, they are inextricably bound together. Mitchell describes the organizational processes 3M advocate to keep innovation flowing. We look at two very different products – heavy engineering and that doyen of the consumer electronics field, the Sony Walkman. Lorenz describes the transformation at Baker Perkins and the chairman of Sony offers his own story of the development of the Walkman.

Part of the challenge here is in comparing the personalities, the routes they choose and the points of achievement. Do innovators have certain specific characteristics in common or are there a few broad types? Are they mavericks, and if so how can they be integrated into the discipline of organizations? Are the methods of successful businesses reducible to a few rules? Are there recurring obsessions with customers and products?

SECTION 5

IDEAS INTO INNOVATION

14

The innovators

William Davis

Innovation is surely the most exciting part of business life. It can also be one of the most frustrating, but there is nothing to compare with the thrill of finding a new idea and turning it into concrete reality. This section is about people who have done just that. It covers a wide range of activities, because innovation is clearly not confined to any particular field.

The past century and a half has seen advances in technology which are without parallel in history. As a result, it has become commonplace to associate the word 'innovation' with technological change; but it has a much wider application. We live in what Peter Drucker has called 'the age of discontinuity'. People everywhere are constantly looking not only for new products but for new ways of doing things – in manufacturing, in finance, in services, in management, in the arts, in economics. Some innovations, such as instalment buying and the supermarket, have made as much of an impact on our lives as the great advances in technology.

Perhaps, at the outset, a distinction should be made between the two terms 'inventor' and 'innovator', because they are so widely confused. The inventor produces ideas; the innovator makes new things happen. Many talented people do both, but someone who is good at inventing is not necessarily good at turning his concept into a viable commercial proposition. Many inventors are more interested in the idea as such, and in the challenge it represents, than in the business of making it into a marketable – and profitable – product or service, with all the difficulties and hazards which that involves.

The successful innovator is a *doer* – someone with imagination who can visualize the possibilities of an idea and who has a strong desire to see it realized in concrete form. He or she usually encounters considerable scepticism and even determined opposition. There may be discouraging setbacks. It takes a lot of nerve to press on despite all the doubts and uncertainties.

Adapted from Introduction in *The Innovators* by William Davis, copyright The White Rabbit Ltd and William Davis, published by Ebury Press, London (1987), pp. 1–11

Sometimes, of course, the sceptics turn out to be right. Ideas which look brilliant on paper may prove unworkable, or too costly to implement, or too limited in their appeal. There may come a point at which it is plain that to press on would be a foolish waste of time and money. But one of the most noteworthy characteristics of the many people featured here is that they are not the kind of men and women who give up easily.

King C. Gillette had the idea for a safety razor while he was shaving one morning in 1895. 'In a moment', he later recalled, 'I saw it all.' He wrote to his wife: 'I've got it! Our fortune is made!' The jubilation was decidedly premature. He made many experiments with steel blades, but the 'experts' whom he consulted advised him to forget it; they insisted that he would never succeed in putting an edge on sheet steel that would shave. He persisted, but the venture did not get off the ground until 1903 – after a young graduate from the Massachusetts Institute of Technology, William E. Nickerson, had found the answer to the technical problem.

Sir Alastair Pilkington, who developed the 'float' method of glass-making, struggled for seven years to prove that his theories had practical value. People, he says, used to ask him: 'When will you succeed?' All he could say was: 'We will know the answer to that only when we have succeeded.' His process eventually made all the existing ways of manufacturing plate glass obsolete, and the company earned millions from licensing fees. But there must have been many times when his board of directors wondered whether to go on supporting him.

This situation occurs more often than is generally realized, and not everyone gets the chance to see things through. The man with a new idea is frequently regarded as a crank until the idea succeeds. Then, of course, people are only too eager to claim at least part of the credit.

Ironically, some of the strongest resistance to innovation sometimes comes from people who have played a major role in the previous innovation. They not only dislike the suggestion that there might be a better way, but may have a vested interest in defending the status quo. One of the most famous examples is Edison's rejection of the argument that alternating electrical current had advantages over direct current. To accept it would have meant that he was wrong and his great rival George Westinghouse was right; it would also have meant that the plant which Edison's firm already had in operation was obsolete.

This reluctance to abandon familiar concepts is by no means confined to individuals. Many corporations reject innovative ideas, which they regard as disruptive and risky; they prefer to defend their existing business. The same is often true of entire countries. Britain, for example, has been much slower to accept the need for change in the last few decades than competitors like Japan.

It would clearly be unfair to suggest that large companies cannot innovate. They can, and do. In some fields they are the only ones who can afford the massive outlay on research and development, or on capital equipment, which is required to convert an idea into successful reality. But there is no doubt that the bureaucratic structure of some big organizations presents a formidable obstacle to innovation.

Employees are generally expected to follow established procedures; conformity is valued more highly than initiative. The individual who attempts to do things differently can easily get into trouble. This is why so many outsiders who try to sell ideas to large firms find it hard to make any headway. The executive who listens to the proposal (if anyone listens at all) has to weigh up the personal risks involved in supporting it. There is bound to be internal opposition. Do the potential rewards of success outweigh what he or she can lose if the idea fails? It is much safer to say 'No' than 'Yes', and that is what usually happens. The outsider is told that it can't be done because it hasn't been done before, or that 'It isn't right for us', or because the risks are too great. Sometimes it is adopted at a later stage – *after* a competitor has made it work so well that the company's position in the marketplace is threatened.

If one works for a large and apparently solid corporation it is all too easy to assume that tomorrow will be more or less like today. The emphasis tends to be on making the operation even more cost-effective, rather than on innovation. But tomorrow may *not* be like today; indeed, in a rapidly changing world it is very likely that it won't be. Innovation is risky, but it may be even more risky *not* to innovate.

Henry Ford was one of the business leaders who acknowledged this back in the 1920s. In *My Life and Work* he wrote:

> If to petrify is success, all one has to do is to humor the lazy side of the mind; but if to grow is success, then one must wake up anew each morning and keep awake all day. I saw great businesses become but the ghost of a name because someone thought they could be managed just as they were always managed, and though the management may have been the most excellent in its day, its excellence consisted in its alertness to its day, and not in slavish following of its yesterdays. Life, as I see it, is not a location but a journey. Even the man who most feels himself 'settled' is not settled – he is probably sagging back. Everything is in flux, and was meant to be. Life flows. We may live at the same number of the street, but it is never the same man who lives there.

And later in the same book:

> It could almost be written down as a formula that when a man begins to think that he at last has found his method, he had better begin a most searching examination of himself to see whether some part of his brain has not gone to sleep.

Ford was a great innovator, but even he fell into the trap. He made the classic mistake of the production man: he failed to keep pace with the changing demands of the market, contemptuously dismissing fashion and style, which allowed his competitors to exploit what he had begun.

The attitude of senior management is of vital importance: if it gives low priority to innovation, little will be done. The most innovative companies tend to put in influential positions people who, although they may come up with few original ideas of their own, possess an emotional commitment to creative work and do their best to encourage it. It also helps to have two separate budgets: an operating budget and an innovation budget. The first contains everything that is being done at the moment; the second contains the things that could be done differently and the different things to be worked on.

Small and medium-sized companies tend to be more innovative than entrenched large ones. They are more flexible, more willing to try new ideas and approaches. New product development is a crucial factor in determining their financial success, and they have the attacker's advantage. Management–employee relationships are better because people feel more closely involved, have a greater sense of achievement and spend less time on corporate in-fighting. Communication resembles consultation rather than command. The leaders of such companies usually have considerable entrepreneurial flair.

Bright, creative people tend to perform well in that kind of environment. Some large companies, recognizing this, have adopted various ways of instilling entrepreneurial attitudes into their employees. One is the setting up of independent task forces – groups which operate outside mainstream management with the maximum possible freedom to carry out specific tasks. IBM created such a force to develop a personal computer and catch up with Apple. Another method is to encourage team competition within the company. The prototype is Hewlett-Packard, in whose early days autonomous teams competed with each other to develop products and sell them to the sales forces. In many cases, these people take over the running of a new subsidiary set up to exploit the ideas.

At 3M, one of the most innovative of the big US corporations, senior management has long believed in the concept of the 'champion' – the man or woman with a fanatical faith in the specific product that he or she has in mind. The product champion is protected by an 'executive champion' (someone who knows how to deal with the corporate staff) and supported by a new venture team, which consists of people with expertise in various areas, including manufacturing and sales. If anyone wants to stop a project aimed at developing a new product, the burden of proof is on the one who wants to stop it, not the one who proposes it. Paperwork is kept down to a minimum. Many experiments fail, but failure is forgiven. The management at 3M wants its people to keep on trying. Each division is required to ensure that at least 25 per cent of its sales is derived from products that did not exist five years ago. The system seems to work: 3M has introduced more than fifty thousand new products to date.

The risk, of course, is that real champions may eventually take the plunge into starting on their own. Having developed a taste for independence and adventure they may decide, perhaps in partnership with others, that they want to be free to make the most of their endeavours.

The desire for independence, for doing one's own thing, has always been a strong driving force in business. It is often regarded as more important than money, though naturally most entrepreneurial people would like to get rich. A vast number of new companies are launched each year. Management buy-outs have become a familiar feature of the business scene. Many of these enterprises run into trouble and go bust, but the high failure rate among small companies clearly does not deter others from having a go.

Independent entrepreneurs are mavericks. There is something about them that sets them apart from the crowd. They love to make things happen. They are not content with reacting to events; they want to control them. They are opportunists who are constantly on the look-out for new worlds to conquer. They are innovators.

The individuals featured here come from widely different backgrounds. Some were born into poor families and there is no doubt that the urge to acquire wealth – and the sense of security that it provides – has been a powerful factor in their behaviour. Many did not complete their formal education. Soichiro Honda, the Japanese mechanical genius who created the company that bears his name, was dismissed from technical high school. Steven Jobs, the founder of Apple, dropped out of college. Britain's Sir Clive Sinclair left school at seventeen 'because I can only concentrate when I can do what I want'.

There is, however, one common factor: a great enthusiasm for new challenges. Carnegie, the steel magnate, coined the much-quoted phrase 'Pioneering don't pay.' But his subsequent career showed that he simply couldn't resist it: he became one of the most successful pioneers in the US steel industry, not only in the technological area but also in the organization and management of resources.

Carnegie started small and went on to build a giant corporation. Many others have done the same: some of the biggest enterprises in the world today, including IBM and ITT, were launched by independent entrepreneurs. But it is an interesting (though not altogether surprising) fact of business life that creative people often find it difficult to adjust themselves to new disciplines when the company they have started grows big and successful.

Steven Jobs is a much-publicized example. His innovative talents made him a genuine American business hero while he was still in his twenties. His personality, however, didn't fit easily into a large organization. He was enthusiastic, hard-working and full of ideas; but he was also restless, easily bored and blunt to the point of tactlessness. In 1985 the board of directors decided that he would have to leave. The power struggle was bitter and very public, and it ended in defeat for the man who had created the business. He was worth $150 million or so, and could easily have opted for a life of leisure. He tried it for a while, but he missed the challenge which Apple had provided. So he put up $7 million of his own money, hired people who had worked for him and who had left when he did, and launched a new company. 'We are going to take the technology to the next level,' he told the press.

H. Ross Perot, founder of Electronic Data Systems, is another innovator who ran into problems. A brashly unconventional Texan, Perot left the US Navy as a young man because he was frustrated by the slow system of promotion. 'I have no patience for red tape and inactivity,' he later said. He joined IBM, where he quickly became one of their star salesmen. While in that job, he proposed that IBM should create a service organization that would design, install and operate electronic data processing systems on a fixed contract basis. IBM's senior management thought the idea was absurdly impractical, so he left and started EDS with $1000 of savings. Six years later he went public, and the shares received a warm welcome on Wall Street. In 1984 General Motors made him an offer which he felt he couldn't refuse: it bought EDS for $2.5 billion.

GM's chairman, Roger Smith, wanted EDS primarily because of its computer expertise, but he also expressed the view that Perot's drive and 'entrepreneurial spirit' would be good for the vast organization. Whether he meant it or not, it soon transpired that Perot's attitudes and tactics were far from welcome. He chastised General Motors for its volume of rules and for not seeing that car-making is the economic equivalent of war. He also made it clear that he wanted to break down the corporate hierarchy.

Inevitably, it made him a lot of highly placed enemies. But what really upset Roger Smith and the other directors was Perot's insistence on breaking one of GM's most fundamental rules: never go public with criticism. Perot told workers that the management was out of touch with its employees. At a meeting of car dealers, he said that GM wasn't making the cars that customers wanted. Interviewers were told that changing GM's corporate culture was like 'teaching an elephant to tap-dance'. In December 1986 the board decided that enough was enough. In an extraordinary move it voted to pay him about $700 million to shut up and get out. The experiment was probably doomed from the start. Men like Perot flourish in an entrepreneurial format and need to be in charge. The remarkable thing is that apparently GM did not recognize this obvious fact when they took him on.

Jobs and Perot are typical mavericks: opinionated, aggressive, opportunistic, in a hurry. They made their reputations and fortunes in the computer industry, but the same kind of people can be found everywhere.

One of the great growth areas is what is loosely called the 'service sector', a term which encompasses everything from airlines, hotels, stores and supermarkets to health care, entertainment, communications and financial services. It attracts more newcomers than any other area because in many cases less capital is needed since there is no manufacturing element, and because it offers so much scope for the development of new ideas.

Franchising, itself a splendid innovation has given many people an opportunity to share in the success of clever marketing concepts like McDonald's and Kentucky Fried Chicken. The entertainment business has grown at an impressive rate, and communications has become a vast, worldwide industry, aided by new technology. The range of financial services on offer today is staggering, and travel has become a far bigger business than pioneers like Thomas Cook could have foreseen. It has not only led to the creation of international hotel chains like Hiltons and Holiday Inns, and made fortunes for imaginative tour operators and others, but it has also made it easier for innovations to cross national frontiers.

Not so very long ago, people thought themselves lucky if an idea made money in their own country. Many still do. But, increasingly, innovators think in terms of world markets. Ray Kroc, the founder of McDonald's, started with the dream of building a chain of hamburger franchises in the USA. It was a lofty ambition. How pleased he must have been when he discovered that his concept also appealed to the British, the Italians, the Japanese and even the French.

They, in turn, picked up ideas on visits to America. Masaru Ibuka of Sony went to the USA to enquire into American uses of the tape recorder; instead, he found out about transistor technology. He got a licence from Bell and, with his partner Akio Morita, went on to develop a highly successful range of consumer products. Alan Sainsbury 'discovered' the supermarket on a trip to the USA, recognized the potential and introduced the concept to Britain. The charge card, too, was an innovation which originated in America. A Chicago businessman, Frank McNamara, found that he couldn't pay for dinner at a New York restaurant because he had forgotten his wallet. That embarrassing evening led him to create the Diners Club, a simple idea which has spawned a multi-national industry.

Travel has been of benefit to many others. Helena Rubinstein got into the cosmetics business because, on a visit to Australia, she was shocked by the dry, rough skins of Australian women and reckoned – correctly – that they would welcome the creams her mother made in her native Poland. Anita Roddick, founder of the Body Shop, had the idea for her business during a year-long trip around the world at the age of twenty-five. She learned how women in unsophisticated societies cleaned and cared for their skin and hair, and thought that products made from their natural recipes might also go down well in Britain. The scope turned out to be greater than she had expected, and today there are more than 250 Body Shops all over the world.

For many innovators in Europe and Japan, America has long been the Promised Land – the country which, if it likes a concept, will happily help them to make a lot of money. It worked for Masaru Ibuka and Soichiro Honda. It also worked for Britain's Mary Quant, who exported the mini-skirt and other London fashion ideas to the USA in the 1960s, and for Laura Ashley, who re-created the style of the Victorian era and found that Americans, too, were fond of the past.

The market is so huge that success can bring immense rewards. The Japanese, as we all know, have shown an exceptional talent for making the most of their opportunities. They have also been good at developing the inventions of others or finding new uses for them. This, too, is part of the innovative process.

Americans who complain about the 'invasion' by foreign companies should remember that it was they who showed the way: US corporations have been 'invading' others' markets for years. Their impact on the international scene has been enormous: IBM, Ford, ITT and others are vast multi-national corporations whose influence is felt everywhere.

This section is not about companies, or teams, or projects, but about *individuals* – their ideas, their hopes and dreams, their struggles, their successes and failures; innovators whose lives are particularly fascinating, and whose thoughts and actions seemed to me to hold valuable lessons for the rest of us.

15

Soichiro Honda: 'supply creates its own demand'

William Davis

Although he came from a very different culture, Soichiro Honda had much in common with Henry Ford. He, too, was a small-town boy with an intuitive mechanical genius who created a business empire that still bears his name. He also shared Ford's disdain for formal education.

'I am not impressed by diplomas,' Honda told me when I interviewed him in Tokyo in 1968.

> They don't do the work. I went to a technical high school, but was dismissed. I was twenty-eight when I joined, and I had already held down a job. I attended only the classes I wanted to go to. Other students memorized the lessons, but I compared them with my practical experience. My marks were not as good as those of others, and I didn't take the final examination. The principal called me in and said I have to leave. I told him I didn't want a diploma. They had less value than a cinema ticket. A ticket at least guaranteed that you would get in. A diploma guaranteed nothing.

The son of a blacksmith, Honda was fascinated by mechanical things almost as soon as he could walk. Impatient and ambitious, he left school at sixteen to become an apprentice in an auto repair shop. He later devoted much time and effort to the technique of casting, in an attempt to make a piston ring. He went to the technical high school primarily because he hoped he might learn something to help him in this endeavour.

Within a year of being asked to leave, he succeeded in manufacturing identifiably sound and functional devices. After a slow start, he gained Toyota's financial support. During World War II he invented machinery for automatic piston ring manufacture and automatic planing for aircraft propellers, allowing relatively untrained women to produce these goods as the men went off to battle. He even managed to find uses for the aluminium wing tanks that American planes dropped while bombing his home town. 'Truman's gifts,' he called them. But he lost two factories to fire bombs, and after the surrender he decided to break away from Toyota. He sold what was left of his piston ring business for $125,000 and looked

From *The Innovators* by William Davis, copyright The White Rabbit Ltd and William Davis, published by Ebury Press, London (1987), pp. 187–92

around for new challenges. His next step was eventually to lead to world-wide fame, though he did not know it at the time.

Honda's car had been immobilized by the fuel shortage, along with many others, which made it difficult to get around. He solved the problem by the novel device of attaching a motor to a bicycle. His neighbours were impressed enough to ask him to make more. Using a small gasoline engine which had been used for electrical generators during the war, he contrived a makeshift motorbike. When the surplus engines ran out, he decided to build motors himself. Faced with government controls on gasoline and restrictions on the manufacture of gasoline-using machines, he built a motor that ran on pine resin, which he recalled had been used as a substitute for aircraft fuel towards the end of the war. This innovation, based on a temporary problem, was the start of what later grew into the world's leading motorcycle company.

With the income from his contraptions, he set out to design and manufacture a real motorcycle, which he called the Dream. There was not yet a market for such a machine, but as he said later: 'We do not make something because the demand, the market, is there. With our technology we can create demand, we can create the market. Supply creates its own demand.'

The Dream was a sleek and powerful motorcycle with a four-cycle engine. Honda hired an experienced businessman, Takeo Fujisawa, to look after sales and the business side generally. Fujisawa wrote a letter to all the eighteen thousand bicycle shops in Japan. Five thousand dealers, who came to make up one of Japan's first and largest distribution networks, responded favourably. But Honda recognized that his Dream appealed only to a limited section of what was potentially a huge market: he would have to come up with something likely to command a more popular following. In 1952, a year after the launch of the Dream, he introduced a small, cheap, and efficient Cub engine that ran either on Honda's red-and-white frame or clipped conveniently on to a bicycle. It was a tremendous success.

He went on to produce the Super-Cub, which combined the power and excitement of big machines with the convenience and efficiency of scooters. It was built in his own modern factory, priced well below the competition, and advertised to a mass market. ('You meet the nicest people on a Honda.') By the 1960s the company was exporting motorcycles all over the world, decimating the competition and dominating the industry.

It then began building cars. This did not suit the plans of MITI (the Ministry of International Trade and Industry, a sort of super-agency that plays a major role in Japan), which wanted to mould the auto industry into an international force and saw no room for Honda. He defied MITI and spent several years making a succession of cars that were, for the most part, forgettable and not very well received. But he kept on trying. 'Success', he later told a graduating class at Michigan Technology University, 'can be achieved only through repeated failure and introspection. In fact, success represents 1 per cent of your work which results only from the 99 per cent that is called failure.' In less than twenty years, the company's annual auto production went from twenty thousand cars to over a million.

From the beginning, Honda ran his business in his own special way. He hired young people and gave them responsibility immediately. He was contemptuous of the *gakkubatsu*, the old-boy network of university graduates, and scorned the *zaibatsu*, the industrial monoliths like Kawasaki and Mitsubishi. In the west Honda would have been considered a maverick; by Japanese standards, he was a radical.

He told me, in that interview, that he hated the Japanese seniority system, under which promotion is governed by length of service rather than merit. 'I promote by ability,' he said. 'Many people take pride in saying, at their retirement ceremony, that they got through their working lives without making mistakes. I prefer them to say that they made many errors, but always tried to advance. People who never made mistakes simply did what their boss told them to do. They are not the kind we want.'

What qualities did he look for? 'First,' he said, 'I try to find out what a man is good at, and whether he has ideas of his own. Then I assess whether he can get along with others. A man must have self-confidence, but he must be modest enough to learn from others.' And the secret of his own success? 'Imagination, resourcefulness, fresh ideas, sound theories, and economy of time. Life is based on seeing, listening, and experimenting. But experimenting is the most important. This company has grown to today's dimensions because it had no traditions.'

Japan, he went on, had done well out of losing the war.

> We'd never have the freedom we have now. I'd never have been allowed to get where I have got. With everything flattened, we could start from scratch, plan from the word go, and think big. You can see it in Tokyo to this day: the blitzed arcas are booming, but those which escaped are backward. I love this new freedom. It allows me to go down to the shop floor. I couldn't bear sitting in the presidential suite, as I should have had to do in an old-fashioned firm, supposing I had risen to the top.

Honda rarely appeared at his own office. He much preferred working among the hundreds of technicians employed on basic research. The actual running of the business was left to bankers and accountants. 'Every man', Honda said, 'should concentrate on the things he can do best.'

When we met, at the company's research centre on the outskirts of Tokyo, he was wearing grease-stained overalls. He was a small man with rosy cheeks, a healthy tan and a mouthful of gold teeth. He laughed a lot, and generally seemed to be enjoying life. Wealth, he told me, had given him the freedom to do what he wanted to do – which, in his case, meant experimenting with new ideas. He didn't get much time for leisure, and he didn't have a yacht or anything like that. 'I have three cars – a Lotus Elite, a Fiat and a Honda sports car. But I drive them myself.' My house? 'Yes, it's large and luxurious. When I go abroad I get invited to a lot of big houses, and I have to have somewhere to entertain people who come to Tokyo.'

I asked him what advice he would give to his sons. 'Simply to do what they would like to do. One must be happy at work. That's the most important thing of all.'

On the wall of the small room where we talked was a large notice headed 'Management Policy'. It listed five points: proceed always with ambition and youthfulness; respect sound theory, develop fresh ideas and make the most effective use of time; enjoy your work and always brighten your working atmosphere; strive constantly for a harmonious flow of work; be ever mindful of the value of research and endeavour.

Soichiro Honda and Takeo Fujisawa retired on the company's twenty-fifth anniversary in 1973. Neither man was remotely approaching his dotage, and their departure was unusual in a nation accustomed to a gerontocracy. But Honda had been held back by his youth in the early days and he wasn't about to place the same obstacle before others. The company was left to the younger generation, men considered middle-management at other Japanese firms. Honda's successor, Kiyoshi Kawashima, was forty-three; when he retired, ten years later, another young man, Tadashi Kune, stepped in.

16

Steven Jobs: genius in a garage

William Davis

Steven Jobs is one of the most remarkable young innovators in the computer business; as the founder of Apple, he became a genuine American business hero while still in his twenties. His career to date also shows how difficult it often is for truly creative people to adjust themselves to new disciplines when the business they have started grows big and successful.

Jobs grew up in California and, like so many teenagers of his day, found himself attracted to eastern philosophy. He dropped out of college, let his hair grow long, smoked dope and frequently went without shoes. He wanted to go to India but couldn't afford the passage. To earn money, he began doing bits of work for the Atari Corporation, helping to build video games. Jobs was no engineer, but he was quick and smart. In the summer of 1974, he finally made it to India. He had his head shaven by a guru, and attended religious festivals and visited monasteries. He contemplated going to Japan to join a monastery, but returned to California instead.

There he met Stephen Wozniak, who was five years older, and they became good friends. Wozniak was also a college drop-out, but he was fascinated by digital electronics and computers and managed to get himself hired by Hewlett-Packard. He was assigned to calculators, not computers, and found the job disappointing. After hours, Wozniak worked hard building a small, easy-to-use computer. The invention of the microprocessor had made such a machine theoretically possible, and Wozniak became obsessed with the idea of creating one. In 1976, he succeeded. The machine was smaller than a portable typewriter, it could perform the feats of much larger computers. Hewlett-Packard turned him down when he asked if he could pursue his hobby for the company. The one person who recognized that these smaller machines might have some kind of broader appeal was his friend Steven Jobs. They talked about it endlessly and finally Jobs persuaded him that they should start a little company of their own.

Jobs, then twenty-one, opened a makeshift production line in the garage of his parents' home. He raised $1300 by selling his Volkswagen Microbus

From *The Innovators* by William Davis, copyright The White Rabbit Ltd and William Davis, published by Ebury Press, London (1987) pp. 204–8 and Wozniak's Hewlett-Packard scientific calculator. Recalling a pleasant summer that he had spent working in the orchards of Oregon, he christened the new computer Apple. He looked around for capital and they eventually agreed to take on another partner, a former marketing manager of a computer company who not only knew something about running a business but also put in $250,000 of his own money and helped arrange other finance, including a credit line with the Bank of America.

Sales in 1977 were $2.7 million. By 1980 they had soared to $200 million and Apple went public. Jobs was chairman of the board and, at twenty-six, a wealthy man. Wozniak, incredibly, decided to go back to Berkeley to finish his studies!

The runaway progress continued: in 1981, revenue was close to $331 million, heading towards $1 billion and beyond. It was one of the great American success stories. With the computer selling so well, Jobs and his colleagues decided to create a new product, one that could get a foothold in the increasingly important office market. Jobs called it Lisa, after one of his ex-girlfriends. The importance of the Lisa project guaranteed that the new division was where the action was going to be. He naturally wanted to be in charge of it. Much to his surprise, however, his business partners turned him down. Their reasons were that he was too young and inexperienced to manage an organization as large and complex as the Lisa division was bound to become.

The real problem with Jobs, as perceived by the others, was that his personality didn't fit easily into a big organization. He was enthusiastic, hard-working and full of ideas. But he was also restless, easily bored and blunt to the point of tactlessness. He frequently told subordinates that their plans were 'dogshit' and expected everyone to work a ninety-hour week, as he did. In short, he was what one Apple executive described as 'a royal pain in the butt'.

The job of running the Lisa division went to a former Hewlett-Packard man who brought in other people from HP to build the machine. Jobs became increasingly agitated over the shape it was taking but, because he did not have financial control of the company, could do nothing about it. His judgement was later proved correct: Lisa turned out to be an expensive fiasco. Meanwhile, he decided to build a computer that, as he saw it, would save Apple from itself. His colleagues agreed to let him have a go, and he started work on a machine he called the Macintosh. With the Macintosh project, Jobs was attempting to recapture those glorious days when he and Wozniak were alone, dreaming their dream, in a garage. 'The metaphysical garage,' he called the venture. He even moved the Mac group into its own 'garage', a building away from the rest of Apple, and fostered a culture in which the Mac people thought they were somehow divorced from the company that paid their salaries.

When the new computer was unveiled at the annual stockholders' meeting in January 1984 it was greeted with a standing ovation that lasted for a full five minutes. Jobs later called it the greatest day of his life. He said it was an intense experience – 'I think I know what it must be like to watch the birth of your child.' But the Macintosh did not create the revolution that the original Apple computer had done. The company eventually merged the Lisa division with the Macintosh division, and put Jobs in charge. But he couldn't change his style: he was simply not cut out to be the manager of a large enterprise in which people led normal lives. By the spring of 1985, Apple was about to announce its first quarterly loss ever, and the board of directors decided that Jobs would have to leave. The power struggle lasted for three weeks. It was bitter and very public, and it ended in defeat for the man who had created the business.

Jobs was worth $150 million or so, and could easily have chosen to lead a life of leisure. He tried it for a while, reading and travelling. He toyed with the idea of going back to university, or even getting into politics. But he was only thirty, and he missed the challenge which Apple had provided – and he missed the work. Then, one day in late August 1985, he had lunch with Paul Berg, Stanford's Nobel Prize-winning biochemist. The conversation turned to the subject of recombinant DNA, on which he had been reading up. Why, he asked Berg, weren't scientists speeding up the lengthy, arduous DNA experiments by simulating them on a computer? Because, Berg replied, any hardware powerful enough to simulate such experiments cost close to $100,000; and the software didn't exist at all. Jobs immediately became enthused: he had to build the computer that Berg – and every other scientist and professor and student in America – was waiting for. He had a purpose again.

Within weeks of that lunch, Jobs was talking excitedly to the press about his new dream: to build the first personal computer specifically designed for universities – a machine for learning, a machine at least three times faster, ten times more powerful, than any personal computer ever made. Precise enough for science professors to re-create DNA experiments. Powerful enough to allow pre-med students to simulate the mechanics of the nervous system. Inexpensive enough for both students and professors to buy them 'by the millions'.

He put up $7 million of his own money, hired people who had worked with him at Apple and who had left when he did, and launched a new company, called NeXT Inc. He rented office space: small, cramped quarters at first – 'to get back to the purity of the garage' – and then larger offices as NeXT grew. 'We are going to take the technology to the next level,' he told an interviewer in 1986.

It is still too early to tell whether the venture will succeed. Jobs has also bought a controlling interest in another company, Pixar, the computer graphics division of George Lucas's Lucasfilm. As chairman, he is overseeing the development of the Pixar, a machine that he says will generate some of the world's finest photographic-quality computer images. Jobs, typically, envisions yet another machine that will change the world. Doctors will use the Pixar to read CAT scans; engineers for computer-aided design; and oil companies for analysing seismic soundings. Even defence contractors, interpreting data beamed from satellites, will, Jobs hopes, find the Pixar indispensable.

There are, of course, plenty of people who would like to see him fail. Men like Jobs invariably make enemies – partly because of their behaviour but also because there is a natural tendency to envy those who make a lot of money early in life. Time will tell whether the management of Apple was right to drop him, but one can't help admiring his enthusiasm and dedication to whatever tasks he decided to tackle.

17

Edwin Land: inventor of the instant camera

William Davis

Dr Edwin Land is chiefly remembered as the inventor of the Polaroid camera, though he holds numerous other patents. He is both a gifted scientist and a shrewd businessman, a combination which has made him enormously wealthy.

Land's first product was a transparent plastic sheet capable of polarizing light – a type of light filter soon familiar to almost everyone in the form of sunglasses. His interest in the subject had begun when he was a seventeen-year-old freshman at Harvard; walking along Broadway in New York at night, it suddenly struck him that polarizing filters could eliminate head-light glare and thus reduce the hazards of night driving. He took leave of absence from the college and spent day after day in the New York Public Library, reading everything which might be relevant. At night he carried out experiments in a small laboratory he had set up in a rented room nearby. For the next three years college was forgotten, but when he patented his sheet polarizers Harvard not only welcomed him back but also offered him one of its laboratories. He spent the following three years there, but never got around to taking his degree: the 'Dr' attached to his name is strictly honorific.

In 1937, at the age of twenty-eight, he launched the Polaroid Coporation with the help of a group of Wall Street financiers who relished the prospect of putting his filters on every car headlight and windshield in the country. He made such an impression on them that they left Land with a majority of the voting stock and placed him in complete control of the company for ten years. But Detroit turned Polaroid down, and he had to find other uses for his invention. During World War II the company was kept busy manufac-turing lenses and gunsights for the military, but Land also spent a great deal of time in his lab trying to invent an 'instant camera'.

He later said that it was his small daughter who provided the inspiration. When he was taking pictures of her on a family holiday she asked impa-tiently how soon she could see them; he explained that it took time to get

From *The Innovators* by William Davis, copyright The White Rabbit Ltd and William Davis, published by Ebury Press, London (1987), pp. 225–7.

them developed, and then thought about what he had said. There was something basically wrong with photography if people had to wait hours, or even days, to see a picture. He started to experiment with ways of getting a finished picture directly out of the camera that took it. By 1947 he had come up with the answer, and his new sixty-second camera went on the market in the summer of 1948.

The trade was sceptical, but the public liked it. Land had the good sense to hire an outstanding general manager, J. Harold Booth, who had a great talent for promotion. He conceived the plan of offering one department store in each major city an exclusive on the product for thirty years, provided it would advertise prominently in local newspapers and give the camera intense promotion throughout the store. When it went on sale for the first time, at Jordan Marsh, the big Boston department store, it was an instant hit. Booth subsequently opened a dazzling promotion in Miami, supplying a squad of pretty girls and lifeguards with Land cameras to snap pictures at pools and beaches and give them away to astonished tourists. Within a few weeks most Miami stores had sold out their stocks – and the tourists went back home to show off their new toys. Every owner became, in effect, a Polaroid salesman.

Land later developed a simple system for instant colour photography and produced all kinds of other ideas: by 1980 he had more than four hundred patents in his own name. He played a key role in the development of cameras which can take pictures at high altitude; the cameras used in the famous U-2 espionage project, and those which detected the Soviet missiles in Cuba, were his.

Land has always maintained that the ability to create and invent was not rare; in his opinion, it was commonplace but generally uncultivated. 'My whole life', he once said, 'has been spent trying to teach people that intense concentration for hour after hour can bring out resources in people that they didn't know they had.'

18

Alastair Pilkington: inventor of float glass

William Davis

Sir Alastair Pilkington – he was honoured with a knighthood in 1970 – invented the 'float' method of glass-making which revolutionized the industry in the 1960s. He had the idea in the early 1950s, allegedly while washing up: the sight of a plate floating on water, it is said, made him think that the same principle could be applied to the manufacture of glass. But it took seven years of hard work to prove that he was right, and the cost of developing the process brought his employers close to financial ruin. Although it was announced to the public in 1959, it was not until 1962–3 that it became uninterruptedly profitable. Since then it has made a vast amount of money for Pilkington Brothers: income from licensing and technical fees is running at a rate of £30 million (about $50 million) a year.

Alastair Pilkington was educated at Sherborne School and Trinity College, Cambridge. He became an officer in the Royal Artillery just before the outbreak of World War II, and later fought in the Mediterranean, where he was taken prisoner after the fall of Crete. When the war ended, he returned to Cambridge and gained a degree in mechanical science. He joined Pilkington Brothers (there was no family connection) as a technical officer in 1947.

When he started work on his process, the target was to make, more economically, the high-quality glass essential for shop windows, cars, mirrors and other applications where distortion-free glass was necessary. At that time this quality of glass could only be made by the costly and wasteful plate process, of which Pilkington Brothers had also been the innovator. Because there was glass-to-roller contact, surfaces were marked. They had to be ground and polished to produce the parallel surfaces which bring optical perfection in the finished product. Sheet glass – glass made by drawing it vertically in a ribbon from a furnace – was cheaper than polished plate glass because it was not ground or polished, but it was unacceptable for high-quality applications because the produc-

From *The Innovators* by William Davis, copyright The White Rabbit Ltd and William Davis, published by Ebury Press, London (1987), pp. 298–301

tion method imparted some distortion. It was suitable for domestic and horticultural glazing, but could not replace polished plate. Many people in the glass industry had dreamed of combining the best features of both processes. They wanted to make glass with the brilliant surfaces of sheet glass and the flat and parallel surfaces of polished plate. Float glass proved to be the answer.

In the process, a continuous ribbon of glass moves out of the melting furnace and floats along the surface of a bath of molten tin. The ribbon is held at a high enough temperature over a long enough time for the irregularities to melt and for the surfaces to become flat and parallel: because the surface of the molten tin is flat, the glass also becomes flat. The ribbon is then cooled down while still on the molten tin, until the surfaces are hard enough for it to be taken out of the bath without rollers marking the bottom surface: so a glass of uniform thickness and with bright, fire-polished surfaces is produced without the need for grinding and polishing.

Alastair Pilkington encountered numerous setbacks during his seven years of hard labour. People, he recalls, kept asking him: 'When will you succeed?' All he could say was: 'We will know the answer to that only when we have succeeded.' The cost was far higher than anyone had bargained for, and it took considerable courage for the board of directors to go on supporting him. When he finally made it, they decided to license the process, chiefly to get some income but also in order to ensure that others would not find it worthwhile to research their own technology. The first foreign licence went to the Pittsburgh Plate Glass Company in 1962, and this was quickly followed by manufacturers in Europe, Japan, Czechoslovakia, the Soviet Union and others in the USA. Today the float glass process is licensed to thirty-five companies in twenty-nine countries and the Pilkington Group itself operates fourteen plants – six in North America, three in Britain, three in Germany, one in Sweden and one in South Africa.

Under the licensing arrangement the group gets a disclosure fee, a once-and-for-all payment for each float glass plant put down, and a royalty on sales. An improvements clause which gives all manufacturers an incentive to undertake development work is built into the licence. Any improvements made by Pilkington go automatically and freely to all licensees, but any patented improvements made by any of them can be sold to other licensees – with the exception of Pilkington, who receive it free.

Pilkington glass is used in everything from shop windows to skyscrapers. The company is the world leader in supplying windshields to jet aircraft, from Boeing's fleet to the most advanced jet fighter planes. Elsewhere in aviation its glass is used as a heatproof shield for generations of guided missiles, which puts it in the forefront of Star Wars research. It also provides submarine periscopes and the glass for NATO's Challenger tank. It makes 20 per cent of all the spectacle lenses in the world. One in five of all the cars made in the world use Pilkington glass, and the company is now developing a range of glass auto components, from engine parts to body panels, which are so tough and shatter-proof that within the next decade they could replace much of the steel used in the industry.

Alastair Pilkington's endeavours, all those years ago, *could* have led to disaster. But his persistence paid off. It is one of the most remarkable success stories in British industry.

19

Clive Sinclair: the innovator who lacked business flair

William Davis

Sir Clive Sinclair – he got his knighthood in 1983 – is a classic example of the inventor who has good ideas but who cannot match technical innovation with business acumen. His career has been marked by an extraordinary series of ups and downs.

Born in London, he left school at seventeen. His mother wanted him to go to university and become an academic, but Clive was far more interested in emulating his father, who ran his own business. He wasn't sure what he wanted to buy and sell, but he was keen on electronics and liked the notion of inventing new products. He had no capital, so he got himself a job as a technical journalist, which he reckoned would give him the opportunity to study the market and ask a lot of questions. He worked for *Practical Wireless* and wrote small handbooks for the electronics hobbyist. Later he said that in the process he learned more about his subjects 'than anyone who ever read the things'.

In 1962 he founded a company called Sinclair Radionics to sell amplifier kits by mail order. He designed the product (a radio amplifier), ordered the parts, and placed half-page ads in the specialist magazines, hoping that by the time he had to pay for the parts he would have enough orders to pay his suppliers. It worked, and he added hi-fis to his list.

His primary interest, though, was still in innovation. A friend agreed to look after the mail order side, and this helped to persuade Sinclair that he should concentrate on inventing and subcontract everything else. It meant a considerable saving in time and capital, but it also put him at the mercy of his subcontractors, which gave him a lot of problems as the business developed.

In 1972 he launched a cheap pocket calculator and soon became the UK market leader. From there he went on to digital watches and the world's first pocket television set. He also devised new digital metering equipment. All these projects encountered difficulties, and Sinclair Radionics slipped into the red. He was bailed out by the government-sponsored National

From *The Innovators* by William Davis, copyright The White Rabbit Ltd and William Davis, published by Ebury Press, London (1987), pp. 349–53

Enterprise Board, but Sinclair did not get on with the Board's officials – they disagreed about which way the company should go – and in 1979 there was a formal parting of the ways.

Sinclair set up another company, called Sinclair Research, and brought out an inexpensive computer. The following year he produced one that cost even less – the highly successful ZX81 – and sold more than a million, worldwide, in the first eighteen months. This was followed by the equally successful Spectrum, and the more sophisticated QL. Sinclair also launched the latest version of his mini-TV, the Microvision.

But again things started to go wrong. His licensing agreement with Timex for the North American market ran into problems and was cancelled. In Britain, customers started to complain about over-long delays in meeting orders already paid for, and the company got a lot of bad publicity. Sinclair was characteristically frank. 'We are', he said, 'in the business of innovating. We're not proud of our delays and we're not at all happy that we've let people down. But as bad as we got it, we're probably better than the competition.' Inevitably, though, business was hit and in 1985 Sinclair also had to cope with a sudden downturn in the home computer market. His response was yet another innovation – the C5 electric trike, which he called a 'car' and which he said would transform in-town motoring.

The electric car was not a new idea. General Motors had tried one but couldn't make it work economically enough, and of course every golfer was familiar with battery-operated carts. Sinclair's trike was an open-topped three-wheeler with no reverse gear. Its top speed was fifteen miles an hour, it needed pedals to go up hills, and it had room for just one person. But it was cheap and Sinclair thought he had a winner. He sold some of his shares in the company to raise money for the project and engaged a subcontractor, Hoover, in Merthyr Tydfil. The public, however, was distinctly unenthusiastic. Only eight thousand C5s were sold in the first three months, leaving so many in stock that production had to be cut back. Sinclair conceded that he had misjudged the market. 'People', he said, 'are much more resistant to change than I imagined.' In 1986, following staggering losses, he was forced to sell his once-thriving computer range (and his name) to arch-rival Amstrad for a paltry £5 million. But Sinclair has a remarkable capacity for coping with the most daunting setbacks. He formed a new business, the Cambridge Computer Company, and early in 1987 he launched his latest invention, the Z88, which he described as 'the first truly portable and completely comprehensive personal computer'. He also revealed that he was working on several other ideas, including a cheap portable telephone and a revolutionary wafer-scale integrated circuit which, he said, was 'potentially worth hundreds of millions of pounds'.

Sinclair's basic approach, over the years, has been to identify what people want but still can't afford: he then tries to create a product which they *can* afford. But, of course, he has not been alone in this. The NEB felt he could not stay in consumer electronics in competition with the Japanese, and one can well understand why it should have been sceptical. Creative genius is not enough: one needs volume to keep prices down, and that requires formidable skills in sales and marketing. Sinclair badly damaged his credibility by announcing innovations before they were available. He says that he did so because 'it helps to attract talent for work on the project'. But that is an attitude more suited to an inventor than to a businessman trying to serve a mass market. He has always felt that he has to move on – to keep ahead of the rest of the field. But there are obvious dangers in expanding in too many directions at the same time, especially if you are heavily dependent on the contribution of others.

Sinclair likes to work with a relatively small team of bright people who share his enthusiasms, and to remain as flexible as he can. He doesn't care for the details of management, and he is impatient. He accepts that he can't be right all the time, but reckons that making mistakes now and then is very much part of the game. He would undoubtedly be far wealthier if he had been more cautious, but he insists that money is not very important to him – 'It's just another tool.'

One of his favourite topics of conversation is the so-called fifth-generation computer, a machine that thinks and could ultimately become more intelligent than man. In 1984 he told the US Congressional Clearing House of the Future:

> I think it certain that in decades, not centuries, machines of silicon will arise first to rival and then surpass their human progenitors. Once they surpass us they will be capable of their own design. In a real sense they will be reproductive. Silicon will have ended carbon's long monopoly. And ours, too, I suppose, for we will no longer be able to deem ourselves the finest intelligence in the known universe. In principle it could be stopped; there will be those that try, but it will happen none the less. The lid of Pandora's Box is starting to open.

He has also lectured on the subject as a visiting professor at London's Imperial College, and would clearly love to be the man who makes it all happen. But he is not the only one: numerous rival teams are working on the concept, and many have far greater resources than he does.

20

Anita Roddick: adventurer

Interviewed by Ronnie Lessem

All our early recipes were natural and earthy including seaweed, nettles, orchids, henna ... Our shops are like a cross between a chemistry set and a toyshop. You can try anything ...

Anita Roddick, Director, Body Shop

I've always worked terribly hard. From the age of ten, when my father died, there was no alternative but to work for survival and that never leaves one. My parents were Italian immigrants to this country. My father had been interned, during the war, and we children were sent to a Catholic school. Being foreign set us apart.

My mother ran a restaurant café in a coastal resort in Sussex. The cafés in the fifties played the part of modern youth clubs. In fact, before he died, my father had installed the first juke box in a café in this area. I used to change the decor about to make the atmosphere in the café more pleasant. I loved playing about with the display, especially in the soda fountain bar. It was great theatre. In retrospect, this background must have done me an enormous amount of good.

After school I went on to college. I was training to be a teacher. The same showground. During the holidays I used to work at Butlins, from six in the morning to twelve at night, to earn more money. I seem to have inexhaustible energy.

At college I had this extraordinary lecturer in aesthetics. He showed us ways of presentation, of understatement and overstatement. I went on to teach history, and was lucky to have this amazingly free-thinking headmaster. He let me do anything. I created my own special classroom atmosphere evoking the subject we were covering with the music and visual art forms of the period. The kids became totally involved.

So I did well as a teacher – it's all theatre, you know, all acting – but I wanted to go to Geneva, and work for the United Nations. I had such gall in those days that I just appeared on their doorstep and got a job in the women's section of the International Labour Organisation. Having made lots of money, tax free, I decided to travel around the world, to North Africa, India, Australia, South America and Polynesia. What preoccupied

Adapted from R. Lessem, *Intrapreneurship* (Aldershot: Gower, 1987), pp. 148–54 me was the local women's skin. In those hot places it should have been dry and crèpy, but it was like satin. In Tahiti, for instance, it didn't take me long to work out why. Women rubbed their bodies with a lump of stuff that looked like lard. It was cocoa butter. In Morocco women were washing their gorgeous silky hair in mud. In Mexico, I saw a mother treat her child's burn by snapping off a cactus leaf and applying the slimy juice – aloes – to his skin. When I returned to England I started looking around for these natural products. I had no luck, and my interest waned.

In the meantime, in exotic Littlehampton, I had met my husband to be, Gordon, who had been an agricultural student in Scotland. We set off to start up a pineapple plantation in Australia, but decided to get married in San Francisco instead. We came back to Sussex, bought an old Victorian pile and converted it into a hotel. Our combined Scottish and Italian work ethic soon got things going. A restaurant we took on did good business too. The combination of rock music and lasagne went down well with the locals.

But we began to get tired of the hotel and restaurant business after a while. What with two children and the work till midnight, it became exhausting. Gordon decided that he wanted to ride a horse across the South American desert for a year, and I thought I'd do something with more regular hours, like open a shop. Then a whole lot of threads came together, all at once.

I'd been over to the States for a short while and noticed all over the country car repair places called 'Body Shop'. The name struck me as odd. Then I remembered, after returning from America, going into a green-grocer, a sweet shop, a department store: I could get a choice of quantity of applies, of vegetables, confectionery, and so on, but not of skin lotions, or cosmetics. Wouldn't it be lovely, I thought to myself, if I could go into a place, without feeling intimidated, and get something, in whatever size I wanted, for my skin. I remembered the women in Morocco and Tahiti and the natural ingredients they used, and planned on opening our first shop.

All the success that we subsequently reaped stemmed from the same source. We had no money. I had gone to the bank bursting with enthusiasm. But the manager obviously wasn't impressed by this fresh faced young woman in jeans, carrying a baby on her back. They turned down my request for a loan. Eventually we raised £4000, but that was hardly anything. So the ideas of re-fill containers, no packaging, and subsequently franchising, arose because we had virtually no finance. Had I been given £30 000 I'd probably have sought the advice of some design and packaging consultants, and come up with the usual sort of thing. When you don't know about something you get frightened, and you listen to business advice, even if it goes against your social principles.

Anyway, I opened this first 'Body Shop' in Brighton. The name was evocative, quite risqué in the early seventies. We set up shop next to a funeral parlour and had the solicitors after us forthwith. That got into the Press and gave us some good PR. But it wasn't easy to start with. Gordon took off on his desert trip and didn't come back till his horse fell off a cliff.

By then I'd opened a second shop, and people were clamouring for new shops.

I knew exactly the ingredients I wanted to develop for my range, but knew nothing about how to make them up. I tried all the big contract manufacturers and supply houses of cosmetics, and they weren't in the slightest interested. I went to them saying, 'I've got this wonderful idea, can I have two gallons of lotion with cocoa butter in it? Just as it is please, no packaging.' Of course they weren't interested. Packaging is where they make all their money. So I had to do it myself.

In fact the greatest buzz for me has been developing new products. But, having been rejected by the majors, I had to find someone to make them. Not knowing where else to go I looked for a herbal cosmeticist locally. I found one, in the area, willing to make what I wanted. I was over the moon. And then I came across my protégé. A young herbalist rang up after he'd heard about me. He is, like me, a committed ecologist. He's produced some incredible stuff for me over the years. It's fun. Such fun.

The timing of everything, when we started in March 1976, was perfect. Many people had become frightened by recent chemical scare stories. There was a great swing towards health foods, and people were beginning to become more concerned about the environment. The development of jojoba plant-based products, for example, was in direct response to calls to save the endangered sperm whale. All our early recipes were natural and earthy including seaweed, nettles, orchids, henna and so on. People came back again and again. Our shops are like a cross between a chemistry set and a toy shop. You can try anything, mix your own perfumes, play around and have fun.

When Gordon came back, after I had opened our second shop, we decided to go into franchising. Potential franchisees were queuing at the door. In any case, we didn't have the money to finance ourselves. To open up a shop in a prime site on the high street now will cost you £80 000. That's a huge bite into your resources. Franchising is also a fantastic motivator. In retailing the biggest problem is staff. Yet when people run their own business they discover hitherto untapped energies.

We now have 54 franchised outlets in Britain, and 56 abroad. Girls who started here as assistants, or on the stalls in Camden market, now have their own business, turning over a million pounds a year. To see it now is my pat on the back. When, in 1984, we got our placing on the Unlisted Security Market, people expected us to feel an incredible achievement. Certainly we felt, by then, that we had made it financially. But I get my real sense of achievement out of seeing these women running their own successful businesses. It's easy for people who have the money, but a lot of our women started with as little as I did. In the old days it was very inexpensive to buy in. And even today we have a system where the bank guarantees 50 per cent of the start-up capital.

Only 7 of our 110 shops are owned by us. Our most popular locations abroad are Canada, Finland and Sweden. We produce something like 300 different products, notably hair shampoos, hair conditioners, skin creams, cleansers, oils, lotions, soaps and perfumes. We are essentially in the business of skin and hair care. Our target market is women of 18–35, but the range is expanding all the time. None of our creams is priced at more than £3.00, so we are accessible to all. I look after product development, shop design, publicity, marketing and staff, while Gordon looks after the finance and administration. Our turnover is currently running at about £5 million, with an anticipated pre-tax profit of nearly £1 million.

As far as the cosmetics industry is concerned, we have broken just about every rule in the book. We've never marketed hope. We've never packaged. We've never advertised. We're not controlled by design groups. We're the only company who offer six sizes of one product, who refills, the only ones who offer a choice of mud, herbal and conventional shampoos.

Our herbalists will come out of the laboratories to talk to the customers and the assistants are trained on how the products are made and on their suitability for the individual's needs. I continue to develop new products via my travels to overseas countries. Wherever I go I do a lecture on cosmetics, in a hall, or in the marketplace. I then turn the talk inside out and get information from my audience. I find out about their birth and death rituals. Extraordinary folkloric information. They fill in question-naires for me on how their mothers or grandmothers wash their hair, and that kind of thing. I look for old recipes, and then go to Kew, or write to their university, to find out more about them. I get more detail on a particular material or crop. That way we amass an amazingly comprehensive collection of indigenous recipes. Often I get them substantiated by scientific data, because that's what some people want.

A year ago I wrote to Quaker Oats in Chicago. We use lots of oats in our products. I asked them whether they have developed cosmetic uses for oatmeal. They sent me information on Oatpro, a by-product of theirs, which can be used for eye make up. We've now converted it into liquid foundation. It spurred me on to writing to the Milk Marketing Board. There are these milk mountains, and people want milk baths. But the Board came up with nothing, so we'll have to develop a product ourselves.

Aside from developing new products, I've always enjoyed the momentum of the High Street. There's a constant coming and going. You cannot stand still. The basic house in which you accommodate your product changes. The products don't. I love that change area. There's a buzz. I also love knowing that we have unique and individual strengths. Who else has a perfume bar where you can try things out, and even mix your own products? I've learnt a lot about window display, and we're improving all the time. It's also important to educate your customers, in one or two sentences!

We'll always be adding new products. The problem is deciding which ones to drop. We're influenced by current developments. Our now famous peppermint foot lotion was produced after meeting sponsors of the London Marathon who expressed a hope that something could be formulated for bruised, sweating and aching feet! The elderflower eye gel was a direct response to pleas from girls operating computer terminals who were suffering from eye strain. But we draw a line at anything that doesn't involve skin or hair care. After all, we're so good at what we're doing, why should we go elsewhere? We're not tempted to diversify.

But we're going to open many more shops. We control them extremely well. There's going to be incredible growth in Europe. Germany is bizarre! It's absolutely biting. That's going to be a huge market. We should have 30–40 shops in Scandinavia over the next two years. Once we have 20 shops in a country we contract out the manufacturing. At the moment most of the manufacture of our products in England is also sub-contracted out.

The other thing we want to do in the near future is to establish a training school. Our sales are only as good as our girls. We're converting part of our Marlborough Road store into a training establishment, where we'll bring in lecturers on merchandising and motivation, as well as top herbalists, masseurs, and make-up artists. You sell by having the knowledge. If it works we'll want to open the place up to the schools.

At the moment, we are in the process of producing for schools, an information project pack on the cosmetics industry – exploding the myths, current and historical data, employment in the industry, opening areas for class discussion, all aspects of this vibrant industry. When that pack and 'The Body Shop Book' are completed we'll really have something!

Finally there's the proposed massage school. I believe absolutely in the healing power of touch. Massage is the one way you can instantly relieve stress. They should be using it in mental institutions and hospitals.

I opened up as an alternative business. The wealthy have choice, but other people often don't. I like to think of my customers as if they were one-parent families. Those are the people we opened our shop for. Now that we have gained financial security, we want to give something back to society.

SECTION 6

PROCESSES INTO PRODUCTS

21

Masters of innovation: how 3M keeps its new products coming

Russell Mitchell

It was 1922. Minnesota Mining & Manufacturing inventor Francis G. Okie was dreaming up ways to boost sales of sandpaper, then the company's premiere product, when a novel thought struck him. Why not sell sandpaper to men as a replacement for razor blades? Why would they risk the nicks of a sharp instrument when they could rub their cheeks smooth instead?

The idea never caught on, of course. The surprise is that Okie, who continued to sand his own face, could champion such a patently wacky scheme and keep his job. But unlike most companies then – or now – 3M Co. demonstrated a wide tolerance for new ideas, believing that unfettered creative thinking would pay off in the end. Indeed, Okie's hits made up for his misses: he developed a waterproof sandpaper that became a staple of the auto industry because it produced a better exterior finish and created less dust than conventional papers. It was 3M's first blockbuster.

Through the decades, 3M has managed to keep its creative spirit alive. The result is a company that spins out new products faster and better than just about anyone. It boasts an impressive catalog of more than 60,000 products, from Post-it notes to heart–lung machines. What's more, 32% of 3M's $10.6 billion in 1988 sales came from products introduced within the past five years. Antistatic videotape, translucent dental braces, synthetic ligaments for damaged knees, and heavy-duty reflective sheeting for construction-site signs are just a few of the highly profitable new products that contributed to record earnings of $1.15 billion in 1988.

At a time when many big US corporations are trying to untangle themselves from bureaucracy, 3M stands apart as a smooth-running innovation machine. Along with a handful of other companies that might be called the Innovation Elite – Merck, Hewlett-Packard, and Rubbermaid among them

– 3M is celebrated year after year in the rankings of most-respected companies. Business schools across the country make 3M a case study in new-product development, and management gurus trumpet 3M's methods. Peter Drucker's *Innovation and Entrepreneurship* is peppered with 3M tales. A star of the bestseller *In Search of Excellence*, 3M remains a favorite of co-author Thomas J. Peters. 'It is far more entrepreneurial than any $10 billion company I've come across,' he says, 'and probably more entrepreneurial than a majority of those one-tenth its size.'

The publicity has attracted representatives of dozens of companies from around the world to tour 3M headquarters near St. Paul, Minn., in search of ideas and inspiration. While such companies as Monsanto Co. and United Technologies Corp. have adopted some of 3M's methods, it's hard to emulate a culture that has been percolating since the turn of the century.

Lose some

So how does 3M do it? One way is to encourage inventive zealots like Francis Okie. The business of innovation can be a numbers game – the more tries, the more likely there will be hits. The scarcity of corporate rules at 3M leaves room for plenty of experimentation – and failure. Okie's failure is as legendary among 3Mers as his blockbuster. Salaries and promotions are tied to the successful shepherding of new products from inception to commercialization. One big carrot: the fanatical 3Mer who champions a new product out the door then gets the chance to manage it as if it were his or her own business.

Since the bias is toward creating new products, anything that gets in the way, whether it's turf fights, overplanning, or the 'not-invented-here' syndrome, is quickly stamped out. Divisions are kept small, on average about $200 million in sales, and they are expected to share knowledge and manpower. In fact, informal information-sharing sessions spring up willy-nilly at 3M – in the scores of laboratories and small meeting rooms or in the hallways. And it's not unusual for customers to be involved in these brainstorming klatches.

Peer review

That's not to say that corporate restraint is non-existent. 3Mers tend to be self-policing. Sure, there are financial measures that a new-product team must meet to proceed to different stages of development, but the real control lies in constant peer review and feedback.

The cultural rules work – and go a long way toward explaining why an old-line manufacturing company, whose base products are sandpaper and tape, has become a master at innovation. And a highly profitable one at that. Earnings spurted 25% in 1988 from a year earlier. It wasn't always so. The company hit a rocky stretch in the early 1980s. But stepped-up research spending and some skillful cost-cutting by Chairman and Chief

Executive Allen F. Jacobson have revived all of 3M's critical financial ratios (see Figure 1).

A 3M lifer and Scotch-tape veteran, Jake Jacobson took over the top job in 1985 and laid out his J-35 program. That's J as in Jake, and 35 as in 35% cuts in labor and manufacturing costs – to be accomplished by 1990. 3M is well on its way to reaching those goals, and the push has already improved the bottom line. Last year return on capital climbed almost three points, to 27.6%, and return on equity had a similar rise, to 21.6%. Jacobson has clamped down on costs without harming his company's ability to churn out new products one whit.

Motley crew

3M was founded not by scientists or inventors but by a doctor, a lawyer, two railroad executives, and a meat-market manager. At the turn of the century the five Minnesotans bought a plot of heavily forested land on the frigid shores of Lake Superior, north-east of Duluth. They planned to mine corundum, an abrasive used by sandpaper manufacturers to make the paper scratchy. The five entrepreneurs drummed up new investors, bought machinery, hired workers, and started mining. Only then did they discover that their corundum, alas, wasn't corundum at all but a worthless mineral that the sandpaper industry wanted no part of.

The company tried selling its own sandpaper, using corundum shipped in from the East, but got battered by the competition. How perfect: the company that tolerates failure was founded on a colossal one. 3M was forced to innovate or die. Most of the original investors got swept out of the picture, and the remaining 3Mers set about inventing. First, the company introduced a popular abrasive cloth for metal finishing. Then Okie struck gold with his Wetordry sandpaper. They drew inspiration from William L. McKnight, who is revered to this day as the spiritual father of the company. He started out as an assistant bookkeeper and worked his way up through sales. His approach, unusual for its day, has stuck with the company. Rather than make his pitch to a company's purchasing agent, McKnight talked his way onto the factory floor to demonstrate his products to the workers who used them. After he became chairman and chief executive, he penned a manifesto that said, in part: 'If management is intolerant and destructively critical when mistakes are made, I think it kills initiative.'

Loyal lifers

That kind of thinking breeds loyalty and management stability. The company rarely hires from the outside, and never at the senior level. Jacobson, 62, a chemical engineer, started out in the tape lab in 1947. And all his lieutenants are lifers, too. The turnover rate among managers and other professionals averages less than 4%. 'It's just not possible to really under-

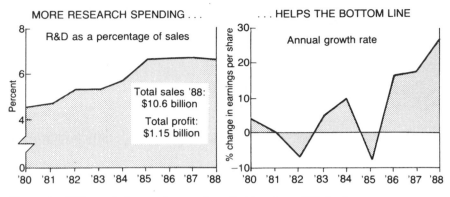

Figure 1   3M's push for products and profit (data from 3M Co.)

stand this company until you've been around for a long while,' says Jerry E. Robertson, head of the Life Sciences Sector.

Don't let 3M's dull exterior fool you. The St Paul campus, home of company headquarters and most of the research labs, is an expanse of brick buildings with a high-rise glass tower that could have been designed by a kid with an Erector set. But inside is an army of engineers and technical experts and platoons of marketers just raring to innovate.

Here's how it typically works: A 3Mer comes up with an idea for a new product. He or she forms an action team by recruiting full-time members from technical areas, manufacturing, marketing, sales, and maybe finance. The team designs the product and figures out how to produce and market it. Then it develops new uses and line extensions. All members of the team are promoted and get raises as the project goes from hurdle to hurdle. When sales grow to $5 million, for instance, the product's originator becomes a project manager, at $20 million to $30 million, a department manager, and in the $75 million range, a division manager. There's a separate track for scientists who don't want to manage.

Many paths

As a result, 3M is big but acts small. There are 42 divisions, so ladders to the top are all over the place. Jacobson reached the pinnacle by cleaning up old-line operations, while his predecessor, Lewis W. Lehr, invented a surgical tape and then rode the company's burgeoning health care business all the way to the chairman's post.

So what are the corporate guidelines? A prime one is the 25% rule, which requires that a quarter of a division's sales come from products introduced within the past five years. Meeting the 25% test is a crucial yardstick at bonus time, so managers take it seriously. When Robert J. Hershock took over the occupational health division in 1982, it was utterly dependent on an aging product category, disposable face masks. By 1985 his new-product percentage had deteriorated to a mere 12%.

Inspiration from the plant floor

When I worked as a tape slitter at 3M, we called them The Ties. They were the buttoned-up members of the 3M Co. quality control team who would occasionally venture onto the grimy factory floor.

'They were the bad guys,' says Leo Vernon, who runs a slitting machine that converts huge rolls of tape into the small ones you buy in the store. 'They used to tell you rather than listen to you, assuming they even spoke to you in the first place.' I worked alongside Vernon 15 years ago, running my own machine, slitting masking tape so I could come up with college tuition. 3M paid me well and, by the standards of the day, treated me well. But despite all the talk I had heard about 3M and innovation, nobody ever asked me for ideas on how to do my job better – least of all the guys from quality control.

That was 1973. Today, 3M's tape business is under assault from Japanese and European manufacturers. Over the years, while researchers at head-quarters in St Paul spewed out new products, innovation in 3M's factories lagged. By the early 1980s costs were out of control, and quality wasn't up to snuff. Productivity became a top priority for Chairman and CEO Allen F. Jacobson, who worked his way up through the tape division. By 1990, he aims to cut labor and manufacturing costs by 35% each.

On a roll

The edict forced major change at 3M's far-flung factories. At its tape plant in Bedford Park, a Chicago suburb, Vernon is in charge of his own quality now. 'The difference,' he says, 'is night and day.'

The manufacturing process has been completely overhauled. Tape is made by coating a backing with adhesive and creating a giant roll about the size of an office desk. These 'jumbos' are then taken to slitting machines. Until recently, all tape at the plant – masking tape, industrial tapes, closure tape for diapers – was coated in one area and transported for slitting to the other end of the factory. The coating and slitting functions had separate supervisors, and they didn't always communicate well. Production rates weren't coordinated, and hundreds of jumbos were stockpiled throughout the plant.

Now slitters are placed near the coaters, and management duties are determined by product line, not function – that is, a supervisor will be in charge of masking tape, not just coating or slitting. The new setup puts a lot more responsibility on the shoulders of individual workers. A slitting operator is expected to identify quality problems immediately so he or she can have the coater stopped after only two or three bad jumbos are produced, rather than the dozens botched in the past. As a result, inventory has been trimmed dramatically. And manufacturing time has improved by two-thirds.

The workers with whom I talked appreciate the new responsibilities. I had hated feeling like an automaton when I worked in the 3M plant, but it's an entirely different story these days for my former colleagues. They don't miss The Ties at all.

Employees from various disciplines discuss the design of a respirator

That set off alarms. He and his crew had to come up with plenty of new products – and they had to do it in 18 to 24 months, half the normal time. Using technology similar to the division's face-mask filters, Hershock's action teams created a bevy of products. One team came up with a sheet that drinks up the grease from microwaved bacon. Another devised a super-absorbent packing material that was widely welcomed by handlers of blood samples. The idea came from a team member who had read a newspaper article about postal workers who were panicked by the AIDS epidemic. The division's new-product sales are back above 25%.

Then there's the 15% rule. That one allows virtually anyone at the company to spend up to 15% of the workweek on anything he or she wants to, as long as it's product-related. The practice is called 'bootlegging,' and its most famous innovation is the ubiquitous yellow Post-it note. Arthur L. Fry's division was busy with other projects, so he invoked the 15% rule to create the adhesive for Post-its. The idea came out of Fry's desire to find a way to keep the bookmark from falling out of his hymn book. Post-its are now a major 3M consumer business with revenues estimated at as much as $300 million.

Cultural habits

A new-product venture isn't necessarily limited by a particular market's size, either. Take Scotch tape. It was invented in 1929 for an industrial customer who used it to seal insulation in an airtight shipping package. Who could have known that it would grow into an estimated $750 million business someday?

Post-its, demonstrated by 3M engineers Art Fry (left) and Spencer Silver, began life as a way to keep bookmarks from slipping out

Another recent example: the market for 3M chemist Tony F. Flannery's new product, a filter used to clean lubricants in metalworking shops, was a mere $1 million. But Flannery got the go-ahead to dabble with it anyway. He hooked up with a customer, PPG Industries Inc., which sells paint-primer systems to auto makers. The filters they were using to strain out impurities weren't doing the job. Flannery made prototypes of filter bags using a fibrous 3M material. They not only turned out to be bang-up primer filters, but the new bags are also being used to filter beer, water, edible oils, machine oil, and paint. Flannery figures that the filters could become a $20 million business in a few years.

Getting close to the customer is not just a goal at 3M – it's an ingrained cultural trait. Back in the 1920s, 3M inventor Richard G. Drew noticed that painters on automobile assembly lines had trouble keeping borders straight on the two-tone cars popular at the time. He went back to the lab and invented masking tape.

In-house grants

Even with 3M's emphasis on innovation, new ideas do fall through the cracks. In 1983 some employees complained that worthwhile projects were still going unnoticed despite the 15% rule. Guaranteed free time doesn't guarantee that there will be money to build a prototype. So the company created Genesis grants, which give researchers up to $50,000 to carry their projects past the idea stage. A panel of technical experts and scientists awards as many as 90 grants each year.

CORPORATE INNOVATORS: HOW THEY DO IT

3M Relies on a few simple rules . . .

Keep divisions small. Division managers must know each staffer's first name. When a division gets too big, perhaps reaching $250 to $300 million in sales, it is split up

Tolerate failure. By encouraging plenty of experimentation and risk-taking, there are more chances for a new-product hit. The goal: Divisions must derive 25% of sales from products introduced in the past five years. The target may be boosted to 30%

Motivate the champions. When a 3Mer comes up with a product idea, he or she recruits an action team to develop it. Salaries and promotions are tied to the product's progress. The champion has a chance to someday run his or her own product group or division

Stay close to the customer. Researchers, marketers, and managers visit with customers and routinely invite them to help brainstorm product ideas

Share the wealth. Technology, wherever it's developed, belongs to everyone

Don't kill a project. If an idea can't find a home in one of 3M's divisions, a staffer can devote 15% of his or her time to prove it is workable. For those who need seed money, as many as 90 Genesis grants of $50,000 are awarded each year

. . . While other companies have their own approaches

RUBBERMAID 30% of sales must come from products developed in the past five years. Looks for fresh design ideas anywhere; now trying to apply the Ford Taurus-style soft look to garbage cans. A recent success: stackable plastic outdoor chairs

HEWLETT-PACKARD Researchers urged to spend 10% of time on own pet projects; 24-hour access to labs and equipment; keeps divisions small to rally the kind of spirit that produces big winners such as its LaserJet laser printer

DOW CORNING Forms research partnerships with its customers to develop new products such as reformulations of Armor-All car polishes and Helene Curtis hair sprays

MERCK Gives researchers time and resources to pursue high-risk, high-payoff products. After a major scientific journal said work on anticholesterol agents like Mevacor would likely be fruitless, Merck kept at it. The drug is a potential blockbuster

GENERAL ELECTRIC Jointly develops products with customers. Its plastics unit created with BMW the first body panels made with thermoplastics for the carmaker's Z1 two-seater

JOHNSON & JOHNSON The freedom to fail is a built-in cultural prerogative. Lots of autonomous operating units spur innovations such as its Acuvue disposable contact lenses

BLACK & DECKER Turnaround built partly on new-product push. Advisory councils get ideas from customers. Some new hot sellers: the Cordless Screwdriver and ThunderVolt, a cordless powertool that packs enough punch for heavy-duty construction work

Data: company reports

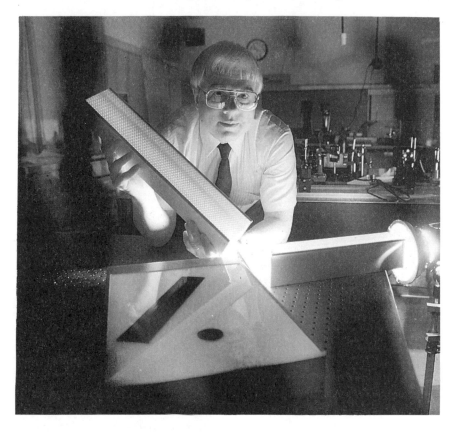

Sanford Cobb won an in-house grant to develop the use of plastic film in lighting – a profitable breakthrough

One recipient was Sanford Cobb, an optics specialist at 3M. In 1983 a bulb went on in his head at a scientific conference when he ran across something called light pipe technology. Plastic is inlaid with nearly microscopic prisms so it can reflect light for long distances with little loss of energy.

Cobb knew the heavy acrylic used in the original invention was impractical because it would be difficult to mold, but he figured he could use 3M technology to make a light pipe out of a flexible plastic film. Because 3M isn't in the lighting business, though, Cobb couldn't find a division manager willing to fork over prototype money. So he applied for a Genesis grant. He got it, and made his idea work.

City lights

3M licensed the basic technology from the inventor, and now its light pipes are used in products offered by several divisions. One use is in large highway signs. The new ones feature two 400-watt bulbs, replacing 60 to 70 fluorescent tubes. Manufacturers of explosives use light pipes to illuminate their most volatile areas. And the top of One Liberty Plaza, the new office tower dominating Philadelphia's skyline, is decorated with a light-piping design. Cobb's development is part of a major new technology program at 3M, with potential annual revenues amounting to hundreds of millions of dollars.

It's a surprise, given 3M's strong predilection toward divisional auton-omy, that its technology gets spread around. But 3M is a company of backscratchers, eager to help fellow employees in the knowledge that they'll get help when they need it in return. For example, when the non-woven-fiber experts got together with the lab folks at abrasives, the result was Scotch-Brite scrubbing sponges. A Technology Council made up of researchers from the various divisions regularly gets together to exchange information.

The result of all this interconnection is an organic system in which the whole really is greater than the sum of its parts. It's no coincidence that 3M is never mentioned as a possible breakup candidate. Bust it apart, sever the interconnections, and 3M's energy would likely die. Even if a raider decided to leave it intact, an unfamiliar hand at the helm might send the company off course. The possibility of a raid on 3M was taken a bit more seriously in the early 1980s, when financial performance slipped as the result of a strong dollar and skimping on R & D in the 1970s.

Jacobson's cost-cutting has done wonders for 3M. But his next challenge is formidable. The company's fortunes tend to track the domestic econ-omy, so with a slowdown on the horizon, he must now find ways to spur growth. For one, he wants to expand internationally, boosting overseas sales from 42% of revenues to 50% by 1992. It may be slow going, how-ever. Just as Jacobson was about to win a beachhead for a plethora of 3M products by buying the sponge unit of France's Chargeurs, the French government blocked the sale on antitrust grounds.

Jacobson is also starting to insist that 3M's divisions develop bigger-ticket products. The company has been taking core technologies and com-ing up with hundreds of variations. But those market niches can be pretty skinny – often only a few million dollars or so. Now the company's strate-gists are focusing on 45 new product areas, each with $50 million in annual sales potential three to five years out. One example: a staple gun that replaces pins for broken bones. A 50% new-product success rate would contribute $1.2 billion in sales by 1994 from this program alone.

Sincere flattery

Jacobson's latest achievements have yet to be reflected in 3M's stock price, which has been hovering in the 60s since the 1987 crash. Analysts are concerned that despite the company's diversification into health care, it still makes about 40% of its sales to the industrial sector, so it could get socked in a recession. And 3M is still considered vulnerable in floppy disks and videotape and related media, which account for about $800 million in sales. The unit has been locked in a bruising battle with the Japanese for years, and lost an estimated $50 million in 1987. While those products finally became profitable in last year's fourth quarter as a result of cost-cutting and wider distribution, the area could remain a trouble spot. 'It's a fragile turnaround,' says analyst B. Alex Henderson at Prudential Bache Securities Inc.

Other companies would love to have 3M's problems if its successes came with them. Indeed, 3M constantly finds itself playing host to companies trying to figure out how to be more creative. Monsanto has set up a technology council modeled on 3M's, and United Technologies has embarked on an effort to share resources among its not-so-united operations. Eight years ago, Rubbermaid Inc. began insisting that 30% of its sales come from products developed in the previous five years.

While other companies may pick up ideas piecemeal from 3M, it would be impossible for any big corporation to swallow the concept whole. 'We were fortunate enough to get the philosophy in there before we started to grow, rather than trying to create it after we got big,' says Lester C. Krogh, who heads research and development. 3M has a simple formula: Find the Francis Okies and don't get in their way. But for managers of other companies, large and small, that's often easier said than done.

22

Baker Perkins: oddball convert

Christopher Lorenz

Michael Smith is a marketing man who for many years ran one heavy engineering company, Baker Perkins, and went on to head part of another: APV, the process machinery maker which merged with Baker Perkins in 1987. Smith is not the most likely enthusiast for industrial design. But ardent enthusiast he very definitely is.

Why does a manufacturer of machinery for baking, biscuit making, and – for many years – printing, use industrial designers *at all*, let alone give them a central role in the product development process? The products made on APV/Baker Perkins machines over the years have certainly been glamorous enough, from French croissants to glossy magazines, but the machines themselves have not been. So why did Smith and his cohorts of engineers and marketers become convinced that industrial designers were capable of strengthening the company's position so forcefully in world markets?

Baker Perkins' imaginative use of industrial designers first came to light in 1981, when Smith made a speech on quality and competitiveness at a major conference of top executives in London. To illustrate his case he took the example of his company's biscuit-cutting machines. The traditional ones had been very much geared to the home market: heavy and of solid construction. They were only occasionally sold overseas. But now, said Smith, Baker Perkins had a range of products which, despite being more expensive than their competitors, had gained a competitive edge in international markets because of superior performance. Its market share was growing and its margins were improving.

To enforce the company's golden rule that the product, not the organization, is paramount, Smith and his technical director, Charles McCaskie, had created product management teams to bring marketing, engineering, finance and manufacturing together to define and execute a product plan.

Then came the comments that really surprised Smith's audience:

> We gave the industrial designer a much greater role as the product planner, at a very early stage in the cycle. He no longer designed pretty guards to wrap our products in, but became the translator, the bridge, the catalyst. He turned the marketing specification of the product into reality before the design, the ma-

From Chapter 10 in C. Lorenz, *The Design Dimension* (Oxford: Basil Blackwell, 2nd edition, 1990), pp. 114–19

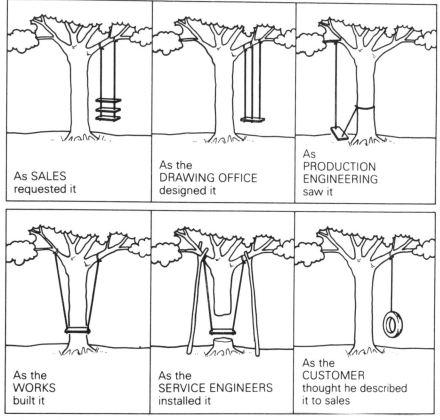

| As SALES requested it | As the DRAWING OFFICE designed it | As PRODUCTION ENGINEERING saw it |
| As the WORKS built it | As the SERVICE ENGINEERS installed it | As the CUSTOMER thought he described it to sales |

Mike Smith's secret weapon: the salutary tale of 'How not to design a swing, or the perils of poor coordination'

terials or the manufacturing methods had been established.

We now had a product range suitable for a world marketplace, with product quality the known responsibility of all the people involved. We had brought the marketplace into the factory. Product quality had beforehand probably had most to do with the field engineers, who kept dark secrets because no-one else wished to know.[1]

Without this organization, said Smith, Baker Perkins would have suffered from the notorious 'swing syndrome'. His set of slides, which gradually unveiled the perils of poor interdepartmental coordination, brought him considerable applause. Smith went on to recount how the company had produced a better product than its German and other competitors, with sales and market share to match.

Eighteen months after this first revelation of Baker Perkins' surprising commitment to industrial design, an even more graphic illustration emerged into public view: the story of its latest printing press, which at the time of Smith's speech had still been under development at the company's headquarters in Peterborough, 75 miles north of London.

The new press had emerged from a dilemma that had faced Baker Perkins as far back as 1976. At that time, its printing machinery division was selling just one type of web offset machine, known as the 'satellite' design. Its main competitor, Harris Corporation of the US, had backed an alternative type of design, the 'blanket-to-blanket' press. (Don't worry about the jargon, just enjoy the rich images it evokes.)

As 'blanket-to-blanket' technology improved, other competitors followed suit. So, especially in the US, where Baker Perkins was already well established, did the most rapidly growing and lucrative part of the market – not newspapers, with which the company had done considerable business, but the printers of magazines and brochures. As a result, the company had to scrap its range of half a dozen 'satellite' products, plus a major new development project. Instead, it embarked on a costly £2 million development programme designed to leapfrog the competition into the very top end of the 'blanket-to-blanket' market, with a machine that could print 32 pages at once, at a very high speed.

It was a bold, all-or-nothing step, and cost several times what Baker Perkins was used to; this is true even if one takes account of a 25 per cent grant from the British Government, which reduced the risk to measurable (though still uncomfortable) proportions.

Less than three years later, first orders for the new 'G16' machine were being delivered. This was in spite of all the intricacies of using computer-aided design and manufacture for the first time, and having to develop microelectronics expertise at a rapid rate of knots. The G16 went on to outsell the US competition, and to take about a fifth of the world market for these big machines, including 70 per cent of the North American market.

By late 1980, Smith, McCaskie and the management of their printing division had begun to get to grips with how to penetrate down-market with a slightly slower, 16-page machine. Not only were potential customers starting to invite them to do so, but they had to broaden the product range in order to reduce the division's vulnerability to a single product/market segment, and at the same time gain economies of scale from a range of modular products sharing as many common components as possible.

This is where the work of the industrial designers came in. It had been in the late 1960s, when he was working in the company's baking division, that McCaskie had hired his first industrial designer (from London's famous Royal College of Art). The job of the new arrival was essentially to do what McCaskie called 'clean-ups' on the machinery's casing. As McCaskie climbed the ladder – he was appointed technical director of the whole company in 1971 – industrial design grew with him. First the industrial designer was allowed to use his sketching ability to work on alternative product concepts, and then to go a stage further by making alternative models.

As McCaskie recalls, 'during this period we were developing marketing – and we realized that industrial designers also had a role to play'.[2] As more designers were recruited they became increasingly involved in specification setting. By 1980, when the specifications for the new press were first debated, they had become fully involved in the development process. This is now the standard pattern: together with a senior design engineer (the team leader) and a production engineer, one of the company's half-dozen designers forms the core of each product team. Marketing, sales and service provide input, and are involved in decision making, but are not part of the three-person core.

The industrial designer on both the printing press projects was Martyn Wray, a former church organ builder and subsequently a student at London's Central School for Art and Design. In a book about the work done for manufacturing industry by former Central graduates, Wray summarized the pivotal role of the industrial designer in modest fashion. He had particular responsibility for appearance, ergonomics, hygiene and safety, he wrote, and 'his sketching ability is also used as a link between members of the design team, other parts of the business and the customer'.[3]

McCaskie sees the industrial designer's role very much in terms of the classic comment that engineers are good at analysing, industrial designers at synthesizing. But he also goes much further, stressing the extreme importance of the designer as communicator: the communications skills of industrial designers are of an entirely different order of magnitude from those of the engineers, he says. Himself a mechanical engineer, he argues that engineers tend to focus on cogs, wheels and mechanical forces, rather than on the product as a whole.

It is not just engineers and marketing people who don't speak the same language, but also the design engineer and the production engineer. In McCaskie's words, 'a manufacturing guy doesn't understand the process of printing at one speed rather than another. It's not part of his culture.' Industrial designers are needed to help the two communicate.

On the second printing press project, christened the G14, Martyn Wray began synthesizing the analysis of his various colleagues (and adding some of his own) in early 1981, right from the start of the all-important specification phase. It was through specification writing that the industrial designers had really begun to be influential at Baker Perkins. To synthesize the specifications of marketing, engineering and production can be an appallingly difficult task, which is why many companies find that their new products are difficult and expensive to make. Or they prove easy to manufacture, but fail to meet consumer requirements. It is equally possible, as the 'swing syndrome' shows, that the various sides settle on a weak compromise which suits nobody.

During the specification phase of the G14 Wray played a key role in challenging the proposals of several specialists, including some which concerned the question of which market segments to go for, and therefore precisely which performance characteristics to specify. And during the subsequent 12 weeks, when the product team was trying to establish whether it would be possible to make the new press to the extremely tough cost targets which had been agreed (30 per cent cheaper than the G16, on a comparable basis), Wray's sketching ability proved vital in establishing a basis for the intricately detailed communication which had to take place between the various parties.

His imaginative proposal of several new concepts for certain components was also of considerable assistance in getting the cost down. Most engineers find it difficult to sketch (they're not trained to) and their lack of practice at applying their imagination often makes them miss even simple solutions.

And so the catalogue of industrial design virtues at Baker Perkins continues, right down to the 'bottom line': their ability to help shorten the product development cycle not just indirectly, by helping specialists communicate with each other, but also directly, by accomplishing through a few quickly done sketches what would take an engineering draughtsman weeks to do, even with the help of CADCAM. The entire development-to-delivery process of the G14 took only two years, a third less than it would have done in the late 1970s.

Added to this contribution was some more obvious but nevertheless important work on aesthetics and ergonomics, including requirements for easy field installation and maintenance, plus the resolution of some very tricky safety aspects to do with access to the top of the press.

The first G14 was installed in Chicago in early 1983, and within two years over 30 had been sold, including 200 printing units – which is a large number in the printing market. Along with continuing sales of G16, the success of the machine helped to quadruple turnover of the printing division to £40 million in 1984, and to boost profitability dramatically.

Following the Baker Perkins merger with APV, however, the printing division became something of an oddity, outside the enlarged group's main focus of process machinery for the food and beverage industries. As a result, the division was sold in 1989 to one of its main competitors, Rockwell International.

But some of the Baker Perkins industrial designers – still located at their original Peterborough base, though now within various of the APV group's operating companies – continued to work on a consultancy basis for the printing division under Rockwell. The successful development of a new printing press, which was launched in 1990 as the G-44, again owed much to the designers' involvement.

So, within APV, did two products also launched in 1990, a flaking roll for breakfast cereal production, and an innovative skinless sausage-making machine. In both cases, Martyn Wray was one of the industrial designers.

If a former church organ builder can play a crucial part in dismantling departmental barriers within a capital goods company, and can help it improve its commercial performance, then anything is possible. The common denominator is industrial design.

Notes

1   Smith, M.R.H., paper to National Conference on Quality and Competitiveness, London, November 1981. Reported in the *Financial Times*, 25 November 1981.
2   Interview with Charles McCaskie, Peterborough, October 1983.
3   Woudhuysen, J. (ed.) *Central to Design – Central to Industry*, London, 1982.

23

Selling to the world: the Sony Walkman story

Akio Morita

I came to realize from my earliest experience in trying to sell the tape recorder that marketing is really a form of communication. In the traditional Japanese system for distributing consumer products, the manufacturers are kept at arm's length from the consumer. Communication is all but impossible. There are primary, secondary, and even tertiary wholesalers dealing with some goods before they reach a retailer, layer after layer of middlemen in between the maker and the ultimate user of the product. This distribution system has some social value – it provides plenty of jobs – but it is costly and inefficient. At each layer the price has to go up, even though some of the middlemen may not even come in contact with the goods. The system is adequate for commodities and low-technology items, perhaps, but we realized from the beginning that it could not serve the needs of our company and its new, advanced technology products. Third or fourth parties simply could not have the same interest in or enthusiasm for our products and our ideas that we had. We had to educate our customers to the uses of our products. To do so we had to set up our own outlets and establish our own ways of getting goods into the market.

We were bringing out some products that had never been marketed before – never made before, actually, such as transistorized radios and solid-state personal television sets – and were beginning to get a reputation as a pioneer. In fact some people called us the 'guinea pig' of the electronics industry. We would produce a new product; the giants of the industry would wait to see if our product was successful; and then, if it was, they would rush a similar one onto the market to take advantage of our efforts. This is the way it has developed over the years; we have always had to be out in front. We have seen this in most of our major product developments, from small solid-state radios and transistorized TV sets (we built the very first one) up to today's portable stereo player, Walkman; our small hand-held flat television, Watchman; and our compact disc player, Discman. We introduced stereo into Japan. We built the world's very first video cassette recorder for home use; invented the Trinitron system, a new method of projecting a color image onto the TV tube; and we innovated the 3.5-inch computer floppy disk, which now has the highest storage capacity in the world for its size. We revolutionized television news gathering and broadcasting worldwide with our hand-held video cameras and small videotape players. We pioneered the filmless camera, Mavica, the compact disc system, and invented eight-millimeter video. That's only to name a few of the more easily recognizable things we have done.

In the beginning, when our track record for success was not established, our competitors would take a very cautious wait-and-see attitude while we marketed and developed a new product. In the early days, we would often have the market to ourselves for a year or more before the other companies would be convinced that the product would be a success. And we made a lot of money, having the market all to ourselves. But as we became more successful and our track record became clearer, the others waited a shorter and shorter time before jumping in. Now we barely get a three-month head start on some products before the others enter the market to compete with us with their own version of the product we innovated. (We were fortunate to get a whole year's lead on the portable compact disc player, Discman, and almost six months with the Walkman.) It is flattering in a way, but it is expensive. We have to keep a premium on innovation. For many years now we have put well over 6 per cent of sales into research and development, and some years as much as 10 per cent. Our plan is to lead the public with new products rather than ask them what kind of products they want. The public does not know what is possible, but we do. So instead of doing a lot of market research, we refine our thinking on a product and its use and try to create a market for it by educating and communicating with the public. Sometimes a product idea strikes me as a natural.

As an example, I can cite a product surely everybody knows of, the Walkman. The idea took shape when Ibuka came into my office one day with one of our portable stereo tape recorders and a pair of our standard-size headphones. He looked unhappy and complained about the weight of the system. I asked him what was on his mind and then he explained, 'I like to listen to music, but I don't want to disturb others. I can't sit there by my stereo all day. This is my solution – I take the music with me. But it's too heavy.'

I had been mulling an idea over in my mind for a while, and now it was coming into focus as Ibuka talked. I knew from my own experience at home that young people cannot seem to live without music. Almost everybody has stereo at home and in the car. In New York, even in Tokyo, I had seen people with big tape players and radios perched on their shoulders blaring out music. I remembered that one time when my daughter, Naoko, came home from a trip she ran upstairs before even greeting her mother and first put a cassette in her stereo. Ibuka's complaint set me into motion. I ordered our engineers to take one of our reliable small cassette tape recorders we called Pressman, strip out the recording circuit and the speaker, and replace them with a stereo amplifier. I outlined the other details I wanted, which included very lightweight headphones that turned out to be one of the most difficult parts of the Walkman project.

Everybody gave me a hard time. It seemed as though nobody liked the idea. At one of our product planning meetings, one of the engineers said, 'It sounds like a good idea, but will people buy it if it doesn't have recording capability? I don't think so.'

I said, 'Millions of people have bought car stereo without recording capability and I think millions will buy this machine.'

Nobody openly laughed at me, but I didn't seem to be convincing my own project team, although they reluctantly went along. I even dictated the selling price to suit a young person's pocketbook, even before we made the first machine. The Pressman monaural tape recorder was a relatively expensive unit, selling for forty-nine thousand yen in Japan, and I said I wanted the first models of our new stereo experiment to retail for no more than thirty thousand yen. The accountants protested but I persisted. I told them I was confident we would be making our new product in very large numbers and our cost would come down as volume climbed. They thought we should start from a cheaper base than the Pressman, but I chose the basic configuration of the Pressman because many parts for the Pressman were available worldwide at our service centers, and we knew the unit was reliable. Therefore we could start out without worrying that the thing would turn out to be a mechanical failure.

In a short time the first experimental unit with new, miniature headphones was delivered to me, and I was delighted with the small size of it and the high-quality sound the headphones produced. In conventional stereo with large loudspeakers, most of the energy used to produce the sound is wasted, because only a fraction of it goes to the listener's ears. The rest of the sound vibrates off the walls and the windows. Our tiny unit needed only a small trickle of battery power to the amplifier to drive the tiny lightweight headphones. The fidelity that came through the small headphones was as good or better than I expected. I rushed home with the first Walkman and was trying it out with different music when I noticed that my experiment was annoying my wife, who felt shut out. All right, I decided, we needed to make provision for two sets of headphones. The next week the production staff had produced another model with two headphone jacks.

A few days later I invited my golfing partner, the novelist Kaoru Shoji, for a game of golf, and as we settled down in the car for the ride to my club I handed him a set of headphones and started playing a tape. I put on the other set and watched his expression. He was surprised and delighted to hear his wife, Hiroko Nakamura, a concert pianist, playing the Grieg piano concerto. He smiled broadly and wanted to say something, but he couldn't because we were both hooked up to headsets. I recognized this as a potential problem. My solution was to have my staff add a button-activated microphone to the machine so the two people could talk to each other, over the music, on the 'hot line.'

I thought we had produced a terrific item, and I was full of enthusiasm for it, but our marketing people were unenthusiastic. They said it wouldn't sell, and it embarrassed me to be so excited about a product most others thought would be a dud. But I was so confident the product was viable that I said I would take personal responsibility for the project. I never had reason to regret it. The idea took hold and from the very beginning the Walkman was a runaway success. I never really liked the name Walkman, but it seems to have caught on everywhere. I was away on a trip when the name was chosen by some young people in our company, and when I got back I ordered them to change the name to something like Walking Stereo, or anything a bit more grammatical, but they said it was too late: the advertising had already been prepared and the units were being made with that name. Sony America and Sony UK feared they couldn't sell a product with an ungrammatical name like Walkman but we were stuck with it. We later tried other names overseas – Stow Away, in England, and Sound About in the United States – but they never caught on. Walkman did. And eventually, I called up Sony America and Sony UK and said, 'This is an order: the name is Walkman!' Now I'm told it is a great name.

Soon we could hardly keep pace with the demand and had to design new automated machinery to handle the flood of orders. Of course, we helped stimulate sales by advertising heavily, and in Japan we hired young couples to stroll through the Tokyo Ginza 'Pedestrian Paradise' on Sundays listening to their Walkmans and showing them off. Although I originally thought it would be considered rude for one person to be listening to his music in isolation, buyers began to see their little portable stereo sets as very personal. And while I expected people to share their Walkmans, we found that everybody seemed to want his or her own, so we took out the 'hot line' and later did away with one of the two headphone jacks on most models. I had been convinced the Walkman would be a popular product, but even I was not prepared for the response. I posed with my once-skeptical project team at the five million mark and I predicted they had only seen the beginning. Since the first Walkman went on sale, we have sold more than twenty million in more than seventy different models – we've even made waterproof and sandproof models – and there are more versions to come.

It is interesting that what has happened with Walkman is that something that began by taking away features from a full-scale recording and playback unit has now come almost full circle. We have put back – or made available with add-on devices like tiny speakers – all the features we removed in the first place, and even added some new ones, like the capability of copying from one tape to another.

My point in digressing to tell this story is simple: I do not believe that any amount of market research could have told us that the Sony Walkman would be successful, not to say a sensational hit that would spawn many imitators. And yet this small item has literally changed the music-listening habits of millions of people all around the world. Many of my friends in the music world, such as conductors Herbert von Karajan, Zubin Mehta, and Lorin Maazel, and virtuosos like Isaac Stern, have contacted me for more and more Walkmans, a very rewarding confirmation of the excellence of the idea and the product itself. As a result of developing small, lightweight options for the Walkman series, we have been able to miniaturize and improve the quality of our standard headphones and introduce dozens of new models, and so we have become one of the world's largest makers of headphones. We have almost 50 per cent of the market in Japan.

It was this kind of innovation that Ibuka had in mind when we wrote a kind of prospectus and philosophical statement for our company in the very beginning: 'If it were possible to establish conditions where persons could become united with a firm spirit of teamwork and exercise to their hearts' desire their technological capacity,' he wrote, 'then such an organization could bring untold pleasure and untold benefits.'

He was thinking about industrial creativity, something that is done with teamwork to create new and worthwhile products. Machines and computers cannot be creative in themselves, because creativity requires something more than the processing of existing information. It requires human thought, spontaneous intuition, and a lot of courage, and we had plenty of that in our early days and still do.

PART THREE

THEMES – CASE STUDIES

In Part Three we explore some of the major themes of innovation which emerge from the earlier scan of examples.

The innovation process and the style of entrepreneurship depend naturally upon the size and history of the organization, but also upon the ability of top management to encapsulate the aims of their organization. Traditionally this has been described as management by objectives, offering targets and milestones. Under the influence of the new management paradigm this ability is described now in grander words reverberating with literary overtones – scenarios, missions and visions. Section 7 looks at several papers which offer ways of building scenarios and mission statements. Burnside describes the process of visioning. Wack outlines the scenario planning procedures that saved Shell in the 1973 and 1981 oil crises and Shirley explains how she relates vision to strategy when directing her own company.

The next major theme concerns how the targets are realized and how missions are fulfilled, or not. Creativity is then fulfilled against the grain, within the cracks of the organization. The extracts in Section 8 cover the use of creativity techniques, integration of technology and market sense, but above all stamina and persistence by a few dedicated individuals in the face of a resistant framework. The examples include the development of the ubiquitous Post-it pads in a large multinational, cake decorations in a relatively small family business, and the struggle individuals face in attempting to develop a potentially lucrative technical development in a large organization.

Section 9 concerns mature organizations seeking renewal. In the natural evolution to middle age there comes a time when the original impulses are lost, either buried in bureaucracy or diversification or complacency. The examples here are of the rare organization which can originate and sustain new ideas in dire circumstances of decline. To quote from the Reid chapter on Harley-Davidson – 'If we can do it, *any* company can.' Evans and Russell show us a creative way of tackling the topical issue of environmental concerns within the chemical industry. Like many Western companies Xerox has had to face fierce competition from Japan. Kennedy describes how Xerox is learning from its failures and setting about changing its culture. Rover has had a chequered history, yet since its partnership with Honda it too has managed to turn itself around, and as Walker explains, adopting Japanese engineering techniques involves fundamental attitude change.

SECTION 7

DIRECTION FINDING

24

Visioning: building pictures of the future

Robert M. Burnside

In many organizations today, people feel isolated and overwhelmed by complexity; they have no clear sense of the future and cannot, consequently, see the meaning of what they do. These problems can be addressed by a process called *visioning*, in which a picture of the future is created. Although visioning techniques vary, they all have one thing in common – they are fundamentally nonverbal, relying on visual images as a basic element. Because it allows one to think in a way that avoids the constraints associated with language in an organizational context (its tendency to be mechanical, analytical, and thus emotionless), the process can be liberating and creative and may thereby address additional problems in the organization. In this chapter I describe how the Center for Creative Leadership assisted two very different clients in their visioning. But first I should say a few words about what a vision is.

What is a vision?

A vision can be described as a living picture of a future, desirable state. It is living because it exists in the thoughts and actions of people, not just in a written document. It is a picture because it is composed not of abstractions but of images. As Bernard Lievegoed noted in his book *Man On The Threshold*,[1] 'Images are more meaningful than abstract definitions. Images always have a thought content, an emotional value, and a moral symbolic value.' A vision is thus integrative because it brings these dimensions together.

The focus of a vision is on a desirable future, where circumstances are different and better than current ones. It does not, however, concentrate on how to achieve that future.

A vision orients, and thus steadies, a person. It can be used to organize materials and thereby control complexity. By establishing future goals, it can give meaning to current thoughts and actions. When it is shared by people within an organization it helps define relationships and overcome alienation. The more it is held as a common picture, the more powerful it can be in helping overcome the inertia of the present state.

There are a variety of ways to accomplish visioning. Techniques range from structured to very loose and free. With our clients we used one highly structured and one free-flowing technique.

Chemical, Incorporated

Chemical, Inc., is a $2-billion division of an oil company. The Vice President of the R & D Department approached us two years ago to do an Innovation Assessment Process to determine what was stimulating and obstructing employee creativity in the organizational climate. The company had recently completed a downsizing process that eliminated ⅔ of the workforce. Despite the fact that growth was beginning again, and the R & D budget was increasing, employee morale remained very low.

In the assessment process, all employees received a questionnaire to complete, and 35 employees were personally interviewed for one half hour about the stimulants and obstacles to creativity in their organization. During these interviews, employees were cynical, mistrustful of management, and discouraged about the future.

The results of the questionnaire confirmed that employees mistrusted management, management's style was overly directive, and the atmosphere was highly political. The management team of ten people came to CCL for a three-day meeting to review the results. We started with the first day being a visioning process, reasoning that 'If you don't know where you're going, you'll end up somewhere else!' (David Campbell).

The technique we used with the team to stimulate their imaginations was toward the analytical, structured side: they were told to imagine that the 1992 version of their industry's trade magazine *Chemical Week* had just come out, with the lead article describing the incredible success of Chemical, Inc. R & D department – how it had become the model for the industry – and describing the process used to change it. Each manager, working alone for an hour, was told to draft a version of that article. Then each prepared a flip chart presentation of his article, which he presented to the group. When all had presented, common themes were noted. From these, the group drafted a vision statement, which read:

> Technology is crucial to the success of Chemical, Inc. Research and Development will provide a continuous stream of innovative technologies to drive the company's growth. Freedom and respect for each employee are essential for Innovation and Growth.

This vision statement was tremendously exciting for this group of managers. The next day they received the feedback from the assessment process. There were no surprises here – just confirmation in objective data of the hallway talk. They put the findings of the CCL survey into their own words and themes. On the third day, we reviewed with them possible feedback strategies with the rest of their organization, emphasizing face-to-face meetings with the employees to review the survey results and the new vision statement.

The open discussion of their many problems, and the codification of a new vision of how they would operate, was exhilarating to the management team. Much to our surprise, they called together the employees immediately on their return to the organization and shared the overall results and the new vision. Then they quickly organized and pulled off two-and-a-half-hour meetings with all employees in groups of 30. At the conclusion of each session employees spontaneously volunteered for 'Vision Action Teams' to handle the problems identified. It was just as if a flash fire had ignited and spread through the organization. Of course, as with flash fires, there was the danger of a quick surface interest and then back to the same old ways.

However, despite the confusion of the quickly formed teams, many of whom were inadequately trained, the management team's commitment to change allowed the change process to take root and hold. Management took three actions that helped sustain the change process.

First, the employees had suggested two changes to the vision statement both of which were accepted by management. First, they added the words 'and people' to the statement: 'Technology and people are crucial to the success of Chemical, Inc.' Second, they added the word 'teamwork' to the statement: 'Freedom, respect, and teamwork are essential for Innovation and Growth.'

Second, management allowed the structure of the Executive Committee to be changed to allow more participation by employees, and named the new group the 'Vision Steering Committee.'

Finally, management allocated funds to support the actions of the Vision Action Teams, and scheduled 6-month interval group meetings with all managers to assess the efficacy of the change effort.

The latest of these review meetings was held in November, 1989. All 80 managers were invited to the day-and-a-half meeting. The meeting was divided into three parts: Look how far we've come; Where are we now; and, Continuing to build the vision. The format for the first section, Look how far we've come, reviewed results of a recent survey that measured how much progress employees felt had been made in the past two years. These results were very positive. Then, managers were put into eight mixed groups with the assignment to discuss how the organizational climate today compared with the climate two years ago. They were told to prepare a picture or display that captured how it was two years ago, and how it is today. Finally, they had to prepare a 'celebration sound' other than clapping to conclude their presentations. What a difference in how these managers acted compared to their behavior in the interviews two years ago! They were enthusiastic, exuberant, creative, and uninhibited in their presentations. One group prepared an 'idea machine,' meant to represent the ideas developed within R & D. In the 'before' picture, the group of ten people milled around aimlessly, bored and sad, stuffing ideas into the 'idea machine,' with no results. In the 'after' picture, the ten people joined together, smiling, coordinating their efforts around stuffing ideas into the machine, and results came out! Another group compared the before and after to the opening of the Berlin wall. It is the same as the opening in Eastern Europe, they said. The only difference is a matter of degree. For their celebration sound they mimicked the Czechoslovaks by jingling their keys. One of them, a Czech, said 'The vision is the key that unlocks us from the prison of conformity.' Three of the groups designed models that incorporated sunlight-receiving cells. These cells 'brought in the light of the vision to guide and power our efforts'. All of the models described the present as much improved over the past, though all were careful to note that there still was much left to be done.

The exuberant behavior of these managers compared to two years ago was strong testimony to the power of the visioning process, even with the rather structured and rational approach used to kick it off at the start. The enthusiasm experienced by the management team in the beginning had been successfully extended into the ranks.

Advertising Agency, Incorporated

Advertising Agency was a very different organization. It was a private family business, consisting of a total of 100 employees, doing advertising business in the northeast United States. The five-member management team wanted to look at improving its leadership style and the creativity of the organization. The leadership mantle was in the process of being passed from the father to the son. The management team spent two days at the Center for Creative Leadership during which they identified the need to develop their own vision of the future of the agency. They felt strongly that to grow, they had to move away from being a local advertising-only firm, to a national comprehensive communications firm. They developed the vision on their own, and presented it to employees two months later. This was the second of a series of one-day-per-month interventions by CCL at the client's site.

Management gathered all 100 employees at an off-site training center to present their vision of the future. The lights went down, and a slick multi-media presentation began, using slides of employees, music, buzz words from the new vision, and a voice-over describing employees in the future company as 'new age communicators.'

At the end of the ten-minute show, the new head (the owner's son) stood up and delivered a speech that summarized what the management team hoped for in the future company. Then, each of the other management team members stood up and delivered a brief view from their functional area. Finally, in an emotional speech, the father 'passed the mantle' to the employees. The employee group was young, most in their late 20s and 30s, and expressed a lot of enthusiasm. After the presentation, the hourly employees went back to work, and the 40 exempt employees stayed for the remainder of the training day, which was to be led by CCL.

I felt it was important to let them imagine from their point of view what the future might look like. Management had given them a clear logical description of what the agency must become to survive the marketplace changes. But these would remain 'just words' unless we developed them into living pictures through exercising their imagination – i.e. doing visioning. I explained to the group that visioning the future means going there now, a suspension of time and space, that imagines the future state as successfully attained. We would 'wake up' in this attained state, and using all our senses, would note what we saw, heard, felt, etc. This would be a non-rational non-analytical approach to attaining the future. We were not worried about how to get there, but rather what there looked like. Many times people confuse visioning with how to get there, without ever really examining what the there looks like that they are trying to achieve.

Because this was a younger group than at Chemical Incorporated, and in a profession more open to free use of the imagination, I decided to use a visioning technique that was more free-wheeling than the one used at Chemical, Inc. This technique is called 'guided imagery.' I had the 40 people close their eyes and get relaxed as I played some soft new-age type music in the background. After a couple of minutes, I told them to wake up in the future (in 1994, which was the target year given by management that morning). 'You have successfully attained that which you were seeking as a firm. You are in your work place. What do you see around you? What sounds do you hear? What are you doing? How are you feeling?' After each question, a pause of a minute or so was allowed. 'Now, walk away from your work area and join a meeting of your colleagues. What do you see occurring? How are you interacting? What do you see, hear, feel? How has this changed from before? Now, walk around the building. What does the architecture look like? Notice an interaction between management and an employee. What occurs? Finally, attend a client briefing session. What is happening? Who is there? What is the client saying? How is it different than before?'

Altogether, they spent about 8 to 10 minutes with their eyes closed in this guided imagery tour of the future. Then I turned down the music, asked them to return to the present, and gave them 15 minutes of alone time to 'make notes, pictures, that capture for you the significant images and events you saw occurring.' Next I put them into six groups of about seven people each. They had one hour to share their pictures of the future with each other. They were required to report out what was in common in their pictures, and what they brought that was unique.

The groups worked hard with a lot of energy and laughter. At the report-outs, I was surprised how much there was in common in each of the six groups' summaries. Every group had a similar picture of the architecture of the building: 'a gutted warehouse, with lots of windows that let in huge amounts of light . . . flexible office walls with walls for the introverts, and open areas for the extroverts . . . sunken living rooms for the cross-functional client-focused teams . . .' There was much more in the employees' vision about relationships and how people would treat one another than in management's vision earlier that morning. In fact, after every group had in some way described how 'management would stop treating employees like children, and speak honestly about what they were going to do,' I began to get nervous. What exactly had I unleashed here with this visioning process? Management had given a clear if dry presentation that morning, and here this afternoon I had 40 employees clearly set on, among other things, reforming how management interacted with them. How would I resolve this without causing a disturbance within the organization?

After the summaries, I put the employees into six groups by department to work on identifying the top issues that needed attention. During this time I reflected on the employee groups' report-outs. Their vision of the future had more emphasis on the relational aspects of the workplace, while management focused more on the strategic exterior aspects of the firm. Although the employees' vision was somewhat different in emphasis, it fitted in well with the strategic objectives management had set. They had not challenged these; in fact, they underlined and supported them. Therefore, I decided to use the analogy of a conversation between management and employees, noting that management set the picture strategically, focusing on the external relations of the organization, while the employees focused on the internal relations. I called the strategic picture the 'head' side and the relational picture the 'heart' side of the organization. Management had worked on the head issues, while employees had worked on the heart issues. Together, the two visions made a whole.

The employee group wanted to produce a slick version of their common vision to present to management and the rest of the organization. They elected one representative from each of the working groups to make a 'Gang of Seven' who would produce the employees' response vision during the next month.

A month later, the employee group's vision was presented to the combined organization. It was received with great enthusiasm by management: 'an excellent and exciting picture of the future that fits with what we had envisioned.' I was very moved by the presentation – it featured music and slides, and then a produced audiotape of a new employee's first day joining the firm and what she experienced. The employees were excited and proud of what they had attained. As the facilitator, I was pleased that the two visions went so hand-in-hand, complementing each other and building a greater whole.

Conclusions

Essentially, both at Advertising, Inc. and at Chemical, Inc., the visioning process had released great quantities of creative energy from the employees, with the only stimulus being that they free their imaginations from the use of only words and the focus on the present, and allow themselves to dream in complete images of the particular future state that they wished to attain. The future states that emerged were characterized by having both strategic 'hard' aspects of bottom-line delivery, and the soft side of relationships and values. Even better, they had particular detailed descriptions of what the future would look like, toward which they could strive.

In conclusion, almost all firms contacted today express a need to have a clearer picture of the future, to understand and answer why they do the work they do. The release of the individual human imagination through visioning techniques is a powerful way to begin forming a clear picture of what they want to achieve. Not only does a clear picture emerge, but a great release of energy and creativity comes with it.

Notes

Marjorie Parker, of the Norwegian Center for Leadership Development, Oslo, Norway, has conducted visioning work with Norwegian organizations; the various conversations I had with her on the subject in 1989 were helpful in developing the thoughts in this chapter.
1   Lievegoed, Bernard, *Man on the Threshold*, 1983, Driebergen, p. 75.

25

Scenarios: uncharted waters ahead

Pierre Wack

Few companies today would say they are happy with the way they plan for an increasingly fluid and turbulent business environment. Traditional planning was based on forecasts, which worked reasonably well in the relatively stable 1950s and 1960s. Since the early 1970s, however, forecasting errors have become more frequent and occasionally of dramatic and unprecedented magnitude.

Forecasts are not always wrong; more often than not, they can be reasonably accurate. And that is what makes them so dangerous. They are usually constructed on the assumption that tomorrow's world will be much like today's. They often work because the world does not always change. But sooner or later forecasts will fail when they are needed most: in anticipating major shifts in the business environment that make whole strategies obsolete.

Most managers know from experience how inaccurate forecasts can be. On this point, there is probably a large consensus.

My thesis – on which agreement may be less general – is this: the way to solve this problem is not to look for better forecasts by perfecting techniques or hiring more or better forecasters. Too many forces work against the possibility of getting *the* right forecast. The future is no longer stable; it has become a moving target. No single 'right' projection can be deduced from past behavior.

The better approach, I believe, is to accept uncertainty, try to understand it, and make it part of our reasoning. Uncertainty today is not just an occasional, temporary deviation from a reasonable predictability; it is a basic structural feature of the business environment. The method used to think about and plan for the future must be made appropriate to a changed business environment.

Royal Dutch/Shell believes that decision scenarios are such a method.[1] As Shell's former group managing director, André Bénard, commented: 'Experience has taught us that the scenario technique is much more condu-

Extracted and reprinted by permission from *Harvard Business Review* (Sep–Oct), 1985, pp. 73–89. Copyright © 1985 by the President and Fellows of Harvard College; all rights reserved

cive to forcing people to think about the future than the forecasting techniques we formerly used.'[2]

Many strategic planners may claim they know all about scenarios: they have tried but do not like them. I would respond to their skepticism with two points:

- Most scenarios merely quantify alternative outcomes of obvious uncertainties (for example, the price of oil may be $20 or $40 per barrel in 1995). Such scenarios are not helpful to decision makers. We call them 'first-generation' scenarios. Shell's decision scenarios are quite different, as we shall see.
- Even good scenarios are not enough. To be effective, they must involve top and middle managers in understanding the changing business environment more intimately than they would in the traditional planning process. Scenarios help managers structure uncertainty when (1) they are based on a sound analysis of reality, and (2) they change the decision makers' assumptions about how the world works and compel them to reorganize their mental model of reality. This process entails much more than simply designing good scenarios. A willingness to face uncertainty and to understand the forces driving it requires an almost revolutionary transformation in a large organization. This transformation process is as important as the development of the scenarios themselves. . . .

I will describe the development of scenarios in the early 1970s as they evolved out of the more traditional planning process. As you will see, the concept and the technique we arrived at is very different from that with which we began – mainly because there were some highly instructive surprises along the way for all concerned. The art of scenarios is not mechanistic but organic; whatever we had learned after one step advanced us to the next.

The 1972 scenarios

Having all these building blocks, we could begin to understand the forces driving the system. In response, we presented the revamped scenarios to Shell's top management as an array of possible futures, gathered in two families, A and B, in September 1972.[3] The A-group timed an oil supply disruption to coincide with the scheduled renegotiation of the Teheran price agreement in 1975. (In reality, it came, of course, in the fall of 1973 – after the imposition of the oil embargo.)

Most oil-producing countries would be reaching the technical limit of their capacities by 1976, while others would be reluctant to increase output further because of their inability to absorb the additional revenues. Accordingly, producer countries' oil prices would increase substantially by the end of 1975. Confronted with possible energy supply shortages and increased oil import bills, consuming countries would feel economic shock waves.

Because we had identified a predetermined element, we used the A-family of scenarios to examine three potential solutions to the problems it presented: private enterprise (A1); government intervention, or *dirigiste* (A2); or none (A3), resulting in an energy crisis.

The A-family of scenarios emerged as the most likely outcome, but it varied sharply from the implicit worldview then prevailing at Shell. That view can be characterized loosely as 'explore and drill, build refineries, order tankers, and expand markets.' Because it was so different, how could our view be heard? In response, we created a set of 'challenge scenarios,' the B-family. Here the basic premise was that, somehow, a sufficient energy supply would be available. The B-family scenarios would not only challenge the assumptions underlying the A-family but also destroy many of the business-as-usual aspects of the worldview held by so many at Shell (like their counterparts in other companies).

Under the B1 scenario, for example, some ten years of low economic growth were required to fit demand to the oil supply presumed available. While such low growth seemed plausible in the 1971 downturn, by 1972 signs of a coming economic boom began to show. B1 was also implausible since governments and citizens of industrialized countries viewed rising unemployment as unacceptable and would consciously seek growth no matter what. The implausibilities under B1 made the inevitability of a major disruption more plain to managers.

B3 was also an important educational tool because it postulated a very high supply of oil as a way to avoid major change. We called it the 'three-miracles' scenario because it required the simultaneous occurrence of three extremely unlikely situations. The first was a miracle in exploration and production. The Shell exploration and production staff estimated a 30% chance that the reserves necessary to meet 1985 demand would be found in each of the oil provinces individually, but only a very small chance that these high reserves would be found in all areas simultaneously. Meeting the forecast 1985 demand under B3 would require not only 24 million barrels daily from Saudi Arabia, but also 13 million barrels from Africa and 6 million barrels from Alaska and Canada – clearly an impossibility.

The second miracle was sociopolitical: B3 foresaw that all major producing countries would happily deplete their resources at the will of the consumer. Countries with low capacities to absorb the excess revenue would agree to produce huge amounts of oil and put their money in the bank, exposed to the erosion of inflation, rather than keep it in the ground. That miracle projected the values of consuming countries onto oil producers – a kind of Western cultural imperialism that was extremely unconvincing, even to the most expansion-minded manager.

The final miracle started with the recognition that no capacity would be left above projected demand. Previously, when minor crises developed, additional oil was always available to meet sudden short-term needs.

Under B3, however, there would be no spare production capacity. The miracle then was that there would be no need for it – no wars in the region, no acts of God, no cyclical peaks of demand higher than anticipated. Again, this was nothing short of miraculous. The improbability of B3 forced Shell management to realize how disruptive the change in their world would be.

B2 was a totally artificial construct. It premised that – despite all the problems – the world would muddle through. This reflects the sentiment that, as William Ogburn said, 'There is much stability in society. . . . Social trends seldom change their directions quickly and sharply. . . . Revolutions are rare and evolution is the rule.' We couldn't rationally justify this scenario, but we realized that the worst outcome does not always develop. So we imagined a B2 scenario in which everything positive was possible. Oil producers would live and let live to obtain concessions from the consumers who, in turn and with great foresight, would immediately curb oil consumption.

We quantified both the A- and B-family scenarios in terms of volume, price, impact on individual oil producers and consumers, and interfuel competition. Our presentation gained the attention of top management principally because the B-family of scenarios destroyed the ground many of them had chosen to stand on. Management then made two decisions: to use scenario planning in the central offices and the larger operating companies and to informally advise governments of the major oil-consuming countries about what we saw coming.

We made a series of presentations to the governments of the major consuming countries and stressed the coming disruption by tracing its impact on their balance of payments, rates of inflation, and resource allocation.

Banging the drum quickly

Shell first asked its major downstream operating companies to evaluate current strategies against two A-type scenarios, using the B2 scenario as a sensitivity check. By asking 'what if,' the B2 checked strategies already conceived in another conceptual framework (the A-family).

To this intent, we presented the A and B scenarios to the second echelon of Shell's management – its first exposure to scenarios. The meetings stood in stark contrast to traditional UPM planning sessions, which dealt out forecasts, trends, and premises – all under an avalanche of numbers. The scenarios focused less on predicting outcomes and more on understanding the forces that would eventually compel an outcome; less on figures and more on insight. The meetings were unusually lengthy and the audience clearly appreciative. We thought we had won over a large share of these managers.

The following months would show, however, that no more than a third of Shell's critical decision centers were really acting on the insights gained through the scenarios and actively preparing for the A-family of outcomes. The scenario package had sparked some intellectual interest but had failed to change behavior in much of the Shell organization. This reaction came as a shock and compelled us to rethink how to design scenarios geared for decision making.

Reality was painful: most studies dealing with the future business environment, including these first scenarios, have a low 'existential effectiveness.' (We can define existential effectiveness as single-mindedness, but the Japanese express it much better: 'When there is no break, not even the thickness of a hair, between a man's vision and his action.') A vacuum cleaner is mostly heat and noise; its actual effectiveness is only around 40%. Studies of the future, particularly when they point to an economic disruption, are less effective than a vacuum cleaner.

If your role is to be a corporate lookout and you clearly see a discontinuity on the horizon, you had better learn what makes the difference between a more or a less effective study. One of the differences involves the basic psychology of decision making.

Every manager has a mental model of the world in which he or she acts based on experience and knowledge. When a manager must make a decision, he or she thinks of behavior alternatives within this mental model. When a decision is good, others will say the manager has good judgment. In fact, what has really happened is that his or her mental map matches the fundamentals of the real world. We call this mental model the decision maker's 'microcosm'; the real world is the 'macrocosm.'

There is also a corporate view of the world, a corporate microcosm. During a sabbatical year in Japan, for example, I found that Nippon Steel did not 'see' the steel market in the same way as Usinor, the French steel giant. As a result, there were marked differences in the behavior and priorities of the two corporations. Each acted rationally, given its worldview. A company's perception of its business environment is as important as its investment infrastructure because its strategy comes from this perception. I cannot overemphasize this point: unless the corporate microcosm changes, managerial behavior will not change; the internal compass must be recalibrated.

From the moment of this realization, we no longer saw our task as producing a documented view of the future business environment five or ten years ahead. Our real target was the microcosms of our decision makers: unless we influenced the mental image, the picture of reality held by critical decision makers, our scenarios would be like water on a stone. This was a different and much more demanding task than producing a relevant scenario package.

We had first tried to produce scenarios that we would not be ashamed of when we subsequently compared them with reality. After our initiation with these first sets of scenarios, we changed our goal. We now wanted to design scenarios so that managers would question their own model of reality and change it when necessary, so as to come up with strategic insights beyond their minds' previous reach. This change in perspective – from producing a 'good' document to changing the image of reality in the heads of critical decision makers – is as fundamental as that experienced when an organization switches from selling to marketing.

The 1973 scenarios – the rapids

More than 20 centuries ago, Cicero noted, 'It was ordained at the beginning of the world that certain signs should prefigure certain events.' As we prepared the 1973 scenarios, all economic signs pointed to a major disruption in oil supply. New analyses foretold a tight supply–demand relationship in the coming years.

Now we saw the discontinuity as predetermined. No matter what happened in particular, prices would rise rapidly in the 1970s, and oil production would be constrained – not because of a real shortage of oil but for political reasons, with producers taking advantage of the very tight supply–demand relationship. Our next step was to make the disruption into our surprise-free scenario. We did not know how soon it would occur, how high the price increase would be, and how the various players would react. But we knew it would happen. Shell was like a canoeist who hears white water around the bend and must prepare to negotiate the rapids.

To help reframe our managers' outlook, we charted the 1973 scenarios (Exhibit I). From the calm upriver of the traditional environment, the company would plunge into the turbulence of the rapids and have to learn to live in a new habitat.

We could eliminate some of the original scenarios. We could dam off the alternate branch of the river (the B-family scenarios of 1972). The no-growth-no-problem scenario (B1) was clearly implausible as economies, fully recovered from the 1971 recession, boomed. The three-miracles scenario (B3) remained just that – three supply miracles. Finally, our discussions with governments about the impending crisis had allowed us to conclude that their reaction would occur only after the fact. (Obviously, we hadn't yet learned how to affect governmental microcosms.)

Because the B-branch of the river was dammed, we needed to explore other potential streams that dovetailed with management's current optimism, an optimism based on the booming economy of late 1972 and early 1973 – in which growth exceeded that of any period since the Korean War. In an oil company having an affair with expansion, many executives were naturally reluctant to slow or suspend the expansion of refineries, the building of tankers, and so forth. In response, we created two 'phantom' scenarios – alternatives to our main scenarios but ones we considered illusions. In Phantom Scenario I, we assumed a delay of 5 years in the onset of the disruption; in Phantom II, 15 years. (These represented typical times needed to first, bring a new oil facility into service and second, amortize it.) These phantom scenarios were used to measure the 'regret' Shell would

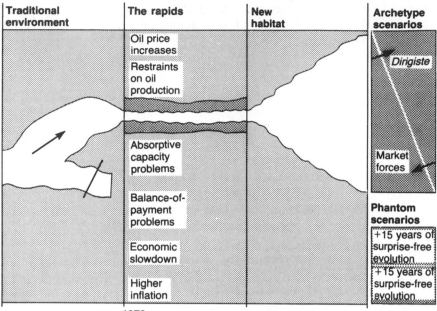

Traditional environment	The rapids	New habitat	Archetype scenarios

Oil price increases

Restraints on oil production

Dirigiste

Absorptive capacity problems

Market forces

Balance-of-payment problems

Phantom scenarios

+15 years of surprise-free evolution

Economic slowdown

+15 years of surprise-free evolution

Higher inflation

1973

Exhibit I   *1973 scenarios*

feel if it planned for a discontinuity that never occurred for 5 or even 15 more years.

Only two developments could delay the inevitable and both were ruled out: (1) the discovery of new Middle East-sized oil reserves in an area that would have no problem in absorbing revenues, or (2) political or military seizure and control of producers by consuming countries.

More than water on a stone

On the surface, the 1973 scenarios seemed much like the A-scenarios constructed in 1972. Driven by a new sense of urgency, however, we saw them in a different light. The time we had to anticipate, prepare for, and respond to the new environment had shrunk greatly.

More important, we wanted the 1973 scenarios to be more than water on a stone: we wanted to change our managers' view of reality. The first step was to question and destroy their existing view of the world in which oil demand expanded in orderly and predictable fashion, and Shell routinely could add oil fields, refineries, tankers, and marketing outlets. In fact, we had been at this job of destruction now for several years.

But exposing and invalidating an obsolete worldview is not where scenario analysis stops. Reconstructing a new model is the most important job and is the responsibility of the managers themselves. The planners' job is to engage the decision makers' interest and participation in this reconstruction. We listen carefully to their needs and give them the highest quality materials to use in making decisions. The planners will succeed, however, only if they can securely link the new realities of the outside world – the unfolding business environment – to the managers' microcosm. Good scenarios supply this vital 'bridge'; they must encompass both managers' concerns and external reality. Otherwise, no one will bother to cross the bridge.

If the planners design the package well, managers will use scenarios to construct a new model of reality by selecting from them those elements they believe relevant to their business world. Because they have been making decisions – and have a long track record to show that they're good at it – they may, of course, not see any relevant elements. Or they may go with what their 'gut' tells them. But that should not discourage the planner who is drawing up the scenario.

Just as managers had to change their worldview, so planners had to change the way they viewed the planning process. So often, planning is divorced from the managers for whom it is intended. We came to understand that making the scenarios relevant required a keener knowledge of decision makers and their microcosm than we had ever imagined. In later years, we built some bridges that did not get used. The reason for this failure was always that we did not design scenarios that responded to managers' deepest concerns.

Building blocks for new microcosms

In developing the 1973 scenarios, we realized that if managers were to reframe their view of reality, they would need a clear overview of a new model. Exhibit II, one way to portray that model, summarizes the anticipated business environment and its key elements: the predetermined events, which are shown on the left, and the major discontinuities, which are shown in the center.

We focused attention on the following features of the business environment (shown in Exhibit II):

● Alternative fuels, which we could develop only very slowly. Even under a wartime crash development program, none could be available before the 1980s. We analyzed the cost in three stages. First, even though other fuels might replace oil for generating power and steam in large industrial settings, the oil-producing nations would not be impressed. On the contrary, they welcomed the alternative of coal and nuclear power in what they considered low-value markets. Second, oil used for heating was a different story. Burning coal was not a satisfactory alternative. You would have to gasify or transform coal into electricity, with accompanying thermodynamic loss. The price for this alternative was high; the price for oil would not exceed this threshold in

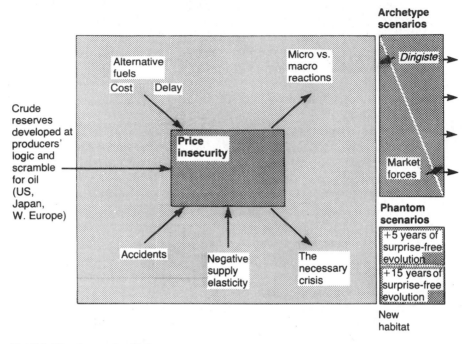

Exhibit II   *A new worldview*

the near future. The third possibility, oil used in transport, had an even
higher fuel cost than oil used for heating and was obviously irrelevant.

- Accidents, which included both political and internal and physical inci-
  dents, are events that any oil executive considers a matter of course. In
  the same way, a Filipino knows that a roof must be built carefully; even
  though the weather in the Philippines is usually balmy, typhoons are
  frequent enough that the only uncertainty is when the roof's strength
  will be tested.
- Negative supply elasticity, which means that unlike other commodities
  the supply of oil does not increase with increases in its price, at least for
  a number of years. On the contrary, the higher the price, the lower the
  volume of oil it would be in the interest of the major exporting countries to produce.

As planners at the center of a diverse group of companies, we faced a
special problem beyond the construction of a new worldview. We had to
make its message useful not only to managing directors but also to operating companies from Canada to Germany, Japan to Australia. And yet the
dramatic changes we anticipated would affect each differently. What basic
message could we convey to all of them?

To construct a framework for the message, we borrowed the concept of
archetypes from psychology. Just as we often view individuals as compo-
sites of archetypes (for example, part introvert and part extrovert), so we
developed governmental archetypes to help us examine differing national

responses. In our view, nations would favor either a market-force or government-intervention (*dirigiste*) approach. No country would follow one path exclusively. We expected, for example, that West Germany's response would be more market oriented, whereas France's would be more *dirigiste*. We analyzed the actions anticipated under each archetypal response in terms of price increases, taxes, alternative fuel development, and regulations by market class.

We led the managers to water ...

While we didn't fully comprehend that influencing managers required a tailor-made fit between the scenarios and their deepest concerns, we knew intuitively that events in 1973 gave us this fit in several ways. The arrows on the right side of Exhibit II symbolize four of the implications stressed.

We told our upstream managers, engaged in exploration and production, that the unthinkable was going to happen: 'Be careful! You are about to lose the major part of your concessions and mining rents.' The traditional profit base in the upstream world would be lost and new relationships would have to be developed between the company and producing nations.

To the downstream world of refiners, transporters, and marketers, we said something equally alarming: 'Prepare! You are about to become a low-growth industry.' Oil demand had always grown more rapidly than GNP, something Shell's management took for granted. In the past, we did not have to consider the consequences of overinvestment; one or two years of normal market growth would cure any premature moves. Now oil consumption in industrial countries would increase at rates less than the increase in GNP, and Shell would have to develop new instincts and reflexes to function in a low-growth world.

A third serious implication was the need to further decentralize the decision-making and strategic process. One basic strategy would no longer be valid for operating companies in most parts of the world. Shell companies had generally – and successfully – aimed for a higher share of conversion in refineries than did the competition. Now we understood that the energy shock would affect each nation so differently that each would have to respond independently. Shell, which was already decentralized compared with other oil majors, did in fact decentralize further, enabling it to adjust faster to the turbulence experienced later. (For some time now, it has been the most decentralized of all the major oil companies.)

Finally, we made managers see that because we didn't know when the disruption would come, they should prepare for it in different phases of the business cycle. We developed three simulations. In the first, the oil shock occurred before the cyclical downturn; in the second, the events were simultaneous; and in the third, the oil shock followed the downturn. These simulations led us to prepare for a far more serious economic decline than might otherwise have been expected.

... and most finally drank

We hit planning pay dirt with the 1973 scenarios because they met the deepest concerns of managers. If any managers were not fully convinced, the events of October soon made them believers. We had set out to produce not a scenario booklet simply summarizing views but a change in the way managers view their world. Only when the oil embargo began could we appreciate the power of scenarios – power that becomes apparent when the world overturns, power that has immense and immediate value in a large, decentralized organization.

Strategies are the product of a worldview. When the world changes, managers need to share some common view of the new world. Otherwise, decentralized strategic decisions will result in management anarchy. Scenarios express and communicate this common view, a shared understanding of the new realities to all parts of the organization.

Decentralized management in worldwide operating companies can adapt and use that view for strategic decisions appropriate to its varied circumstances. Its initiative is not limited by instructions dictated from the center but facilitated and freed by a broad framework; all will speak the same language in adapting their operations to a new business environment. Companies from Finland to New Zealand now knew what 'the rapids' meant, were alert to the implications of producer logic, and recognized the need to prepare for a new environment.

From studying evolution, we learn how an animal suited to one environment must become a new animal to survive when the environment undergoes severe change. We believed that Shell would have to become a new animal to function in a new world. Business-as-usual decisions would no longer suffice.

Notes

1 Throughout this article, I use 'Royal Dutch/Shell' and 'Shell' to refer to the Royal Dutch/Shell group of companies. The terms also serve as a convenient shorthand to describe the management and planning functions within the central service companies of that group in London and The Hague. I am generally excluding Shell Oil Company of the United States, which – as a majority-owned public company – had undertaken its own operations planning. I use words like 'company' as a shorthand for what is a complex group of organizations with varying degrees of self-sufficiency and operational independence. Most are obliged to plan for a future in their own national economic and political environments and to be integral parts of the Royal Dutch/Shell group of which they are members. I would not like to mislead anyone into thinking that any single person, manager, or planner is able to have a clear view of it all.

2 André Bénard, 'World Oil and Cold Reality', *Harvard Business Review*, November–December 1980, p. 91.

3 With hindsight, this set of scenarios was still clumsily designed. Six are far too many: they had no proper names to convey the essence of what drives each scenario. The sequel to this article includes a discussion of design.

26

Corporate strategy and entrepreneurial vision

Steve Shirley

Like Molière's Monsieur Jourdain who found that he had been speaking prose all his life, I believe that entrepreneurs are strategic planners without realizing it.

Certainly we think long term. Certainly we lay claim to vision; and that vision is subsumed into a leadership role. Leadership is not the antithesis of professional management. It may include the skills of the professional manager. Or again, it may not. Entrepreneurs are traditionally considered eccentric, impossible to manage, egocentric, egotistical – the list of qualities is long and generally unflattering. Female entrepreneurs, of course, have an enormous rarity value. Our characteristics can be disguised with joint activities with a spouse. Debbie Fields, Sophie Mirman, Anita Roddick, Mary Quant and others have very businesslike husbands, as had the late Laura Ashley.

As the business world over the last few years has filled with more and more MBAs and business school managers I had begun to wonder whether there was any longer a place for the softer sciences of vision, human values and a genuine sense of corporate mission in the management world today. Perhaps I was lucky and I started my company before management became professionalized. Perhaps such an operation as the FI Group would not have established itself today. But, as Professor Henry Mintzberg said recently, any new company, once it has sorted out its financial needs, must be driven by a vision, a dream, by something that energizes and motivates the company from top to bottom. Vision is not just a mirage, a chimera of half-developed ideas and concepts.

The test, I suppose, is whether that dream is actually related to reality. By reality I mean the needs of the marketplace and the cost/benefit factors that motivate the purchasing decision. There is little point in having a dream of making the best quill pens or making a new improved steam locomotive. The vision must be based on customer needs and a foundation of truth that will stand up to both market analysis and gut feeling. I suspect the road to bankruptcy is paved with ex-entrepreneurs who had a gut feeling about a new product, yet failed to support it with proper market analysis. The difference between visionary marketing plans bedded in concrete and those in sand must have something to do with how well the entrepreneur understands business in the first place.

Certainly when I started my company 26 years ago, I had a vision. From that vision we developed a clear strategy which managers would accept in terms of logic and rational analysis. That vision would not have seen the light of day if one of the market research companies had gone out and tried to discover a trend first and then attempted to quantify it.

What I then saw as a growth market, an unsatisfied need, would not I suspect have been statistically significant enough to show up on their data. It would have been no more than a blip on the graph. It was worse than that because it was the time of flower power and hippies so what I was suggesting was often dismissed as Beatlemania.

As a computer analyst and programmer, as a woman, and as an observer of changing life-styles, a number of things appeared to me to be happening all at once – what is now called a 'paradigm'. More women were coming off the University conveyor belt just at the time when a knowledge-based service revolution was about to break. All around me in the computing field I saw highly-qualified business analysts, software engineers, computer managers, leaving jobs to have babies, and get married (it was the 1960s so it was often in that order) and somehow never really returning to work at the level they deserved.

Industry was not properly organized at middle and senior management level to take back its staff after a 2-year gap. There were still just enough males to go around the computer job market and they would get preference for promotion over women trying to return to jobs after a 2–3-year interval. The first signs of the computing explosion were there but had not registered with top management. There was a massive talent loss by women. The impending female executive explosion was too small to be noticed, and on top of all this there was an underlying life-style change. This was apparent to me even beneath the glamour of the flower power nonsense. There was still a smidgen of something more serious. People, men and women, were becoming less sure that they wanted to be locked into a 9–5 future which entailed appalling commuter travel, dehumanized office environments and a sense that even if salaries and disposable incomes were expanding, fewer and fewer people had the time to enjoy their new found wealth. There was talk of flexitime, but few companies used it; there was talk of new out-of-town office centres in Southend and Croydon, with new towns growing at Milton Keynes, Hemel Hempstead and Basildon, yet this was still not the new life to which most of the post-1950s generation were aspiring. So, there was a niche, only we did not talk of niche-making then, it was just 'will somebody buy our product?'

The point that comes out of this is that when I founded the company, despite my original vision I still had to ensure that all the ducks were in a row. An expansion in the availability of well-qualified women took place just when a skill shortage was about to be created through the explosion of the new knowledge-based service industries, which in turn needed computers to drive it. All this came at a time of underlying attitude change and an interest in new values among the British workforce.

The scene was set therefore, thanks to Information Technology, for a new way of looking at work – what today in FI we call *the distributed office*. We now have over 1000 people (male and female) working from their homes or neighbourhood work centres at whatever time of the day or night they prefer, writing highly sophisticated software systems for clients that range from the big clearing banks to the Ministry of Defence, and in alliance with the computer manufacturers. With last year's profits in excess of £1½m, and the possibility of a stock exchange quote, the company is developing by the hour. The original strategic vision is now being replaced by a mature second generation company. While the original decision to respond to the confluence of forces that became apparent to me in the 1960s *was* more visionary than planned, yet somehow if analysed, it was not just a piece of psychedelic dreaming.

Earlier I used the word paradigm and I wonder if this is perhaps the key to corporate strategy by vision – what, in effect separates vision from *foundationless dreaming*, the type of loose thinking that all too often leads to a desert of dwindling cashflow and under-capitalization. *What separates this from effective strategic 'vision' planning* is an ability to pull a number of divergent strands together. My analysis of the situation 25 years ago enabled me to distinguish between blips in the business culture and the beginning of an underlying trend. It was an ability to pick up the faintest echoes of change in different parts of the business world, in my case it was new management techniques coming available, a skills shortage, and fundamental social change – and by making a jump out of reality into what we today would probably call an 'exponential extrapolation' and then to put my money where my prophecy was. This of course is the key. Plenty of visionaries may identify the paradigm change. They might be able to articulate it better than I can. But can they turn ideas into action?

Strategic planning by vision is a dangerous concept. It can be an excuse for poor analysis, a narrow interpretation of a paradigm or even a failure to see its existence at all. Then, too often, there is a lack of conviction or courage to put money where their mouth is. How right are the clearing banks and venture capitalists when they demand a financial commitment by the applicant at a level that will really hurt if things go wrong. There is nothing like the loss of your own cash to concentrate the mind at night and push you into more work rather than an evening at the theatre.

Strategic vision works in practice if you use the phrase to cover the factors I have described. It must include personal career or financial involvement. It only works if all the factors come together. Take away one leg of the three-legged stool of accurate trend analysis, conversion of that analysis into action and a willingness to lay your own money on the line, take away any one of those legs and like Kipling's stool, it will crash to the ground. All these factors produced not just another company with another product. It allowed us in FI to mobilize some of the highest quality talent available (our distributed staff typically have twice the years' equivalent experience of our competitors' staff), and it enabled us through geographical flexibility and a lack of normal time constraints to produce work faster and closer to client needs. Vision is no use if it only produces another mouse-trap. As Michael Porter says, you have to offer a price advantage or a differentiation by added value if you want competitive advantage. My concept of corporate vision had to be market-led otherwise I might as well have stayed home and written books about it. The scribbling professions of journalism and authorship are full of futurologists and astrological soothsayers. It is when they actually turn that forward thinking into action that I get interested and when, I suspect, most managers get interested too.

SECTION 8

REACHING THE MARKET PLACE

27

3M's little yellow note pads: 'Never mind. I'll do it myself'

P. Ranganath Nayak and John M. Ketteringham

Of all ways to devise new products, probably the most inefficient is to invent some substance with novel properties and then cast about for ways to use it – especially when the ultimate goal is a product people have to pay for. Faced with an irrational commercial challenge, Spence Silver applied an unnatural irrationality to the Post-it adhesive. To understand his persistence, it's necessary to go back to his moment of discovery.

Silver's role in the development of Post-it Note Pads began in 1964 with a 'Polymers for Adhesives' program in 3M's Central Research Laboratories. Since the time of William L. McKnight, a 3M salesman who interviewed furniture makers in 1912 in order to find ways for the company to make better sandpaper, 3M has had a tradition of periodically reexamining its own products, inside-out, to look for ways to improve them. Sometimes this policy turns into a problem of not seeing the forest for the trees, and sometimes it results in 3M 'fixing' something that 'ain't broke.' But it's a tradition that, at its best, results in incremental 'innovations' that occasionally lead to new markets, new technologies, even whole new product lines. 'Every so many years,' said Silver, 'they would put together a bunch of people who looked like they might be productive in developing new types of adhesives.'

In the course of that 'Polymers for Adhesives' research program, which went on for four years, Silver found out about a new family of monomers developed by Archer-Daniels Midland, Inc., which he thought contained

Extracted and reprinted with permission of Rawson Associates, an imprint of Macmillan Publishing Company, from Chapter 3 in P. Nayak and J. Ketteringham, *Breakthroughs* (New York: Arthur D. Little, 1986; London: Mercury Books, 1987), pp. 53–69. Copyright © 1986 Arthur D. Little, Inc.

potential as ingredients for polymer-based adhesives. He received a number of samples from ADM and began to work with them, with the full approval of 3M. This was an open-ended research effort, and Silver's acquisition of the Archer-Daniels Midland monomers was the sort of exploration the company encouraged.

'As long as you were producing new things, everybody was happy,' said Silver. 'Of course, they had to be new molecules, new patentable molecules.'

Silver went on, 'In the course of this exploration, I tried an experiment with one of the monomers in which I wanted to see what would happen if I put a lot of it into the reaction mixture. Before, we had used amounts that would correspond to conventional wisdom.' Silver had no expectation whatsoever of what might occur if he did this. He just thought it might be interesting to find out.

Already, Silver was venturing into the realm of the irrational. In polymerization catalysis, scientists usually control the amounts of interacting ingredients to very tightly defined proportions, in accordance with prevailing theory and experience.

Silver said with a certain measure of glee, 'The key to the Post-it adhesive was doing the experiment. If I had sat down and factored it out beforehand, and thought about it, I wouldn't have done the experiment. If I had really seriously cracked the books and gone through the literature, I would have stopped. The literature was full of examples that said you can't do this.'

Reliable, published experts could have told Spence Silver there was no point in doing what he did. But there is a charm in Spence Silver that supplied him both with indefatigable good spirits and, eventually, an irrational loyalty to his odd semi-sticky adhesive. He understood that science is one part meticulous calculation and one part 'fooling around.' . . .

Silver went door-to-door to every division at 3M that might be able to think up an application for an adhesive with the curious charm of hanging around without making a commitment. The organization never protested his search. When he sought slots of time at in-house technical seminars, he always got a segment to show off his now-it-works, now-it-doesn't adhesive. At every seminar, some people left, some people stayed. Most of them said, 'What can you do with a glue that doesn't glue?' But *no one* said to Silver, 'Don't try. Stop wasting our time.'

In fact, it would have violated some very deeply felt principles of the 3M Company to have killed Silver's pet project. Much is made of 3M's 'environment for innovation,' but 3M's environment is, more accurately, an environment of nonintervention – of expecting people to fulfill their day's responsibilities, every day, without discernible pressure from above. Silver, no matter how much time he spent fooling around with the Post-it adhesive, never failed in his other duties, and so, at 3M, there was no reason whatsoever to overtly discourage his extracurricular activities.

The positive side of this corporate ethic is the feeling of independence each worker experiences in doing his job. The disadvantage is that, when you have a good idea that requires more than one person to share the work and get the credit, it can be hard to convince people to postpone their chores and help with yours.

As Silver pursued his lonely quest, his best inspiration for applying his adhesive was a sticky bulletin board – a product that wasn't especially stimulating even to its inventor. He got 3M to manufacture a number of them – through a fairly low-tech and inexpensive process – and they were sent out to the company's distribution and retail network. The outcome was predictable. 3M sold a few, but it was a slow-moving item in a sleepy market niche.

Silver knew there had to be a better idea. 'At times I was angry because this stuff is so obviously unique,' said Silver. 'I said to myself, "Why can't you think of a product? It's your job!"'

Although Silver had overcome the metaphorical trap of always striving for stickier stickum, he, too, at the next stage of development for his adhesive, became trapped by the metaphor. The bulletin board, the only product he could think of, was coated with adhesive – it was sticky every-where. The metaphor said that something is either sticky or not sticky. Something *partly sticky* did not occur to him.

More intellectually seductive was the fact that, until Silver's adhesive made it possible, there was no such thing as a self-adhesive piece of note paper. Note paper was cheap and trivial, and the valuable elements in the conveyance of these bits of paper were their durable fasteners. The world is an ocean of pins, tacks, tapes, and clips – so Silver was immersed in an organization whose life-blood was tape – Scotch brand tapes, like cello-phane tape, duct tape, masking tape, electrical tape, caulking tape, secur-ity tape, nappy tape, and surgical tape – to name a few. In this atmosphere, imagining a piece of paper that eliminates the need for tape is an almost unthinkable leap into the void. . . .

Arthur Fry's benign exterior belies the playground of curiosity that capers within him. He is the person who took the baton from Silver's weary grasp, infused the quest with substance, and carried it over a jumble of discourag-ing hurdles. Fry, unlike Silver, had support from above, from Nicholson, but the technological problems he dealt with were far more daunting than Silver's.

Even before joining the new venture team in Commercial Tape, Fry had seen Spence Silver show off his adhesive. Like Archimedes pondering the tyrant's crown, Fry kept the idea turning slowly in the back of his mind. He agreed with Silver that this adhesive was special, but he wondered what to do with it.

'Then one day in 1974, while I was singing in the choir of the North Presbyterian Church in north St Paul, I had one of those creative moments,' Fry explained. 'To make it easier to find the songs we were going to sing at each Sunday's service, I used to mark the places with little slips of paper.'

Inevitably, when everyone in the church stood up, or when Fry had to communicate – through gestures – with other members of the choir, he would divert his attention from the placement of his array of bookmarks. One unguarded move, and they fluttered to the floor or sank into the deep crack of the hymnal's binding. Suddenly, while Fry leafed frantically for his place in the book, the North Presbyterian Church was gripped with a moment of sweaty anticipation. 'I thought, "Gee, if I had a little adhesive on these bookmarks, that would be just the ticket,"' said Fry. 'So I decided to check into that idea the next week at work. What I had in mind, of course, was Silver's adhesive.'

What had happened in Fry's ever-searching curiosity was what Arthur Koestler called a 'bisociation,' the association, at once, of two unrelated ideas. After Fry went to 3M, mixed up some adhesive and paper, and tried different concentrations, he had invented what he called 'the better bookmark.'

By then, certainly encouraged by Silver's enthusiasm and the Nicholson push for new products, Fry began to realize the magnitude of his 'creative moment.'

'I knew I had made a much bigger discovery than that,' said Fry. 'I also now realized that the primary application for Silver's adhesive was not to put it on a fixed surface, like the bulletin boards. That was a secondary application. The primary application concerned paper to paper. I realized that immediately.'

What Silver and the rest of 3M had not realized in five years, Fry realized in a flash. It was one of those ideas that contemplation doesn't seem to generate: it either pops into one's head or it doesn't happen at all. For Arthur Fry, that moment of insight has had effects more extensive than the success of Post-it notes. Through a sort of conspiracy among journalists, business analysts, and 3M executives, Fry has been ordained as the Post-it notes champion, a title which, in ensuing years, has imposed some unusual burdens on him. Today, rather than working side-by-side in a lab with old friends like Silver and Oliveira, Art Fry is ensconced in his own laboratory. To a chemist, this is the equivalent of the corporate corner office, lofty among the echelons of the organization. According to 3M, 'The thrust of his day-to-day corporate activity is far-ranging across many 3M laboratories.' Being 'far-ranging' appears to be a lonely job. . . .

Spence Silver seemed relieved and grateful at the comparatively short shrift given to his role in the Post-it story. Silver is still in 3M's basement, working out of a cramped, windowless office in a large, open, multi-hood laboratory – a place where experimental ferment still seems to seep from the grouting of the breezeblock walls.

In Silver, the scientific playfulness that gave birth to the Post-it adhesive still seems intact. In fact, without much prompting, he will find, somewhere jammed in an overflowing drawer, a glass cylinder filled with the old Post-it polymer. He holds it up, showing it in its restful state. It is milky white in colour. But then he squeezes the polymer with a plunger and, under pressure, the contents become – magically, crystal clear. Silver releases the pressure and the adhesive becomes opaque again!

Silver doesn't know why it does that. 'Isn't that wonderful?' he says. 'There must be some way you can *use* that!'

In 1974, after Silver had been making the same exclamation for years already, Fry provided the first truly affirmative response. But with the 'Eureka moment' at the North Presbyterian Church came an immediate problem. On the bulletin board, Silver's adhesive was attached to a favourable 'substrate.' It stuck to the bulletin board better than anything else. Move it to paper, though, and it peeled off onto everything it touched. If you couldn't change this property, you still couldn't make a future for Silver's Post-it adhesive.

The two members of the Nicholson team who invented a paper coating that made the Post-it adhesive work were named Henry Courtney and Roger Merrill.

Silver said, 'Those guys actually made one of the most important contributions to the whole project, and they haven't got a lot of credit for it. The Post-it adhesive was always interesting to people, but if you put it down on something and pulled it apart, it could stay with either side. It had no memory of where it should be. It was difficult to figure out a way to prime the substrate, to get it to stick to the surface you originally put it on. Roger and Hank [invented] a way to stick the Post-it adhesive down. And they're the ones who really made the breakthrough discovery, because once you've learned that, you can apply it to all sorts of different surfaces.'

Courtney and Merrill's contribution was the first in a series of actions that definitely were not accidents. Although there was still organizational resistance after early 1974 and Fry's choir book epiphany, every action thenceforth – including Courtney and Merrill's research – was directed towards the development, production, and market success of the Post-it note. Fry was a tenacious advocate of the product through all phases from development to production scale-up.

While Silver's task had been simply to convince his corporation that his glue was not just a footnote in the obscure history of adhesives, the job Fry assumed when he joined in the fatherhood of the Post-it note was to help his division manufacture something that was (a) not sticky at all on one side, (b) only sticky on part of the other side, and (c) wasn't actually *very* sticky anywhere. It had to be produced in big sheets, not in rolls, and then the big sheets had to be laid together and cut into smaller sizes. This might sound hard, but what added to the difficulty was the natural resistance of people. The engineers in 3M's Commercial Tape Division were accustomed to tape – which is sticky all over on one side and then gets packaged into rolls. To apply glue selectively to one side of the paper, and to move the product from rolls to sheets, the engineers would have to invent at least two entirely unique machines.

In war and politics, the best strategy is divide and conquer. In production engineering, the reverse seems to be true. Fry brought together the production people, designers, mechanical engineers, product foremen, and machine operators and let them describe the many reasons why something like that could not be done. He encouraged them to speculate on ways that they might accomplish the impossible. A lifelong gadgeteer, Fry found himself offering his own suggestions. 'Problems are wonderful things to have, especially early in the game, when you really should be looking for problems,' said Fry.

Inevitably, from these discussions people started thinking of places around 3M where they'd seen machines and parts they could use to piece together the impossible machines they needed to build. And they thought of people who could help. 'In a small company, if you had an idea that would incorporate a variety of technologies and you had to go out and buy the equipment to put those together, you probably couldn't afford it, or you'd have to go as inexpensively – or as small – as possible,' said Fry. 'At 3M, we've got so many different types of technology operating and so many experts – guys that really know all about any subject you want – oh, and so much equipment scattered here and there, that we can piece things together when we're starting off. We can go to this place and do Step A on a product, and we can make the adhesive and some of the raw materials here, and do one part over here, and another part there, and convert a space there and make a few things that aren't available.'

And then there was Arthur Fry's basement. He had had arguments with several mechanical engineers about a difficult phase of production, applying adhesive to paper in a continuous roll. He said it could be done; they said it couldn't. He assembled a small-scale basic machine in his basement, then adapted it until he'd solved the problem. The machine worked, and it would work even better once the mechanical engineers had a chance to refine it. But the next problem Fry had was worse – the new machine was too big to fit through his basement door. If he couldn't get it out of his cellar, he couldn't show it off to the engineers.

Fry accepted the consequences of his genius and did what he had to do. He bashed a hole through his basement wall and delivered his machine by caesarean section.

Within two years, Fry and 3M's mechanical engineers had tinkered their way to a series of machines that, among other things, coated the yellow paper with its 'substrate,' applied adhesive, and cut the sticky paper into little square and rectangular note pads. All of the machines are unique, proprietary to the company (and secret) – and they are the key to the Post-it notes' marvellous consistency and dependability. The immense difficulty of duplicating 3M's machinery – without the slightest notion of what Fry and the Commercial Tape Division engineers did – is part of the reason few competitors have made it to the market with Post-it note imitations.

Fry and the engineers worked on their unique machines and mass production methods in a pilot plant in the Commercial Tape lab. They produced more than enough Post-it note prototypes to supply all the company's offices. All the sticky pads went to Nicholson's office. From there his secretary carried out a program of providing every office at 3M with Post-it notes. Early in the program, secretaries on the fourteenth floor, where the senior managers work, all received Post-it notes and became hooked. Jack Wilkins, the Commercial Tape Division's marketing director at the time, described the process of discovery that hit people the first time they encountered the Post-it notes.

'Once people started using them it was like handing them marijuana,' said Wilkins. 'Once you start using it you can't stop.'

But strangely, the personal enthusiasm of secretaries and marketing people like Wilkins did not impress the people responsible for putting Post-it notes into the market. For the division's marketing organization, fear of the unfamiliar repeatedly raised its unsightly head and threatened to scuttle the program. The marketing department had got out of the habit of dealing directly with consumers. This is ironic, because that 3M ancient warrior, William L. McKnight, had established a tradition of direct contact with consumers in 1914. That year, as the company's brand-new national sales manager, the first act performed by the twenty-four-year-old McKnight was to visit furniture factories in Rockford, Illinois, and find out from labourers what was wrong with 3M's mediocre sandpaper – which was then the company's only product. That trip to Rockford was the first instance of an executive from 3M walking in the door, approaching a worker, and saying, 'Here! Try this! Tell me what you think!'

By 1978 the Commercial Tape Division's marketing department was involved in the introduction of half a dozen new products that met easily identified needs for clearly defined markets – products like book binding tape for libraries and PMA adhesives for the art market. The Post-it note was just another new product, and not a high-priority product at that. While the company's marketing people had become mesmerized by Post-it notes in their own offices, they couldn't imagine that other people would feel the same way.

Although most of the marketing group had used Post-it notes, when they created marketing materials to present the new product they included no samples. Instead they wrote brochures describing the note pads, then sent boxes of samples separately – which people would open only if they got excited by the brochures.

The 3M marketing group was trapped, just as Spence Silver had been trapped by the metaphor of the adhesive bulletin board and could not envision his adhesive group onto paper instead. As marketing experts, it was their job to explain products, not to demonstrate them. And as explainers, they had no words to overcome the 'scratch paper' metaphor. If they couldn't explain them, they couldn't sell them.

Nicholson, who had spread Post-it notes like an infection within 3M, only had limited power to push them outside the company. When the four-city test failed, he might not have had the influence alone to keep the product alive. But by this time Nicholson had a heavyweight ally in Joe Ramey, general sales manager of the Commercial Tape Division and Nicholson's boss. Ramey was a marketing troubleshooter. He knew that some market problems are too far advanced to be saved. He had gone to Richmond because he liked Nicholson, not because he liked Post-it notes' chances.

But the reactions, face-to-face, when people in Richmond started 'playing' with Post-it notes, were so dramatic that Ramey had all the evidence he needed to throw all the artillery into Boise. It was a moment when Nicholson and Ramey must have felt a little like William McKnight among the furniture makers of Rockford.

It's remarkable that two of the company's greatest breakthroughs, sixty-six years apart, grew out of a similar style and faith in the wisdom of sitting down with customers and asking questions – without any of the trappings of corporate protocol. It could be just a coincidence, but according to most business analysts, Post-it notes finally succeeded because 3M's corporate culture creates a positive environment for innovation. Although *corporate culture* is one of those fragments of business jargon that eventually will pass from the English language without ever being defined, suffice it to say that there is something in 3M's style that tends to encourage a measure of individual ingenuity among its workers.

One of 3M's corporate strengths for more than fifty years has been its perpetual efforts to improve the product line. The development of cellophane tape in the 1930s was a breakthrough that came from 3M's work on developing insulation for railway carriages. From that point, 3M sustained its interest in tape, improving cellophane tape constantly, always devising an improved product that left their imitators behind, culminating (most recently) in the Scotch brand Magic Tape revolution in the 1960s.

Whenever 3M's constant search for improvement led in a slightly different direction, the company let a few people follow that direction. If the detour resulted in a product line, even of modest profitability, 3M allowed the effort to proceed.

'3M . . . operates on a simple principle,' *Forbes* magazine once said, 'that no market, no end product is so small as to be scorned; that with the proper organization, a myriad of small products can be as profitable, if not more so, than a few big ones. More firmly than most, 3M management appreciates that the beach is composed of grains of sand, the ocean of drops of water.'[1]

This tolerance of the small-scale certainly helped Spence Silver, and then Art Fry, to keep the company from stomping on the Post-it notes project before the project had developed a life of its own. But there was also the benefit of bigness. Over the years, 3M has grown into a loosely integrated cluster of divisions, with senior management in the St Paul corporate headquarters. One of the results of this corporate sprawl is that it permits the clever researcher to hide in the crevices and carry out his own version of the '15 per cent principle.' Silver benefited more from this 'neglect of magnitude' than from anyone overtly encouraging him to innovate. Fry also enjoyed this dispensation from scrutiny as he fostered the Post-it project through the touchy and costly labor of product development. . . .

But one thing 3M has proven is that when it gets self-conscious about managing its innovation, it doesn't innovate any better than any other company. As Nicholson said, Post-it notes came from accidents, not calculations.

The Post-it note accidents were Spence Silver's polymer discovery, Arthur Fry's bookmark epiphany, and Geoff Nicholson's dragging Joe Ramey off to Richmond. Each accident occurred after one person took an entirely independent course of action from the one assigned by the corporation. Each time, the individual got frustrated either by the indifference or the resistance of the organization.

Similar accidents had occurred in the past. In 1956 a researcher spilled a tube full of totally useless fluorocarbon compound on her shoes – and from that accident, chemists Patsy Sherman and Sam Smith created Scotchgard fabric protector. In 1950, after three polite 3M requests to stop wasting money, researcher Alvin W. Boese squeezed synthetic fibres mixed with wood pulp through a makeshift comb and created one of the most successful types of nonwoven decorative ribbon ever devised.

These accidents happened because when the organization – or management – discouraged people from doing something, the cancellation orders didn't carry much conviction. Ego is not popular at 3M, and it is clear that the people thinking up things often have more room to express their egos than the people who are supposed to be running things. If there is an organizational key to breakthrough at 3M, a significant element of corporate culture, it is in the fact that people there don't believe in placing the values of the corporation above the values of the individual. People keep the organization vital by not taking the organization very seriously. As a result, when the creative people, Silver and Fry and Nicholson, inevitably ran into the resistance of the organization, they felt the freedom to say, 'Well, okay. Never mind. I'll do it myself.' The organization simply did not have an equal measure of persistence in response. 3M gives in to people who are sure of themselves.

Just as important, everybody at 3M knows that if someone's pet project blows up in his face, it isn't the end of the world. If Silver, Fry, or Nicholson had failed, they wouldn't have been dismissed or disgraced. As long as they had their chores done, they would always have a place at the table.

Note

1   Quoted in *Our Story, So Far: Notes from the First 75 Years of the 3M Company*, St Paul: Minnesota Mining & Manufacturing Company, 1977.

28

G.T. Culpitt & Son Limited

R. Charles Parker

Inherited businesses are less likely to experience the same economic and social scene which gave them birth, and can, therefore, only be perpetuated by a Darwinian type of adaptive behaviour. This chapter offers an example of such a family business, which is encountering economic difficulties that stem from considerations largely outside the company's control. It is an exciting study since, at the instigation of the company chairman, successful use has and is being made of current management techniques.

Culpitts manufacture cake decorations, and, at their headquarters in Hatfield, they mount a most impressive display of their products. Their cake decorations meet the needs of every conceivable occasion, ranging from sugar-based edible flowers, motifs and nursery figures to gold and silver lacquered ornaments, wedding sprays, bells, horseshoes and many other novelties; stands, pillars, and cake-bases are produced in a wide variety of designs. All of their products are illustrated in a colour catalogue which is most attractive, as indeed are the products themselves. Figure 1 shows three typical decorations.

The company is currently under the control of two brothers, Peter and David Culpitt, who are chairman and managing director respectively. Their father and grandparents began the business in about 1920; their grandmother was an artificial flower-maker to the millinery trade and, when orders fell short, she extended her artistic talent into floral bouquets for weddings and then cake decorations. With her husband and son they then started the present company from what was virtually a cottage industry. (Peter Culpitt's daughter is now in the business and his son is undergoing training with a view to joining the firm in the near future.)

In the beginnings of the company there were many competitors and German imports imposed a serious threat since 'they were not made of sugar and were not, at that time, very expensive'. However, 'Culpitt's share of the market had to be fought for and was greatly improved'. At the end of World War II it was decided to make a supreme effort to build up

Adapted from Chapter 3 in R. Parker, *Management of Innovation* (Chichester: John Wiley, 1982), pp. 34–45. Copyright © 1982 by John Wiley & Sons Ltd. Reproduced by permission of John Wiley & Sons Ltd

Figure 1 *Typical cake decorations*

their production and stocks to satisfy the home market completely prior to a recovery of the German import trade; this policy was both courageous and successful. Using all available finance they took on many more staff and moved up to a new factory at Ashington in Northumberland, which was a development area. About this time a family friend began making small imitation Christmas trees for them near his home in Eastbourne, Sussex. Somewhat fortuitously, this small spur grew and extended into bigger premises and now, together with the Ashington factory, has a turn-over in excess of £2m per annum.

There are obvious communication and transport penalties in having a business so widely split geographically, but Culpitts survive these without serious hardship, largely by carefully selecting the staff to manage their factories and by giving them a vested interest in the success of the company. This leaves the two senior partners free to concentrate on the more important tasks of policy-making and management, whilst the day-to-day production ripples are sorted out quite competently by the people responsible for them.

The situation in 1978

Over the years Culpitts have expanded steadily. Their share of the home market, 60 per cent and 80 per cent of their business, is with wholesalers and cake-manufacturers. Today, they have a very dedicated board including company secretary, marketing and production directors. (See Figure 2 for company organization chart.) They have a staff of over 350, of whom half are non-productive. It is a successful, lively, enterprising company enjoying a pleasant atmosphere and good labour relations. Like many other small- to medium-sized businesses, however, Culpitts have not been without their problems and these have been particularly exacerbated by the adverse economic climate of the last decade. Many of Culpitt's operational problems stem from two particular characteristics of their type of business – it is seasonal and it is very labour-intensive.

Their dependence on manual labour in their factories causes the Culpitt board concern. The high minimum wages they have to pay – even for low-grade jobs – causes them to raise the price of their products to a level which endangers their survival. Furthermore, they feel extremely vulnerable to doctrinaire policies of present-day trade union control in labour-intensive factories such as theirs. Culpitts do have very good labour relations with their workforce; they achieve this by having the right people managing their factories. This enables them to maintain a contented pleasant atmosphere, to anticipate problems before they get too serious, and to delegate the authority to put things right.

Nevertheless, whatever plans the company might have for expansion do not include any increase in their workforce. On the contrary, it is now their aim to replace manual labour with automated machine processes wherever possible. The chief obstacle to implementing this policy, however, is the high cost of production machinery, most of which is highly specialized and, with profits of only about 3–4 per cent of turnover, they just do not have the spare capital to invest in such plant to the scale they would wish.

It is well known that large quantities of small cut-price products are imported from the Far East, including plastic decorations, and should this trade expand its repercussions could be serious. As Peter Culpitt explained, 'We have always had competition from Hong Kong and Taiwan but, with rapidly rising labour costs in Britain, it is likely to become serious.' In an attempt to counteract this, the company has begun a small production factory in Mauritius, where labour is very much less expensive and where the Mauritian government offers considerable incentives to encourage foreign business development. The manager in charge is Mauritian and he is on the board of directors. Products and raw materials are despatched to the Mauritian section from the UK for painting and finishing by hand. Mauritian girls are extremely good at artistic work. Certain edible products are unsuitable for this treatment due to the hot, humid climate, but this would not prevent expansion of that section in other areas. At

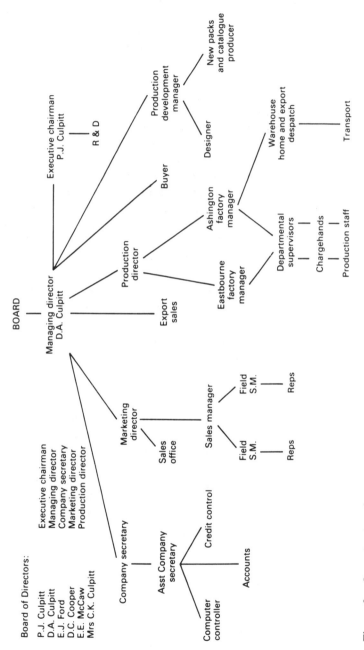

Board of Directors:

P.J. Culpitt — Executive chairman
D.A. Culpitt — Managing director
E.J. Ford — Company secretary
D.C. Cooper — Marketing director
E.E. McCaw — Production director
Mrs C.K. Culpitt

Figure 2 *Organization chart*

present, only twelve people are employed there. It will be more profitable with a larger workforce to offset export overheads.

They have a further problem in that 50 per cent of their business is done in three months of the year, from September to November, for the Christmas trade. This causes them severe problems with cash flow. Normally they have a credit balance for only a few months in each year. After paying off their overdraft and creditors, they are again overdrawn for several months. With this situation it is clearly important that they maintain strict budgetary control of their stock and order schedules and, to do so, they recently installed a computer which has proved invaluable. They have a particularly good operator on this, working in liaison with their company secretary.

The seasonal nature of their business is exacerbated by the inflationary situation in the UK. Three years ago, for example, they failed to anticipate the unprecedented rise in the cost of raw materials. As is the nature of their business, their stocks and orders to which they were committed had been arranged six months previously and they had pitched their prices too low. They could do little about it and they made a major loss that year. The bank refused to increase their overdraft and they were forced to seek help from a merchant bank, which requested 25 per cent of their equity before making the finance available to the company to cover their requirements. It is confidently believed that their computer-based budgetary control system will now prevent this type of crisis recurring.

Their North American business is covered by a full-time sales representative but 'by the time we've processed the orders he's secured, inflation has forced us to raise our prices and the customer doesn't want to know any more'. Perhaps it was not unexpected but, on being asked whether quality, delivery or price was considered to be the most important factor, Peter Culpitt replied: 'Price was definitely first, followed by quality and then delivery.' As he explained: 'These kinds of problems are always with us. A business like ours cannot be run to a mathematical formula. We have to make decisions on what we should buy and produce, based on what we think we can sell at a price we think people will pay. But the balance is so delicate; a mistake of 2 per cent can cut our profit in half. One lorry-drivers' strike at the wrong time and our profits for the year are gone.'

So this was the position of Culpitt & Son Limited at the beginning of 1977 – a family company which had enjoyed relative stability and security in the operation of its business for over fifty years being forced into changing its policies to stave off the threats and pressures of adverse economies and political climate. Basically the board knew what had to be done. Less-seasonal lines from new marketing areas would improve their cash-flow problems and automated processes would reduce their dependence on manual labour – this would go a long way towards stabilizing their prices and counteract the threat of cheap foreign imports. But how was this to be achieved? A single machine for automatically producing edible flower petals – even if it could be found – would cost over £30 000.

Manufacturing operations in the Eastbourne factory

The manufacturing processes in the factory are indeed very labour-intensive, and many of the operations rely on the skill of the operator: for example, flower petals were hand-made individually by squeezing out the appropriate amount of material from a bag. Considerable initiative had been shown in the construction of semi-automatic plant from standard components. It transpired that much of this equipment had been designed and adapted by Peter Culpitt himself, at home with his own lathe, milling machine and other tools. He refused to call himself an engineer, yet the skill and ingenuity evident in his creations were far superior to those of many people who claim that title. Silk-screen printing was used to print designs and messages on edible wafers. Orders for these ranged from 10 000 to 150 000 at a time and the production rate was around 2500 per day. This method of silk-screen printing on edible products had been developed by the Culpitt brothers and was one of several patents held by them to protect their processes. One product which uses the printing is a decorated waferette. In another room, circular hand-made communion wafers were made from starch on which was embossed a small cross. An edible dye was applied by a silk-screen process. They were then cut and stored automatically. There was, incidentally, a 50 per cent wastage of material cut from around the disc in this process which amounted to £150 per month. The manufacturing of tiny Christmas trees was another standard line. These were made largely by hand: small lengths of green Mexican fibres were hand-placed between pairs of wires which were twisted to form the radial 'branches'; these were trimmed to a conical shape and given a snow-covering by dipping in a paste solution and spinning by hand so that only the tips of the branches were coated with little white blobs.

In another section, edible spheres were made from sheets of a starch solution pressed between heated male and female platens, which were machined with hemispherical undulations. This machine operated on a 20-s cycle and on removal from the press the resulting hemispheres were cut by hand from the pressed sheets; another operator then stuck two together to form hollow spheres; these formed the head and body of small decorated figures for birthday cakes. The painting of all their cake decorations was done separately by hand. It was indeed evident that, with so much manual work, the company was heavily dependent on a stable and consistent workforce. The seasonal nature of the employment ran counter to this since, outside the festive season, much of the staff would either be stock-piling or under-employed – either way, cash-flow problems would clearly be paramount during the summer months.

There was one new project that the company was in the process of developing which had the potential to even out the business cycle during the lean periods. This was an order for small imitation trees to be used in United States' flight-simulator models measuring 100 ft × 40 ft. These trees had to look realistic when magnified by television cameras and about 17 million were needed. During the visit the manufacturing techniques for this order were far from complete and the company was behind schedule. The apparatus for making the trees from cork and wire was quite ingenious and two people were working on this at the time of the visit. The device was largely home-made – again to a design conceived by Peter Culpitt.

This project, and possibly others like it, seemed well within the capabilities and expertise of the company and, as stated above, it might go a long way towards solving their irregular order schedules. It seemed rather surprising, therefore, that more effort was not being made to push ahead with this opportunity or to investigate similar market areas. The order for the trees came in the first place from the Americans but, despite its obvious importance, there was no mention of a marketing enquiry having been made to other airlines, filming organizations, scenic model-makers, etc.

During the visit there was a problem with a machine for producing starch-based wafers. This was a gas-heated press – a large, fairly old, Baker Perkins model, which had been bought second-hand for £750 and cleverly adapted to perform its current role. Inside, a chain of eighteen platens were sequentially opened, fed with a mix, and closed; they passed into an oven and were 'pressed' together by steam with a force of 4 tons. The machine was producing an inconsistent and unsatisfactory product, and a cure was being sought by a number of senior staff and workers on an *ad hoc* basis. The corporate spirit with which the problem was being tackled clearly exemplified the very good labour relations enjoyed by this family business but it really was uneconomic in staff deployment. The cut-and-dry technique adopted, although requiring a fair degree of skill, lacked any real methodology or system.

Process problems of this nature are particularly difficult, since the ultimate solution would be likely to involve alterations to a number of factors, e.g. temperature, viscosity, time, pressure, etc. Indeed, the recommended approach is to use a statistical planning technique designed to measure the combined effect of sets of possible interacting variables. However, it was perhaps inevitable that the management kept hoping that the next experiment would succeed and did not seek help with an alternative approach. In fact, eight months elapsed before this machine fault was determined and rectified – eventually, by chromium-plating the platens and applying an anti-sticking agent. The delay clearly cost an estimated £30 000, to which should be added the lost opportunity costs.

Conclusions after factory visits

Notwithstanding the difficulties associated with seasonal production in a labour-intensive industry, Culpitts were seen to be a reasonably successful family business, enjoying pleasant and cordial staff relations. They were coping with their problems and showing a profit, albeit a small one. The company was keeping its head above water largely due to the enthusiasm and initiative of the senior partners, for whom the staff had considerable respect. Nevertheless, they did have cause for concern, and their current state of affairs could very quickly change for the worse if something was not done in time.

First, Culpitts appeared too reliant on traditional outlets and were becoming increasingly vulnerable to overseas competitors. To protect themselves against this threat, new market opportunities had to be sought and a planned marketing policy formulated and put into practice quickly. Second, an attempt had to be made to even out their cash-flow situation so that the new market outlets should take account of this.

Under the inspiration of the chairman there was considerable evidence of ingenuity in the construction of semi-automatic equipment in the factory but innovation was really needed on a much broader front to embrace entire work-processes. Furthermore, these processes would need to be designed in such a way as to be less dependent on manual labour – particularly if they could not be fully utilized all the year round. This desire for fully automatic processes was, in fact, the objective which prompted Peter Culpitt to seek outside advice in the first place, but their current methods of operation conflicted with this form of development; there was little evidence of planning which operations would be best automated having regard to profit capital, market importance, etc.

During many years of evolution and development of a factory it is inevitable that much of the development occurs fortuitously and in several unco-ordinated directions. This indicates a healthy determination to follow up particular ideas and projects. To give one example, one order from a large supermarket chain amounted to 20 per cent of the business and its many 'specials' made high production efficiency almost impossible to attain. Periodically, however, it becomes necessary to stand back and take an overall look at a situation, with the object, for example, of reorganizing the layout more efficiently. It was felt that the Culpitt factory had reached such a stage and the time had arrived when a more purposeful direction might be given to the innovation of work process – especially in the establishment of criteria for development in relation to in-house and external sources of expertise.

Further action

It was believed that the firm would benefit considerably from the expertise of external planning consultants to enable them to rationalize their production and marketing methods. They were given details of the Manufacturing Advisory Service offered by the Production Engineering Research Association (PERA), which has all the facilities and expertise to provide information and assistance in all areas of manufacture, materials, marketing, financial control, etc. PERA is a non-profit research and development consultancy, training and information centre set up by British Industry and the government in 1946 to provide individual firms with help to overcome specific production and management problems.

Although it was not the function of the 'Management of Innovation' project team to act as planning consultants it was felt that in this particular case, when the company might be at a crossroads, there would be benefit to both the team and the company in undertaking a small work programme to help steer the firm towards better planning and regionalization of its operations. Given the goodwill and co-operation of the chairman, an effort in this direction could increase their profit margin significantly. To continue as they were might easily result in their being forced out of business if overseas competition based on cheap labour were to undermine their traditional lines.

Synectics session

To identify new market opportunities which would be less vulnerable to overseas competition and offset the seasonal fluctuations of traditional business the project team suggested the use of the synectics creative problem-solving technique. A group of seven was selected and comprised Peter Culpitt, Dr Parker, the plant director from Ashington, and four other staff members representing different functions and levels of hierarchy. An external specialist conducted the sessions.

After a brief explanation of the principles of synectics, including suspension of judgement, use of fantasy and apparently irrelevant material, constructive evaluation, etc., the group addressed the question 'What products can we develop using existing technology?' Initially they generated twenty-five goal/wish statements, covering a wide range of possible approaches, wishes, embryonic ideas, etc. Three of these were selected for further development:

1   A new kind of sweet using Culpitt's printing technology;
2   Mail-order sales of complete cake-decorating packs; and
3   Metallized plastic products.

Four specific variants of the first concept were developed – sugar chocolate and printed wafer petals. Each idea was given a percentage rating by the participants for its newness, appeal, feasibility, and probability of success. The next session was devoted to the concept of mail-order cake-decorations. The concept was rated as before and scored high on all counts. Possible problems were identified and ideas generated on selling methods, products to be offered, designs, etc. The session ended with a listing of the action steps to be taken to pursue the idea. The third session dealt with metallized plastic products: a list of products for metallizing was generated and each participant selected their preferred idea from the list.

After a lunch break the group reassembled for one further session involving a high level of speculation with the object of developing a novel idea. The group generated a further twenty-seven goal/wish statements, with a much higher level of fantasy (lower practicality) than in the first session. They then used imaging techniques to generate fantasy material and developed intentionally absurd ideas. By a process of triggering and association a highly novel concept emerged: 'A wafer containing the ingredients of medical pills cut into strips, with symbols printed on, for underdeveloped countries.' The idea was considered by the group to be highly novel, appealing and feasible, and the chairman decided to put in a patent application and talk to a pharmaceutical consultant about it.

Subsequent to the synectics session (which took about 4½ hours) the planning director from Ashington attended the five-day synectics course with a view to using the techniques in the company on a regular basis. Some two months later Peter Culpitt held a 'think-tank' session concerned with their corporate planning exercise and explored the company objectives, corporate image, current position, threats, strengths and weaknesses. Additionally, they had five ideas for new products, and it was interesting to note that, from those five ideas, three were identical to those obtained in the seven suggestions from the synectics session, although the two groups only had two members in common.

The current position of the main suggestions is that the research and development team has been asked to design a machine to produce a sugar-wafer sprinkle. Peter Culpitt commented that 'No other person in Europe has such a machine, so a large market could develop of a non-seasonal nature.' It was, however, decided to postpone direct mail-order selling because of staff wage problems. Again, while metallizing plastic was believed to have a future, it was deferred because of lack of spare production capacity and of finance to purchase machinery. Chocolate-containing projects had to be abandoned since the company had insufficient expertise with this material. A new product in new market segments, namely drugs in wafers, is being patented and considered by a drug company.

Corporate planning

The success of the synectics session appeared to help the company accelerate its move towards a more progressive management of its business. Perhaps for the first time, the board started to take a really critical look at their situation. They drew up a corporate plan which was based on an appraisal of their expertise, their strengths and their weaknesses. They evaluated the threats and risks to which they were exposed and they considered alternatives to overcoming these. They stated their objectives carefully and realistically and set specific targets to be attained within a given time-scale. In addition, they have made 'brainstorming' sessions a regular feature of their company policy.

Culpitt's new strategy for forward planning involved four major policy changes:

(1) They made a critical assessment of all sections of their production department and used the simple criterion of profitability to decide which plant should be automated, semi-automated, or dropped. This, of course, involved accurate forecasting of market potential, capital outlay, and labour-savings.
(2) They would make further use of external expertise, manufacturing advising services, etc.
(3) They intensified their efforts to find new markets. One idea that stemmed from the synectics session was direct selling of their products by mail-order. They carried out market research to determine the demand for communion wafers. (This was done for them by two students from Buckingham Management College.) To Peter Culpitt's surprise here was a considerable market, possibly worth £35 000 in 1979 which, together with the model trees, could help to even-out their cash flow. Greater efforts were also to be made to increase their sales abroad. Fifteen per cent of their production was currently exported, with Canada being the best overseas market, but it was believed that this could be increased significantly. A major asset of the company was its highly motivated sales force – two in Europe, one in Scandinavia, and one in North America. It is of interest to note that the European market is restricted because several countries have no tradition of decorating cakes. New markets in Canada and the USA were thought to have considerable potential, and these would be served by the Mauritian factory.
(4) Research and development of new products would be made a key factor in their future strategy. To this end, a small development section was set up at Radlett near the company headquarters. Only two engineers were initially employed there, one aged thirty-eight and the other twenty-five, but both had served apprenticeships and both had obtained their City and Guilds Certificate. Additionally, a development engineer was appointed to the parent factory at Ashington, whose principal duties were to adapt and improve machines to suit the Culpitt processes. The first project to be worked on at Radlett was an automatic tree-making machine for the American flight simulation model based on Peter Culpitt's original idea but better suited to production in terms of safety and reliability.

The current situation and change

In the current inflationary climate things are still far from easy for the company. The reorganization of the factory has to be undertaken without disrupting current production schedules and there is little spare capital for this development. Profits are only 3 per cent of turnover and are daily eroded by price-increases in raw materials, mounting administration costs, and ever-increasing wage demands. In October 1978 the company's wages bill was increased by 22 per cent and the mark-up in profits was not sufficient to redress this higher expenditure; there seemed little prospect of improvement during 1979. The attitude of the TUC to our economy gives little incentive to growth and, to survive and prosper in such a climate, Culpitts are more than ever determined to reduce their workforce. The projections made in their corporate strategy and the planned automation of machinery were all aimed at increasing production and profits with fewer staff and, until this situation was achieved, the hardships would have to be borne without any real net increase in individual incomes. In the future, more consideration is to be given to licensing as a means of evening-out cash flow; indeed, this possibility has become part of their current thinking and discussions are currently being held with one British manufacturer.

Undoubtedly, Culpitt's new strategy contained a large element of innovation and it required considerable courage and dedication to carry it out. This was a healthy attitude, which had all the hallmarks of success for the future prosperity of the company. But perhaps the most innovative and courageous move of all was that made by Peter Culpitt of his own free will – to recognize the shortcomings of his own organization and to do something about it before it was too late; given the will, all things are possible.

Since completing the body of this report, Peter Culpitt has written: 'I would just add that, out of all the multiplicity of ideas, we only needed two or three to work out successfully to considerably change and improve the company's financial position and, in this connection, the effort put into the model trees for flight simulators has just resulted in a £75 000 order being received which, in itself, will be extremely profitable due to the fact that these items are manufactured completely automatically from start to finish as a result of producing one machine specifically to do this job. Several of the other new items are in the pipeline, the main one being the production of a machine to produce sugar wafer sprinkle – so here again a large market could develop of a non-seasonal nature.'

29

From idea to implementation: pitfalls along the stony road between idea creation and the market place

Walter K. Schwartz

Initially encouraged by management, several employees of Ogden Silks International (OSI) identified a totally new business opportunity which would make use of state of the art material handling and fabric printing techniques.

The method would also allow customizing of fashionable garments, scarves and ties to user specifications. The new products were intended particularly to appeal to individuals who could afford higher cost silk fabrics and wanted unique fashion products.

This chapter shows examples of how brilliant ideas with a revenue potential of several hundred million dollars for the company struggle through a labyrinth of bureaucracy, national and personal prejudices, procrastination, or the ever present 'not invented here' syndrome before they finally succeed – or die.

The persons, departments and organizations affected are:

- Idea Originators – compulsive, capable, dedicated but sometimes dreamy or hopelessly optimistic, rarely equipped with adequate salesmanship.
- Expert Advisers – helpers in the fine tuning of a proposal who too often superimpose their own thinking onto someone else's idea and thus weaken identification and the originator's pride.
- Decision Makers – with power and resources to make things happen in the end but sceptical of solutions or apparent opportunities unless almost outwitted into believing they were part of the creation of the idea.
- Departments – overburdened with measurable responsibilities and therefore unwilling to allocate resources to new tasks which come about late and totally outside the routine planning cycle.
- Corporations – aware of the need to innovate, prepared to endorse efforts but reluctant to diversify into unknown avenues, particularly where radical changes of marketing methods would be required.

This chapter also attempts to identify common originator mistakes which either delay the acceptance of an innovation or eliminate it altogether.

- Idea Selection – ideas which generally reflect very personal needs or interests are assumed to be welcomed by everyone else as well.
- Concept Presentation – the 'selling' of ideas to the wrong address. Frequently the targeted manager or group is not easily enthused by radically new concepts. Lack of decision power to act upon a proposal, by an otherwise receptive manager, can also be the end of a good idea.
- Originator's loss of drive and confidence – the originator is unprepared to deal with great resistance to change within the company.

Market attraction, sustainable competitive advantages and rock bottom costing are critical to the success of innovation. But without the right corporate climate, management with a visionary spirit, unbiased consultants and exceptionally diligent innovators, ideas would not even see the light of the day. Nothing improves the likelihood of success more than the constructive attitude of stakeholders during idea development. Innovation is a 'people issue'.

This chapter is based on the trials and tribulations which confront innovators in their desire to affect change. In most organizations the hurdles which confront the avant garde are ever present but rarely admitted, so we have changed the names of companies, individuals and products. For reasons of simplification secondary decision makers have not been given much exposure here, primarily because they could have been bypassed and thus not have influenced the real outcome of the case. But in a critical sense of the word, just about everyone in a company is a stakeholder as everyone contributes to corporate climate.

The chapter is intended for aspiring 'Change Agents' and practitioners of Innovation. It aims to sensitize those interested in avoiding the typical pitfalls in the innovation process. It is left to the scholar of innovation to categorize the dominant attitudes of stakeholders: Are they opposing, indifferent, supportive or even proactive? How can the available power of the first two groups be turned to advantage? How can existing positive forces be made even more effective? Which are the 'power lines' in the organization? Who can really influence what? At the same time it is important to avoid 'overpowering' a proposal. Driving a project regardless of its strategic and monetary value, is as much a waste of company resources as it is not to pursue the right opportunities.

Modo Mondiale

MM (Fashion Ware International) was established just before the turn of the century by Riccardo Rosso, a small silk producer, outside Milan, Italy. The company had only seven employees initially but by 1915 there were eighty. At that time the product mix was only 40% silk garments, and the rest wool and cotton, but the company was still called Seta Rosso (Rosso Silk). World War I brought further expansion and a shift to nearly 95% wool and cotton, primarily with government and military applications. Only when Riccardo Rosso II took over in 1937 was the present name adopted.

Paradoxically by then silk had again become the predominant fabric used by MM. There was a clear market/materials split: 75% of silk production was exported and almost exclusively designer fashion-oriented. On the other hand all of the cotton and wool line (40% of total production) remained in Italy for continuing government and professional applications.

World War II again forced a switch, partly because the domestic farming of silkworms gave way to alternative crops (imports from China and India were not possible) and partly because the alliance with Germany had eliminated the bulk of exporting opportunities. Germany then advocated 'plain lines and practicality': silk was reserved for a very select minority.

But MM had another boom. The war demanded nearly all of the production capacity of the company and it was necessary to expand the manufacturing facilities and substantially upgrade equipment. Because of the priority status of military garment supply it was necessary to increase the labour force to 1600, nearly all women except about 110 male engineers, mechanics, truck drivers, the big boss, Signor Rosso II and his brother-in-law, Bruno Bianco, whom Rosso called 'direttore', although it was clear to everyone who the real director was. In October 1944 the imminent end of the war brought an abrupt termination of employment to all but a handful of the by then 2150 labour force.

The postwar years were disastrous for MM. Government contracts were unavailable, Europe had more pressing interests than fashion and synthetic fabrics began to make enormous inroads into the garment business. Some of MM's manufacturing plant had also suffered war damage and needed renewal or at least repair, although on the whole the company was still equipped for mass production.

Help came in the form of a major investment by a forgotten Rosso family member, Claudio, who had done well after his emigration to the USA in 1936. Claudio was also able to pull strings with the Italian Government for loans, for contracts and deals with the unions. By 1956 MM was back on the map. Employment was below the wartime level but at an impressive 1300.

At this time the company adopted the logo 'Clothing by Nature', a kind of statement of the direction its business activities would take. This statement gave the hopeful and constantly growing staff a strong sense of identity, but in the core management group it was the cause of constant conflicts.

In 1982 Claudio's daughter brought in another player and the scene was set. She married Alfredo Alancio, a Harvard graduate and a real visionary, but with scant respect for the traditional ways of running MM. Two weeks after his arrival at the plant, on taking office as marketing manager, he publicly expressed the view that the company was in for challenging years ahead (without first consulting his father-in-law or the ageing Rosso II). Alfredo could see the day 'when head-on competing with the Koreans and other cheap sources would be the only way out' and felt this was what Modo Mondiale should prepare for.

By the end of 1988 MM had 2620 employees in one main and two subsidiary production facilities in Italy. The company also had excellent channels of distribution bringing the whole product range of primarily very attractive and popular fashion wear to all of Europe, North America and Japan. About a dozen well-known freelance designers guaranteed them a fashionable look at more affordable prices.

Modo Mondiale's position in the market

The company's total sales value for 1988 was $670 million, with a revenue of $81 million. The total value of the clothing business in the region is $178 billion, 28% (or $50 billion) of which is spent on dresses, blouses, shirts, scarves and ties. Seven billion dollars of this goes into the quality/price category which MM is competing for. Its share is short of 10%, but along with one US and one West German manufacturer MM is clearly a key contender. Sixty per cent of this market was served by 72 small but mostly well branded companies.

In the mature industrial markets, and in 'medium fashion', a trend towards quality, individuality and health concerns has heightened interest in natural fibres. This is particularly true of Europe. North American and Japanese consumers still prefer the easy care synthetics or mixes.

The leading players

Riccardo Rosso II, 85, CEO, the real 'ruler' of MM, feels responsible for the continuation of the tradition of the Rosso credo: 'We are the best. As long as we all work towards this goal we are safe.' The employees refer to him as 'Papa' and bow when they meet him.

At the annual Christmas get-together every employee is personally handed by Rosso II an MM garment (always red as the company colour is also red – rosso!). Yet the tough old man has, just like his father, kept MM wages at a minimum. He is a feared negotiator with the unions and has never ceded this task to the personnel manager. He wins as a rule, since the community of Melegnano, the main company location, depends entirely on the existence and growth of Modo Mondiale. For 20 years from 1951 Rosso II was even mayor of the town. For 20 years now he has talked of retiring but he seems not to want to relinquish power. But finally, because of his doctor's urging, he said that by 1989 he would step down. No indications were given as to who his successor would be. No wonder, for ever since Claudio Rosso returned to Italy, Rosso II had been fearful of giving up his reign to an 'intruder'. He has never once admitted that the company would probably not have survived without Claudio.

Claudio Rosso, 62, managing director, a self-made entrepreneur of Italo-American style and accent, is a doer who spends much time on the shop floor talking to employees. He is very analytical and has a keen understanding of finance and a reliable instinct for the clothing business. Unlike the original Rosso clan, who from day one saw themselves as a silk company and would have liked still to call the company 'Seta Rosso', he predicted that MM would depend on a second product line, not silks.

Francesco Verde, 46, production manager, with an engineering background in printing technology, must be considered one of the world experts in garment manufacturing equipment and workflow for this industry. He is constantly called upon to air his knowledge at international professional conferences for the garment industry. He does not claim to understand the marketing mechanism of big business, nor does he have to. He is well liked by employees, is quite open to suggestions and participation by his staff and is probably the only higher manager who commands some respect from the CEO, at least with regard to his 'grease monkey skills', as Rosso II calls it.

Alfredo Alancio, 38, marketing manager, Harvard Business School graduate, for 3 years advertising manager for a leading airline, knows a good deal about information technology and speaks four languages fluently. He is an amateur racing driver but also enjoys spending as much time as possible with his wife and their two small children. Only very gradually has he been accepted as a capable and trustworthy leader in the company. His approach is still totally different from the Rossos'. His track record at MM is good: the company has improved sales volume by 82% since he joined 6 years ago. But a year ago he was seen to lose the company's most lucrative account in France, the leading French hypermarket chain, by making delivery promises which MM could not meet. According to Signor Verde, the production manager, the promises were quite unrealistic. Alancio blames the 'disinterested teams' in the factory. He will have to do a lot of mending in order to be accepted again. Rosso II temporarily fired him but the family persuaded him to reconsider. This, incidentally, was the day Papa first mentioned his definite retirement.

Antonio Grigio, 59, financial and administration manager, is, along with the production manager one of only two non-family members of the management group at MM. He is a detail-oriented bureaucrat, punctual to the point of obsession; the staff snigger behind his back, although no one really understands what he thinks and wants. Justice is top priority and it is more important to do things right rather than to do the right things. His books are in perfect order and because of his 39-year involvement in international finance he has also acquired an impressive feeling for the trends and timing of the world money markets. At least one and a half percent of profit must be attributed to Antonio's creative handling of the company's finances.

Carlo Nero, 42, sales manager Europe and North America, brother of Signora Rosso II, got his job through his sister when she was helping him to get over a personal tragedy. Since then brother and sister have had some major disagreements because of Carlo's critical behaviour towards Rosso II. It was agreed that he could keep his job because he does it well and because he is rarely home anyway. It was thought that putting him on commission would starve him, but quite unexpectedly he is now one of the best earners in MM.

Franco Marrone, 30, building maintenance assistant since he started with the company at 17, is a jack of all trades and helpful when asked but rather a 'loner', a little introvert but ready to be involved with everything as soon as trouble arises. He is perfect for his job. Only his manager, Signor Grigio, finds him much too disorganized and unable during a performance interview to articulate what he does. He has been twice bypassed for promotion and while he is not bitter at MM he is always on the look-out for another job. His hobbies are model railways and computing, which keep him up late at night.

Angela Aureo, 37, secretary to the production manager (Verde) is capable, fast, pleasant, and likes to help underdogs. Her boss is totally dependent on her as she knows the company inside out, most of the staff and even the customers, as she previously worked in the sales support department. Her boss boasts about her and says that 'if she has the measles, MM might as well shut down.' On her birthdays she has 15 bouquets of flowers on her desk, but she is single: she is in love with her job.

The coming of innovation overture at Modo Mondiale

When Alfredo Alancio, the marketing manager and Francesco Verde, the production manager, were on the plane home from the annual Garment Manufacturers' Association meeting in Paris, they agreed that MM was in need of reform. They felt that the one Swedish speaker who talked of the resource 'people' made a lot of sense when he said that employees only need to be given a chance and they will make a contribution to their company. While the Italians were a bit sceptical, they were going to sell the idea to Papa, have a sort of idea contest for the entire company. Rosso II did not like it at all, and it took his wife's encouragement for him to reluctantly agree.

Three weeks later the old man signed an invitation on the bulletin boards which asked anyone with an idea for turning the company into a gold mine to fill in an idea form available at Angela's desk. Someone scribbled on the notice 'Papa's Gold mine', but in total 140 forms were filled in and about 30 of these had proposals which were attractive enough to consider further. Alancio felt that the ideas should be discussed after a special presentation arranged for the innovators to 'show and tell'.

Rosso II made a little speech and it looked as if it had all been his doing. The judging managers were pleased with what they found in the ideas; at least they said so. One proposal seemed to arouse anger. When the quiet Franco Marrone unpacked his home-modified ink jet printer and claimed that he could write 'Rosso' on a silk tie with it, Grigio, the bureaucrat, left the room, saying that the process was a waste of time. Much to the amazement of the rest of the group Marrone showed that his device worked. Alancio offered to spend time with Marrone to give it some enhancement and help with some of the marketing aspects.

The appendix shows Marrone's original proposal, embellished with the help of Alancio. The company provided the format, with questions to help individuals who are not skilled in all disciplines. Most of the forms had a title and a brief idea description filled in only. It was a good start. At least the aims of the individual proposals were clear. Alancio felt the ink jet idea was so good he wrote a very detailed business plan before Verde and his technical staff could provide a technical feasibility statement. He said he had seen it work and that was all that counted. Marrone at first was overwhelmed by all the attention he got from Alancio but, when Angela congratulated him on his brilliant idea, he said that Alancio had really done most of the work.

When Carlo Nero was home for a few days he learned of the ink jet proposal and asked Marrone to give him a demonstration. Bluntly he told Marrone that there were probably some eccentrics who would buy 'hand painted' silk wear, but his customers were too sophisticated to go for stuff like this. Besides, why not go for somewhat larger runs and use conventional printing techniques for which the equipment was already in house?

Marrone was destroyed. He was about to go back to his model railways when Angela Aureo suggested she talk to Verde. Sure enough she got him to pay full attention to the case again and also to discuss it with the two Rossos. Rosso II in the end could not see how this method could ever work in mass production, because it would now take 3 minutes for the ink jet printer to finish some 8 inches of full width fabric. Alfredo Rosso in a flash of inspiration suggested contacting a school friend who was an expert with ink jet printing. The friend's response was very encouraging and the project seemed to be back on course.

Verde, the production manager, allocated some reserve funds and put a small team of technicians to work to build a larger transport unit and to incorporate several print heads to speed up the printing. Just as the first results came back from this test Signora Rosso II and Angela Aureo were discussing Marrone's dream machine which would let them design their own summer dress on Friday and wear it to the picnic on Saturday.

What an opportunity. They even had Rosso II fully on their side now. Only Grigio saw absolutely no chance of this 'gadget', as he called it, bringing anything but debt to the company. He would not agree to the investment which would be necessary to go into production before the next season. Why not try it out in a garage first? Between this cost and the expansion of the train loading dock, he felt the latter was by far the more important. Also he cautioned that the unions would not accept another production method which potentially replaced manpower.

When the salesmen in Italy and abroad were asked by Alfredo Rosso, in a note accompanied by a sample of material imprinted with the ink jet method, to obtain customer opinions about market potential another critical stage had arrived. Carlo Nero, who learned of the letter to 'his' sales team, called Rosso II and said that the reps would only make fools of themselves if they went around and showed this 'painting by numbers invention'. Rosso was furious but was not willing to have another family crisis by arguing with Carlo.

The answers from customers via the sales team were sporadic and not very encouraging. But then came the lucky break. An American mail order company with a nationally distributed catalogue requested immediate rights for the exclusive handling of dresses, blouses and ties designed by the user. They would offer their customers the opportunity to send in designs or patterns and pick one of 23 different garments to combine with their 'personal art'. The originals would be scanned on the day of arrival and transmitted via modems to the factory in Italy. There they would be printed by the computer-controlled ink jet printer, cut and sewn on the same day. They wanted a 24-hour service as an added sales incentive.

MM seized the contract. Alancio was happy, Marrone was proud. It had only taken 14 months to bring this idea to market. However, the sales are not yet very impressive. Two of MM's original US customers changed supplier because the exclusive agreement between MM and their competitor upset them. The net outcome in the first year of market availability is negative. But the jury is still out and only time will tell if ink jet printing was a worthwhile innovation.

Appendix: Modo Mondiale business proposal

I. TITLE

Descriptive phrase (7 words max.) conveying essence of idea such as technology, applications and target market.

Ink jet printing on silk fashion wear.

II. ABSTRACT

A one paragraph summary of the Idea Memorandum.

Existing dyeing and imprinting methods for silk garments and accessories are costly and inflexible. The idea utilizes ink jet printing which is computer controlled and thus permits infinite colour and design variations at affordable prices for a receptive world fashion market.

III. BACKGROUND

What needs (established or latent) and trends does the idea satisfy?	*Higher priced fashion wear often lacks the 'one of a kind' appeal. Middle income consumers would like to afford high-class fashions. There is a slight trend back to natural fibres.*
How is the market now served, however inadequately?	*Cheap imports from China and India, which do not meet Western design and colour expectations, or unimaginative synthetics are offered to the market now.*
What are the limitations of what is out there now?	*Conventional natural fabric imprinting methods depend on medium to high volume to be economic, making the end product rather ordinary. Cheap synthetics do not accept subtle dyes for the classic look.*
Who benefits? What and where is the market potential?	*Fashion-conscious middle income consumers worldwide would be attracted to personalized silk fashions. 250 million individuals fit this category.*
What is the value?	*About two purchases/year/person would account for a global value of $9 billion.*
What is the cost?	*Associated ink jet printer investments, including some cooperative research, are about $300K.*
For how many years will this opportunity be valid?	*A window of opportunity for at least 10 years is realistic.*

IV. IDEA DESCRIPTION

Is this an extension of a current Modo Mondiale business or a new venture?	*It is proposed to set up a separate MM division to serve the ink jet garment imprinting market.*
What is your product or service? (Briefly describe concept supported by one or two simple sketches if applicable.)	*The product to be offered depends on a specially designed fabric ink jet imprinting device, computer controlled, to permit design and colour changes at a minimal effort and cost. Hardware and software would be proprietary to our company.*
How does the proposed idea overcome the above mentioned limitations?	*The method would substantially reduce the production costs of printed silk materials for the fashion industry.*

Are there additional advantages to the customer?	*Infinite design and colour variations, much finer print resolution, and variations for individual stores with imprinted branding are also a simple matter.*
What is your key success ingredient?	*Short term availability of the ink jet printer, a well co-ordinated campaign which takes full advantage of our leading edge.*
What unique strengths does Modo Mondiale have that relate to this idea? (Technology, marketing, etc.?)	*Modo Mondiale's recent re-entry into the high fashion arena and the company's quality and brand image along with worldwide distribution capabilities.*
If this business is successful, does it lead to more opportunities?	*It is readily possible to apply the same printing technique to cotton and wool goods.*
What is your price/cost position?	*Compared to conventional silk imprinting, production costs with the above method will be less than 1/3 allowing for healthy margins.*
Assumptions and prerequisites for implementation:	*It is assumed that world silkworm production can satisfy new demand levels for lower cost silks and that the trend to use natural fibres will continue to grow. A prerequisite for the anticipated success is market availability prior to 1989 as other suppliers are likely to pursue the same opportunities.*
Issues and unresolved questions:	*One issue to be resolved concerns whether dye stability is impaired by the combination of high intensity jet pressure and delicate silks.*

V.   CONCLUSION

A brief wrap-up statement. In what way will Modo Mondiale benefit most from this proposal? (Strategically, financially, image-wise, share-wise.)	*By following this proposal, Modo Mondiale would diversify into a totally new market segment at a very attractive rate of return.*

ORGANIZATIONAL RENEWAL

30

Using the creative process to resolve a strategic conflict over environmental issues at Berol

Roger Evans and Peter Russell

One area in which many companies are having to reconsider established patterns of thinking and behaviour – and very rapidly so – is in response to environmental concerns. Global disaster is clearly not in the long-term interest of any company, yet its threat has seemed so far removed from such day-to-day considerations as sales and marketing, budget forecasting and production planning that environmental issues have, until recently, remained low on most boardroom agendas. In part this tardiness has been due to a lack of awareness of the long-term impact of various industrial processes, and in part it has been due to an inherent conflict between the values of a corporation, driven by its need to stay in business, and the more human needs of people who wish to stay alive and healthy.

The chemical industry, in particular, is beset by this conflict between corporate and human concerns. It is, by its very nature, not very friendly to the environment. It can have problems with the effluents it produces; there can be hazards associated with the production; and many chemicals may be difficult to transport. In addition, the products themselves may have to be handled carefully; some may be of immediate danger to living systems, or they may not degrade easily, thereby accumulating in the eco-systems once their job is done. For people working in the chemical industry this conflict can be the source of considerable tension and unease; the company's need, as seen in the short term, to stay in business may require that people respond in ways that are contrary to their own personal values.

One might argue that people who find themselves in this situation should leave and find work in what is for them a more compatible industry. But for most this is not practical. Personal and family needs do not allow them the flexibility of retraining, they would probably have to suffer an unacceptable reduction in salary, and in many cases relocation would present severe disruption to family life.

Towards the end of the eighties this internal conflict came to the fore in Berol Kemi, an international chemical group based in Sweden. A number of the employees, including some of the directors, wished to see the company adopt a policy of 'environmentally sounder chemistry'. They believed that the company should produce only products that were safe for the environment, the user, the public and the employee – and for these products to be produced by equally safe means. This group wanted to see their company adopt the goal of becoming, within five years, one of the cleanest chemical companies in the world. Other members of the company felt that these objectives were impractical and unrealistic, to say the least. They argued that to attempt such a shift, given the current state of the industry as a whole, would be financial, and hence corporate, suicide.

The process

The situation came to a head at the annual strategy meeting, which we were helping to facilitate. Strategy meetings in Berol did not follow the norm of most corporations. Under the inspiration of its then president, Ralph Edebo, the company had adopted a decentralized structure and had included production workers and administration staff in its decision-making processes in addition to board members and departmental chiefs. As a result the strategy meeting consisted of about 40 people representing a cross-section of the company – and a cross-section of views on the green issue.

The question of a strong environmental strategy had been fermenting in the company for quite a while and by the time of the meeting feelings were running high in both camps, their positions becoming increasingly entrenched. Rather than rushing in and trying to resolve the polarization by argument and debate – a process that tends to produce capitulation on the part of the minority rather than any genuine resolution – we invited them first to step back and look at some different perceptions on the issue.

During the first morning we showed the group several short videotapes – an astronaut describing his experiences in space; an exploration of the long-term implications of accelerating change; and a summary of the ways in which human civilization was degrading the environment. These inputs were followed by a general discussion of the world-wide environmental issue and participants' personal feelings about it.

This setting of the issue in a broader context is a very important part of any creative process. The most common response to any problem is to rush in and get a solution. But rarely are such solutions the best ones. Spending a good period of time (often as much as half the problem-solving time) exploring the greater context of the problem is almost always time well spent. It not only leads to an approach that is more thought through; it can itself trigger completely new approaches to the problem.

The sharing of feelings is also a crucial part of this initial process. If we keep our emotional responses to ourselves (as most people north of the Alps are prone to do) we inhibit our own thinking around an issue. Having people simply express their feelings, without any judgement, can play a very important role in helping the group open up to each other, and results in much freer and more productive conversations.

At this stage we also introduced people to the creative thinking model that we use. This is not to give a technique of creativity, but to help people recognize the stages that they are passing through – particularly the periods of frustration that can come up with issues such as the one we were tackling. Too easily people dismiss their frustration as something that is standing in the way of their arriving at a satisfactory solution, rather than seeing it as signal of what is needed at that time – perhaps more preparation, or a period of quiet incubation.

We also spent some time introducing people to mind-sets – what they are and how they affect our perception, thinking and decision-making. When people start debating different points of view, they are often debating their different mind-sets on an issue – too easily we become stuck in our own beliefs and do not see the other side's point of view. Nor, for that matter do we recognize that our side of the argument is strongly coloured by our own mind-sets; more often than not we feel 'I am right, they are wrong'.

Following through on the mind-set model, we asked everyone in the room to explore their own attitudes and assumptions on the question of the company becoming a leader in 'environmentally sounder chemistry'. Collecting all the different mind-sets together, we put them up around the room – there were so many different points of view that this took most of the wall space available. The purpose of this was to help everyone stand back and see the issue from beyond their own particular point of view. Each person could see that their views were there, and were being taken into consideration; and they could also see more clearly why other people might take a different position. People on opposite sides of the issue were able to step back from their position without feeling they were giving in. In other words, everyone could feel heard without having to over-ride others.

Moreover, not only did they feel heard, they each began to recognize that they also had some sympathy for opposing points of view. So long as they remained in a position of having to defend their own side they were not able to acknowledge this in themselves.

After considerable discussion of all the different mind-sets that were in this group, we asked them to see if there was any common ground to them – anything they could all agree upon. What came to the surface was the fact that no-one in the group felt happy about working in an industry that had a negative impact on the environment. As one participant put it: 'I cannot put my hand on my heart and say that I am proud to earn my salary in the chemical industry.'

This was the turning point for the group. When one of the union leaders heard the president state that he too felt this way, he said, 'If that is what you feel then you have my full support.'

The conflict now had a larger context within which it could be explored, and which did not leave people polarized. The 'pragmatists' were able to acknowledge the values and needs of the individual. And the 'greens', feeling heard, were in turn able to hear the very real concerns of the pragmatists. The conflict between the needs of the individual and the needs of the company was now a conflict everyone could share.

The action

Having established common ground we then set about finding a common path that could satisfy the different facets of the issue, i.e. a path that both respected individuals' concerns about the environment and their wish to work for a company that was doing everything it could to improve the situation, and the need of the company to remain a healthy competitor in its field.

The group decided that the first step should be to carry out an audit of the company's environmental performance in key areas. Five action groups were set up to carry this through, to recommend appropriate changes and to co-ordinate implementation. The areas tackled were:

1 The internal environment in the company
2 The external environment
3 Our products today: how environmentally sound are they?
4 New business opportunities
5 Logistics.

Results

While the results that follow cannot be attributed solely to the 'environmentally sounder chemistry process' (ESC) that was initiated, there is agreement that this process certainly assured that some key results were achieved much earlier than otherwise would have been the case.

Plants made substantial reductions in emissions and are setting standards well beyond those likely to be required by future law. New research into more acceptable products is underway. An important idea to emerge in screening the development of products was an 'environmental matrix' that is applied to all new business opportunities, from exploration through to final use and waste of the product. Internal safety standards have been significantly improved throughout all production facilities in four different locations.

And perhaps most important as far as the long-term alignment of company and individual objectives are concerned, a company-wide environmental education programme (Ekolyfkt) was established. Although participation has been on a voluntary basis, held outside work hours over a three-month period, 60% of the total work force has participated in this

programme. All participants in the programme were given free member-
ship by Berol of either the Swedish Environmental Protection Foundation
(SNF) or to Greenpeace.

The effect of this educational programme has been widespread through
many parts of the company and served to raise awareness in many people
about the critical significance of the environmental issue at this stage in our
history. What is interesting is that this exercise was organized approximately one year before a major push by the environmental movements in
the EEC, and at the same time as the Green Party in Sweden obtained 5%
of the total vote in a general election and took seats in the Swedish
Parliament. The synergy of these events is, we believe, significant and the
willingness of Berol Kemi to undertake this level of education has been
very important for the morale of the employees within the company.

The momentum that the whole of the environmentally sounder
chemistry (ESC) programme started to build at Berol Kemi was considerably inhibited during the process of selling the company to Nobel Industries in 1988 and its merger with Kenobel to form Berol Nobel.

With new leadership at Berol Nobel now, a new strategic development is
underway to put the environment again in the forefront of its development.
Since the Spring of 1990 we have been engaged by the new President,
Christer Andersson, to help facilitate a new position on the environmental
question. Once again this has involved about 50 of the senior managers of
the company in a creative process and dialogue to help them look at
positive steps that need to be taken.

This time, four years later, although some momentum has been lost
there is a strong commitment to deal not only with the external and internal environment but most important with a need to develop new environmentally sound products. This commitment is backed by a group of company-wide project leaders who are looking at different areas of the
business to stimulate and challenge line management to make the environment a central plank of their local strategy.

Conclusions

As we look back over this creative process with Berol Kemi/Berol Nobel
we see learning points for both ourselves and for the company.

While the initial creative process in the first strategy meeting was an
important way to empower and create a new attitude in Berol Kemi towards the environment and enable a number of separate initiatives to be
started, it did not in our view realize its full potential in the first instance.
What was required was not only an on-going, sustained commitment by
senior management but a significant re-commitment and re-statement by a
new leadership to ensure that the creative process continued.

Our key conclusions can be identified as follows:

1 It is not enough to initiate a process of change, such as environmentally

sounder chemistry, from the top. It is vital that this support is sustained strongly after the initial process.

2   The groups set up in each of the key areas were very interested and committed, but most were not empowered with enough authority to carry the initiatives through to completion.

3   Our role as facilitators was used fully in the early part of the process and in the strategy meeting. In order to ensure that the action groups were empowered to achieve their results we could have played a more significant and facilitating role with them. Groups such as these, working with the edge of new ideas, need continual support, encouragement and creative coaching to deliver.

4   While it happens, an interactive process such as ESC becomes an integral part of the culture of the company. This must be considered and taken into account when trying to merge two companies and their activities.

5   Education is an action, an event and a process with many different aspects and levels. One aspect of the Ekolyfkt was that it created a neutral platform where burning issues of the company could be discussed.

31

Xerox charts a new strategic direction

Carol Kennedy

The myth of the paperless office

The paperless office, that technological mirage which beguiled us in the 1970s, is not going to happen. Xerox Corporation, a company built on the single most profitable invention in US history – the photocopier – has designed its strategy for the 1990s around the firm assumption that the paper document will continue to be 'the primary tool of the office' and its principal measure of work output.

After a period of restructuring and corporate soul-searching in the early 1980s which succeeded in reversing a serious Japanese threat to its survival in the mass copier market, Xerox adopted intensive new planning techniques to identify its strengths for the future in office products and systems. Out of these has come a new strategic direction for the company, based on a family of technologies covered by the term 'document processing'.

Xerox has concluded that, for most businesses, enormous investments in information systems have not paid off in increased productivity because office technology, in most cases, reaches only a small portion of a company's information base – up to 80 per cent of which is carried on paper. Former Xerox president Paul A. Strassmann, an internationally recognized guru on information technology, has pointed out that paper usage in US offices has been growing steadily since 1946 at three times the rate of the country's GNP, and shows no sign of slowing down. Instead of replacing paper, electronic workstations have actually generated more of it.

Documents, in the words of Roger E. Levien, Xerox Vice-President responsible for corporate strategy, are 'the lifeblood of the office, its raw material and its final product'. Document processing, as the new strategy defines it, is broadly the technique of building bridges for documents to pass easily between the two worlds of paper and electronics, to enable a company to make the best use of its entire information base. Although electronic printers enable computer-held data to be transmitted to paper,

Reprinted with permission from *Long Range Planning*, 22 (1), 1989, pp. 10–17; © 1989 Pergamon Press PLC going in the reverse direction is less easy. Huge amounts of data are therefore being held on paper, electronically inaccessible to many parts of a company.

Technology, says Levien, is just beginning to close this loop. The next big step will be for paper documents to be converted to electronic documents – not simply as images but with words, graphs, charts, pictures, scanned into digital storage systems to be called up as required and reformatted, edited, or put together in a brand new document. Xerox has the technology and its strategy for the remainder of the century will be to deliver products and systems to the market that bridge the present chasms between paper and electronic filing and retrieval.

It is potentially an enormous market. Including electronic printing, Xerox president Paul Allaire estimates it at around $80bn by 1995 – ten times its present size. Allaire believes that small companies, even doctors' and lawyers' offices, could be part of it within 10 years.

Linking electronic and paper documents

In the larger business context, Allaire states:

> Connecting the company's document base to its electronic environment is a key to realising the full potential of its investments in information systems. We believe that a company's ability to gain a competitive edge in the future will depend on its ability to effectively utilise its entire information base. Our strategy is designed to enable our customers to do that – by providing products and software that will enhance the ease with which people can create, reproduce, distribute and file documents, and by enabling users to move seamlessly back and forth between electronic and paper documents.

In Allaire's view,

> the biggest requirement in industry today is to improve office productivity. It has not kept up with productivity improvements on the manufacturing side. To compete in the nineties, a company has to be cost-effective in all areas: for most businesses, most of the jobs are in the white-collar area.

David T. Kearns, chairman and chief executive officer of Xerox since 1982, enlarged on this theme when he explained some of the basic findings which emerged from the first major strategy review, 'Xerox '95'.

> It will become increasingly imperative for American businesses to improve office productivity. Office expenditures now account for about 75 per cent of the national wage. They are the largest expense item in business today, and they are increasing.

> While data processing and communications have automated many office functions very well, this is not true in the document area. With office workers spending 30 to 70 per cent of their time interacting with documents, this area accounts for a large percentage of office costs.

Paper will continue to be the primary medium for documents well into the future.

We can expect electronics costs to continue to fall and capability to continue to rise at incredible rates over the next 5 to 15 years. This will make new document processing applications affordable for most businesses.

Kearns, a man with a crusading belief in quality that extends to dinner-table arguments with his wife over whether 100 per cent fault-free quality is consistently attainable (he thinks it is, she doubts it), has achieved something remarkable, if not unique, in US industry. By his quality cultural revolution in the company, coupled with fierce cost-cutting and decentralizing the businesses, he has made Xerox the only US corporation to regain market share lost to Japanese competitors. (In 1986, a hard year for the office equipment industry, Xerox increased overall market share in copiers.) That battle, although won, instilled awareness of the need for longer and deeper planning horizons. Kearns explains how the strategy emerged:

Narrowing the focus

> We took a long, hard look at our weaknesses. We saw that we were not going to succeed selling office information systems that were computing or communications oriented. We also recognized that we could not sell 'generic' systems. Nobody buys a generic anything – they buy something to help them meet a specific need. We saw that our initial strategy – offering operating systems that were developed uniquely for our equipment – was the wrong way to go.
>
> We considered our strengths, too. This company began in the document image processing business, and that has always been our greatest strength. We also have tremendous knowledge and experience in the information systems business, having pioneered many of the important advances in the application of information processing to the office. We believe our expertise in the office, and particularly in the document area, gives us an important edge over companies that will attempt to compete in this market from a data processing or telecommunications point of view.

Several alternative strategies were considered, as Roger Levien explains in detail later. There were some vigorous differences of opinion over how broad or narrow the company's focus should be, and over how quickly Xerox customers would take to the new concept of document processing. 'I can't say we all agreed on all the points we debated, but we did get a pretty good consensus,' says Kearns. 'We ended up by narrowing the focus of the company considerably. We reorganized to reflect our new emphasis on document processing, cutting back on a number of programmes and bolstering or consolidating others.'

The strategic reconnaissance

The idea of 'Xerox '95' was to establish a 10-year corporate strategy, based on the company's best assessments of where office technology and global markets were heading. Before Kearns launched the exercise in 1985, however, a great deal of spadework had already been done under the direction of Levien, who joined the Xerox corporate strategy office in Stamford, Connecticut, in 1982 after 20 years experience in long-range planning, two-thirds of that with the Rand Corporation.

'Xerox did not have a tradition of thinking more than a few years into the future,' explains Levien. Some strategic work had been done in the early 1970s, but it was never built into the regular planning process. Levien volunteered on his appointment to undertake a study called Xerox 1992, looking at what was then a 10-year horizon for the sort of market environment in which the company might expect to be operating.

Levien employed a technique analogous to a military staff exercise, which he had practised both at Rand and at the International Institute for Applied Systems Analysis, a body set up jointly by the United States and Russia in 1972 and sponsored by non-government agencies in 17 countries; its purpose being long-range thinking on global, bridge-building issues between east and west.

> We called it a 'strategic reconnaissance', the idea being to fly out over the future and try to determine the key features of the strategic terrain; where the hills and valleys and swamps were, not so much to pick out each house and telephone pole, but to understand the terrain and then to look at some possible paths through it, as if you were flying a reconnaissance out ahead of an army and wanted to understand where the enemy is and what the opportunities are, and where the breaches and defences are.

If a technique like this had been part of Xerox's strategic planning 10 years earlier, the company would undoubtedly have woken up much earlier to the Japanese threat that materialized between 1976 and 1982 to deprive it of half its worldwide business in copiers. During those 6 years, Xerox's market share of copier sales plummeted from 82 to 41 per cent under an onslaught from Canon, Minolta, Ricoh and Sharp, all of whom were producing small compact machines – a market niche neglected by Xerox – at half Xerox's manufacturing costs, and selling them at the US company's cost price.

The classic success story

The cultural shock was almost as severe as the financial one for a company that had regarded itself as virtually unassailable in its field. Xerox had, after all, been one of the century's classic business success stories, ever since the entrepreneurial Joseph Wilson's Haloid Corporation acquired the rights in 1947 to the process of xerography invented by Chester Carlson in 1938. More than 20 major US manufacturers had turned down Carlson's invention of dry copying; among them blue-chip names like IBM, RCA, Kodak, General Electric and Remington Rand. None could see the point of an expensive machine performing the function of cheap carbon paper.

Carlson went on to earn more than $200m from his invention, and Wilson more than $100m. On 16 September 1959, Xerox announced its model 914 copier, later to be described by *Fortune* magazine as 'the most successful product ever marketed in America' (one of the original 914 copiers is now in Washington's Smithsonian Museum). The 914, so called because it could reproduce documents up to 9 inches by 14 inches in size, was easier to use than rival copiers from Kodak and 3M: it used ordinary paper, and all the operator needed to do was dial the number of copies required and push a button.

The innovation that really established Xerox's market leadership, however, was not so much the product as Joe Wilson's brilliant idea of leasing the machines while his competitors sold theirs outright. For $95 a month and a 15-day cancellation clause, customers could make 2000 free copies and pay four cents a copy after that. So rapidly did the photocopier become indispensable to business life that the volume of copies soon exceeded the wildest forecasts: in 1967 a research company estimated that each leased machine was generating an average of 100,000 copies a year – a clear $4500 of pure profit for Xerox.

'The 914 killed carbon paper,' said Peter McColough, who succeeded Wilson as CEO in 1968. But the real, unexpected volume came through the copies made from copies. As McColough is quoted in *Xerox: The American Samurai*, by Gary Jacobson and John Hillkirk: 'It was the forerunner of making graphic communications possible ... It allowed people to share information inexpensively and easily.' In the mid-1950s, 20m photocopies a year were made in the United States: by 1965 the figure had reached 9.5bn and by 1966 it was 14bn. In 1985, more than 700bn copies were being churned out around the world.

The Jaws Chart

One of Xerox's key mistakes in the 1970s was to phase out its lucrative leasing base in favour of outright sales; a move which generated cash in the short term but ate away fatally at the long-term seedcorn. The strategy began in the European subsidiary, Rank Xerox, on the assumption that new products would soon fill the gap, but these were 2 to 3 years behind schedule. As a result, Rank Xerox profits dived from £255m in 1979 to £200m in 1981 and then fell by half in 1982 to £105m. Xerox executives ruefully drew what they called the 'Jaws Chart' after the killer shark in the movie: the upper line of the open jaw represented short-term profits rising, the lower line represented leasing revenue declining. Without new products to fill it, the gaping jaws would eventually bite deep into earnings. Using another metaphor, a Xerox Vice-President commented: 'We had this gigantic cash cow and we almost milked it dry.'

So successful was the 914 that 2 years after it was introduced, the Haloid Corporation – by then renamed Xerox – was in the *Fortune 500*. Today, including its revenues from financial services (a $1.6bn diversification in 1982, appropriately mainly in insurance, to armour the company against over-reliance on the vulnerable business products market), it ranks among the top 40 US companies.

The name Xerox was personally chosen by Wilson from the Greek-derived 'xerography', meaning 'dry writing'. He adopted the principle used to create the Kodak trade name – a short, easily remembered word, starting and finishing with the same letter.

Xerox had the field virtually to itself for more than a decade. Serious competition arrived only in 1970 with the first IBM office copier. Xerox promptly sued IBM for infringement of 22 patents, but during the 1970s it was itself the target of many anti-trust suits. Then in the mid-1970s Eastman Kodak entered the fray with a copier that was technically more advanced than the 914. It forced Xerox on to the defensive for the first time. Simultaneously, the Japanese began to produce their low-cost copiers, making the technology affordable on a large scale to companies which could now buy cheaply instead of being locked in to a long-term leasing agreement. Kodak then joined forces with Canon of Japan to challenge Xerox directly across a wide range of copying machines.

The Japanese attack

The crunch for Xerox came in 1980 when it discovered that, far from narrowing the production-cost gap with Japan, it was actually falling farther behind. 'We were horrified to learn that *the selling price of the smallest Japanese machines was our manufacturing cost*,' says Kearns, who at that stage was company president but not yet CEO.

Kearns began to study the example of Xerox's Japanese partner, Fuji Xerox, which had already adopted total quality control. This was to become a cornerstone of Kearns' philosophy as CEO. With consultancy help from McKinsey, the company was radically restructured into more than 20 entrepreneurial business units and an R & D drive begun which resulted in successful new products such as the Memorywriter.

A group of Xerox engineers went to Japan and discovered that *Japanese firms could produce copiers in half the time as well as at half the cost of the American manufacturing plant* in Rochester, New York, although the daily amount spent on R & D in both cases was much the same.

Benchmarking

One key new practice which came out of this trip was 'benchmarking' – identifying the company's best competitors and working out how to improve on their methods at even lower costs.

Kearns set about implementing the new policy with vigour. Not only design and manufacturing but every single department of Xerox was henceforth required to measure its performance against the 'best of breed', in the old IBM terminology. So deeply was the philosophy eventually seeded through the corporation that the distribution department studied the mail-order business of L.L. Bean, based in Maine and an acknowledged leader in the field, to see how Bean organized such factors as inventory held in the warehouse.

Benchmarking, together with a marked upsurge in employee motivation and participation, helped Xerox chop its product development costs to a third of what they had been, and saved the corporation $120m a year on its entire design process. At the same time, in 1982/1983, Kearns cut 15,000 jobs and reduced the labour needed to bring out a new machine by 40 per cent and the time to bring it to market by 30 per cent.

Leadership through quality

The company's philosophy is now essentially one of 'zero defects'. As Jacobson and Hillkirk say in their study: 'The entire focus of today's product development process at Xerox is to have a design, testing and manufacturing system that assures quality with the first machine out the factory door.'

The commitment to quality and the customer is visibly led from the top: on one day a month, each of Xerox's 20 most senior executives at the Stamford, Connecticut headquarters takes it in turn to answer all customer phone calls. That includes CEO Kearns, who will break meetings to take calls.

The campaign is known as 'Leadership Through Quality' and by 1987 all 100,000 Xerox employees around the world had undergone up to 48 hours of formal quality training. Kearns and his senior managers personally went through 6½ days training. On the assumption that poor quality can cost a company up to 20 per cent of its annual revenue, Xerox believes that the campaign has the potential to triple its yearly sales figure to $30bn by 1992.

The quality revolution by itself, however, could not assure Xerox of sustained leadership in a market driven by rapidly evolving technological, social and economic factors. Levien's appointment from outside the corporation in 1982 marked a basic shift in management philosophy on planning. He says it represented 'something of a gamble': in the years of easy growth in the 1960s and early 1970s, 90 days had been considered long-term in Xerox planning.

Revenue growth prospects

Speaking rapidly but with deliberation in a 40-minute interview carved out of a hectic schedule of meetings, Levien explained how he had addressed his task, which was purely related to the office products and systems side of the business, not financial services. (The former still account for 75 per cent of Xerox's annual $10bn revenues.)

We had some very good people who had been doing competitive analysis, market analysis, economic analysis and technological analysis, but it had never been put together in a framework before.

I looked at the kind of questions which I felt could be capably addressed and decided there was one that gave a focus to the work: what are the revenue growth prospects for Xerox over the next 10 years? Not, what is the outside world going to be, but given what the world is going to be, what are the trajectories of revenue growth Xerox ought to be able to obtain? The main theme had to be: how large was the market going to be, and what share of that market could we get?

So in order to determine the size of the market we looked at the economics. What is the general growth of the world GNP going to be, because the office marketplace is only a proportion of that. What are the demographic changes going to be? How many new office workers are there going to be? Where are the factory workforces going to be? What are the social forces at work that might affect the office – for example, the movement of women into the labour force, the increase in information use in society . . .?

Then we looked at technology. How was that going to evolve and what new technological possibilities would there be? Adding all these up – economics, demographics, social forces and technology – would enable us to get a sense of how the markets in which Xerox was going to operate would evolve over those years.

In a sense, this is the 'playing field' we have, this is 'the size of the pie'. But two things then affect how much of that pie we can extract in value for Xerox. One is government policies as they affect a multinational: some governments are hospitable and some are not; others let you in, then build a barrier round you; some others won't let you in at all. Then there's the competition, which is also going to be extracting value from that same marketplace.

So you add up all of these markets, subtract the parts that government policies are going to affect and the part the competition is going to get, and then you can make estimates, using a set of assumptions about what market share you are going to get; which markets you are going into; various revenue trajectories. Then you get a series of strategic consequences, things the company should do.

This first study took 7 months, using a large team of people. The work began in May 1982, and the week before Christmas Levien presented each member of the senior management team with a 300-page book, tied in festive ribbon.

Over the following year, he made a series of presentations to the company's top 240 managers, in 12 groups of 20. As yet, however, there was little impact on strategy-making: people viewed it as an interesting 'staff exercise' but not as a part of their existing planning procedures or decision-making practices.

Xerox '95

In January 1985 Levien became head of the corporate strategy office with the rank of a senior Vice-President of the company. He decided it was time for a new 10-year horizon exercise, but one with a more participative approach. To manage the new programme, Levien selected Dave Bliss of the strategy office, a man with 20 years' experience in product planning, marketing and sales at Xerox. 'The key to it was the marketing focus that he brought,' recalled Levien.

The Xerox '95 programme succeeded from within, by involving senior management in terms they could apply to their own areas of the business. 'You want senior management to internalize the strategy, not have it externally applied,' said Levien. 'They need to think through the issues; it should be their strategy, one they are comfortable with implementing, and on which they don't need constant guidance.'

The key point, Levien identified, was 'direct linkage with the planning process'. That process had been reshaped in 1981 when Xerox had been decentralized into more than 20 business units, eliminating some of the main corporate functions and giving more responsibility to the individual units.

At the same time a corporate strategy office was set up with six principal officers, all of director level and most with 15–20 years' experience in the company in a variety of functions. Their task was to think about the long-term future, balance the company's different 'portfolios' and help senior management review the planning of the business units without engaging obtrusively in their planning processes. As Levien explained: 'We had to find a simpler way in which senior management could discuss with the divisional management the critical strategic issues from the corporation's point of view without getting bogged down in detail.'

The Business Resource Management Statement

The outcome was a five-page document known as BRIMS, or Business Resource Management Statement; an adaptation of an existing form used for appraising senior personnel in the company. BRIMS was to be the prime tool of strategy 'linkage' between corporate planning and the 20–25 business units, each of which had been assigned 'missions and boundaries' based on corporate targets for return on assets (always the key Xerox measurement) and other performance criteria.

Each unit completed a BRIMS, the first page of which described its 'mission', its market, its basic strategy, together with a 5-year history of its financial performance and projections of ROI, revenue, market share and other variables. Subsequent pages detailed the unit's market horizons in terms of size and competitive environment, and listed critical factors for success along with the unit's definition of its customer requirements. The final section summarized the general manager's view of his unit's current and future position in the context of Xerox strengths and markets, including a list of 'deliverables' needed to accomplish the strategy, requirements from other parts of the business, an assessment of external uncertainties and a page of detailed financial data.

The corporate strategy office responded in turn to each BRIMS with a list of questions. Unit general managers were given a week to prepare for a tough 2-hour session with senior management in which they would be expected to answer those questions without using any material already presented in the BRIMS.

Early in each year's planning calendar the BRIMS and their corporate reviews were put together in a 'Consolidated Strategy Review' to test whether the business unit planning added up 'both financially and conceptually' to the strategic direction of the corporation as a whole. Out of the Consolidated Strategy Review would come directions and targets for the operating units and functional units reporting to them such as manufacturing or engineering. They in turn would come back with business plans that were reviewed at corporate level: finally, a Consolidated Plan Review provided direction to the business units to create their 1-year operating plan.

Xerox strategic planning, apart from the special 10-year exercises, is regularly done on three time horizons: 5 years (the BRIMS and Consolidated Strategy Review); 3 years (the business plans) and 1 year (the operating plans). More consolidation is done on the 1-year plans to ensure that they are, as Levien says, 'the first step in the 5-year direction' (see Figure 1).

The system worked both 'bottom up' and 'top down' throughout the calendar. The process has since been somewhat simplified by dropping the BRIMS document and covering that data as part of the operational reviews that go on through the year.

Strategy development

One thing, however, was missing from this otherwise comprehensive process – an overall context of corporate strategic direction into which the individual businesses could fit their 'missions and boundaries'. This was the gap Xerox set out to fill with Xerox '95, designed to involve the management of the business units in longer and deeper horizons.

Xerox '95 got under way in August 1985 with a series of meetings between unit and corporate management, conducted off site away from the Stamford headquarters. Before the first of them, David Bliss of the corporate strategy office asked each of 15 senior corporate managers a basic question: How did they see a successful Xerox 10 years ahead? What would be the critical external and internal forces affecting that view, and what were Xerox's current strengths and weaknesses?

'We took everyone's answers and put them on the same page,' said

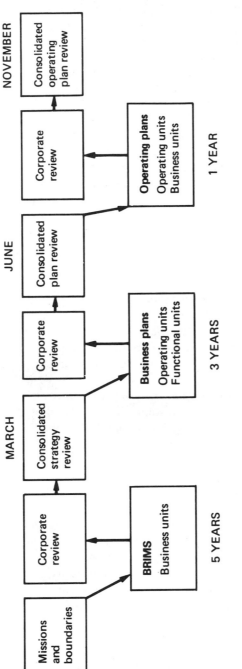

Figure 1   *Xerox planning process – the context for strategy*

Levien. 'Then we stripped away the names of the respondents, so that you could see the range of the answers given, and we gave them back to each participant before the meeting.' Kearns chaired the round-table gathering, which opened with a video of Joe Wilson, the company's founder, giving his personal vision of the future.

'We used that one-day meeting to discuss key issues like the nature of success, critical success factors, and what businesses we should be in,' said Levien. 'It became clear there was a wide range of views, even among those 15 people, about what a success Xerox would be, 10 years on.'

Between the first meeting in August and the second in November, more questionnaires were constructed in the corporate strategy office. They posed such questions as: 'What kinds of products do you think we should sell? In what geographic regions? What are the critical success factors?'

The 'high concepts'

'In analysing those questionnaires, we thought we had found a number of underlying world views on implicit strategies for the company,' Levien recalled. From those,

> We isolated four strategic themes that we thought a group among the respondents were implicitly pursuing. For each of these we gave a brief description, using the Hollywood notion of a 'high concept'.

(A one-sentence encapsulation of a movie theme such as 'great white shark terrorizes beach community' for *Jaws*.)

> One of these strategies, for example, was for Xerox to be a complete financial animal, to look at each business purely on its short-term returns and to get out of any business which couldn't promise a profit fairly quickly. In other words, to manage a portfolio as a conglomerate would, strictly according to the profitability of each element, without any synergy.

> Another was to put together a complex set of businesses which could compete across the board with an IBM. Another was to 'mind our knitting'; to be a first-class copier and printer business and forget about anything else. The fourth was to emphasize our distribution channels and build on that.

> We then took 16 people and divided them into groups of four and asked each group to take one of those four strategies and spend the first part of the afternoon elaborating it in some detail. Each group contained one person who was a strong supporter of that strategy and one who was not too enthusiastic about it. When they came back and made their presentation, using flip charts and spelling out the strategy in further detail, it became apparent that support for this or that strategy depended largely on that person's view of the world.

> One key issue that emerged was the future of paper: was paper going to play an important role in the office in the future?

In between this second 1-day meeting and the third in the series, which covered a 3-day weekend, more work was done at corporate level on external economic and political research. The assignment was to spell out in more detail the four strategic alternatives in a BRIMS-like format.

The consensor

At the weekend meeting, groups of four were asked to decide what they felt were the most important external and environmental influences likely to affect the company's future strategy. These were then 'polled' anonymously by a device called a consensor, a small box with two dials numbered 0 to 7 on which individuals registered the issues in terms of numerical rating. A central console read the settings, consolidated them and displayed the result as a bar chart on a screen.

> We used the consensor to narrow the group of 20–25 assumptions about the world down to a handful, perhaps a dozen, which people agreed were the key assumptions about the external environment. That became what we call our 'view of the world'. There are now 24 assumptions of that kind which we keep evergreen; these are our beliefs about the external environment which we see as strategically critical and which we continue to monitor in the corporate strategy office.

Those 24 assumptions – about the future of paper, the way competition is seen as likely to evolve, the way marketing channels may develop and other key factors – became a small printed booklet within Xerox, highly classified to outsiders. It was the blueprint upon which Xerox would build its strategy for the 1990s.

The last stage of that weekend meeting began with members of the corporate strategy office sitting with each of four small groups discussing in detail the four 'high concept' strategies and analysing them through to financial and market projections. On the Saturday evening, each person was given an hour to collect his thoughts and then the group gathered round a large table. Kearns asked each in turn to spend 5 minutes describing which strategy, or combination of strategies, he favoured and why. The result was 15 different options. After dinner, a small group gathered with Kearns to discuss them before retiring to bed. On the Sunday morning Kearns gave his verdict on which strategic direction the company should follow.

The whole exercise was typical of Kearns' methods, said Levien: 'He likes to build teams, he likes to listen, but he's willing to make the tough decisions himself.'

Out of this came the strategy built around document processing, although Kearns did not use those words when making his choice. The corporate strategy office took the direction he had outlined and formulated a one-page 'statement of strategic intent'. That was followed, in 1986, by an exercise called 'strategy validation', in which the ideas in that statement of intent were rigorously tested, with external consultants as well as internally. A thick and detailed document resulted, and further refinements were made as the 1986 planning process unfolded.

In January 1987, coinciding with another corporate restructuring, principally in the marketing area, a second Xerox '95 meeting was held which produced a very precise statement of missions and boundaries for each of the business units as well as for overall strategic direction (see Figure 2).

'We are continuing these Xerox '95 meetings twice a year to bring senior management together, and in 1989 we will probably start working on a Xerox 2000', said Levien.

Rethinking market segmentation

The concept of document processing is seen as requiring change in the way the company perceives and meets its customers' needs. 'We're also in the process of rethinking market segmentation', said Levien, explaining that traditionally, Xerox has segmented markets 'in terms of customer size and geography rather than in terms of vertical industry markets or horizontal function markets'.

'But we recognize that is what we have to do in order to meet the needs of our customers in this particular business. Market segmentation is an absolutely critical part of it, and this is something we are in the process of doing.'

Marketing organization has now been split into three groups based on different methods of dealing with customers: one responsible exclusively for dealers and re-sellers; one for the traditional business customer base, and a new organization called the public systems division, targeting government and other large-scale buyers. Within each of these groups the company will now be looking at specific industries where there is a heavy role for document processing and trying to develop applications and solutions for them.

The figure of \$80bn which Xerox has put on the document processing market is, says Levien, 'necessarily speculative, but it's certainly big enough to support a reasonably good-sized Xerox with a substantial market share. We think it's the right business for Xerox; it relates to our traditions, it's what we think people will understand. But it's not going to be something that just falls into our lap. There is a lot of work to do. . . . Senior management has set the general directions, now it's up to the operational units to take those and give them life.'

All this is not to lose sight for one moment of the 'Leadership Through Quality' campaign which Xerox executives say has wrought a genuine 'cultural change' throughout the company. 'It's built a culture in which constant, incremental improvement is part of the way of life, and this is a great strength of the Japanese,' says one. '*In the United States we have a saying, "if it ain't broke, don't fix it", but to me the Japanese always seem to be saying, "if it ain't perfect, don't leave it".*'

'The culture here now is to identify problems and then fix them. That is a

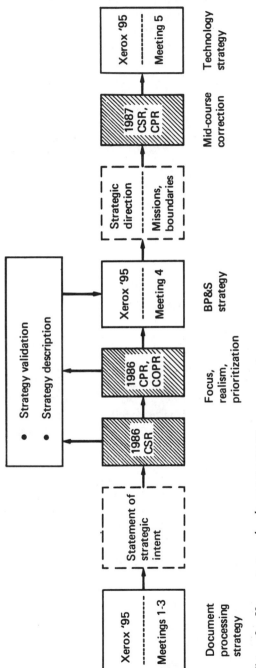

Figure 2 *Xerox strategy development process*

very, very powerful message that has been successfully disseminated throughout the company. I don't think we've seen the major benefits yet that will come out of it.'

Bibliography

Gary Jacobson and John Hillkirk, *Xerox: The American Samurai*, Macmillan, New York (1986).

Benchmark, Xerox quarterly publication, Spring (1988).

'Meeting of the Research Board', Xerox Corporation, San Francisco, 4 March (1987).

Remarks by Paul A. Allaire, *Business Week*, 22 June (1987).

Roger E. Levien, *Making Strategic Concepts Work*, Xerox Corporation (1983).

32

'If we can do it, *any* company can!'

Peter Reid

To understand why Harley-Davidson's executives make this claim with total conviction, consider this scenario: You're a senior manager in a US company that makes big-ticket leisure products and belongs to a conglomerate seeking to shift its focus *away* from leisure products to industrial products. When the parent puts your company on the block, you and other top managers see an opportunity to purchase it in a leveraged buyout (LBO). You're looking at the following facts about your company's current situation:

- You are losing sizable chunks of market share to your much bigger Japanese competitors.
- The economy is beginning to slide, and many blue-collar workers – your core customers – are facing layoffs.
- Sky-high interest rates are also making it hard for people to buy your product.
- Your manufacturing systems and product quality are inadequate to meet world-class competition.
- Your product line is seriously out of date.
- Your product has been stereotyped with a rough, tough image.
- Your Japanese competitors are unloading thousands of products on American shores that compete directly with yours.
- The Japanese products not only have higher quality, but they also have lower prices.

Sounds like a good deal? Few observers thought so in 1981 when the Harley-Davidson Motorcycle Company was put up for sale by American Machine & Foundry (AMF), the conglomerate that had owned it for 11 years. It looked like just another sad case of an old-line US manufacturer being hammered into oblivion by Japanese competitors whose basic strategy was to invade American markets with high-quality products at substantially lower prices. All of AMF's worldwide attempts to sell Harley-Davidson were unavailing. No one wanted it.

Next, consider what happened after 13 Harley-Davidson managers –

despite all these negatives – still went ahead and bought the company in an $81.5-million LBO:

- The market for heavyweight motorcycles declined by 20 per cent within a year.
- Harley lost more market share as the Japanese flooded the United States with Harley look-alikes at discounted prices.
- For the first time in almost 50 years, Harley lost money.
- Harley had to lay off more than 40 per cent of its work force.
- Saddled with a staggering LBO debt, Harley had to borrow even *more* money just to service its debt and keep going.
- Harley's major lender, Citicorp, seriously considered withdrawing its support and taking steps to liquidate the company for whatever the assets would bring.

Small wonder that industry observers concluded that Harley-Davidson was not long for this world.

'There's something about a Harley'

Why did 13 apparently astute executives buy a company that the Japanese were literally blowing away? Like many business decisions, this one was both rational and emotional.

On the practical level, Harley-Davidson did have solid business assets: an extraordinarily loyal customer base, a well-established dealer network, a high added-value product, and a strong, in-place management team.

But those factors aren't enough to explain the buyout. The buyout team was also motivated by strong feelings about Harley-Davidson, and to understand them it is necessary to understand the Harley-Davidson 'mystique.' Or as one Harley rider, an investment banker, calls it, 'the value of intangibles.'

From its first appearance in 1903, the Harley motorcycle has been unique, one of the few US consumer products destined to evolve into an 'American institution' with a committed constituency. To Harley owners, Harleys have heart, Harleys have soul. Harleys have raw power and a 'voice': a basso-profundo thump that makes other motorcycles sound like sewing machines. To many riders, Harley-Davidson is the *real* 'heartbeat of America.'

These Harley riders run the gamut. About half are supervisors, machine operators, and other skilled workers. But Harley riders also include lawyers, doctors, bankers, entertainers, engineers, and scientists. Perhaps 1 percent belong to the Hell's Angels end of the spectrum.

Despite their diversity, Harley riders all have something in common: a fanatical dedication to their Harleys. It's a feeling that many cannot articulate, and for them there's a Harley T-shirt inscribed: 'Harley-Davidson – If

I Have to Explain, You Wouldn't Understand.' Actor Mickey Rourke
says, 'It's a personal thing that can't be described. It's part of you.'

One thing is certain: this incredible brand loyalty is emotional. It is
based on a pattern of associations that includes the American flag and that
other American symbol, the eagle (which is also a Harley symbol), as well
as camaraderie, individualism, the feeling of riding free, and pride in
owning a product that has become a legend. On the road, one Harley rider
always helps another in distress – even though one may be a tattooed biker
and the other a bank president.

Some of these feelings obviously spilled over into the decision of
Harley's managers to buy the company in 1981. Though not all were
motorcyclists, they all shared the Harley rider's emotional commitment to
Harley-Davidson – and they had an intense desire to see the last US
motorcycle manufacturer live to fight again. They had the greatest incentive in the world to improve: survival. They firmly believed that Harley-
Davidson would go under at the hands of its Japanese competition unless
they assumed ownership of the company and turned it around – no matter
how much sweat it took.

*Organized activities sponsored by the Harley Owners Group are part of
Harley-Davidson's efforts to make motorcycles a way of life, not just a
product. One activity is the Ride-In Show, which gives riders a chance to
show off their 'iron' and win prizes for the Best of Show in various
categories*

And now the good news

In the five years following the LBO, Harley-Davidson again became a thriving company. Shortly thereafter, it recaptured its market-share lead from Honda, its major Japanese rival, and Honda has since sharply cut back its participation in the US heavyweight motorcycle market.

Harley quality is at an all-time high. The company sells every motorcycle it can make – at the premium end of the market – and at this writing is failing to meet market demand.

By going public, Harley was able to pay off its heavy LBO debt, with enough money left over to acquire a leading maker of premium recreational vehicles.

Now Harley is on full throttle.

How Harley-Davidson came back from the dead and achieved its remarkable turnaround is a classic story of the little guy against the big guys, of a small company that fought a fierce battle against industrial giants with far greater financial, technological, production, and marketing resources – and survived. Much of this story has never been told before.

At another level, however, the Harley-Davidson saga carries some clear lessons for all US companies on what it takes to become a world-class competitor in today's global economy – and a strong message of hope to those who fear that US competitiveness may be finished and done with.

The most important lesson, says Harley-Davidson chief executive officer Richard Teerlink, concerns people:

> Without the dedication of all its employees, no company can have long-term success. Top management must recognize that it has the responsibility and obligation to provide an environment in which an employee feels free to challenge the system to achieve success. Once the employee is committed, the techniques become easy. For Harley-Davidson, the techniques involved *all* functional areas of the business.

Harley-Davidson learned many other lessons – often the hard way – along the road from the euphoria of independence in 1981 to the brink of bankruptcy in 1985 to market leadership today. These lessons have a major theme: to survive in today's competitive world, US manufacturers must make customer satisfaction their ultimate goal and must adopt (1) the Productivity Triad techniques of employee involvement (EI), just-in-time inventory (JIT), and statistical operator control (SOC); (2) a 'close to the customer' marketing approach; and (3) a 'cash is king' financial strategy.

Supporting this theme, the following key conclusions can be drawn from Harley-Davidson's turnaround:

- Competitive success requires a corporate strategy based on continuous improvement in *all* areas of company operations.

- Quality-improvement programs do not require large cash investments; on the contrary, they *generate* cash.
- The key to finding out what the customer perceives as 'quality' is to create occasions and opportunities for customers to tell you what they think about your product and then to *listen* to the customers carefully. And 'close to the customer' should be a way of life for top management and all employees, not just the marketing department. (Harley senior executives make a point of riding and talking motorcycles with their customers.)
- Particularly in this era of heavy LBO debt, a company must focus on having enough cash to operate on a daily basis; otherwise, it will not survive long enough to become a world-class competitor. Having cash doesn't ensure success, but not having it can ensure failure. Harley-Davidson learned several key techniques for improving its cash flow in difficult times: (1) understand the terms of a loan agreement better than the lender does, because loan terms can reveal hidden opportunities to maximize cash flow; (2) know a lender's objectives, which makes it possible to negotiate more effectively; (3) sell off assets that don't fit the company's long-term strategy; and (4) exploit untapped profit opportunities that exist within the business.
- The secret of continuous improvement in manufacturing quality does not lie in high technology but rather in the development of three major programs in unison: EI, JIT, and SOC (also known as statistical process control). The potential of these programs that make up the Productivity Triad can only be realized if they are adopted together: (1) There can be no quality improvement without full *employee involvement*. Employees can no longer be asked to check their brains at the door. They must be trained in new skills and new ways of thinking about their jobs so they can make timely decisions on the shop floor instead of bucking them up to a supervisor. When the employee is given the right tools and is listened to, problems start getting solved. (2) High inventories are simply an excuse for inadequate systems and production processes. *Just-in-time inventory* not only generates cash, it also increases quality. (3) With *statistical operator control*, employees can focus on reducing variability instead of on conforming to specifications.
- There can be no quality improvement without the involvement of *management* – first-line to the top. Managers must forgo certain management prerogatives they may have previously taken for granted and let employees make more and more decisions.
- The Japanese work processes and methods can be adapted to any work force, anywhere, regardless of culture. That has been proved by Harley-Davidson – an all-American culture if there ever was one – as well as by the growing number of other US companies that are providing useful models for any company willing to commit itself to meaningful change.

Portrait of a survivor

Since its founding in 1903, Harley-Davidson has made it through five major crises that threatened its very existence. That it overcame the first four – all brought on by external events – can be credited to the ability of its tough-minded founders, who simply refused to let it succumb.

- *Survival Crisis 1.* After zooming from 150 motorcycles in 1907 to 28,000 in 1920, production drops precipitously to 10,000 because of an economic downturn and a consumer switch from motorcycles to cars for basic transportation.
- *Survival Crises 2.* The Great Depression hits just as the company is regaining previous production levels. In 1933, production collapses to a meager 3700 motorcycles. (As one Harley-Davidson senior executive says today, 'One can only have admiration for a management group that figured out how to adjust to the almost 80 per cent drop in shipments the company suffered from 1929 to 1933!')
- *Survival Crisis 3.* With the military's need for motorcycles in World War II, production reaches 1920 levels once more – only to nose-dive when the war is won.
- *Survival Crisis 4.* Postwar demand from returning veterans takes production to record levels temporarily, but the market sags again as veterans turn their attention to housing and other necessities. Indian Motorcycle Company goes out of business in 1953, leaving Harley as the only motorcycle company in the United States.

All of these crises were externally generated. The fifth was generated by the failure of Harley-Davidson – and its parent, AMF – to answer the Japanese motorcycle invasion of the 1970s with better quality, increased productivity, and fresh new products. Instead, production was expanded so fast that it flew out of control, and product development was neglected, throwing Harley-Davidson into a crisis that few thought it would ever survive.

Surmounting the 'insurmountable'

Can the United States reverse its industrial slide? Can it compete in a global economy? The Harley-Davidson story answers those questions with a resounding yes. Will it be easy? An equally resounding no.

No for a lot of reasons, which have to do with both the internal and external environments that US companies must deal with in trying to improve their competitive position.

Internal environment

In 1980, Harley-Davidson's internal environment was fairly typical of many US manufacturers. The company had:

- A corporate management that focused mostly on short-term returns
- A management that didn't listen to its employees or give them responsibility for the quality of what they made
- High inventories of parts that gobbled up cash and reduced productivity
- Inefficient production systems that generated poor quality, low productivity, and excessive costs
- A 'meeting specifications is good enough' attitude toward quality, rather than a constant drive toward higher standards
- A belief in quick fixes for problems – such as throwing in computers and state-of-the-art machinery to improve productivity
- Slow design and development time that allowed foreign competitors to reach the market first with new products
- A high breakeven point that left the company vulnerable to unpredictable market fluctuations
- A management that woke up too late to the threat of foreign competition because of the 'it can't happen here' syndrome.

For the most part, you won't find these conditions and attitudes in Harley-Davidson today. But that's not true of a majority of US manufacturers – it is difficult to change beliefs and systems that have been entrenched so solidly for so many years. What does it take? Most of all it takes top management's total commitment to change. It takes tremendous energy and dedication from the whole management team. And it takes the full involvement of every employee in the organization. Add patience, perseverance, and obstinacy and you have the necessary ingredients.

Easy it is not – but it can be done. Look at what Harley accomplished:

- Productivity improvement   +50%
- Inventory reduction   −75%
- Scrap and rework   − 68%
- Increased US revenue   +80%
- Increased international revenue   +177%
- Increased US market share   +97%
- Increased operating profit   +$59 million

External environment

It is tempting for US corporate chieftains to blame their difficulties on the many advantages enjoyed by their foreign competitors, particularly the Japanese. As James C. Abegglen and George Stalk Jr point out in *Kaisha: The Japanese Corporation* (1985), Japanese concerns live in an environment characterized by:

- A free, competitive domestic market in Japan
- Plenty of low-cost funds for investment, provided by a high savings rate and a supportive financial system

- An educated, disciplined labor force at moderate wages
- A government that nurtures the private sector.

Yes, it would be easier for US companies to become world-class competitors if we could transfer these economic benefits to our shores. But waiting around for that happy day will be self-defeating.

This is just a sampling of the wide variety of official licensed products that help Harley-Davidson build on its name. Harley-Davidson licenses its name and logo to about 60 companies

Harley-Davidson's position is: Our environment may not be ideal, but we must learn to improve our competitive position despite it. We must focus on the Japanese advantages we *can* transfer to our own operations: better management methods, more effective production systems, faster product-development cycles, and full employee involvement.

Making it against your competition – anywhere in the world

The manufacturing revolution now going on in the United States was forced on us by the Japanese, so it is natural for us to consider them our major competitors. But as the quality and productivity revolution spreads throughout the world, your competition can come from anywhere – including your competitor down the street. Those who join the revolution will become the survivors, while those who prefer the status quo will be the casualties. If foreign competitors don't get you, a domestic competitor will.

So the story of Harley-Davidson's resurgence is both a warning and a promise. The warning is that companies in your business are right now adopting progressive systems and methods that will give them a competitive edge. The promise is that if a small, underfunded US company like Harley-Davidson can meet and beat the toughest competitors in the world, you can, too.

Reference

Abegglen, James C. and Stalk, George Jr (1985) *Kaisha: The Japanese Corporation* (New York: Basic Books).

33

Creative empowerment at Rover

David Walker

The first Rover vehicle was a bicycle. The original Rover company was founded by J.K. Starley, the inventor of the diamond frame safety bicycle which was itself a very significant innovation and the archetype of every modern bicycle since its introduction in 1885. [1,2]

Rover began making motor cars in 1904. After a chequered career of prewar success and postwar mergers, the company attracted increasing government support until it was nationalized as part of British Leyland in 1975. In 1982 it became part of the Austin Rover Group, which in turn became the Rover Group in 1986. At that time Graham Day was appointed Chairman and began the process of shedding acquisitions, such as the computer company Istel and the truck division Leyland, which lay outside Rover's normal product focus. In 1988 the Rover Group was purchased from the government by British Aerospace.

During the mid-1960s the federation of companies which formed BLMC (British Leyland Motor Corporation) were Austin, Morris, Rover, Land Rover and Leyland. Between them they accounted for 50% of the total UK home market. Imports of foreign cars were very low at this time. The market share of Rover is currently running at 13–15%. The reduction in UK market share has been offset in part by a significant increase in vehicle exports. In 1990 the Rover group exported 115,660 vehicles from a total production of 384,458 units.

Currently Rover employs 42,000 people. The company has reported a profitable performance for the last three years. In 1989 its turnover was £3,430 million, which gave a trading profit of £64 million. [3]

The partnership between Honda and the Rover Group dates from 1979. For the first five years there was a reluctance to accept that Japanese methods could work in a new context. Only in the last five years have attitudes changed sufficiently for a whole new way of managing to take effect.

> We did not believe they could teach us anything about making cars. Now we know different. [4]

The new style of management has had profound effects on the products of the company. The users of cars now perceive a remarkable difference in quality and performance in the most recent vehicles – the 200 series and

400 series. The latter has been favourably compared to its BMW equiva-lent.[5] The advertising campaigns of the company make sly use of the comparison, reprinting a press cutting about a Rover police car chasing a BMW and catching it.[6] More recent reviews favourably compare the Rover 216 GTi with the VW Golf GTi.[7] All in all, there is widespread public acknowledgement of the improvement and competitiveness of Rover products.

How have these changes come about? What are the organizational shifts which have generated such dramatically improved products?

There are several interconnected organizational changes which have raised Rover products to new heights. For convenience I have listed them below in a sequence moving from technology-centred to people-centred, from hard to soft management.

- Integrated technical database
- First choice suppliers
- Minimal inventory control
- Cell management
- Total quality management
- Project team working
- Corporate culture

I shall briefly outline the first five techniques and spend a little longer thinking about the wider and more pervasive implications of the last two factors.

Integrated technical database

The company has developed a computer-integrated engineering pro-gramme, wherein *product master database* contains a three-dimensional model fusing all data from design engineering and manufacture.

Updating and revisions during development can be conveyed to all specialist functional areas through an integrated *format*. In turn this has meant standardization through a single supplier for all computer graphics applications and for all CAD/CAM hardware.

First choice suppliers

Approximately 60% by cost of each Rover vehicle is provided by external suppliers (these components are known as *bought in* components). There-fore suppliers are an extremely important, if external, part of the organiz-ation. Two radical steps have been taken to integrate their work with that of internal activities. Firstly a central supply centre is responsible for coor-dination and timing of all purchasing activities; secondly a shortlist of first choice suppliers (sometimes referred to as preferred suppliers) becomes part of the vehicle project development team. There are three supply centres, dealing with small cars, medium/large cars and 4×4 vehicles. Appropriate sections of the CAD/CAM database are made available to the chosen suppliers who, through electronic exchanges, become more involved in component design and component quality. A key factor is the *early involvement* of suppliers. Rover recognizes the expertise of its suppliers in specialist areas and tries to use this expertise from a very early stage.

The other key factor is *quality*. Rover has adopted a much broader view of quality than traditionally held. Purchasing objectives are directed towards obtaining the lowest overall cost rather than the lowest purchase price. To do this the company encourages its suppliers to adopt the same set of total quality management principles (TQM). (These principles are covered a little later in this chapter.) This has mutual benefits. On the one hand the lead times are reduced, while on the other hand the suppliers are assured of long term business, provided they continue to meet Rover criteria in all its dimensions (quality, delivery, cost control, minimum inventory).

Minimum inventory

Just in time (JIT) is a repertoire of manufacturing techniques committed to eliminating waste, eliminating inventories and minimizing set up times. In its purest form, as practised by companies such as Toyota, JIT calls up components externally and internally *only* when required. This means holding the absolute minimum of stock. Components are delivered in end use containers to the lineside. An operator on the line passes work in progress along only when a signal (*kanban*) is received from the next operator in the manufacturing chain. The JIT system is based on a *pull* philosophy rather than *push*.

The *push* system has been widely used in the West in an attempt to use all available capacity (that is, minimizing downtime) regardless of whether production was required by customers. This generates finished stock to be held and an accumulation of work in progress. Within this system there tends to be a build up of bottlenecks which are aggravated by production problems and demands for variety. The inflexibility and slowness of response of this system has been a prime factor in making UK cars uncompetitive.

The *pull* system, on the other hand, is triggered by customers' demands and creates a chain reaction through the whole production process. The control by use of *kanbans* is visual and easily understood.

Rover is committed to adopting JIT policies but so far has taken only the first steps. While kanban control operates in one area of power train production, vehicle production generally is still largely geared to push flowline production. Minimal inventory control (MIC) diminishes inventory holdings within such a system. Supplier deliveries to Rover are normally timed to minimize queuing and components are packaged to facilitate their delivery straight to trackside.

The push system of inventory control is driven by *forecasts of* build requirements whereas the pull system is driven by *actual demand*. At the time of writing Rover is working hard to generate a more responsive production system which can be largely driven by sold orders.

Cell management

The production line at Rover is organized into a series of work cells. Because JIT and MIC require changes in attitude and organization, they depend upon the creation of manufacturing work cells wherein plant, equipment and operators take on more responsibility for a whole product or component. Work cells create an environment of high autonomy and product ownership. Within the cells individuals are encouraged to look for improvements in the production environment and the quality of their output.

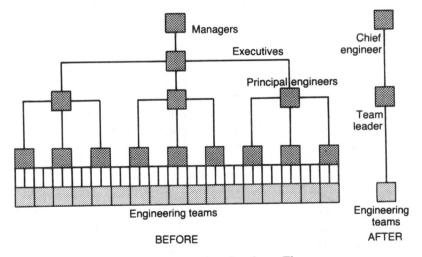

Figure 1 *Five levels of management reduced to three. There are approximately 100 engineering teams within the company*

The Rover assembly line is divided into work cells of around 80 people. The impulse to shorten lines of communication to the manufacturing cells has led to five levels of management being reduced to three.

At the base level is a new-style production manager with a much broader role than the old-style foreman. Typically this mini-managing director will be in charge of the whole cell of 80 people. Apart from the responsibility for technology and production, this role also entails the welfare, training and education of employees.

However, the dictates of flowline production constrain autonomy. Each cell cannot influence the levels of output and input achieved over a long run – the line rate determines scheduling requirements and sold orders determine what will be built. Yet in a broader sense each team takes on a greater responsibility for quality.

Total quality management

Rover is evolving to a TQ company. The commitment to see this evolution through exists at the highest level and examples of TQ in action are very widespread. Total Quality Improvement can be defined as achieving total quality by harnessing everyone's commitment. It can be pictured as having a strategic and a tactical dimension. The strategy entails definition of company-wide principles, the tactics embody means of implementation.[8]

Everyone in the company is encouraged to portray themselves within the chain of production. Each individual therefore has unique individual 'suppliers' and 'customers' to whom they respond and for whom they perform. The standards and measurement of performance are agreed locally and undergo local monitoring and revision. These tactics take place within a framework of general knowledge and understanding of corporate aims.

At Rover the explicit principles are:

Philosophy – Prevention not detection
Approach – Management-led
Scale – Everyone responsible
Measure – Costs of quality
Standard – Right first time
Scope – Company-wide
Theme – Continuous improvement

Total Quality is defined as the achievement of quality at the lowest cost by eliminating errors and waste. Therefore one vital element of employee training concerns quality. At Rover all employees are involved in a programme of Total Quality. They are trained both in the concept and its detailed application. Similarly the network of suppliers and sales staff are also involved in the training programme.

This programme is an initiative launched and supported from the top echelons of management. TQ is founded upon the identification of customers, understanding and meeting their requirements, measuring success and continuous improvements.

Project teamworking

In the realm of developing new products, somewhat larger and more dispersed groupings than the manufacturing cells are necessary. Since the

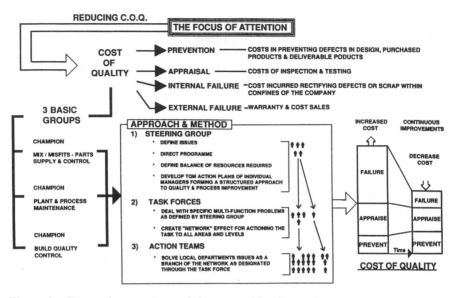

Figure 2 *Extract from an internal document,* 'Quality and Communications Strategy for 1991'

Spring of 1988 the Rover Group has been completely committed to team-work not only in manufacturing but in its development of new products. The main elements of that teamworking derive from Japanese practices and have been directly influenced by Honda.

Product development is divided into teams both within and across functions. Each team leader is responsible for reaching specific *business objectives*. These objectives vary between teams but they have in common the imperative to satisfy their internal and external customers.

In its first phase, members of a team were seconded from their departmental home base (in finance, engineering, marketing, purchase or wherever) to take part in new product conceptualizing. This dual loyalty and matrix organization has given way to a more wholehearted relocation of key personnel within teams. This is a radical advance from the structure of three years ago, when projects were controlled by groups of programme managers who became isolated from their engineers and their customers.

The metaphor offered to the team at the outset is rugby football.

> When we talk about teams it is not the relay team approach where one group fully completes their task before handing over to the next group, but more the rugby team approach where the whole team is involved and are moving forward to a common goal. As in a game of rugby the degree of involvement of the participants during the game will vary, but the team will know who the key players are at any one time.[9]

The vehicle development team in total could be as large as 150 persons and includes not only internal seconded staff but external first choice suppliers.

Running such a large multidisciplinary team, of course, presents several headaches for management. The resolution of these difficulties takes two main forms:

- map of involvement of all parties
- clear authority and reporting lines

The involvement of subgroups within the time frame changes according to the balance shown in Figure 3. Within each phase the mix of specialisms will vary and each specialism has those moments when its ideas, knowledge and skills are particularly crucial. At such times natural opinion leaders emerge from the temporarily dominant specialism. This is viewed within the company as an *organic* process.

For example, take the point of Programme PDL (product development letter) in Figure 3. Here the dominant voices are product engineers. As you can see design and concept engineering has peaked earlier in the process. The supply centre, representing and consolidating the demands of suppliers, while having a voice from the beginning of the process, has a greater share of the debate in the later stages.

Overall authority is vested in the vehicle directorate, that is, in a few individuals who guide the programme of development not just through planning design and development, but through manufacturing, sales and marketing, and service. The vehicle directors take responsibility for the programme. They are the product champions and take *ownership* of the ideas that go into making up a new vehicle.

Corporate culture

Teamworking and total quality management and the other techniques which derive from them, are not enough on their own. They are the outward symptom of more profound changes. These mechanisms are driven by a whole new management ethic.

> By British standards, Japanese management is amazingly brave. It gives responsibility to younger people, guided perhaps by experienced employees who do not interfere that much. It gives responsibility to the work force in a way which runs right across the traditions in the UK. Decision making is driven right down to the shop floor. There they can take responsibility for making changes. They have all the information which is necessary to understand the implications of those changes, in cost and knock on effects and so on. Management then becomes very largely providing an *information service* which enables those changes to be made.[10]

By comparison to these new attitudes, the traditional management of UK firms is made to look impossibly hierarchical, fearfully territorial, jealously tribal, pessimistic and mistrustful.

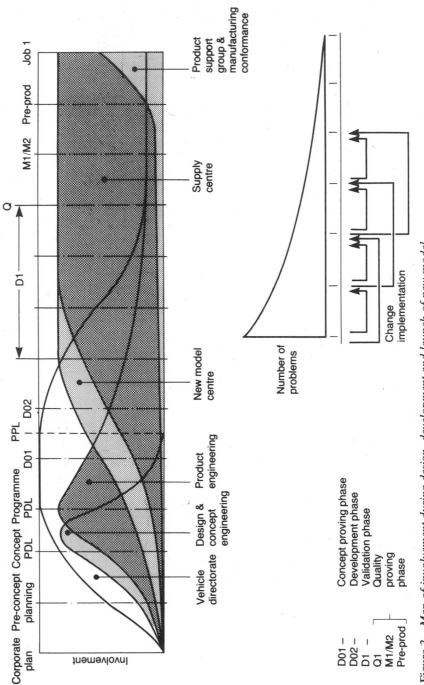

Figure 3 *Map of involvement during design, development and launch of new model*

The starting point of any re-invigoration, as exemplified by Rover, is that the main asset to the company is quite simply *people*, their energy and their skills. Management cannot continue to neglect and undervalue the corporate value of those assets, but must seek ways to protect, engender and maximize them. This deeply held set of convictions we might call *creative empowerment* – in which decisions and responsibility are driven downwards, and the workforce as a whole is nurtured through customized programmes of training and education. One of the main conclusions of an important study of industrial America stressed the vital importance of educating the workforce in the broadest sense.[11] This might seem a costly investment but the costs of *not* doing it are greater.

> You can try to gain competitive advantage through technology, but within six months everyone has caught up. You can try to achieve it through style, but it's very difficult these days to find a style which meets aerodynamic specifications and is still significantly different from everything else on the market, and you can try to achieve it through fittings but nearly every car nowadays is a Christmas tree of goodies. We believe we have a real chance of achieving it through our people.

> In Rover we have got 40,000 very good people, some of them extraordinary. If we could get to a situation where we had 40,000 people who were totally committed to us, multi skilled, highly flexible, and with us all the way, we would have that competitive advantage.[12]

With this attitude, the policy of the company is to draw out the hidden skills of its employees. For example, comprehensive suggestion schemes run in 1989 netted 13,000 suggestions from a total workforce of 40,000. Of those suggestions 20% were implemented – generating a massive saving of £4 million.

Similarly, in 1990 the company established Rover Learning Business, with an annual budget of £30 million. This business within a business has its own chairman, managing director and board responsible for its products – that is, schemes of learning and development. One early discovery was that the vast majority of Rover employees saw project work as the way to maximize their education: only 10% of those polled thought formal training courses were useful. This has led to RLB to pilot self-directed personal development files.

Some aspects of training are part of the mainstream educational task, for instance in total quality management and attitudinal training. In 1989, 88,000 days, the bulk of voluntary training, were taken in company time. Other developments include Rover Employees Assisted Learning (REAL) which offers up to £100 per annum to each employee for any form of education that may or may not relate directly to their jobs, such as learning French, computer skills or woodwork.

Crucially the Japanese partners have driven home a fundamental lesson to their UK partners. They used to say to Rover, rather smugly, '*You do not know how to get the best out of your work force ... but we do.*' For

Rover and a few UK companies this is fortunately no longer true. For others changes are very slow. Changing attitudes and changing minds is perhaps the hardest part of a manager's job.

> We at Rover are moving away from an organization which was based upon management direction and instruction provided from on high, and pursued through the deep layers of a highly structured organization to a frustrated employee body, to a much looser/flatter organization in which leadership, team working, appreciation of goals and scope to make a contribution at every level is the order of the day.
>
> It is this recognition that no organization can succeed without effectively harnessing the talent and effort of all its employees – wherever they work, no matter what their educational background – which could turn out to be the biggest factor in Rover's success.[13]

Rover provides not merely an object lesson in managing complex manufacturing but a lesson in how a corporate culture can radically shift. The lessons are not so much about a way of managing, as a way of thinking.

Notes

1   I.K. Starley, 'The evolution of the bicycle', *Journal of the Royal Society of Arts*, vol. 46, 20 May 1898.
2   F.R. Whitt and D.G. Wilson, *Bicycling Science*, MIT Press, 1982.
3   Randall Jackson, Product Engineering, December 1990.
4   Royden Axe, Design Director, Interview, October 1990.
5   *CAR* magazine, 4 January 1990.
6   *The Guardian*, 17 September 1990.
7   *Autocar and Motor*, 12 December 1990.
8   Most of the information in this section came from Gavin Hall, SCUL, Rover, January 1991.
9   I.G. Inglis, 'Team work in Rover Engineering', Internal publication, 1988.
10   Nick Stephenson, Vehicle Director, Interview, September 1990.
11   Suzanne Berger et al., 'Towards a new Industrial America', MIT study reported in *Scientific American*, June 1989; also ch. 34 this volume.
12   Rob Meakin, Personnel Director, Rover Group, *Personnel Management*, April 1990.
13   George Simpson, Managing Director, October 1990.

PART FOUR

CONTEXT – LESSONS FROM THE WIDER PICTURE

The final part of the book steps back to give a digest of managerial strategies, to look at the factors which critically influence innovation, and to place these things against their economic backdrop. The economic decline of the USA runs in parallel and maybe is even deeper than that of the UK. From the MIT study, reported by Berger et al., it seems that the underlying causes are very similar. If they have to be boiled down to one phrase then we would suggest: *neglect of human capital*. The remedies offered by the Berger paper flow from that thought – employee involvement, economic citizenship at the workplace, group working, and investment in training and education. Peters advises companies from an international perspective. Pilditch offers recipes for success culled globally from the best practices of what are sometimes called *winning companies* and reviews a digest of factors from more local UK experience.

So we come full circle, wherein the collapse of economies, and the decline of the West, is connected to the inhibition of human skills and the imprisonment of our best capacities.

SECTION 10

INNOVATION AND ITS IMPACT

34

Toward a new industrial America

Suzanne Berger, Michael L. Dertouzos, Richard K.
Lester, Robert M. Solow, and Lester C. Thurow

The US economy is a perplexing mix of strengths and weaknesses. It is now
in the seventh year of the longest peacetime expansion in this century.
Since the early 1980's large numbers of new jobs have been created, and
both unemployment and inflation have remained low. American exports
have recently surged (helped by a decline in the exchange value of the
dollar), and in late 1988 American factories were operating at close to full
capacity.

On the negative side, the trade deficit remains formidable (although it is
beginning to shrink). In 1988 the US bought about $120 billion more goods
and services from other countries than it could sell overseas. The US
automobile and steel industries, which once dominated world commerce,
have lost market share both at home and abroad, and newer industries are
also struggling. The American presence in the consumer-electronics
market, for example, has all but disappeared.

There are other disturbing signs that American industry as a whole is not
producing as well as it ought to produce or as well as the industries of other
nations have learned to produce. Growth in productivity, a crucial indicator of industrial performance, has averaged only slightly more than 1 per
cent per year since the early 1970's. Productivity has grown more rapidly in
several Western European and Asian nations, and US firms are increasingly perceived to be doing poorly in comparison with their foreign competitors in such key aspects as the cost and quality of their products as well as
the speed with which new products are brought to market. In many new
fields with broad commercial applications, such as advanced materials and
semiconductors, America's best technology may already have been
surpassed.

In spite of such disquieting developments, some observers maintain that
there is nothing fundamentally wrong with American industry itself. The

From *Scientific American*, 260 (6), June 1989, pp. 21–9. Reprinted with permission.

trade deficit, in this view, is the result not of intrinsic deficiencies in industrial performance but rather of such macroeconomic factors as natural differences in rates of economic growth among countries, fluctuations in currency-exchange rates and the enormous US budget deficit. Then, too, the rise and fall of industries is said to be a normal part of economic evolution; at any given time a certain number of industries are sure to be in decline while others are growing.

Yet if the unfavorable trends in industrial performance are real (and we believe they are), then the US has reason to worry. Americans must produce well if Americans are to live well. The sluggish growth in US productivity is barely sufficient to sustain an improvement in the nation's standard of living. (Real wage rates have in fact hardly increased since the early 1970's.) That, in itself, would be of concern regardless of what is happening in the rest of the world. As it is, the more dynamic productivity performance of other countries is also resulting in a relative decline in the US standard of living. Moreover, because political and military power depend ultimately on economic vitality, weaknesses in the US production system will inevitably raise doubts about the nation's ability to retain its influence and standing in the world at large.

Late in 1986 the Massachusetts Institute of Technology established the Commission on Industrial Productivity (with funding from the Sloan and Hewlett foundations) to determine whether there actually are pervasive weaknesses in US industrial practices and, if so, to identify their causes and formulate a set of recommendations to counter them. Unlike many observers of contemporary US industry, the commission did not view the problem entirely in macroeconomic terms. We believed that we could best contribute to the understanding of the problem by focusing on the nation's production system: the organizations, the plants, the equipment and the people – from factory workers to senior executives – that combine to conceive, design, develop, produce, market, and deliver products.

In keeping with this 'bottom-up' approach, the commission began its task by dividing into eight teams, each of which would examine in detail one of eight manufacturing industries: automobiles; chemicals; commercial aircraft; consumer electronics; machine tools; semiconductors, computers and copiers; steel; and textiles. These industries combined account for 28 per cent of US manufacturing output and about half of the total volume of manufactured goods traded by the US (exports and imports). American firms in each industry were evaluated for what we have come to call productive performance: their efficiency, product quality, innovativeness, and adaptability, as well as the speed with which they put new products on the market. Such factors are not explicitly captured in conventional measures of industrial productivity. Altogether, the commission's teams visited more than 200 companies and 150 plant sites and conducted nearly 550 interviews in the US, Europe and Japan.

In choosing to focus on the production system itself, we did not underes-

The MIT Commission on Industrial Productivity

Michael L. Dertouzos (Chairman)
    Department of Electrical
    Engineering and Computer Science
    Director, Laboratory for Computer
    Science
Robert M. Solow (Vice-chairman)
    Institute Professor Department of
    Economics
Richard K. Lester (Executive
    Director)
    Department of Nuclear
    Engineering
Suzanne Berger
    Head, Department of Political
    Science
H. Kent Bowen
    Department of Materials Science
    and Engineering
    Codirector, Leaders for
    Manufacturing Program
Don P. Clausing
    Department of Electrical
    Engineering and Computer Science
Eugene E. Covert
    Head, Department of Aeronautics
    and Astronautics
John M. Deutch
    Provost

Merton C. Flemings
    Head, Department of Materials
    Science and Engineering
Howard W. Johnson
    Special Faculty Professor of
    Management, Emeritus President,
    Emeritus Honorary Chairman,
    MIT Corporation
Thomas A. Kochan
    Sloan School of Management
Daniel Roos
    Department of Civil Engineering
    Director, Center for Technology,
    Policy and Industrial Development
David H. Staelin
    Department of Electrical
    Engineering and Computer
    Science
Lester C. Thurow
    Dean, Sloan School of
    Management
James Wei
    Head, Department of Chemical
    Engineering
Gerald L. Wilson
    Dean, School of Engineering

Members of the Commission on Industrial Productivity were drawn from the faculty of the Massachusetts Institute of Technology. The interdisciplinary group included economists, technologists, and experts on organization, management, and politics.

timate the importance of the macroeconomic factors that regulate the economy in the large; on the contrary, we could not avoid observing their manifestations time and again as the teams proceeded with their work. It is clear that the nation's productive performance problems will not be solved without some improvement in the economic environment. The reason is that investment – meant here broadly to include not only new plants, equipment and public works but also education, training and research and development – is crucial for productivity, and the economic environment largely determines the level of a nation's investment. Indeed, we believe that the highest priority of US economic policy must be to reduce the huge federal budget deficit, which saps the savings from which investment funds are drawn.

Nevertheless, after two years of study, it seems clear to us that current economic conditions do not fully explain the deficiencies in US industrial performance, nor will macroeconomic policy changes suffice to cure them. The relation of poor product quality to US interest rates and tax policies, for example, seems at best tenuous. The economic environment also does not directly affect the speed with which firms identify and respond to changes in the market and to new technological possibilities. Finally, macroeconomics cannot adequately explain why some US businesses thrive in the very same sectors where others are failing, nor why Japanese manufacturing plants in the US have often achieved better results than comparable American plants.

By looking at what actually takes place in industry – from the shop floor to the boardroom – the commission was able to observe recurring patterns of behavior and to draw certain conclusions about the most important micro-level factors that have adversely affected US industrial performance. To do so the commission worked much like a jury: we assessed the large mass of detailed, diverse, and sometimes contradictory evidence that the study teams had collected, ultimately reaching a verdict.

The verdict is that US industry indeed shows systematic weaknesses that are hampering the ability of many firms to adapt to a changing international business environment. In particular, the commission observed six such weaknesses: outdated strategies; neglect of human resources; failures of cooperation; technological weaknesses in development and production; government and industry working at cross-purposes; and short time horizons.

The industry studies revealed two types of outdated strategies that are impeding industrial progress today: an overemphasis on mass production of standard commodity goods and an economic and technological parochialism. Both are hold-overs from the unique economic environment that prevailed after World War II. For decades after the war US industry was able to flourish by mass-producing undifferentiated goods principally for its own markets, which were large, unified and familiar. Because firms in most other countries had to rebuild in economies devastated by the war, they could mount no significant competition and were largely ignored by US industry.

Not only did US producers sell their wares primarily to the domestic market, they also drew their technical expertise almost exclusively from US factories and laboratories. Such technological parochialism blinded Americans to the growing strength of scientific and technological innovation abroad and hence to the possibility of adapting foreign discoveries. In the 1950's and 1960's, for example, American steel producers lagged behind Japanese and European steelmakers in adopting such new process technologies as the basic oxygen furnace; later they were again slow to adopt continuous casters and such quality-enhancing technologies as vacuum degassing and oxygen injection. The critical error in many of these cases was the failure to recognize the worth of someone else's innovation.

The American industry of the 1950's and 1960's pursued flexibility by hiring and firing workers who had limited skills rather than by relying on multiskilled workers. Worker responsibility and input progressively narrowed, and management tended to treat workers as a cost to be controlled, not as an asset to be developed.

Training practices in the US have been consistent with that strategy. Workers often receive limited training while on the job; typically it amounts to watching a colleague at work. Even in firms offering organized training programs, in-plant training is usually short and highly focused on transmitting specific narrow skills for immediate application. In other countries we observed a greater inclination to regard firms as learning institutions, where – through education and training – employees can develop breadth and flexibility in their skills and also acquire a willingness to learn new skills over the long term. In a system based on mass production of standard goods, where cost matters more than quality, the neglect of human resources by companies may have been compatible with good economic performance; today it appears as a major part of the US's productivity problem.

The neglect of human resources in the US actually begins long before young Americans enter the work force. It is in primary and secondary school that they learn the fundamental skills they will apply throughout life: reading, writing and problem solving. Yet cross-national research on educational achievement shows American children falling behind children in other societies in mathematics, science and language attainment at an early age and falling farther behind as they progress through the school years. The school system – from kindergarten through high school – is leaving large numbers of its graduates without basic skills. Unless the nation begins to remedy these inadequacies in education, real progress in improving the US's productive performance will remain elusive.

The third recurring weakness of the US production system that emerged from our industry studies is a widespread failure of cooperation within and among companies. In many US firms communication and coordination among departments is often inhibited by steep hierarchical ladders and organizational walls. In addition, labor and management continue to expend valuable resources and energies battling over union organizing.

Suppliers and even customers have also been kept at arm's length by the management of many US companies, in spite of the fact that such vertical linkages can be conduits not only for raw materials and finished products but also for technological innovations and other developments that enhance productivity. These companies are reluctant to share designs, technologies and strategies with either their customers or their suppliers for fear that proprietary information will leak to competitors. Yet by keeping that kind of information to itself, a firm misses the chance to work with its suppliers and customers to improve the products it sells and buys. A similar lack of horizontal linkages – cooperative relations between firms in the same industry segment – has led to a dearth of joint projects in such areas as the setting of common standards and industrial research and development, even when they might have been permitted under the law.

Notwithstanding its spotty performance in the global market in recent years, the US remains the world leader in basic research. Ironically that outstanding success may have diverted attention from 'downstream' technological skills in product and process development and production that become progressively more important as new concepts proceed down the path from the laboratory to the marketplace. Simply put, many US firms have been outperformed in the design and manufacture of reliable, high-quality products.

A survey conducted by the International Motor Vehicle Program (IMVP) at MIT found that, despite recent gains, the number of defects reported in the first three months of use was still almost twice as high for cars produced in American plants in 1986 and 1987 as for those from Japanese plants. The commission's automobile study team also learned that American car builders have recently been taking about five years to carry a new design from the conceptual stage to commercial introduction. In contrast, Japanese manufacturers complete the cycle in three and a half years.

Some of the responsibility for the persistent failure to convert technologies quickly into viable, high-quality products lies in the American system of engineering education, which has deemphasized product realization and process engineering since World War II. The professional norms of the American engineering community also assign rather low priority to such essential downstream engineering functions as the testing of product designs, manufacturing and product and process improvements.

Other aspects of the problem can be found in certain practices followed by US industry. For one, many American companies simply do not devote enough attention to the manufacturing process. In a recent comparative study of industrial research and development in Japan and the US, Edwin Mansfield of the University of Pennsylvania found that US companies are still devoting only a third of their R & D expenditures to the improvement of process technology; the other two thirds is allocated to the development of new and improved products. In Japan those proportions in R & D expenditures are reversed.

Many US companies also fail to coordinate product design and the manufacturing process. It has been standard practice for design engineers to end their involvement with a new product once they have conceived its design. They hand over the design to manufacturing engineers, who are then supposed to come up with a process for the product's manufacture. This compartmentalization of tasks has led to serious problems. Product-design groups often neglect manufacturing considerations, making it harder to come up with a manufacturing process.

The Proprinter project of the International Business Machines Corporation is an impressive example of what can be achieved when product designers are brought together with manufacturing engineers and research scientists. Charged with designing a new computer printer that has fewer component parts and no springs or screws (which increase assembly time and decrease reliability), a multidisciplinary IBM design team came up with a product having 60 per cent fewer parts than its predecessor. (Ironically because an individual assembly worker could put the printer together in three and a half minutes, the highly automated and expensive assembly plant that had been built to make it was largely rendered superfluous.)

Multifunctional design teams and an orientation toward simplicity and quality at the design stage have been a long-standing fixture of Japanese industry and have contributed to its comparative advantages in quality and productivity. The IMVP survey showed that Japanese-designed automobiles retain their quality advantage even when they are assembled in American factories, which implies that the Japanese automotive engineers had incorporated quality-enhancing features into the design itself.

American companies also have often lagged behind their overseas competitors in exploiting the potential for continual improvement in the quality and reliability of products and processes. The cumulative effect of successive incremental improvements in and modifications of established products and processes can be very large; it may even outpace efforts to achieve technological breakthroughs.

The federal government deserves part of the blame as well for the technological weaknesses in development and production. Whereas the governments of most other industrial nations have purposefully promoted research and technology for economic development, US policy for science and technology has traditionally focused on basic research. The commercial development and application of new technologies have for the most part been considered to be the responsibility of the private sector.

To be sure, the Department of Defense, the National Aeronautics and Space Administration and other federal agencies have invested heavily in technology development. Indeed, about 46 per cent of all US research and development is sponsored by the Government. Those expenditures are usually in the areas of defense and space activities or in other specific Governmental missions, however. In such cases commercial applications of the resulting technology are considered secondarily, if at all. Furthermore, there are indications that defense R & D, which accounts for almost two thirds of all federal R & D spending, is becoming less relevant to the needs of the civilian market.

More generally the lack of a common agenda between government and industry has produced negative effects across broad stretches of the US economy. Some observers, for instance, have blamed the collapse of the consumer-electronics industry in part on the federal government's failure to enact or implement tariffs and import quotas as well as to amend or enforce antidumping and antitrust laws. Yet while some see the problem as too little government support for key industries, others see it as too much government support for inefficient producers.

The evidence gathered from the commission's industry studies was similarly mixed regarding the charge that too much government intervention, particularly in regulating the environment and occupational safety, has put US companies at a disadvantage in relation to foreign competitors. Where problems have arisen, the fault tended to lie in the nature of the regulatory process rather than in the strictness of the regulations themselves. Indeed, many European countries as well as Japan now have environmental and occupational-safety laws in many areas that are at least as strict as those in the US.

The issue, then, is not simply whether there is too much government or too little. What is clear to the commission, however, is that a lower level of cooperation between government and business exists in the US than it does in the countries of American firms' major foreign competitors and that the frequency with which government and industry find themselves at cross-purposes is a serious obstacle to strategic and organizational change in individual US firms.

American industry has also been handicapped by shrinking time horizons and a growing preoccupation with short-term profits. There have been many recent instances in which US firms have lost market share to overseas competitors despite an early lead in technology or sales, or both. Often these firms effectively cede a potential market by not 'sticking to their knitting'; instead, they diversify into activities that are more profitable in the short run.

The development of the videocassette recorder provides an exemplary case. Video-recording technology was first developed in the US, but the early machines were complex and expensive and suitable only for industrial and professional applications; many years of further development were needed to create low-cost, highly reliable products for the mass-consumer market. No American manufacturer was willing or able to spend the time and money, but several Japanese manufacturers were. The Japanese are now virtually unchallenged as makers of the most important single product in the consumer-electronics market.

Why are US firms less willing than their rivals to live through a period of heavy investment and meager returns in order to build expertise and secure a foothold in a new market? Is it that American managers are incapable of looking as far ahead as their foreign counterparts? Or are they forced by external circumstances to focus on the short term, even though they realize that it is not in their firm's best interest to do so? Or might it be that a short-term focus is actually in the best interest of the firm but not of the US economy as a whole?

Some observers argue that the higher cost of capital in the US compared with its cost in Japan is the overriding reason for the different time hori-

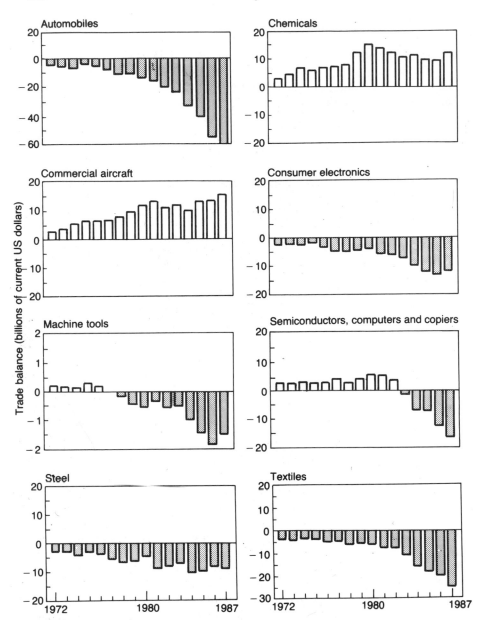

Balance of trade (the total value of exports less the total value of imports) for the eight key manufacturing industries studied by the commission reflects the industries' general condition in the US. A positive balance means that more of an industry's products are sold overseas than are exported to the US by foreign rivals; a negative balance implies the converse. An industry's trade balance is affected by the performance of its firms with respect to product cost and quality, service, and the speed of response to new technological and market opportunities. Macroeconomic conditions – particularly currency-exchange rates – can also affect the balance.

*First commercial videotape recorder was made by the Ampex Corporation
in Redwood City, California, but no US firms were willing or able to
devote the resources to bring unit costs down for sale to retail customers.
Ampex concentrated on high-price, high-performance systems; other US
firms abandoned the field altogether. Japanese companies had the
financial stamina to sustain low returns on investments while perfecting
designs and manufacturing processes. The result is that the Japanese now
dominate the consumer video-recording market. Moreover, by
capitalizing on the profits, technology, and economies of mass production
built up in that market, they have begun to encroach on the upscale
market as well.*

zons of firms in the two countries. Certainly the cost of capital is important,
but we think that other factors are also important.

The nature of the institutions that influence the supply of capital may
affect investment decisions at least as much as the cost of capital. A large
and growing share of the capital of US firms is owned by mutual funds and
pension funds, which hold assets in the form of a market basket of securities. The actual equity holders, the clients of the funds, are far removed
from managerial decision making. The fund managers also have no long-
term loyalty to the corporations in which they invest and have no representation on their boards. (Indeed, legislation prohibits their participation in
corporate planning.)

Although some fund managers do invest for the long term, most turn over their stockholdings rapidly in an effort to maximize the current value of their investment portfolio, since this is the main criterion against which their own performance is judged. Firms respond to this financial environment by maximizing their short-term profit in the belief that investment policies oriented toward the long term will be undervalued by the market and thus leave them vulnerable to a take-over.

At the same time senior executives are also motivated to maintain steady growth in earnings by their own profit-related bonus plans and stock options. A chief executive whose compensation is a strong function of his or her company's financial performance in the current year will naturally stress short-term results.

Explanations that cite the cost of capital and the sources of financing all tend to depict corporate managers as victims of circumstance, forced by external conditions into a short-term mind-set. Yet Robert H. Hayes and the late William J. Abernathy of the Harvard Business School have argued that executive ranks have come to be dominated by individuals who know too little about their firm's products, markets, and production processes and who rely instead on quantifiable short-term financial criteria. These modern executives are more likely to engage in restructuring to bolster profits than to take risks on technological innovation.

As part of its work the commission sought to find not only patterns of weakness in US industry but also patterns of change that are common to successful US firms – firms that are doing well in the international arena. Indeed, we probably learned as much from what such 'best practice' firms are doing right as from what many other US firms are doing wrong.

In particular, we found that successful firms emphasize *simultaneous* improvements in quality, cost, and speed of commercialization. Whereas other firms often trade off one dimension of performance against another, only the best companies have made significant improvement in all three. To gauge progress, one common practice among the successful firms is to emphasize competitive benchmarking: comparing the performance of their products and work processes with those of the world leaders. At the Xerox Corporation, for example, quality improved by an order of magnitude over the past decade after the company instituted detailed comparison tests of Xerox copiers and competing Japanese models.

In addition, the best-practice firms we observed are developing closer ties to their customers. These ties enable companies to pick up more detailed signals from the market and thus to respond to different segments of demand. They also increase the likelihood of rapid response to shifts in the market. Even high-volume manufacturers have combined a continuing emphasis on economies of scale with a new flexibility, reflected in shorter production runs, faster product introductions and greater sensitivity to the diverse needs of customers.

Closer and more tightly coordinated relations with suppliers were also observed among the best-practice firms. In some cases, better coordination with suppliers has been achieved through the coercive power of market domination, in others by new forms of cooperation and negotiation. No matter how it comes about, coordination with external firms is crucial in cutting inventories (and thereby costs), in speeding up the flow of products and in reducing defects.

For example, Greenwood Mills, Inc. (a textile company specializing in the production of denim), brought down its inventory radically over two years, even as sales doubled. To achieve those results the company tightened up its own operations and at the same time negotiated new arrangements with suppliers, who now deliver on a just-in-time basis. In exchange, Greenwood Mills halved the number of its suppliers, leaving itself more vulnerable to price hikes but gaining the advantages of closer collaboration.

Most thriving firms in the US have also realized that business strategies based on throwing new hardware at performance problems are unlikely to work. They have instead learned to integrate technology in their manufacturing and marketing strategies and to link them to organizational changes that promote teamwork, training, and continuous learning. In the generally depressed domestic apparel industry, firms such as the Model Garment Company and Levi Strauss & Company are succeeding by investing heavily in information technologies that allow them to fill orders very rapidly and reduce inventory levels.

In virtually all successful firms, the trend is toward greater functional integration and lesser organizational stratification, both of which promote quicker product development and increased responsiveness to changing markets. The Ford Motor Company was the first US automobile company to experiment with cross-functional teams to speed the development and introduction of a new model. The product-development team for the Taurus model included representatives from planning, design, engineering, manufacturing, and marketing. The specialists worked simultaneously rather than serially.

Flattening steep organizational hierarchies goes hand in hand with dismantling functional barriers. A flatter hierarchy generally enhances organizational flexibility. It also promotes closer relations with customers: a customer with a problem can speak directly with the group that has responsibility for the product instead of having to go through a sales department. In leaner, less hierarchical organizations the number of job categories at each level is reduced, and the responsibilities associated with particular jobs are broadened.

At the Chaparral Steel Company, for instance, there are almost 1,000 employees, and yet there are only four job levels. Production workers are responsible for identifying new technologies, training, meeting with customers, and maintaining equipment. Foremen and crews install new equipment. Security guards are trained as emergency medical technicians, and they update computer records while on their shift.

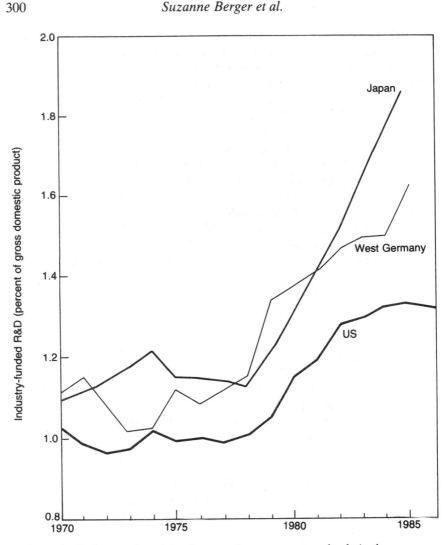

Industry-funded research and development has grown more slowly in the US than in Japan and West Germany. Total spending on R & D as a percentage of gross domestic product, however, is about the same in the three countries, because the difference in industry-funded R & D is made up in the US by federal funding of R & D.

An essential ingredient for greater worker responsibility and commitment is continual training. Large companies such as IBM have the resources to train their own workers. Having lower labor turnover, they also have more incentive to invest in training, because they are more likely to capture the benefits of that investment. Smaller companies do tend to draw more heavily on outside institutions for training, but there is often a major internal component as well.

The Kingsbury Machine Tool Corporation once built dedicated equipment for vehicles; it has since successfully converted to building computer-controlled machines and production lines for flexible manufacturing. Under the old regime the primary demand on the work force was for mechanical skills, but the new product line requires workers with some knowledge of computers. To retrain the employees, the company provided everyone – from janitors to vice presidents – with computers to use at work or at home and offered classes to employees and their families.

Although an increasing number of American companies are recognizing what it takes to be the best in the world, many US firms have not yet realized that they will have to make far-reaching changes in the way they do business. They will need to adopt new ways of thinking about human resources, new ways of organizing their systems of production and new approaches to the management of technology. What distinguishes the best-practice firms from the others in their industries is that they see these innovations not as independent solutions but as a coherent package. Each change for the better reinforces the others, and the entire organization is affected by them.

Of course, today's best practices will surely not remain the best forever. The nature of industrial competition is changing rapidly, and new challenges will undoubtedly emerge. The commission identified three major and pervasive long-term trends that will have broad implications for the future productive performance of US firms.

First, economic activity will continue to become more international. A company's ownership, location, workforce, purchases, and sales are all spreading beyond the boundaries of the nation in which it originated. A growing number of countries will acquire the capacity to produce and to export sophisticated goods and services. Many of these emerging economies have labor costs even lower than those of Taiwan and South Korea and far lower than those of the US, Japan and Europe.

Second, partly because of internationalization and partly because of rising incomes around the world, markets for consumer goods and intermediate goods are becoming more sophisticated. Markets are also becoming more segmented and specialized; not everyone is prepared to accept the same product designs and specifications.

Third, we expect the rapid pace of technological change to continue. Particularly rapid progress seems likely in information technology, materials science and engineering, and biotechnology. Information technology has already permeated nearly every facet of the production of goods and delivery of services, and we expect it to affect the business environment in a number of ways in the future.

The obvious implication of these three trends is that US firms will not be able to compete on the basis of cost alone. The future of US industry lies in specialized, high-quality products; standard commodities will be made in the US only if their production is extraordinarily capital-intensive and

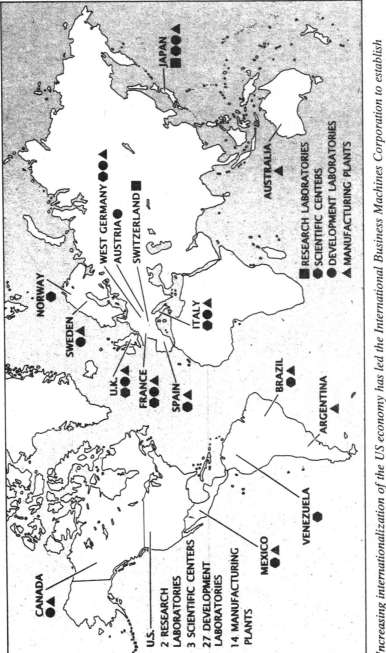

Increasing internationalization of the US economy has led the International Business Machines Corporation to establish numerous research laboratories, scientific centers, development laboratories, and manufacturing plants in foreign countries. Such a geographic distribution helps the corporation remain abreast of technological advances throughout the world. IBM also maintains sales offices in more than 100 countries in order to keep in closer contact with its customers.

technologically advanced. At the same time, competition among US, Japanese and European firms in markets for high-value-added products will become increasingly fierce.

Indeed, the convergence of future consumer preferences, market forces and technological opportunities may lead in some industries to the introduction of 'totally flexible' production systems. In such systems custom-tailoring of products to the needs and tastes of individual customers will be combined with the power, precision and economy of modern production technology.

In a market economy such as that of the US, individual firms have the primary responsibility to correct past problems and find ways to compete successfully in the future. Yet for the US to achieve an economy marked by high productivity growth, all sectors – business, government, labor and educational institutions – will need to work together. Based on its study of current weakness and best practices in American industry, as well as its forecast of long-term trends, the commission believes that five interconnected imperatives should form the core of any such national effort.

First, the US needs to invest more heavily in its future. This means investment not only in tangible factories and machinery but also in research and, above all, in human capital. At the macroeconomic level, as noted earlier, bringing the budget closer into balance should take high priority. In order to encourage firms to develop the necessary outlook for long-term investments, American economic policy should also favor increasing productive investment over private consumption through an approach that combines a more expansionary monetary policy with a fiscal policy that taxes consumption more heavily than savings or investment. Such policies can increase the supply of capital to business. Tax and credit legislation making it harder and more expensive to raise large sums of money for take-overs and buy-outs is additionally needed. Government must also work with industry and academia to ensure not only that investment continues strongly in basic research but also that it expands in the direction of productive manufacturing technologies.

Public resources should be allocated not only to improve the existing economic infrastructure (roads, airports, harbors and the like) but also to invest in new kinds of infrastructure. For example, we think that the time is right for American business and Government to begin developing a national information infrastructure, which would eventually become a network of communication highways as important for tomorrow's business as the current highway network is for today's flow of goods.

The most important investment in the long run is in the nation's schools. A better basic education will be crucial to the technological competence that will be required to raise the productivity of US industry. Without major improvements in primary and secondary schooling, no amount of macroeconomic fine-tuning or technological innovation will yield a rising standard of living.

The second major imperative, closely related to the first, is to develop a new 'economic citizenship' in the workplace. The effective use of modern technology will require people to develop their capabilities for planning, judgment, collaboration, and the analysis of complex systems. For that reason learning – particularly through on-the-job training programs – will acquire new importance.

Greater employee involvement and responsibility will be needed to absorb the new production technologies. Companies will no longer be able to treat employees like cogs in a big and impersonal machine. If people are asked to give maximum effort and to accept uncertainty and rapid change, they must be full participants in the enterprise rather than expendable commodities. Just as important as job security is a financial stake in the long-term performance of the firm. We see in this combination of technological and organizational change an unprecedented opportunity to make jobs more satisfying and rewarding for workers at all levels of a firm.

Third, the US needs to make a major commitment to mastering the new fundamentals of manufacturing. Manufacturing, as we use the term here, encompasses a great deal more than what happens on a production line. It includes designing and developing products as well as planning, marketing, selling, and servicing them. Global competition, changing markets and modern technologies are transforming virtually every phase of the production system.

Managers who are detached from the details of production will lose the competitive battle to managers who know their business intimately. Manufacturability, reliability and low cost should be built into products at the earliest possible stages of design. Innovation must be applied to process development as intensively and creatively as it is now applied to product development. Corporate management and financial institutions must work together to develop indicators that better reflect how well companies are actually doing in developing, producing, and marketing their products than do short-term financial measures such as quarterly earnings. New measures might include indicators of quality, productivity, product-development time, and time to market.

Fourth, Americans should strive to combine cooperation and individualism. The nation's culture has traditionally emphasized individualism, often at the expense of cooperation. Yet in the best US companies (as in other societies), group solidarity, a feeling of community, and a recognition of interdependence have led to important economic advantages.

To this end, steep organizational hierarchies, with their rigidity and compartmentalization, should be replaced with substantially flatter organizational structures that provide incentives for communication and cooperation among different corporate departments. Companies should put less emphasis on legalistic and often adversarial contractual agreements; they should promote business relations based on mutual trust, common goals, and the prospect of continuing transactions over the long run. Management must also accept workers and their representatives as legitimate partners in the innovation process. Both individual and group efforts need recognition and reward.

Americans should think of cooperation among economic entities as a way of overcoming the defects of the market, which often undersupplies collective factors essential to economic success. Cooperative efforts can take the form of research consortiums, joint business ventures, partnerships with Government and standard-setting committees. (To be sure, such arrangements might lead producers to combine forces in order to exploit the consumer. Now and in the future, competition from imports will no doubt provide some protection from domestic monopolies. Still, a little vigilance would help too.)

Fifth, to compete successfully in a world that is becoming more international and more competitive, Americans must expand their outlook beyond their own boundaries. They must gain knowledge of other languages, cultures, market customs, tastes, legal systems, and regulations; they will need to develop a new set of international sensitivities.

Cost considerations will increasingly dictate whether materials and components are best procured at home or abroad. It follows that not only a company's marketing division but also its purchasing agents and production managers will have to be knowledgeable about global conditions. Shopping internationally should go beyond the buying of raw materials and off-the-shelf products to the adoption of effective practices and technologies – wherever they happen to be found.

Americans need to understand that the world they live in has changed. The effortless economic superiority that the US enjoyed in the aftermath of World War II has gone. Strong economic cultures now exist across both the Atlantic and Pacific oceans. The US has much to learn from the rest of the world. Indeed, the rest of the world will force changes in some of the most cherished American operating procedures and assumptions, if the US is to continue to have a standard of living second to none. What Americans must do is determined decreasingly by what they wish to do and increasingly by the best practices of others.

Implementing these five imperatives will not be easy. In many cases, fundamental changes in attitude will be necessary. Just accepting the need for a sense of common purpose – a shared national goal – may require the biggest attitudinal change of all. The commission believes that if industry, government, and the educational system in this country unite in steadfast pursuit of these basic imperatives the next generation of Americans will live in a nation moving into the 21st century with the same dynamism and strength that made it a world leader a generation ago.

Further reading

Made in America: regaining the productive edge. Michael L. Dertouzos, Richard K. Lester, Robert M. Solow and the MIT Commission on Industrial Productivity. The MIT Press, 1989.

35

Thriving on chaos: facing up to the need for revolution

Tom Peters

The winning look is clear

This chapter gives a flavor of the sorts of firms that are turning up winners. Even were most of the recent mergers to reverse history's trend and work, the movement toward specialization and more moderately sized business units would in no way be blocked. A GE swallows an RCA, but its first move is to put each acquired business unit, such as NBC, through a starvation diet, similar to the one GE's homegrown corporate and business unit staffs have been subjected to. The truly close-to-the-market units within GE and its acquisitions, and within Du Pont, IBM, and P&G, are being reshaped to look and act more like The Limited, Minit-Lube, or Worthington Industries.

Take all the evidence together, and a clear picture of the successful firm in the 1990s and beyond emerges. It will be:

- flatter (have fewer layers of organization structure)
- populated by more autonomous units (have fewer central-staff second-guessers, more local authority to introduce and price products)
- oriented toward differentiation, producing high value-added goods and services, creating niche markets
- quality-conscious
- service-conscious
- more responsive
- much faster at innovation
- a user of highly trained, flexible people as the principal means of adding value.

Figure 1 summarizes the case. A series of forces, arrayed on the left side of the chart, are interacting with one another to create a completely new context for doing business, labeled 'outcome.' The outcome can only be dealt with, I believe, by firms which share a common set of traits, labeled 'shape of a winner.'

Extract from Chapter 1 in *Thriving on Chaos: Handbook for a Management Revolution* by Tom Peters. Copyright © 1987 by Excel, a California Limited Partnership. Reprinted by permission of Alfred A. Knopf, Inc.

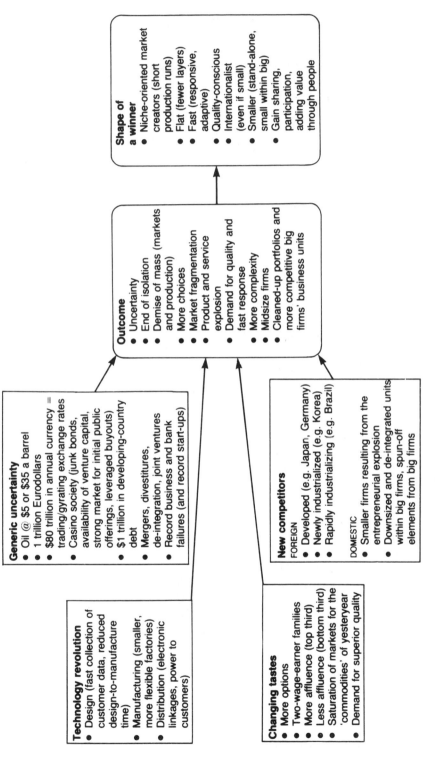

Figure 1   *Forces at work and their apparent resolution*

The good news: there is good news

You want evidence of transformation not led by major mergers? How about Ford at $60 billion, Chrysler at $23 billion, Dana at $4 billion, Brunswick at $3 billion, Milliken at $2 billion, Campbell Soup at $4 billion, McKesson at $6 billion? You want examples of those squarely in the middle of it? Try Du Pont or Procter & Gamble. How about winners who have hiccuped but so far not made a major misstep in tumultuous markets? Consider Cray, Apple, Digital Equipment, Nucor, Worthington, Chaparral, ServiceMaster, American Airlines, Banc One, Federal Express, The Limited, Nordstrom.

But is there anyone big who seems to have known the formula all along? I [have said] that there were no excellent companies. Were I to admit an exception, it would be 3M. If ever there was a perpetual-motion machine, it is this $9-billion firm. Its trick has been to understand value-added differentiation and perpetual market creation long before such tactics became necessary. Every unit of the corporation, whether it serves 'mature' markets or exotic new ones, is charged with continual reinvention. And the firm's minimum acceptable profit margins per unit are astronomical – only attainable with truly superior products and service.

So in every industry there are places to visit, people to learn from. Johnsonville Sausage of Sheboygan Falls, Wisconsin, installed a remarkable organization structure, with little hierarchy, lots of employee involvement, and substantial profit-sharing; its market share in the Milwaukee area soared from 7 to 50 percent in ten years. I wrote about the firm in *U.S. News & World Report* – and was delighted to learn that the column spurred visits by plant managers from 3M and General Mills. Another column, about the stellar customer service and economic performance of Sewell Village Cadillac of Dallas, led to a visit by a team from a Procter & Gamble plant.

So the role models are there – in steel, textiles, and autos, as well as computers, retailing, health care, and banking.

The bad news: pace

General Motors was and remains a pioneer in workplace experiments. From its joint venture with Toyota called the New United Motor Manufacturing, Inc. (NUMMI), to its assembly plant in Lakewood, Georgia, a lot has been going on.

But not enough. The firm's relative cost position has deteriorated. Its management ranks, despite radical (by past standards) surgery, remain hopelessly bloated. Its committee-driven designs still lag and its product development cycles are still two to three times longer than those of its best competitors. And it still can't figure out how to take on small markets. Top that off with a bad case of merger indigestion from Hughes and EDS alike.

Moreover, technology, rather than people, is still its theme. (All of this was, almost certainly, what led to GM's precipitous 20 percent loss of market share in just one year, as of May 1987. Never mind whether or not GM will recover, as it may well do – the simple fact that the world's largest industrial firm could tumble that fast, despite extraordinary incentives to car buyers aimed at stemming the tide, is stunning evidence of the changing times.)

No one is complacent. Ford, though topping GM in profits in 1986 for the first time in sixty-two years, knows it has barely scratched the surface in its attempt to achieve superior quality and shorter product development cycles. It looks to Toyota as the premier firm in its industry. IBM is scurrying, too; one long-time observer of the firm estimates that its payroll has 50,000 more people than it needs to accomplish its current mission.

But is even Ford moving fast enough? It's not at all clear. Radical changes in organizational structure and procedures are called for. Layers of management must be reduced in most big firms by 75 percent. Product development time and order lead time must be slashed by 90 percent. Electronic/telecommunication linkups to customers and suppliers must be developed posthaste. Just listening to customers and dealers needs to become the norm – and as yet it's not.

All this adds up to a requirement, not for structural or procedural tinkering, but for a revolution in organization: more autonomous units – guided by a coherent vision rather than by memorandums and managers-as-cops, and manned by involved workers with a big stake in the action and hell-bent upon constant improvement. And this in turn means that new attitudes are also required – especially commitment on the part of managers to the idea that suppliers, workers, unions, distributors, and customers are all partners in the common endeavor.

But the wholesale changes in attitude have not yet occurred, and without them we are doing immeasurably dumb things. We are, for example, letting work drift offshore in pursuit of the lowest-cost production. But to lose control of the plant is to lose control of the future – of quality, responsiveness, and the source of most innovation, which in manufacturing industries occurs in the palpable, on-premises interaction among plant team, designer, marketer, and customer.

We are misusing automation. Americans still see it as a tool to reduce the need for labor, not as a tool to aid labor in adding value to the product. In consequence, efforts to staff our plants with robots are not working.

We are still churning businesses, via merger and divestiture, in hopes of obtaining some ideal portfolio, fit for the future. There is none. No industry is safe. There is no such thing as a safe, fast-growth haven. The new attitudes toward people and adding value are required as much in financial services and entertainment as in autos and steel. Look at the revolution wrought by The Limited or Federal Express, linking people power and computer network power; most service firms are light-years behind.

Roger Milliken of Milliken & Co, had the genius in 1980 to see that the

answer to competition in the 'mature' textile market was unparalleled
quality attained largely through people. He revolutionized the company
then. But he's almost unique because he saw in 1984 that the first revolution was wholly inadequate to meet the worldwide competitive challenge.
So he made another revolution, reordering every relationship in the firm in
pursuit of unparalleled customer responsiveness. Two revolutions in six
years.

It is Roger Milliken's brand of urgency – and taste for radical reform –
that must become the norm. For Milliken's two revolutions (and the firm
was a star to begin with) are still only barely meeting the competitive
challenge.

Implications for public policy

Management, I believe, holds the key to a competitive resurgence in the
United States. Nonetheless, certain policy prods could help immeasurably
in speeding the necessary transformation.

As a conclusion, I will offer only the barest of outlines – suggestions for
several steps that policymakers can take:

1. *Promote more, not less, competition.*   That is, turn up the heat. *First,
pass no protectionist legislation.* Protect an industry, ancient and recent
history alike suggest, and it gets sloppier, or at least fails to improve at an
acceptable rate. Playing fields are not, and never have been, level. We
should utilize existing trade management legislation, which is fully
adequate, and not add more. The objective is to get better and different,
not to try to hide from a newly energized world economy. (In this regard,
the trade bill which will likely pass in 1987 – the most restrictive since
Smoot-Hawley in 1930 – is a giant step backwards.)

Second, don't tie the corporate raiders' hands. Raiders are no altruists,
and their acts cause much unnecessary pain. And, to be sure, some of the
moves corporations make to forestall raiders are dysfunctional – for
example, making inappropriate mergers so as to create a balance sheet that
scares a raider off, or shuttling jobs offshore in a crash, but ultimately
misguided, effort to slash costs. But on balance, the raiders are, along with
the Japanese, the most effective force now terrorizing inert corporate
managements into making at least some of the moves, such as downsizing,
that should have been made years ago.

*Third, get rid of the entire capital-gains tax after a certain holding period
passes.* The start-up firms are the breath of fresh air in the economy – we
encouraged them with the 1981 capital-gains tax break, and have now
discouraged them with the omnibus tax act of 1986. In general, support
financial incentives that favor start-ups and spin-offs/divestitures such as
leveraged buyouts.

2. *Retool and involve the work force.* The work force must become the prime source of value added. We need to give employers the incentive to hire people and constantly upgrade skills. *First, provide a special tax incentive for all funds, including employee wage costs, spent on training and pay-for-knowledge programs. Provide a further tax incentive for wage increases that result directly from skill upgrading. Provide general tax deductability for employee off-the-job skill upgrading, whether or not it's related to the current job. I also support, to aid displaced workers, some form of Individual Training Account,* as proponents have labeled it. Sizable tax-deductible contributions by employees, similar to IRAs (Inland Revenue Arrangements), might be made over an extended period. The money would revert to the employee at retirement or some such time, but upon displacement would be issued, in voucher form, for use in certified training programs.

A second, sweeping plank is aimed at giving employers an even higher incentive to hire and involve employees. Inspired, in particular, by the ideas discussed by Martin Weitzman in *The Share Economy*, I propose, for employers, that *a major, old-fashioned investment tax credit plan be allowed on wages distributed as bonuses via profit-distributing bonus plans and quality- and productivity-based gain-sharing plans. For employees, I suggest a big tax exemption, possibly with limits, for all income from profit-distribution and productivity-based gain-sharing plans.* (Such a bold incentive would be required to compensate for greater uncertainty – the real possibility of lower pay in bad times.)

Third, greater employee assurance is required as foreign competition heats up even further, and smaller firms become increasingly dominant. *Extended and increased trade adjustment assistance is desirable* to combat the former (though it should be highly skewed to force rapid enrollment in retraining programs, for instance). Portable pensions and other dislocation-ameliorating housing and health-care programs will be required as well.

3. *Stop the mindless offshore job drift.* The loss of jobs per se may be less significant than the loss of control of our destiny, as certain manufacturing activities migrate offshore. *I propose a new form of domestic content legislation.* The term is usually applied to the percentage of domestic content in imports. My alternative is to provide some tax credit for domestic products, based upon the percentage of domestic content, up to, say, 50 percent. A particularly thorny subset of this issue is start-ups – for instance, high-tech firms – that never do establish their own manufacturing operations. The capital-gains tax formula for start-ups could be a sliding one, depending on the percent of value added by onshore manufacture.

4. *Push internationalism.* We need to shed our lingering isolationism. Concepts I support include (a) *a value-added tax (VAT) to pay for the programs I have proposed here, but excluding goods sold for export,* (b) *tax benefits favorable to Americans working abroad,* (c) *provision of more*

readily available financing sources for smaller or mid-sized firms seeking export markets, and (d) *educational incentives to induce much more foreign-language education.*

5. Support expanded research and development. The R & D tax credit and the basic-research credit which supports business and university linkages will both be phased out by the end of 1988, thanks to the 1986 tax act. At the least, they should be restored. Support for high levels of basic research, especially in non-defense areas, is a must. Additionally, we might provide special tax breaks to firms that bring university researchers on board, or that support cooperative education programs, especially in engineering and science.

This brief sketch is not meant to be exhaustive. It does not include any mention of major policy levers that influence the overall business climate (arenas where others are more expert than I), and it includes only some of the types of policies that would hasten the transformation of our firms.[1]

I find myself turning more frequently to public policy considerations because of my growing frustration. The changes are being made – by management. The changes can be made – by management. But they are not being made fast enough by management. The issue is not the unions. Nor is it 'unfair' Japanese practices, unless learning our language or paying attention to details that commercial and individual consumers care about is unfair.

We must look at what's working, and move fast to adapt and emulate the best. The speed of the transition is the most pressing issue.

Note

1   It also flies in the face of the basic intention of tax reform – less use of the tax code to manipulate firms' outcome. While I acknowledge the adverse consequences of thousands of special interest loopholes, I think this is precisely the wrong time to turn our back on the most effective weapon to aid rapid industrial transformation – tax policy.

36

What makes a winning company?

James Pilditch

You've got to have clear objectives and fire in your belly.

John Bertrand, captain of *Australia II*,
the boat that won the Americas Cup in 1983

If evidence taken from many sources becomes repetitive, you may feel it adds up to sound advice. This chapter provides a telegraphic distillation of the findings of experts who have studied companies of all sizes in a number of countries. One hallmark of these companies is that they are introducing new products rapidly and successfully; this is our concern now.

Critics may protest that many of their observations stray from the narrower focus of developing new products. Perhaps that is the main lesson. To be innovative, companies must embrace a whole set of new attitudes. Strengthening the design department, by itself, won't do the trick.

The essentials for winning

Here are the essentials for a company that wants to win, according to Tom Peters and Bob Waterman in *In Search of Excellence* (1982). They wrote primarily about successful US companies that they had studied, but the qualities they found surely have universal relevance. Virtually all are far from the orthodoxy of the modern industrial corporation. That is the bad news. All, encouragingly, are closer to the natural state of smaller companies, especially those in new industries. That is the good news.

1. 'A bias for action', for getting on with it. Who would argue with this? But, we have seen, this does not mean at the pace we are used to. Nor does it mean being satisfied with the best that can be done the way we organize today. Bringing people together in teams is an example of doing things more quickly by doing them differently.

Arthur D. Little has spoken of innovation in management. It is hard to retain much 'bias for action' in a conventional hierarchical company.

Adapted from Chapter 14 in J. Pilditch, *Winning Ways* (London and New York: Harper and Row, 1987), pp. 235–46, now published by Paul Chapman Ltd

Decisions take too long. Forces at work tend to be negative rather than positive. The 'flatter', devolved organization is faster.

2. *'Close to the customer'*.   So many of us say we are but we are not. Not close in the way General Electric was when it wanted to improve its position in the business of making locomotives, or Sony proved it was when it decided to launch an 8-inch TV in the United States, or Honda is when it sends out its designers all the time. Being close to the customer is much safer than being close to the plant or the financier. As the customer shifts, so will you. How many companies have been bemused to discover, too late, that their customer has gone away? That is, at least partly, because they have been looking in the wrong direction.

3. *'Autonomy and entrepreneurship'*.   Peters and Waterman found both, even in the largest corporations. Divide the company into bits, small bits. Encourage all the bosses to achieve their own goals. Don't second-guess every move they make. For example, I know the financial director of one public company who may not write to his accountant without the chairman's permission. Heaven knows how they work lower down in the company. Of that chairman, someone said, 'He's typical. He likes to hold all the marbles.' That is yesterday's world.

Of course, you can't just leave people. There is more to creating the environment of autonomy and entrepreneurship. It includes telling everyone your goals, for instance, and permitting risk, and recognizing success. It includes sharing the same attitudes, brought about through fostering a questioning, open culture.

4. *'Productivity through people'*.   Looking at the winning companies, Peters and Waterman saw a high level of this characteristic. Steve Jobs' experience at Apple is a perfect case. He achieved five or six times the industry average by hiring highly talented, highly charged people and then letting them run.

Almost all of us have far more ability and energy than we are allowed to exercise. But so often, the system holds people back. Procedures are necessary in large organizations, but procedures and rules can be based on trust as easily as they can be repressive. Having layer upon layer of managers, or officials, who feel it necessary to interfere doesn't encourage 'productivity through people'. 'It is not too difficult to motivate innovators,' say Arthur D. Little. 'It is very easy to demotivate them. Indifference and bureaucratic hassles are the most commonly cited demotivating factors.'

Criticizing people for what they don't do, instead of praising them for what they do do, doesn't help either. 'Productivity through people' must be sensible, but a lot goes with it. When it comes to developing new products, there is everything to be said for it. Everyone in the business can help – and will, if they see the point and know they will be appreciated. Ideas, for instance, can come from anywhere, not just from the 'designated thinkers'.

Maybe 'productivity through people' is another of those areas where managers say 'We do that already' because they have personnel managers and pension schemes. This is not the same, not the same at all.

5. *'Hands on, value driven'.*   Peters and Waterman found that these are the companies that win. That means the chairman of Sony carrying his products around with him. It means the head of McDonald's seeing the tables are clean. It means being in touch and on top. There's another, old-fashioned word – 'leadership' – and one way to lead is to show what you think is important by the way you act.

Sir Christopher Hogg, chairman of Courtaulds, told an audience at the Royal Society of Arts in London how he now sees leadership of a company. 'I have been shifted a considerable distance in the spectrum away from administration orientation, in which it is all too easy to forget that a company exists only by reason of its ability to satisfy customers and markets – away from that and towards market, customer and product orientation.'

6. *'Stick to the knitting'.*   If you have found the right way to stay in front, Peters and Waterman say, keep on doing it. There are so many claims on our time it is easy to be distracted. It is also easy, perhaps particularly for imaginative people, to become bored with focused effort. There are so many other possibilities. Sticking to the knitting is not the same as sticking in the mud. Stick-in-the-muds don't alter, don't adapt, don't take risks. People who stick to the knitting do all of these. The key is to drive relentlessly to improve the things that matter.

7. *'Simple form, lean staff'.*   Peters and Waterman noted that the companies whose performance they admire avoided excessive central staffs and bureaucratic systems.

8. *'Simultaneous loose tight properties'.*   Be vigilant about a few issues, delegate the others. As for product development, if I may interpret Peters and Waterman's views, perhaps one needs to be 'tight' about the need to stay close to customers and tight about putting constant product improvement in the front of everyone's mind, but loose about how the team works. Experience shows that teams like to be close to, but not sat on by, the board. Be tight about the need for results, loose about the company's usual yardsticks for good behaviour.

If people in the United Kingdom think 'Well all that might be right for the United States, but Britain is different', they should see the results of the 'Sharp-bender' project carried out for NEDO in 1986. This looked at

British companies that had turned around sharply, that, in a short term, contrived to do much better. Here is what it found:

1 A bias for action. (There it is again.)
2 Willingness to take risks – we've heard that too. Business executives who turn around companies take decisions rather than avoid them and exert continuing pressure for change and improvement.
3 Short-term cutting waste and overheads.
4 Improvement in organization, planning and control.
5 Investment in the future (note, these are companies that turned around quickly).
6 Concentration on the product, market and requirements of the customer.
7 Motivating the workforce and consulting and involving them in the process of change.
8 Flexibility.

As you will note, the two lists of points are much the same.

All very well, I have been told, but that is about management, not about developing new products. My thesis is that if you get the overall attitude in the company right, the new products will come. Roy Rothwell and Paul Gardiner (1984) make the connection better than I may have done. From numerous studies they prepared their own list of 'critical factors for success'. Again there are eight points.

1 Management must establish good communications with customers and other sources of external ideas.
2 Innovation is a corporate-wide task. It is not, they insist, simply a matter of research, design and development. Note that they highlight the importance of good internal communication and co-operation between departments.
3 Watch your product to the marketplace. Too many would-be innovators have produced designs that were technically satisfying in themselves but which failed to meet the needs of potential customers. This is 'a sure prescription for disaster'.
4 Companies should eliminate technical bugs before the commercial launch, urge Rothwell and Gardiner. This, I suggest, need not be at odds with Peters and Austin (1985), who want us to try new products with real people in real situations as fast as possible. That's the best way to find out what the bugs are.
5 Innovation is difficult. Companies need managers of high quality and ability. Top management must be open minded and progressive. Rothwell and Gardiner add 'successful innovation tends to be associated with a participative, horizontal management style, one that emphasizes consultation rather than direction from above'.
6 In-house skills are vital, believe Rothwell and Gardiner. Companies need internal experts to capitalize on external advice. For example,

many attempts at technology transfer have failed because companies did not acquire the necessary in-house skills.

7 After-sales service and user education are important.
8 Companies must have a product champion and business innovator, the latter with overall control of a development project.

In case we find these ideas frighteningly new, it is worth noting that some years ago the Confederation of British Industry arrived at similar conclusions. The stern question is: What have we done about them? In its report *Innovation and Competitiveness*, published in 1979, the CBI found there were consistent and significant factors in successful development. It listed seven characteristics:

1 Responsibility for new product and process development is vested in a member of the board.
2 Support and/or participation by the chief executive.
3 Good rapport between marketing, production and development.
4 Effective use of external sources of technological help and advice.
5 Close collaboration with customers in product design.
6 Presence of technologists on the board.
7 Effective screening of ideas and monitoring of progress of approved projects.

Notice how the same themes turn up again and again.

Focus on developing winning products

You may feel these essentials are too broad for developing competitive products, so then let us focus more narrowly. James Brian Quinn, from his studies of highly innovative companies in several countries (1980), lists the ten characteristics he thinks get results.

1 The need for atmosphere/vision, and a feeling about people.
2 Quinn says you need a technological strategy. It doesn't matter whether you look for major developments, or little-by-little improvement, whether you want to be a leader or fast follower, or whether you want to buy in or do-it-yourself. In whichever dimension of a product you seek technological strength, Quinn believes that having a known strategy gives to a company a unique cohesion and an ability to perform.
3 Third, no surprises any more, the company must be what Quinn called 'market goal-oriented'. The best companies really are, he says; not just the consumer goods companies either. He cited Bell Labs, where technical engineers deal with customer complaints. The way of working he calls for is 'test/feedback/test/feedback'. There are echoes of Peters and Waterman. Make something. Try it. If it goes wrong, improve it. Try it again.

4   Skunkworks and champions exist. There is always a champion who
     drives success.
5   Always develop multiple approaches. We've heard that too. 'The
     nature of innovation is that you don't know.' In any case having
     several lines to choose from is faster. Sony pursued ten major options
     when developing the video recorder. Such internal competition is not
     wasteful. It gets better results quicker.
6   Quinn talks about 'interactive learning', learning from customers,
     learning from people in other disciplines, back and forth.
7   Quinn has the concept of 'key targets and chaos', setting up parallel
     projects, but also placing what he calls 'side-bets', lots of small initia-
     tives beside the main efforts.
8   Don't set up normal structures if you want to develop new products
     quickly.
9   Rewards and incentives, not only financial ones, are crucial.
10 Innovators are task oriented and task driven. Their motivation comes
     from being able to implement their ideas.

The point is this: all the evidence suggests that if you leave innovation to
chance, or leave it to your technical department, or even try to manage it
the way you manage any other part of the business, you probably won't get
far. Arthur D. Little, who have a three-year programme to look at this
subject, are clear about this:

> Companies with a good record on innovation use specific management tech-
> niques to develop new ideas and go out of their way to attract and motivate
> individuals who are good at innovation. These people are rewarded not neces-
> sarily with higher pay but with more interesting jobs and few bureaucratic
> burdens.

What to learn from the winners

The ten lessons Britain's National Economic Development Office learned
from the winning companies are these:

1   *Care about products.* Winning companies care about their products far
     more than most others do. The boards of too many other companies
     are more concerned with finance and short-term profit.
2   *Be obsessive about customers.* They are obsessive about their cus-
     tomers. They have teams committed to studying not only customer
     needs now, but future lifestyle trends.
3   *Integrate design.* They see design as just one part of developing new
     products. In the leading companies design is an integral part of a
     multidisciplinary approach to product development.
4   *Break down the walls.* Today most companies are organized by func-
     tion – engineering, manufacturing, design, marketing, finance, etc.
     Winning companies have largely broken down these walls. They have

Close to the customer: a reminder

multidisciplinary teams, drawn from all these departments, that work together throughout the development of a product. Their communications are more across the company than up and down.

5 *Concentrate on design.* Leading companies give designers and the multidisciplinary design team a much more central place in the company than occurs in most other companies. Design has been lifted from a functional to a strategic role. Designers are expected to imagine the company's future products.

6 *Have a product strategy.* They have a clear product strategy. This may be dual: both to improve incrementally ('little by little') all the time and to take larger, more innovative leaps.

7 *Chase technology.* They chase technology and many buy in all they can. But *note:* they say competitive advantage is not achieved by technology but with 'how you relate it to the needs of the customer'.

8 *Co-operate with your suppliers.* More of these companies are developing long-term relationships with their suppliers. Their choice is based on quality and reliability rather than on low cost. They design components together, and see themselves as partners in growth.

9 *Demand quality.* The winning companies design quality in, rather than inspect faults out.

10 *Communicate.* A characteristic of all winning companies is excellent communications across the company and all through it.

These ten characteristics add up to a remarkable capacity to create products very quickly that their customers buy in preference to others.

More from Japan

Gene Gregory, professor at Sophia University, Tokyo, gave his own summary of the keys to success he has seen in Japan: education, motivation, innovation. Kenichi Ohmae of McKinsey & Co. in Tokyo tells us that the traditional Japanese success recipe includes mass production, incremental managerial improvement, buy-in technology (as opposed to sitting in an ivory tower and developing abstract ideas), fast turnaround time for innovation, small systems and hardware orientation and, of course, strong quality orientation.

Finally, a distinguished American, Robert C. Christopher, who knows Japan well, said in his book *The Japanese Mind* (1984) that the key to Japanese efficiency is not low wages or unfair practice but this: 'Japanese managers manage their companies better.' They get more from their workers because they treat them better. The Japanese worker has pay, pride, security. Everybody, in every job, knows that he or she contributes to the success of the company. They know their products better. They have a higher proportion of engineers in top management, a lower proportion of accountants. They believe in quality – not acceptable quality level (AQL) but zero defects. Quality, they believe, should be designed in from the start. Christopher added that the Japanese take a long-term view. They wait for profit. They call it 'patient money'. Top managers, Christopher said, are more people oriented and more product oriented. 'Disrespect for our products is a prime source of our difference and difficulty.'

'It is one thing to have an idea,' Sir Alastair Pilkington told an audience at London's Royal Society of Arts, 'quite another to turn it into a technical and then a commercial success.' At Pilkington Brothers, he said, they realized that survival would depend on being innovative. But their experience was daunting. When they developed float glass it took them 12 years to break even on their cash flow. Still, he believes, 'If the strategy is good the profits will come.'

Sir Alastair listed three essentials for success. First, he said, the company must believe in the need for innovation. Everyone must see it as vital. 'It simply must not be seen as peripheral,' he claimed. Second, the resources must be made available. A definite commitment, he said, is much more important than is recognized. Third, a major project will not yield quick returns. Everyone has to know that. The man who demonstrated lots of both declared you need 'courage and determination' to see it through.

In his inimitable way, Prince Philip summed up a discussion about 'the management of new ideas' at London's Royal Society of Arts in November 1986. On a scratch pad he listed seven points he thought important. Possibly because he is, inter alia, president of the World Wildlife Fund, he spoke first of understanding the environment we are in. Creatures can remain unchanged for billions of years, he has observed, but that is because their environment has not changed. Where change does occur, Darwin's principles of selection and evolution work. Relating this to corporate life, he believed the market operates the selection process. 'The company that is best adapted to its environment has the best chance of success. The environment in which a company exists decides how it should be shaped,' he said.

Prince Philip then related the management of new ideas to these issues. First, the need to identify the current and future environment in which a company exists. Second, the need to study competition, which imposes restraints and permits opportunities. Third, understanding customer needs and, he added, public attitudes. He gave nuclear power as an example of the gap that can exist between need and acceptability. Next, he urged the audience to be aware of the availability of new materials and new technology. Design talent was vital. Talent was a word he emphasized: 'You need talent,' the Prince said. 'We talk about design education, but perhaps not enough about design talent.' There is an important need for production skills. The next imperative to the introduction of new ideas is, in his view, good management – its attitudes, policy, structure, competence. Finally, he touched on government policy, which can aid or hamper innovation.

Britain's Open University, working with the University of Manchester's Institute of Science and Technology, has interviewed people in 100 companies in various industry sectors. They tried to see whether companies that win design awards, or are recognized to have well-designed products, perform better or worse than companies that have no such accolades. The answer, they say, is unequivocal. Companies that had won design awards or had products accepted for the Design Centre's Design Index showed higher return on capital, higher profit margins, higher growth of turnover and higher capital growth.

Sectors they looked at included the plastics industry, domestic heating, bicycles, office furniture, electronic business equipment and computing.

No less interesting is the way companies with better performance manage their design process. The Open University lists these six common elements:

1   The companies with high profitability and growth provide designers with a comprehensive design brief. Invariably this includes details of the market, guidance on appearance and image, standards (ergonomic and other) as well as the function of the proposed product and its target price.

2   The companies with high asset and profit growth rates employ several sources of market intelligence.

3   The companies tend to evolve products, improving their own or their competitors. Companies that created highly innovative products could succeed brilliantly, but more often found the market hard to develop.

4 These more successful companies put prototypes through systematic customer and user trials, as well as testing the product technically. Less successful firms relied more on 'experience' to judge user acceptance.

5 The companies that performed best shared a commitment to design that ran from top management throughout the firms.

6 The companies with a high proportion of research, design and development staff were more likely to have high levels of profitability and growth.

The same principles come up time and again.

Summary

Listen to authorities in the United States, in the United Kingdom, in Japan, and you hear the same truths time and again. The driving companies, not necessarily those yielding the highest profit this quarter or next quarter, but those that are carving larger and larger shares of our markets, all share the same attributes. This chapter tells us what they are. Put together, they add up to a consistent and compelling picture of what companies need to do or, more precisely, where they need to place emphasis and focus, if they are to compete.

The second salutary point is to note that the general run of companies do not practise the same ideas. The third and most astonishing feature when you come across it, in 3M or Sharp or elsewhere, is the depth and totality of such companies' commitment to these beliefs. These vital attributes are not fashionable management techniques, but inherent in the way such exemplary companies wake up in the morning and go about their business.

References

CBI (1979) *Innovation and Competitiveness*, Confederation of British Industry, London.

Christopher, R.C. (1984) *The Japanese Mind*, Pan Books, London.

Peters, T.J. and Austin, N.K. (1985) *A Passion for Excellence: The Leadership Difference*, Collins, London.

Peters, T.J. and Waterman, R.H. (1982) *In Search of Excellence*, Harper & Row, New York.

Quinn, J.B. (1980) *Strategies for Change: Logical Incrementalism*, Richard D. Irwin, Illinois.

Rothwell, R. and Gardiner, P. (1984) 'Design and Competition in Engineering', *Long Range Planning*, vol. 17, no. 3, pp. 78–91.

Index